SWING TO BOP

Swing to Bop

AN ORAL HISTORY OF
THE TRANSITION IN JAZZ
IN THE 1940S

IRA GITLER

OXFORD UNIVERSITY PRESS
New York   Oxford

Oxford University Press

Oxford   New York   Toronto

Delhi   Bombay   Calcutta   Madras   Karachi

Petaling Jaya   Singapore   Hong Kong   Tokyo

Nairobi   Dar es Salaam   Cape Town

Melbourne   Auckland

and associated companies in

Beirut   Berlin   Ibadan   Nicosia

Library of Congress Cataloging in Publication Data
Gi ler, Ira.
Swing to bop.
Includes index.
1. Jazz music—United States—History and criticism.
2. Jazz musicians—United States—Interviews.
I. Title.
ML3508.G57 1985   785.42'0973   85-5092
ISBN 0-19-503664-6
ISBN 0-19-505070-3 (pbk.)

4 6 8 10 9 7 5

Printed in the United States of America

Acknowledgment is gratefully made to the following for permission to reprint from previously published materials (names and page numbers in parentheses indicate locations of reprinted passages in *Swing to Bop*)

Cadence, Redwood, N.Y., from interview with Bob Rusch, copyright © 1976, 1978 by *Cadence* Jazz Magazine (Allen Eager, p. 307).

Charles Scribner's Sons, from Stanley Dance and Earl Hines, excerpted from THE WORLD OF EARL HINES. Copyright © 1977 Stanley Dance. Reprinted with the permission of Charles Scribner's Sons.

Doubleday & Company Inc., excerpts from *To Be or Not to Bop: Memoirs* by Dizzy Gillespie with Al Fraser. Copyright © 1979 by John Birks Gillespie and Wilmot Alfred Fraser reprinted by permission of Doubleday & Company Inc. (Al McKibbon, p. 45; Dizzy Gillespie, p. 123; Art Blakey, p. 130).

down beat, Chicago (Mose Allison, p. 63; Jackie McLean, p. 63; Charlie Parker, p. 75; Oscar Pettiford, p. 106; Gil Evans, pp. 250, 251, 252; Claude Thornhill, p. 251).

Fantasy Records, *Coleman Hawkins: A Documentary* (Coleman Hawkins, p. 151).

Jazz Hot, Paris (Lester Young, pp. 35–37).

Jazz Journal, London (Dexter Gordon, last three lines on p. 37, pp. 81, 338; Milt Hinton, pp. 44–45, 56–58; Budd Johnson, p. 48, first eight lines on p. 312; Dizzy Gillespie, p. 56; Benny Bailey, first paragraph on p. 97, references to Hubert Kidd on p. 98; Al Levitt, pp. 295, 297).

Macmillan Publishing Company from *Jazz Masters of the Thirties* by Rex Stewart, copyright © 1972 by Macmillan Publishing Company (Rex Stewart, p. 48), and from *Jazz Masters of the Forties* by Ira Gitler © 1966 by (Dexter Gordon, p. 47).

National Endowment for the Arts Oral History Project excerpts courtesy of the Institute of Jazz Studies at Rutgers University (Eddie Barefield, pp. 23–24, 34–35, 41, 82; Kenny Clarke, pp. 52–56, 76–77, 81–82, 102–3, 130, 227; Al Hall, p. 53).

Sonny Rollins, from *Soul* (Sonny Rollins, p. 103).

Ross Russell, from *Bird Lives!* by Ross Russell, copyright © 1972 by Ross Russell (Charlie Parker, pp. 178–79).

Vera Miller Shapiro and Nat Hentoff, from *The Jazz Makers*, edited by Nat Shapiro and Nat Hentoff, copyright © 1957 by Holt Rinehart and Winston General Book (Roy Eldridge, pp. 45, 46, 47).

To the memory of Budd Johnson for his contributions
to the music from the '20s to the '80s.

He bopped with the best and never stopped swinging.

Acknowledgments

Immeasurable thanks to all the people who took the time to contribute their thoughts to the narrative. Gratitude to the Guggenheim Foundation without whose aid the project never would have been carried forward. A tip of my bop cap to my editor, Sheldon Meyer, for contracting the book and having the patience and informed guidance to help me to see it through. Appreciation to assistant editors, Pamela Nicely and Melissa Spielman, for their benevolent nitpicking. Kudos to the transcriber-typists: Patricia Ciro, Sarah McCarn Elliott, and Lora Rosner. Verbal medals to Bill Gottlieb for making his authentic photographs of the period available. The same to Dan Morgenstern, director of the institute of Jazz Studies, Rutgers University, not only for the photos from the Institute's archives, but for resolving the impasse over the book's title between Sheldon and myself, by suggesting *Swing to Bop*, incidentally the name of a Charlie Christian jam on "Topsy." Back in the photography department, a typewritten handshake to Robert Rondon for his inside jacket photo of me in a jazz festival attitude.

To Liz Rose, for the use of her Apple IIe and generous help, I can't say enough. Without them I'd probably still be doing the index. Last, but not least, tulips to my wife, Mary Jo, for her encouragement from inception to the final light at the end of the tunnel.

Contents

SWING TO BOP

Introduction

Big bands were the focal point of the so-called "Swing Era," when jazz reached its greatest popularity, in great part because of its relationship to dancing. Jazz permeated our society from movies through comic strips; found its way into our language, our fashions, and, of course, at its source, was heard in recordings, on the radio (live and on record), in theatres, ballrooms, and nightclubs. The "swing" bands did not play jazz all the time, but even the ballads and novelties were approached from a jazz viewpoint. The "sweet" bands, on the other hand, all had in their books some jazz arrangements, or "flagwavers," as they were called.

Swing, like the styles of jazz that preceded it, was essentially a black expression, but it was the white bands who were accorded the greatest popularity. Duke Ellington, Jimmie Lunceford, Count Basie, Earl Hines, and Cab Calloway all were successful in this period, but not to the extent of their white counterparts. Benny Goodman, utilizing the arrangements of Edgar Sampson, Jimmy Mundy, Horace Henderson, and, most particularly, Fletcher Henderson, sparked the arrival of the Swing Era in the public consciousness. He was dubbed "The King of Swing," and achieved the commercial triumph that had eluded Fletcher Henderson in the latter's years as leader of the first big band to gain wide recognition by playing jazz.

In the mid-1920s, Henderson's trumpet section was graced by Louis Armstrong who, among his other musical accomplishments, defined what swinging—that solid, yet springing, 4/4 propulsion—was all about.

As the '30s segued into the '40s, new ideas were coming together from various sources and directions; different people were developing along similar lines and others were being influenced directly or building their styles in a particular way because they were being shaped by the attitudes dictated by the innovations of these seminal improvisers. Men such as tenor saxophonist Lester Young, trumpeter Roy Eldridge, guitarist Charlie Christian, pianist Art Tatum, bassist Jimmy

Blanton, and drummer Jo Jones were musicians who caught the ears of their peers and inspired them to extend what they heard and create afresh.

The younger black musicians, tired of the repetition of the riff-derived arrangements and lack of solo space in the big bands, began to form a new music that they felt could not be so easily appropriated by the white leaders. Unobserved by many at the time, bebop evolved from the big bands—on the bandstand but more so in the after-hours jam sessions. This was happening in many parts of the country but really began to crystallize in New York at Harlem clubs such as Minton's and Monroe's Uptown House. From there Charlie "Bird" Parker and Dizzy Gillespie introduced their ideas into the Earl Hines band in 1943 for a short stay, unrecorded due to a recording ban. In 1944 came the first large bebop band, led by Hines's former vocalist Billy Eckstine and featuring, among other young stars of the new movement, Parker and Gillespie.

From there bebop moved to 52nd Street (where it had already put down roots), and in 1945 Dizzy and Bird co-led a quintet that offered their music in its quintessential form. When they recorded for the Guild label that same year, the word was spread to musicians and fans far beyond New York.

Although there were still some very important big bands in the Bebop Era, the emphasis shifted to small groups and the individual soloists within them. Then, too, the modern musicians of that time began to think of themselves as serious artists, whether it was someone like Gillespie, who also overtly entertained, or like Parker, who just planted his feet in a wide stance on the bandstand and played. This is not to say that the giants of the Swing Era were not fine artists, but they were coming out of a different milieu, and only people close to the music realized how "serious" their work was.

The advent of bebop came at a time when many of the same venues that the swing players had used—the movie theaters, hotels, and ballrooms—were also the arenas of the modernists, but to a far lesser extent. The boppers, of course, were performing in the small nightclubs, but were also utilizing the concert halls more and more, whether for programs by bands, combos, or the jam session taken from the club context and placed up on the stage. Norman Granz broke through with his *Jazz At the Philharmonic,* and soon there was Gene Norman's *Just Jazz* and other carbons or mutations.

The young black audience, which no longer supports jazz the way it once did (for a variety of reasons, including the cultural genocide of radio), was into bebop in the big cities above the Mason-Dixon Line. I know because whenever I went into a black neighborhood in the years 1945–1949, whether it was at a record store in Harlem, a shoeshine stand in St. Louis, a rib joint in Chicago, or someone's apartment in Brooklyn, I heard bebop coming out of loudspeakers, juke boxes, and an assortment of phonographs from consoles to portables. I was in closer touch with black people because of this music.

It was said that people didn't dance to bebop and, for the most part, this was true, but black people figured out a way to make those fast tempos by cutting the time in half whether they were doing a new dance called "The Apple Jack" or the older Lindy Hop. And when Bird or Lester Young or Gene Ammons played a romantic ballad, you put your arms around your partner, moved to the music, and got groovy. Whether it was Young playing a dance in St. Louis or Parker at the Pershing in Chicago, the ballroom was crowded with listeners *and* dancers.

Bebop was characterized as weird but, to many, it was a music that lifted one with beauty and joy. It was an expression of the finest black musical minds and, besides what it expressed explicitly, offered the human verities that jazz had communicated from its inception.

Though bop became a pervading influence, not only in jazz but, as it filtered down, through all facets of the entertainment and advertising industries, the music, as such, was never fully accepted by the public. Its greatest acceptance was when it was popularized by white musicians. This is not to say that the majority of white players who were drawn to the music came with the thought in mind, "Hey, I'm going to make some money with this." Those who did approach it calculatingly made little impact, for I don't believe even the successful popularizers were armed with that attitude.

All the young musicians, black and white, were caught up in the excitement generated by Parker and Gillespie. As a young fan I, too, was very taken with the new ideas. I think the reason I embraced it quickly was because I recognized all the qualities it had maintained from the previous jazz styles that I had been brought up on and loved so much: rhythmic propulsion and the happy-sad duality of the blues that infused so much of the music even when it wasn't couched directly in the 12-bar form. Additionally, if one could make the connection between the chord structures of the standard songs on which the original bop compositions were based and these new themes, it helped in appreciating the new improvisations.

As important as the harmonic explorations were, it was the rhythmic innovations that were at the core of what made bebop a new and unique expression. The drummers, shown the way by Kenny Clarke, accompanied in a manner that allowed the soloists to fly with eighth-note constructions and extend their lines to include bursts of sixteenth and thirty-second notes. It was a wedding of style and idea that, in new ways, combined elements that had been in existence in jazz for years.

I believe the first time I heard about the new music was when Daniel Bloom, who was a fellow student at Columbia Grammar Prep, was raving about a record called "Bu-Dee-Daht," from the Apollo session that Coleman Hawkins cut in February 1944 with Dizzy Gillespie, Clyde

Hart, Budd Johnson, and Max Roach, among others. It is generally considered the first official bebop recording date and Gillespie's "Woody 'n You" its most celebrated number.

I didn't hear any of the Apollos until after I discovered the Parker-Gillespie Guilds and Gillespie Manors toward the end of 1945 and had set out in search of any and all bebop, be it a chorus on a Johnny Long record of the old Peter Van Steeden chestnut *Home,* or a complete record in the style such as something by the Bebop Boys on Savoy. There were, however, people who heard the Apollos when they were released and were taken with them. Jim Krit, from Chicago, whom I met at college in 1948, said he encountered them when he returned from the Philippines after the war. "We didn't know the word bebop," he said, "but we knew they were different. We called it 'New York' jazz."

It was at that time, through the record program of Sid Torin, known as Symphony Sid, that I really became acquainted with the new "New York Jazz." He played it on WHOM between and among the Basies, Louis Jordans, Wynonie Harrises, and Billie Holidays, and on Fridays, when he came on a little earlier in the evening, he would devote an entire hour to the new releases on labels such as Guild and Manor. Each week he would run a contest in which you had to identify the music or the musician. The reward was free admission to the Sunday afternoon jam sessions at the Fraternal Clubhouse on West 48th Street or the Lincoln Square Center, which was next to the old St. Nicholas Arena on West 66th Street. Jazz promoter Monte Kay (who later went on to manage the Modern Jazz Quartet and Flip Wilson among others), publicist Mal Braveman, and Sid had formed an organization called the New Jazz Foundation under whose auspices these sessions were presented.

One Friday night I called Symphony Sid with the correct answer to his record quiz (I think it was the Slam Stewart trio playing "Three Blind Micesky") and won a pass to the Fraternal Clubhouse on the following Sunday afternoon. The only live jazz of consequence I had heard before was from the theater stage shows but I had never been to a jam session. I was not quite seventeen.

The music that still is remembered vividly from that day is the powerful trumpet blown on "Rose Room" by Bernie Privin, recently returned from overseas and the Glenn Miller Air Force Band; long, tall Dexter Gordon and short, orange-goateed Red Rodney combining on "Groovin' High"; and a slight, dark trumpeter, introduced in an offhand manner by Symphony Sid as "a little student from Juilliard," who was at the back of a large ensemble on stage for the finale and sputtered through a short solo when his turn came. Many, many months later I realized that it had been Miles Davis.

From that time I began to attend other Sunday afternoon sessions and eventually jazz nightclubs, particularly the ones between 5th and 6th Avenues on 52nd Street or "Swing Street," as it was known. Actually, I had already been to 52nd Street once to hear Billie Holiday at the Downbeat. I didn't date that much in high school but there was one girl who excited me, and I guess I wanted to take her to something special. Like all 52nd Street clubs the Downbeat was low-ceilinged, long and narrow. Each wall was lined with banquettes and the tables down the middle were flanked by two thin aisles. There were no dressing rooms to speak of and so the performers, their set over, would go out onto the street and club-hop since there were so many places in that block and the one west between 6th and 7th Avenues. Billie had her boxer named "Mister" at that time, and after she had finished singing she walked by our middle-section table with him on the way out of the club. My date must have tried petting the boxer for a minute later she said to me, "Miss Hollywood's dog almost bit me." It was the last time I took her out.

In the mid-'40s, 52nd Street had several jazz styles going at the same time: New Orleans (or its descendants) at Jimmy Ryan's, swing, and bebop. At the Fraternal Clubhouse and Lincoln Square Center most of the musicians were drawn from people working on the Street or players who might be in town with a traveling big band. There was a mixture of swing and bop that told anyone with ears that, although bop was a new way of playing, it came from and was not incompatible with swing, at least insofar as basic thematic material was concerned. Of course, beboppers were extending the harmonies, and rhythmically there were those marked differences, but there were drummers like Harold "Doc" West who were adapting very nicely.

When Dizzy Gillespie came back from California in the winter of 1946 without Charlie Parker, he opened at the Spotlite on 52nd Street with Ray Brown, Milt Jackson, Al Haig, Stan Levey and Leo Parker, no kin to Charlie, on baritone saxophone. Sometimes J.J. Johnson would sit in, a perforated, grey felt beanie hanging on the bell of his trombone, creating a velvet muted tone not unlike that of a French horn. My first published writing on jazz was a review of this group for the Columbia Grammar newspaper.

There were other great nights on the street: a J.J. Johnson quartet with Bud Powell on piano; Roy Eldridge's big band; Coleman Hawkins quartet with Hank Jones at the piano; and a group co-led by Flip Phillips and Bill Harris after Woody Herman's Herd had disbanded.

I left for the University of Missouri at Columbia in the fall of 1946 with intentions of studying journalism. A couple of record review columns for *The Missouri Student* was all the writing about jazz I did for a while. I visited in St. Louis and Kansas City on some weekends, listening to what music I could catch. On short vacations I would get to Chicago. During the summers, I hung out on 52nd Street, the Royal Roost, and Harlem, bought as many records as I could and read about jazz from Mezz Mezzrow's *Really the Blues* to Leonard Feather's *Inside Bebop*.

In early 1950 I left Missouri and returned to New York. Birdland had opened the previous Christmas and become the main jazz club. I tried to get a job with either *Down Beat* or *Metronome,* the two leading jazz periodicals of the time, but it was not as simple to break into jazz print in those days as it is today.

My professional debut was a set of liner notes from Prestige PRLP 117, a Zoot Sims LP recorded in August 1951. I continued to write for Prestige, also producing records and doing just about everything else—packing boxes, sweeping floors, and serving as liaison with the disc jockeys—intermittently into 1955. I also began to write for other labels and, finally, for *Metronome* and *Down Beat.*

In the 1960s Martin Williams was editing the "Jazz Masters" series for Macmillan and asked me to write *Jazz Masters of the '40s,* a book that concentrates on the major figures of the music called bebop, through the format of biographical chapters. It was first published in 1966, and is now available in hardcover and paperback editions from DaCapo Press.

In the early '70s I felt I wanted to do a new book on the subject from a different standpoint. Rather than biography it would be an oral history, tracing the roots of the style and how it evolved from the musicians of the big bands of the '30s to become a full-fledged force in the big bands and, particularly, the small groups of the '40s. Under a grant from the Guggenheim Foundation the work was begun and interviews conducted with the following people (here listed alphabetically): Joe Albany, David Allyn, Jean Bach, Benny Bailey, Eddie Barefield, Jimmy Butts, Red Callender, Johnny Carisi, Benny Carter, Al Cohn, Sonny Criss, Buddy DeFranco, Charles Delaunay, Billy Eckstine, Biddy Fleet, Terry Gibbs, Babs Gonzales, Dexter Gordon, Jimmy Gourley, Al Grey, Johnny Griffin, Al Haig, Jimmy Heath, Neal Hefti, Woody Herman, Milt Hinton, Chubby Jackson, Henry Jerome, Budd Johnson, Gus Johnson, Hank Jones, Barney Kessel, Lee Konitz, Don Lanphere, Lou Levy, Shelly Manne, Junior Mance, Howard McGhee, Jay McShann, Mitch Miller, Billy Mitchell, James Moody, Brew Moore, Gerry Mulligan, Joe Newman, Red Norvo, Chico O'Farrill, Cecil Payne, Art Pepper, Lenny Popkin, Max Roach, Red Rodney, Frank Rosolino, Charlie Rouse, Jimmy Rowles, Zoot Sims, Hal Singer, Frankie Socolow, Sonny Stitt, Idrees Sulieman, Billy Taylor, Allen Tinney, Lennie Tristano, Charlie Ventura, Mary Lou Williams, and Trummy Young.

« **1** »

The Road

In the period from the early '30s to the war years, the big bands were king and inspired the same adulation that rock bands enjoy today. The jazz fan and the young jazz musician had a very close relationship. Indeed, very often they were one and the same.

❖❖

SHELLY MANNE I remember when I subbed for Davey Tough years ago—when he got ill one night—at the Hickory House with Joe Marsala. I was sitting there playing, and I had been playing drums maybe a year, a little over a year at that time. And Benny Goodman came in 'cause he wanted to hire Davey to join the band. He sat down at the circular bar, right next to the drums. I was playing and it was really nerves time because Benny was there. It's 19 . . . '41 I guess. '40 or '41. Anyway, Benny had, to me, the greatest band he ever had at that time. That was when Charlie Christian and Cootie Williams were on the band—Artie Bernstein and Mike Bryan, Georgie Auld, Gus Bivona. That was a wild band. Eddie Sauter was doing all the writing—"Benny Rides Again."

He left, after he spoke to Joe, and Joe Marsala goes, "Hey, Benny liked the way you played. Maybe he's gonna give you a call." I said, "Hey, you're kidding." About an hour later the phone rang, and Benny said, "Hey kid, what's your name?" And I said, "Shelly Manne." He said, "This is Benny Goodman." I said, "Yes, Mr. Goodman." He says, "You wanta go on the road with my band?" I said, "Yeah." He couldn't get Davey, and I guess he liked the way I played. He said, "Just be down to Grand Central Station tomorrow with your cymbals. I have the drums."

So I put the cymbals under my arm the next day. I think the train was leaving at eleven. I must have been there about eight, sitting there with my one little suitcase, and here they come, about two hours after I'd gotten there, but they start walking in—Cootie, Georgie Auld, Charlie Christian, and Helen Forrest—and, man, I'm sitting there, and

I was really going berserk, you know I really was, and I was scared. I got on the train. I sat there all by myself. In fact, there's a picture I think in one of the jazz history books or something, some place. They took a picture of that band at the station. We were going to the March of Dimes President's Ball in Washington. I sat on the train. I was all by myself, and Benny came up and says, "What are you worried about, kid?" I said, "Well, I haven't seen the book or anything." He said, "You've been listening to my music for years," and he walked away. That night I played with the band. I played with the band I think two, three days, then Davey joined them. He finally got Davey on his phone. It was a funny experience sitting there when you're young, watching these people walk in.

Of course, the big bands were the way a musician could gain national prominence very quickly in a very well-known band. 'Cause everybody knew the third trumpet player, the fourth trumpet player; they'd name me the baritone player, the third alto. They knew everybody's name in the band. That's how guys like Harry James and people like that all became famous in big bands. Like with Benny's band.

I think the big bands were the place where you got your schooling and where you got your experience with other great musicians. 'Cause when we say big bands—when I say big bands—I mean big jazz bands, what I felt were jazz-oriented bands, not just dance bands. Like when we were kids we used to just get in the basement and listen to Duke Ellington records all night.

Of course, big bands gave an individual a chance to be heard nationally and gain a reputation because the big bands had the kind of following the rock bands have now. Maybe not quite as gigantic.

Like the one year with Stan's [Kenton] band when we did concerts. My God, they'd be standing on top of one another to hear the band. It was exciting. It was an exciting time, and the big bands not only paid pretty good salaries for those days for a top-notch sideman, but it was a way of getting, really gaining a reputation. Nowadays it's very difficult to gain a reputation on Woody Herman's band for instance. I know Woody's got a good band, but I can't tell you who's in the band.

Nowadays, most of the young kids come from colleges. They're not well-known. But most of the players in those days were pretty well-known as players before they joined the band. They used to say, "Hey, you know who joined? He joined him." The next thing, you know, you're listening to the band and listening for him, for his solos.

❖❖

The whole big band, road syndrome is something that's virtually finished now. Of course there are a few bands that still travel, but even the small groups don't travel the way they once did. The club circuit is not as extensive, and the airlane to an engagement has replaced the road.

❖❖

SHELLY MANNE   They're not forced—the bands and small bands even today—aren't forced to live together like a family. I think that the big
bands traveling in those days, what we were talking about, being locked
up together, creative juices flowing between twenty guys, created a
whole thing away, another creative thing away from an influence of
someplace else. In other words, I think it was healthy, because it created a thing of your own.

And traveling and constantly living together and exchanging ideas,
creative ideas—playing and creating with your playing on the job at
night created a thing away. You weren't influenced. You didn't say,
"Let's play it like they played it." You didn't hear how they played it.
You said, "Hey, let's play this chart. Let's do this." And you got your
own individual sound that way.

❖❖

If you were a big-band musician in the '30s you played mostly for
dancers in large ballrooms, roadhouses and, in the Southeast, huge
tobacco warehouses. Bands went on location in hotels and theaters, but more often it was one-nighters and the rigors of the road.
They traveled by bus, car, train and sometimes, as with Duke Ellington and Cab Calloway, by private railroad car.

❖❖

MILT HINTON   I'd like to mention this about Cab. Cab had a standard that
he wanted to set. He traveled to the South; he always traveled first-
class. There was no planes, it was always Pullman wherever he could
get a Pullman, and a baggage car next to the Pullman—a huge baggage car where he had a great big, green Lincoln Continental, and he
carried a chauffeur, and we had our trunks in his baggage car, and
when we got to the small towns were you couldn't get a train into, then
he could hire a bus. This kept us out of conflict with the people in the
South that were biased, black and white. Mostly white, but even black
guys couldn't go in a black neighborhood in the South and walk in the
bars because the guys would figure we were pullin' rank on them because we were sharp—we were city slickers—those niggers are from
New York and they've come here to take our chicks. There could be
a confrontation and somebody could get hurt and most likely it would
be us.

It was so competitive, so Cab, to keep this down, he would hire this
Pullman. We would get out, get us cabs to the dance hall. At intermission we'd make whatever connections we wanted with the chicks,
and then we'd tell them, "Meet you at the Pullman." We kept a Pullman porter for six months at a time—the same guy. When we left to
go to the dance, we'd tell him to get fourteen bottles of whiskey, three
watermelons, and a hundred chickens and have it there for us. We'd
leave the money, and the guy would have it all set up so that when
the dance was over, and we'd made our connections at intermission
with all the other chicks we were going to be involved with—we'd tell

them to just come on down to the railroad station. Then we didn't have to go into town and have to compete with the local people, local fellows for the fancy of their local ladies. The ladies who were our choice came down, and when the party was over we'd thank them for their gratuities, and they got off the train, and the train would pick us up and take us on to the next town.

Cab had this feeling that he wasn't very successful playing dances in the South because in the South—as it is, almost now, there were radio stations that sang only blues, and "I'm Gonna Cut Your Head Off," and I'm gonna do this, and "I'm Gonna Kill My Woman," and he didn't believe in this. He thought that perhaps what he intended to do was to try to entertain the people, especially the black community, show them the sharp zoot suit, the hip styles, the new lingo, and this kinda thing, to elevate 'em, but they kept requesting blues, and Cab wasn't a blues band. He didn't believe in these blues, because these blues taught people to fight, and to get under, to make them feel low and degraded, and he didn't feel this.

So Cab consequently would not acquiesce to this type of thing, and of course the people hadn't been educated to his type of entertainment. It was just too sharp for them, and his dances fell off. The white dances were great, even though we had problems with all those who wanted to jump us and all those crackers who wanted to beat us up. They were so rude down there that you could hit a nigger in the mouth—as long as you could get three hundred dollars, and some of them had the money so they wanted to do it—and especially a nigger like Cab. He was a bigshot. So we had these problems along with that, and not being able to play a double dance—play a white dance tonight and a black dance tomorrow night. He was continually losing money in the South, so he decided to give up playing down there. Because the radio stations only plugged blues and race records and whatnots, and not enough of his things. And they did not do that, there, for him, for Cab. The people who could hear him on radio and came just from what they listened to from the Cotton Club on radio programs, but the records, he was never really big in records. Because they never bought his type of records in the South. So he finally gave it up.

❖❖

The private Pullman helped avoid hostile confrontations, but they were an exception. Usually a black band had to stay at black hotels or at private homes in black communities. Sometimes there were no blacks.

❖❖

TERRY GIBBS   I was talkin' with Milt Hinton. There was one town, I'll never forget, Marysville, Kansas, where there wasn't a black section of town, where the guys actually had to sleep on the bus.

❖❖

Nat Towles, out of Omaha, Nebraska, solved this kind of problem by moving his band around in a big sleeper bus. During my hitchhiking experiences, when I was at the University of Missouri, I remember seeing the bus, with the band's name printed clearly on the side, tooling along U.S. 40. A musician once told me, "When that bus used to park for the night, in the morning the ground around the bus would be covered with condoms. And it would get pretty funky inside. They used to clean it out periodically. They called it the 'traveling garbage can.' "

The area Towles traversed was called the "territory." It included Kansas, Missouri, Texas, Oklahoma, Wisconsin, Minnesota, Iowa, and the Dakotas. Bands also made forays into Montana and Wyoming, but these states weren't included when someone referred to the "territory." (When I was in the midwest in the '40s, however, a "territory" band also meant white, "mickey mouse" bands out of Mankato or Sioux Falls.)

❖❖

BUDD JOHNSON   Grant Moore was a band out of Milwaukee, Wisconsin. He had all of these cats with him too, Jabbo Smith, all those cats used to play with Grant Moore.

The only thing about the Dakotas, there wasn't many black people around like us. We used to stay in white homes. They didn't have other hotels, and we would stay with white families in their homes. There was very little prejudice.

I was out in Montana in 1940 and the only place we could stay was in some little, crummy Chinese hotel. They wouldn't even let us in none of the hotels. We couldn't eat in none of the restaurants in town. We couldn't even go to the red-light districts. I don't know about the '20s. But up through the Dakotas, that was different. That was in the late '20s—'28, '29, '30, '31. It started to get a little bad in '31 because some of the cats started messing up, knocking the daughters up and wouldn't marry them and all of that sort of thing. So it got bad about then. We used to feel, we used to feel nothing. A lot of Indians up that way. We used to drink that beer with them and alcohol. We used to put that alcohol in the beer and shake it up and get high. Play all of those state fairs all through Nebraska and Iowa. And no heat. We used to sit up and play with our overcoats and gloves on in some of these barns and things. But a hell of a lot of fun, lot of fun during those times. But I mean all in all . . .

❖❖

Milt Hinton wasn't laughing on the night of June 19, 1936. He was on the road with Cab Calloway, and the experience of that time stays with him.

❖❖

MILT HINTON   In Dallas, Texas, we played the World's Fair. Joe Louis was fighting somebody [Max Schmeling] and got knocked out if I remember properly. It was the greatest disgrace of our lives, 'cause here we were in no black man's country, and they wouldn't even let us listen to it on the radio in the fair grounds, and we had to walk outside the fair grounds to a little bar to listen to the fight on the radio, and after having been saddened by [his knock-out]. . . .

'Cause [Joe Louis] was an impetus to dignity, to manhood, to us. He was a symbol. It was a chance for us to say, "Hey, man, look out. Don't do that. Here we are." And this was a great symbol, and we had to go outside the fair grounds to a bar to listen, and then on top of that, Joe Louis gets knocked out, and officials made us *pay* to get back in where we were working! Made us pay to get back in! So aside from feelin' so low, we came back in and had to pay to get back in.

❖❖

Dexter Gordon was approaching his eighteenth birthday when he left his native Los Angeles for the first time as a member of Lionel Hampton's band. What he saw and did is typical of much of the black band experience.

❖❖

DEXTER GORDON   We left—it was 1940, December 23rd, 1940. We left Los Angeles, and I joined the band like just a few days before we left. I never had a rehearsal with the band. And then we got into this bus. It was a small bus. Gladys [Mrs. Lionel Hampton] was economizing. It was a line called All-American—All-American Bus Line—and the whole band could fit in there, but it was tight, and it was strictly a California bus, and it's December, and so our first stop was Fort Worth, Texas, which I think is about fifteen hundred miles. It took about three days to get there. And after we got out of Arizona, we got into New Mexico, it started getting cold, and so then we got to El Paso, there was a mutiny [laughter]. There was a mutiny in the band. And this cat Jack Lee was the road manager with the band. And the cats said, "No, no, man, shuck this bus. We got to get a real bus." 'Cause that kind of bus was okay for California or a short trip, but being out on the road you needed something like a Greyhound. Something insulated and strong. But then we got the bus, a real bus. I think it was El Paso, 'cause by that time, everybody was wearing overcoats. We were wearing California clothes anyway, but we got everything on.

So then we went to Fort Worth and we played the Hotel Fort Worth. It was a white hotel that was strictly white. And the next day, a couple of days later, we played in some other towns. We played in Dallas. The state fair. For a black dance. And I remember seeing this cat with this beautiful white Palm Beach suit dancing his ass off, swinging. And all of a sudden during the dance, at one point, there was a big circle of people, moving out, moving out and pretty soon it looked like an arena, these two cats in the middle, and this one cat was the cat with the white suit, and then suddenly his suit was red. I'll never forget that.

But for the most part I don't remember too many special incidents, except a funny thing happened one time we were in Mississippi and doing these one-nighters and gettin' food out of the back of the restaurant and all that kind of shit. So we pulled into this filling station, a roadside diner. Everybody's hungry, and nobody wants to get out of the bus and go through all that hassle and shit, so me and Joe Newman said, "Fuck it, we'll get out." And cats are calling, "Why don't you get something, bring me back a pork chop or something?" I said, "Yeah, man." So the cat, the man, is working on the bus, the owner of the gas station, he's filling up the bus, and he's going through all this. So anyway, Joe and I go into the diner, and we stand at the counter—we don't sit down, we stand at the counter. And say we'd like to get something to eat. And there's two young chicks in there. So one said, "Okay, what would you like?" So I said, "I'd like some ham and eggs" or something like that. And Joe said, "Yeah, same for me." She said, "Okay, where would you like to sit?" "Well, here." "Sit down." Just straight life, you know. We're the youngest cats in the band anyway. So we sit down, and then we started eating. By this time the cats in the bus are getting a little curious. They see us go in the front door and expect to see us come right out, and we're in there for a little while, so they start coming out of the bus, stretching, and getting a little curious. They wander over there, they come in. Man, we're sitting there drinking coffee, ham and eggs, toast, napkins, and everything and say, "What the fuck is this?" Next thing you know, the whole fuckin' diner is filled up with the band. And the chicks are ordering this and that. And all of a sudden the front door bursts in, and here comes the cat finished with the bus. And he comes in and sees this diner all filled with niggers eatin', and man this guy got so red. Looked like he was gonna explode—gonna have a heart attack—man, he was really dramatic. And all the cats froze. All gawking and looking. So by this time me and Joe had finished. And the cat's screaming, "Get all these niggers out of here. Uhhh. I'll kill them. Where's my gun?" So then, by this time the manager had come in. So he starts talking to the man and coolin' him off. And the cats are coming out, whether they'd finished or not. And later on he's telling us, that he told him, "All these guys, they're not Southern boys, they don't know nothing about this, they're all from New York or Hollywood or something." And he was talking to him till we got out of there.

❖❖

When blacks and whites gravitated to one another there were problems. The road experience could bring these to the surface.

❖❖

LEE KONITZ   The biggest hassle that I can recall is traveling on tours with Bird and black musicians in the South when we had to stay in different places. This was in '53 we went out, and in Georgia they had to have a white man in the taxi before they could leave the airport, and things of that nature stand out in my mind. Bird invited me to stay at their hotel.

❖❖

When Charlie Rouse, who had been raised in Washington, D.C., went on a deep Southern tour with Dizzy Gillespie's orchestra in 1945 he experienced the kind of incident that cannot be ignored.

Washington is a Southern city, but not in the sense that Memphis or Mobile is a Southern city. As a Washingtonian, Rouse thought of himself more as a Northerner. Most of the men in Dizzy's band were from well above the Mason-Dixon line. Their previous encounters with prejudice more often took a more subtle guise. So going south was a total immersion in a negative atmosphere of separate water fountains, dividing lines at dances, and much worse.

❖❖

CHARLIE ROUSE   We hadn't been to the South at the time, and at the time the South was very bad. And I think it was in Memphis, Tennessee . . . we had to get out of town early in the morning. There was a bass player from Arkansas named Buddy Jones.* Well, I met Buddy Jones in Washington. We were friends there. So he was in the Navy and he was in Memphis, and when we got there with the band we played a one-nighter, and Buddy wasn't supposed to be there, you dig? But he met us in the daytime, and we're walking up and down Beale Street together, and everybody is looking at us weird. We wasn't paying no attention or anything. So when we left each other, Buddy said, "Well I'll see you at the dance tonight." I say, "Okay." And when we got to the dance the police came and beat him and clubbed him out of the dance. They called the SPs and they came and, oh man, they messed him up and they told us we had to get out of town before sundown. It was really weird, man. And the next time I saw Buddy we talked about it. But we felt that it was something happening, 'cause we was walking up and down Beale Street laughing and talking and people turning around looking at us, and we say, "Hey, look at those weird dudes looking at us." And we's just walking up and down the street. We left, but then they put him in, put him in the brig. And he told me later that he stayed in the brig for about two or three months.

❖❖

Despite incidents such as this, black and white musicians continued to interact. Mixed bands were more for jam sessions and recordings—when the Eddie Condon Chicago gang, all white, arrived in New York in the '30s, they cut sides with Red Allen, Sid Catlett, Alex Hill, Teddy Wilson, Fats Waller, Pops Foster, and Zutty Singleton—until Benny Goodman officially broke the "color line" in the mid-'30s when he hired Teddy Wilson and Lionel Hampton as regular members of his orchestra.

Georgie Auld, a Goodman alumnus, led a band in the '40s that was predominantly white but had some black sidemen and played for black audiences at theaters like the Apollo in Harlem.

❖❖

*Influenced to go into music by Charlie Parker, whom he met in Arkansas in 1941, Jones later played with Charlie Ventura, Joe Venuti, Lennie Tristano, Buddy De-Franco, and Elliot Lawrence.

AL COHN   It was the first time that I had ever really been exposed to black theaters and the black neighborhoods, so it was kinda new for me and a great experience. Shadow Wilson played with the band for a while and Howard McGhee, and I don't remember anything happening that was . . . I remember being in Harlem in those days and never thinking there was any kind of "draft"* going on. I don't know how it was for the guys when we played downtown.

When we were with that band we did some one-nighters and, as a matter of fact, I remember hearing something, a little Jewish prejudice going on then too. [In Ohio we were] driving to some gig in the back of the truck when something happened to the bus, and we got a lift from the hotel, and this guy was talking about these Jewboy bands from New York. Being so involved in my own thing, I wasn't even listening to that stuff. I didn't even hear it.

❖❖

Only well enough to remember the remark thirty-five years later. But it was not just about being black or Jewish. It was the state of being a musician, looked down on much as vaudevillians and actors, have been for as long as there have been itinerant entertainers. White bands didn't exactly have a picnic out on the road. Musicians of any race were regarded as interlopers by rednecks or most any provincial and were on a back-door, employees' entrance footing to a great extent. So although they didn't have the problem of "wrong" skin color, white bandsmen, too, knew the rigors and pitfalls of the road. Vocalist David Allyn tells a story that illustrates this and, at the same time, reveals the hipster mentality of a body of white musicians who grew up in the wake of Lester Young, Dizzy Gillespie, and Charlie Parker.

❖❖

DAVID ALLYN   Rocky [Coluccio] and a bunch of buys—Stan Kosow, Stan Levey, Tubby Phillips, and let's see, who the hell was with them? Don Lanphere. We're in Art Mooney's band; we're out on the road. He had a pretty good dance band. Not that show shit that he had all the time, but we had a pretty good book. And we went out to make some money just a few weeks. And we're lost in Cleveland, in Shaker Heights. And the bus driver, it's foggy and kind of dawnish and he didn't know where the hell he's going and we're riding around. And at that time, I was strung out, and I was fucked up. This could have been around '51, '52. Around in there. And it was miserable being out there without shit. You know you're making "croakers"† all the time for Dilaudid. Tryin' to score somewhere. But Jesus we wouldn't hit very much 'cause you'd be missing most of the time. Get beat and all that shit. You'd have to leave town, get on the bus.

*negative feelings.
†doctors.

I think we're just coming into Cleveland. But anyway, the bus driver's lost and there's the gray dawn coming up. And as the fog starts to lift and we're rounding corners, we could see that we're in an area where there's tremendous estates—with great big iron gates and stone walls and houses sitting back, with pillars. Great green lawns and shrubbery. Just fantastic places. And I picked up on it. I used to stand by the driver where I could hold court. "Look at this. Oh, my God, look at this." They would say, "Oh, man." Just like unison, everybody, "Oh, dig that pad. Oh, that's wild. Look at this over here. Look at this. Oh man, look at this." And this went on. The guy's saying, "Jesus, I can't find my fuckin' way." He's trying to drive the bus. And we didn't give a shit about him. The pads were so wild. The houses were just so wild, right? These great big estates. And I said, "We're gypsies. What are we? We're roving, we're wandering, we're stupid." I said, "We're not hip. We're not hip. They're hip. We're square. Look at us. What have we got?" And they're saying, "Oh, you're right, David."

And I say, "What the fuck are we doing?" Who listens to us? Nobody. These people don't even want to hear us. Maybe they turn us on for five minutes and turn us off. And we're working years. They're hip. We're square. That's what it is. We're gypsies. We're bums. That's what we are. And we don't have any shit, and nothing is right." And Rocky Coluccio says, "Yeah, but wait a minute, man, now wait a minute, what do they know about Diz and Prez and Bird?" [laughter]. Oh, God. Fucking classic.

❖❖

Despite the hardships and down days, all was not despair in the big bands. Before 1941 and during the early years of the war, there was no heroin problem. There were soul-testing times, to be sure, but these were men interacting and enjoying the bloom of their youth and experiencing musical and extramusical discoveries.

❖❖

SHELLY MANNE   The important thing about big bands was the fun that you remember having on them. You don't remember the really bad shit that happened. You remember the good things. At least I do. I remember when I was, years ago, with Bob Astor's band or some band in Boston. We were playin' in Boston, and I dress up like the hunchback of Notre Dame. I'd get the girl vocalist to make up my face. I was so skinny and gaunt in those days. I'd stick a pillow in my back, and I remember the Copley Square Hotel—not the Copley Plaza— the Copley Square Hotel. They had fire escapes that ran around the whole building. You could walk all around the building on the fire escapes. Old-style building. So I used to find out what room the guys were in playing cards or something. Oh, there was another band in there. Another good band . . . oh, it was Will Bradley's band. I ran around the fire escape, and I'd run by and I'd peek back and say something and then, all of a sudden I'd jump in the window at them or something.

We used to do crazy things like that. And then I'd run, everybody would scatter. I'd finally run in the bathroom, and they used to have the shower that had a shower curtain, a round one, in the middle of the bathroom. You'd open it, and there guys would be standing there like that. Straight up. Or else we played, I'll never forget it, with Stan Kenton's band. We played a place up in New Hampshire and we stayed in an old house. Like really a hundred, hundreds of years old, the house was. It had a big wicker chair, like a Sidney Greenstreet chair, and at night the hallways were wide and dark, and they didn't have many lights. You just had little, dull lights. Well, I got there real early one night after the job, and I just sat there in the chair like this. I knew a couple of the guys were coming, and I just sat there. They came down this dark hallway in this very spooky kind of house. They flipped. But things like that I remember. We did wild things when we were kids.

I remember on Bob Astor's band, Al Young—Al Epstein. Yeah, used to be Al Young. You know he played trumpet with Babe Russin's band. He played baritone, but on trumpet he could only play middle G to C above high C. He studied with Costello for a little while. And he could only play the high notes, so he used to play all the high notes, like Paul Webster in Lunceford's band. He'd play the end, so we'd play a lot of Jimmie Lunceford arrangements—"For Dancers Only" with Babe Russin's band—and we rehearsed at the Fraternal Clubhouse. Al would put his baritone down and hit the trumpet notes at the end of the chart.

But anyway, we used to do wild things. We were at Budd Lake in New Jersey with Bob Astor's band at the Wigwam, and Al says, "I'll give you fifty cents if you eat that spider and some mustard." You know, you'd do it. You'd do anything, man. One day he put iron glue in my hair while I was sleeping. I woke up—my hair was long in those days, right—my hair stood like that for weeks. I couldn't get it out. Crazy things.

When Neal Hefti first came from Omaha, he came to join Sonny Dunham. Something happened between him and Sonny, and he joined Bob Astor's band. We roomed together. And at night we didn't have nothing to do, and we were up at this place—Budd Lake. He said, "What are you gonna do tonight?" I said, "Why don't you write a chart for tomorrow?" Neal was so great that he'd just take out the music paper, no score, [hums]—trumpet part, [hums]—trumpet part, [hums]—trombone part, [hums], and you'd play it the next day. It was the end. Cooking charts. I never forget, I couldn't believe it. I kept watching him. It was fantastic. And one night we got arrested in Budd Lake 'cause we went out with the guys, had a couple of beers or something—we were just kids. And we opened a big truck where there was ducks, transporting some ducks or something. We opened it out and let them all out. They took us to jail. But those are the things, you remember those things, strange things.

One time with Stan's [Kenton] band, we played a small theater . . . and these things were happening all the time. Played an old theater in New England, and Ray Wetzel used to . . . you know, the trumpet riser in the theater was very high, and Ray weighed almost three hundred pounds or whatever he weighed, and he'd jump off the riser and run down front to sing a vocal. He jumped off the riser this day, and he went right through the stage up to his waist with his trumpet. And there he is stuck in the stage, and of course, like the band couldn't play for like fifteen minutes. We were in tears rolling around. The audience was laughing too, I'm sure. But those things were always happening. Now Stan running for—beating off the band, and running for the piano bench to hit the downbeat on a tune, and the piano bench collapsing on him. Things like that always happened. They were fun days.

Once we were playing a one-nighter in Kansas City in a ballroom, and we're changing clothes. We're late for the job; we're changing clothes in the back. The bandstand was here, and there was an aisleway that led down this little flight of stairs, and the dressing room was behind the bandstand. And the sprinkler system broke, with all our music, our instruments, our uniforms, everything. And Stan was standing there holding the sprinkler, yelling, "Go get a plumber or something." I remember little things like that, that happened.

On Woody's [Herman] band, see I didn't ride on the bus. I bought my own car when I joined Woody's band, and I traveled in the car. Also, I drove with Woody in his car. I made a left turn in a car while I was driving with Woody and drove up . . . I thought it was a street, in Pittsburgh, but it was railroad tracks. I was driving up railroad tracks. The street was to the left.

❖❖

Sometimes playing in a band was just plain hard work, even if you weren't on the road. A location job in a ballroom or hotel was a matter of coming to work in the evening, but the theater stage shows were a different matter, alternating through the day with the feature film.

❖❖

AL COHN   Joe Marsala was my first name band, in '43. We played one week in New York during that time at the Loew's State. That's when I found out what it is to work. I didn't know that you come in at twelve noon, and you're there till eleven o'clock at night. You know, four or five shows a day. That was one week, seven days. But some guys got on a show that really made it, and they spent six weeks doing seven days— you know something like that—playing the same show all the time. You have time off between shows, so you grab a bite to eat. How many times can you see the movie?

Well, it's different if you're working as a musician at Radio City—I never did it, so I don't really know. They have a system. Work a few weeks and then take a few days off.

❖❖

Most major cities had huge movie palaces with the facilities for stage shows, but New York had more of them. Manhattan had the Paramount, Capitol, Strand, and Loew's State. The neighborhood houses, such as the Flatbush (in Brooklyn) and the Windsor (in the Bronx), were otherwise used more for theater presentations rather than motion pictures. Even if one was in grade school it was possible, when school let out at three o'clock, to hear bands such as Count Basie and Charlie Barnet bands in one's own neighborhood. Then there was downtown Brooklyn, where one might see and hear the Jimmie Lunceford band at the Brooklyn Strand in a show headlined by Bill Robinson; and of course, the bright lights of Broadway.

At the Apollo on 125th Street, one often saw Alan Curtis, with his 40-suit wardrobe, as Philo Vance; downtown, one was more likely to view Humphrey Bogart in a Warner Brothers epic while cutting school to catch the morning show of Lionel Hampton featuring Arnett Cobb and Herbie Fields. A classmate once sat through Morris Carnovsky trying to intimidate Alan Ladd in *Saigon* three times just to see four stage shows of Buddy Rich.

The bands were a way of life then, particularly for the strong fans and the budding musicians. Not everyone had the New York advantage, but there were stages all over, and eventually the bands arrived there.

❖❖

JIMMY HEATH   When I was in high school in North Carolina, my uncle used to take me to see the big bands that came down to North Carolina to play, and I saw the Erskine Hawkins band down there. I know 'cause I got everybody in the band to autograph—and the Sweethearts of Rhythm—an all-girls band who nobody realized before the liberation business, but they had a big band. But Erskine Hawkins was one of my favorites. They used to go into some kind of things with the big bands, even with Erskine Hawkins, that would only incorporate the alto, maybe.

❖❖

Many bands had little groups that would come down front, like the Cab Jivers with Cab Calloway.

❖❖

JIMMY HEATH   So now they chased the small group back. It was very difficult. But, I mean, in the beginning there was a small group. Then they went into the big band era. When I was around Philly after I finished school—and I was around there for a few years—I was studying with a guy, saxophone, for about six months or so, and I was frequenting the Earle Theater. Every week I would go over on the day they would open and carry my lunch and see the whole three or four shows a day, and I would know all the arrangements, memorize all their arrangements. I saw Mitchell Ayres. I saw Shep Fields and all them saxophones. I saw Alvino Rey with the steel guitar. I saw Tommy Dorsey's band; Jimmy Dorsey's band; Cab Calloway with Chu Berry; Georgie Auld's band with Shadow Wilson and Howard McGhee; Gene Krupa's band with Roy Eldridge; Andy Kirk's band, with the three tenor players: J. D. King, Edward Loving, and Jimmy Forrest. I saw that. I saw Cootie's band with Eddie Vinson; Charlie Barnet's band when "Cherokee" was out. Let me see . . . well, Lunceford I saw once. And Benny Goodman, of course. He had Georgie Auld with him. "Good Enough To Keep." "A Smooth One." I saw Boyd Raeburn's band. And Lionel Hampton used to come in there and kind of break it up. Basie, of course. But Lionel Hampton was really sensational in the Earle Theater. They had to line up to see him.

❖❖

Hamp's band caused great excitement at the Capitol in late '43. "Flyin' Home" was at its height, and Hamp was jumping off drums and leaping in the air.

❖❖

JIMMY HEATH   Earl Bostic was in the band . . . and Arnett Cobb would be breaking houses down. I saw it once when Johnny Griffin and Arnett did their routine, throwing their coats down and all that.

❖❖

On the road, players encountered bands that never made it to the big city stages.

❖❖

DEXTER GORDON   Texas—well the big cities, Houston and Dallas—there was a little action there. And Houston had some good local bands there. Like Milt Larkins. [Illinois] Jacquet and Arnett [Cobb]—all those cats came out of that band. Then I remember we ran into the Carolina Cotton Pickers somewhere. Had a raggedy old bus, and the cats were wearing overalls. They really looked like the . . . territory band you know. There were a lot of them at that time. A lot of bands.

JIMMY HEATH   I saw lesser-name bands that were good bands, like when I was out with Nat Towles. There was always the Carolina Cotton Pickers band from the Jenkins Orphanage round South Carolina where Cat Anderson came from. And that band was always very good. There was another one called Floyd Ray from out West. That was a very good band, and Ernie Fields' band from Tulsa, Oklahoma. That's the first band I saw Bill Evans playing in—Yusef Lateef—but he was Bill Evans then. So I can say that 'cause he was Bill Evans then. He came to Wilmington, North Carolina, where I was going to school, in Ernie Fields's band. And I remember that big tone, even then. In fact, I got with Yusef last year and was singing some of the arrangements that they had in that band 'cause I could—when I go and hear a band and I really like an arrangement, I sit there until I got it kind of learned.

❖❖

There were all manner of fan clubs for bands and for the individuals who peopled those organizations, but you didn't have to be a club member to know who played what with which band. There was that unofficial club—the jazz fraternity—that supported the bands but, even more so, was aware of the soloists who were surfacing in the sea of orchestration that bubbled with surging ensembles and hot riffs.

However many solo opportunities these players received in the bands (some had entire featured numbers to themselves, but their normal space was more likely to be eight or sixteen bars rather than a full chorus of thirty-two bars) there wasn't enough room for them to do what was becoming an increasing imperative. There was a need for the music of the soloists to expand, while in the confines of the big bands it was being constricted, like the feet of the infant females of ancient China. But if the structure of the big-band performance was sometimes binding, the atmosphere surrounding these bands was conducive to opening new chances for expression.

The big bands brought countless musicians in contact with one another, whether within the same band or in encounters between and among bands. Since these organizations were constantly in motion around the country, they were always rubbing shoulders with one another in the large cities where one or more might be playing at the same time, or at least laying over at the same—or a nearby—hotel or other lodgings. There was also the interaction among the itinerants and the best of the locals in both large and small cities and towns.

The arena of communication became the jam session. It came in all sizes and styles and could happen almost anywhere. It was both proving ground and learning experience; a test of will and ego and a chance to try out and/or learn new ideas. If these jams didn't usually fit the Hollywood image—musicians whipping out their horns on a train or bus and wailing away into the sunset or dawn—there were scenes like the one saxophonist Eddie Barefield describes when he was with Bennie Moten's band in 1932.

❖❖

EDDIE BAREFIELD   We played the dance in Indianapolis that night, and the next day we're to meet in front of the ballroom to go to Terre Haute, Indiana and play the dance that night. And everybody's in the bus, loading up and settin' there. Just as we got to pull out, a guy in a little ol' raggedy Ford runs in front of the bus, and George Johnson jumps out. He says, "Where is Eddie Barefield? I come to cut him!"

And so everybody gets right out of the bus, goes into the ballroom, opens up the piano, and Basie starts to playin'. And we didn't get to the dance that night. Naturally, we sent out and got some booze and things, and we had a jam session right there.

❖❖

This session was strictly for musicians, but there were many others to which the public had access because they were held in nightclubs. Since they were often after hours, however, it was a special nonplaying public that was privy to such affairs. Saxophonists such as Coleman Hawkins, Ben Webster, and Lester Young were always challenging and being challenged. Trumpeters such as Roy Eldridge and Hot Lips Page were always ready to jam and would actively seek out sessions. They were young athletes, anxious to flex their musical muscles, work out with their "chops" and win the musical joust. In the 1930s Kansas City was notorious for its nonstop nightlife and the attendant sessions with their competitive nature.

❖❖

GUS JOHNSON We'd have jam sessions, "head-cutting" sessions, and all like that, you see. Kansas City was one town that all the musicians would come to from Chicago, New York, L.A., St. Louis, just to jam. They always wanted to play in Kansas City because they had so many places to go and sit in and play with the guys. They used to have *good* jam sessions. Ben Webster—you know *him*—and Hawk, Earl Hines would come there—I remember the time he came there. They did a dance out there at, I think Swope Park and, time they finished the dance, they came out on 18th and Vine, got out the bus, the first thing the drummer said was he was there to "cut heads" on drums. Jesse Price, he was nowhere to be found. He was a "head cutter" around at the time. So, I was down there, and we went in a little place down there, and everybody said, "Come on. Play. Come on. Play." I wouldn't play until after he got drunk. After he got drunk, then I'd cut his head.

❖❖

The urge to jam was particularly strong in a band that didn't have too much blowing room within its format. The Billy Eckstine band, although it featured the leader's ballad and blues vocals, was essentially a blowing band, but the young bloods aboard still had more to say after the job. Sometimes jammers were taken advantage of because of the eagerness to play.

❖❖

DEXTER GORDON We'd go out to jam when we were in New York or Chicago maybe or someplace in St. Louis, Kansas City. But down South, it's very seldom you'd run into any place that you could play unless you really just want to play anything. Of course, Los Angeles was always good for sessions. They had plenty of spots like New York, like Chicago.

❖❖

It was a practice in some places to encourage people to jam. Musicians would congregate after the job to eat, drink, and meet women. These clubs wanted to attract musicians who would sit in. That was good for their business.

❖❖

DEXTER GORDON   Well, a lot of times on the road, too, the band got an invitation to some club after the dance. In fact, this was almost everywhere. You go to a club, and there's a band there and you sit in. Some of the cats are playing all that shit. Well, usually, what it was, was just some kind of shuck because after the first drink then they put the bill on you, you dig? At the end of the night, when they'd come up with that shit, they would always take the bottom out of you.

❖❖

If jamming was a way of life, or a way within the band's life, consider the atmosphere and one man's attitude toward the milieu and the answers that jamming gave him.

❖❖

BARNEY KESSEL   I started with traveling bands in North Dakota and Minnesota and playing around there. And finally in 1942, I just decided that I'd better go to California; so I went to California and started playing there. I was there about two months in 1942, in the summer, and finally joined the first professional job I ever was with—that was a band that was funded by, and its musical director was Ben Pollack, who had the Chico Marx band, with Mel Tormé and Marty Napoleon in it. George Wettling was in that. Marty Marsala. It was a very good band. Excellent arrangements by Paul Villepigue. We had eight brass, six saxophones, and a vocal group, and it was tremendous. We played a lot of theaters—we did the Roxy here in New York. We played the Black Hawk restaurant for four months in Chicago, and when [Marx] did his numbers—his stage show—he would lead the band, we'd play with him. He did all of his specialties like with the grapefruit—some of the oranges were so small that when he got to the white keys they sort of didn't roll.

I particularly enjoyed an interesting concept of that band—that Mel Tormé loved the Glenn Miller band, and he made up his own arrangements for vocal groups on all of the Glenn Miller hits. We would do "Chattanooga Choo Choo"—we would do all of these things that Glenn Miller did—and they would be a big-band production, and Mel would write these vocal things, but they were not done in that way. You'd hear a fresh, big-band version of "Chattanooga" and nobody was doing that kind of thing.

There was a lot of jamming. Jam sessions. I would go to as many as I could. I must say, just for the record, and only to give an account of it, not necessarily selling morality or—I've never been involved with drugs or pot or whisky—never been involved. I love the life of playing music. I love the gypsy effect. I love the nomadic life. But I didn't like doing anything that personally would debilitate me and have never been involved in that.

It didn't seem to be a temptation. I felt very sorry for them because I saw guys looking old before their time. I saw a lot of people getting up with hangovers. I saw people trying to play and not having reflexes but believing they were playing very well. I never could see it as a solution to a problem. It was not from a standpoint of wanting to be a good God-fearing man—I just saw too many people that wasted themselves. I was told by many people that if I smoked a lot of grass I could hear a lot of chords. My reply, and it was honest, I would say, I can't even hear the ones I play now.

So there were a lot of jam sessions, and I went to as many as I could go to—not in New York, but wherever I used to play. There were three things that I could see about these jam sessions. One was just a social camaraderie, just the hanging out, being together and meeting new people. Second was learning tunes, learning things and hearing how other people played. I must confess that the third is sort of feeding your own ego and flexing your own egotistical musical muscles. It's kinda like to show people what you can do. And there was a lot of that, too. I never went in what I would call carving contests or cutting contests, but there was always the thing of feeling like that, wherever I played, I was like a gunfighter from out of town coming in, and they had their own local gunfighter, and he's pretty good, and we're very proud of him, let's see what you can do. Always that kind of thing. One thing that was interesting to me as an insight, another lesson, and I've mentioned this in stories; that is, while playing with Chico Marx, at the Black Hawk for four months, I had a lot of solos to play and every time I played I didn't think a thing about it. I just sort of closed my eyes and played whatever came to me, freely, whatever it was. At one point somebody in the band just happened to mention that we had a very large listening audience. He said, "Do you know how many people are listening to us? Millions."

Something happened to me at that point. I started thinking in a particular way. I said to myself, there are millions of people listening when I play a solo, and I'm a professional, and the thing that a professional should do is never make a mistake. Therefore, I should memorize my solos so that I don't.

For one thing, the solos that had been free, that represented a kind of a breathing thing within these arrangements, were now set, so it offered no really fresh kind of an interjection from me, because the band had been playing written parts, and now I came into my solos, and they were all set and the band could sing them with me. Not only did I not change them, but it even got worse because if I made a mistake, everyone knew it, whereas before, if I hadn't played exactly what I thought and it wasn't wrong, nobody knew. And I didn't realize that I'm sort of limiting myself in developing my own ability to improvise. I hadn't been to a jam session in about two months, and I went to a jam session in Chicago, after doing this for a number of weeks, playing this way and memorizing my chords because I didn't want to make a mistake on the radio. When I sat down to play, I realized that my reflexes weren't there, that if I thought of something it didn't come out right away; so something within me told me that I must get back to the way I was before and dare to make a mistake and dare to play freely, and that's the only way to get good at playing. The only way of getting good at making things up on the spot is to constantly make things up on the spot. That was an insight to me. Since that time, it wouldn't matter which show I've been on, I've been on radio shows, TV shows, when it comes time to blow, I just blow, and I could care less about the mistakes.

❖❖

Not only did players discover themselves out on the road, but they also came across musicians who stayed put, recording a few obscure solos or none at all.

❖❖

SHELLY MANNE   If we were playing Texas or someplace, there was always some roadhouse out of town. They said, "Hey, there's a crazy band out there. Let's go out there," and we'd all pack up at night and go on out and play. And it always happened in no matter what town you're in. In Detroit, Chicago, that's the first thing you do after the job is look for someplace to play. And then you'd start exchanging ideas with guys all over.

A lot of very creative musicians came from Washington, D.C. Bernie Miller, "Bernie's Tune." He wrote "Bernie's Tune" and "Loaded." Those things. He played piano. And what was the other guy's name—Romeo or something? I can't even remember. Tenor man in Washington [Angelo Tompros].

And in Philadelphia you know you'd always find the guys that played at all those places. 'Cause most of those guys, even during this time, were very strongly Basie-influenced. Lester Young and Basie School. All the drummers too.

❖❖

Tompros played and recorded with the Joe Timer orchestra (Willis Conover's House of Sounds—Brunswick; and One Night in Washington, Dizzy Gillespie with the Orchestra—Elektra Musician), but another from the Washington area didn't leave any tangible evidence of his talent.

❖❖

CHARLIE ROUSE   There was a kid there—alto player named Gibson. He was from—well, he was playing in Annapolis, Maryland. He had a style closely related to Bird, and I don't think he ever heard Bird at the time, but he was hearing that same type of harmonic structure. This was really in the late '30s—early '30s. Gibson. Gib, they called him. And he was playing, playing different things, and I didn't hear Bird at the time until Ben [Webster] told me about Bird. Because, actually, during that time back then, Diz was playing more like Roy. He was in their thing, that was the whole—that jazz thing.

BENNY CARTER   The only one that I can think of now is Cuban Bennett, who is my first cousin, and it's just a pity that there's nothing been unearthed that he has recorded on. I don't know of anything and this is just a pity, because he had something that was way ahead of its time. He was maybe closer to Clifford Brown, I might say. Yes, I would think so. He lived in a little town called McDonald, which is about eighteen miles out of Pittsburgh. He was really something else, you know. Sound and conception and harmonic structure, everything. He was quite amazing. I think Roy Eldridge is probably the only one around now that remembers him. And being a trumpet player, he could really make a proper evaluation.

HOWARD MC GHEE   Then there was a trumpet player that I had worked with before that I dug, and his name was Charlie Jacobs. He used to play with a girl named Harriet Calloway—she was going as Cab's sister, and everybody would flock to the dance. You used to see her drawing good because everybody thought she was some relation to Cab Calloway.* She was a cute girl; she had this trumpet player, Charlie Jacobs. He loved the ground she walked on. She really messed him up; she went off and left him. He followed her til he caught up with her in Seattle. But, boy, he was in love with that broad. He never did get straight, but he could play the shit out of the trumpet! I think he influenced me as much as Roy did. At that time he was playing all this shit that was as much as you could want to hear. He was using the whole tones, the augmenteds, the raised ninths, the flatted fifths, and he'd do it, and I used to sit and marvel at it because I said, "God-damn, how did this kid . . ." He came from North Carolina, and he had no name whatsoever, nobody never heard of him. I used to listen to him in the band, I said, "Damn! This cat is somethin' else!" He's the one who taught me about augmenteds and shit. I knew the chord changes, but I didn't know about alterations and all of that. This is a year before I came to play around Detroit.

❖❖

Red Allen in Fletcher Henderson's band in the '30s was playing some whole-tone scales and things that were ahead of their time.

❖❖

*Blanche Calloway was Cab's band-leading sister.

HOWARD MC GHEE   I didn't get a chance to hear Red till later on. I didn't know him too well. In fact, I didn't hear many—they told me Frankie Newton was a good trumpet player. I never heard him, period. I heard a record, but I never heard him in person to really hear him play. Another one they always told me about was Jabbo Smith, but I never heard Jabbo but one time, and he only played about two choruses then, but I could tell that he was the damnedest trumpet player. I had never seen a trumpet player that whatever he played he just let the note come out anyway, whether he had the right valve or the wrong valve. We used to laugh 'cause he was funny. Me and Dizzy used to laugh. We'd say, "See that cat?" He'd be playing in the key of G, and he wouldn't be using the first valve. He'd be playing everything in the second or third, and you *gotta* use the first one in the key, but he just bent the note into 'em. Now, Charlie Jacobs was one of my inspirations besides Roy Eldridge. He would take a four-bar modulation and change keys, and most of the time he didn't use nothing but augmenteds, but it was very effective, and I heard him doing it, and I said, "That's nice, I gotta use that," and I started using some of it. Every now and then I'd run across a modulation: going to use an augmented, takes me into another one , then back into the key. And that really sounds good.

TRUMMY YOUNG   I was kinda bred with guys like Louis, and then along came Prez, and I was fortunate enough to work with Budd Johnson in Earl Hines's band in 1934. Now, Budd was getting into something different then. And I hung out with Budd a lot, so I started picking up on a lot of the things that Prez and Budd were doing. Because Budd played with Prez many years before he ever got to Chicago. And I kinda liked what they were doing. It was a little different from what was going along then.

Well, later, we used to go into Kansas City and play quite often. There were some young musicians in Kansas City that we all admired. One of them was Fred Beckett, a trombone player. I thought he was one of the finest trombone men I ever heard in my life. I remember when he was playing things that guys today are playing. And he was doing it back then, and he was a wonder. It's unfortunate that he got in a big band. He got to working with Lionel [Hampton], and he lost a lot of things that he had when he was working in the bands around Kansas City because, in a big band, if you get one chorus, you're very lucky. You get eight bars here, sixteen here. And it was really an injustice to him being in a big band. I would have loved to have seen him in a small band, develop in a smaller group. I thought an awful lot of him. He died in New York, incidentally.

So, Fred told me about Charlie Parker, a guy around Kansas City. But I didn't know Charlie then, but he says, "There's a guy around there that plays an awful lot, man." So next time I went to Kansas City I looked up Prez—I mean, I looked up Parker. I get Prez mixed up because Bird really got it from Prez. But then he extended it. He went on and did something of his own.

Now I met Charlie Christian before he ever left Oklahoma. Long before John Hammond or anybody knew him. Well, I knew him because, traveling with Earl Hines, I went through all those territories, and I knew all the guys that could play. I knew all the territory bands. A lot of guys didn't know those territory bands. Some very good players—Buddy Tate was in those territory bands. I've met some *awful* good players!

In each town you went into, you didn't have to look for musicians. They'd bring their horns and look for you. "Let's get it on, man!" They'd come and tell you. That's the way things were in that day. When I went to Oklahoma City, Charlie Christian and an alto player named Red—I never did know his last name—came up to my room with a guitar and an alto. And I was in bed. And they brought a bottle of liquor up there and said, "Come on, man, let's play something!" And I had to get out of bed, and I didn't even brush my teeth. And I got out of bed, and the three of us just sat there and played for a couple of hours. This was the way the road was back there then. So after that, we'd go and eat a little lunch, and then we'd go somewhere else and find somebody else and play some more. I used to be tired all the time, but I was young, and I didn't pay no attention to it. If you were in a band, and the band was known, well, they'd look for you. Because they didn't have names, but they could play, and they could outplay a lot of us in the big bands. And this was an exchange of ideas. This was how I knew about people like that way before the writers or anybody else knew about 'em.

I wouldn't *take* a million dollars for the guys I came up with around 52nd Street and even prior to that. The guys that I really knew and came up with—guys like Budd Johnson—we go all the way back—and Vic Dickenson when he was with that band over in Cincinnati—Zack Whyte; and Roy Eldridge when he was with McKinney's Cotton Pickers. These are the things that I go back to. And they bring some wonderful memories to me. Milt Hinton, when he was around Chicago; and Ray Nance, when he was around Chicago. I just happened to have come up with people like this, and to prove that these people must have had something, they're still doing pretty good today. And that's been a long time ago. I'd hate to tell you how many years ago that was. You know, there a lot of flash-in-the-pans come up. But for something to last like that—the longevity of the thing, you have to have something special. You have to.

❖❖

That sunny camaraderie was one facet of the road in the '30s. A more desperate aspect was what musicians used to call being "on a panic." In the '40s there were more than a few of these situations.

❖❖

JOE ALBANY   I know a cat that played alto from Bird's hometown, a friend of Bird's named Cliff Jetkins. I stayed at his pad at 11th and Paseo. I was stuck in Phoenix. I had a run-in with my first wife's parents, and I split, and that's how I got to Kansas City, 'cause first I was around thirty miles of Pawhuska, on a farm in Oklahoma. See, my daughter had just been born, and I had to split because my wife's father came in and was gonna have me busted. So some cat gave me a ride and said, "Okay, you sell asbestos siding." So I'm tryin' to sell, a dollar a day to eat on, this asbestos siding. This was '47 or '48—no, it was later, '49. I'm really broke, so I'm passing as an albino like Red [Rodney] in a place called Greenwood Avenue, which is the black section of Tulsa.

The only house where I came close to selling was a black chick who played piano, an entertainer. She had a little place. She might have been singing, but I don't know what happened to that, and then Walter Brown came to a place called the Green Frog or something. And Ernie Fields was the territorial band out there. And Walter said, well, look—because I know I was going to go back into lifting out of cars. And he gave me a fin. I had a fin and got it together. He gave me Clifford's address and he said, "Go there." Clifford put me up for a couple of weeks, and from that I went with some past friends to Chicago. Shelly [Manne] was playing with Kenton and said hello then. And I got the money from loans to finally get back to California. I was born in Atlantic City but from seventeen on, eighteen, I was living out there.

« 2 »

Roots and Seeds

The music developed through musicians influencing one another, a cross-pollination of thoughts and sounds. When we talk
about the roots of bebop we generally bring up names such as
Lester Young, Charlie Christian, Roy Eldridge, Jimmy Blanton,
Art Tatum, and Sid Catlett.

There were also many other, lesser-known players whose ideas
and stylistic nuances were woven into the great tapestry of jazz.
Some were recorded, and some were not, but musicians remember them well for the way they helped shape their musical thinking.

❖❖

JAY MC SHANN   Bird loved Lester. Anytime that Basie was doing a broadcast or anything, he would always say, "Man, Basie'll be on at such and
such time. What time are we gonna take intermission?"—make that
hint for me so we'd take intermission so he could rush out and hear
him.

❖❖

On the recordings that Charlie Parker made with Jay McShann at
the Wichita radio station in 1940 (*First Recordings*—Onyx 221) he
sounds exactly like Lester Young in certain passages.

❖❖

HOWARD MC GHEE   First time I heard him, he sounded like Prez; in fact
the first records that Jay McShann made he sounded like Prez. That's
sayin' that he had a lot of Louis in him, 'cause that's where Prez got
his.

❖❖

Armstrong influenced everybody, directly and indirectly. It didn't
matter what instrument you played. You had to listen to him, to
come through him. He was the first great soloist in jazz and brought
a new beauty and continuity to the solo line.

❖❖

TRUMMY YOUNG   You never do get away from your roots, but I do think every musician—the ones I know—I *know* all of them—they're working constantly on improving themselves, even on what they know how to play. It's always a way of doing it a little different way. Louis was like that. I'd hear Louis play the same solo, but when I listened to it, I'd say, "But he changed it right here or right there!" It would be almost the same solo, but he always thought a little different way, and I've never worked with nobody that had the feeling that Louis had. I don't care who it is. I've worked with some great guys. But I've never worked with nobody that even approached Louis for feeling. And, man, this is something you can't buy in a music store.

Another thing about him, he didn't *care* if he got through to people. He got through to himself. You see, you can't fool yourself. He loved people, but he told me once, "Trummy, when I go on that bandstand, I don't know nobody's out there. I don't even know you're playing with me. Play good and it'll help me out. I don't know you're up there. I'm just playing."

Somebody asked him once. "Louis, you know you've had some awful bad bands that played with you?" He say, "I did?" And this was his answer to him, he say, "I'll tell you. When I played with Joe Oliver at first, I was a pretty bad player myself. Joe didn't bawl me out. He said I could play good but there were a lot of things I didn't understand. And Joe would take time and show me. Well, when you got there, he'd say, 'You shouldn'ta done this. You should have done that. Or this.' "

And, man, Louis say Joe Oliver told him once, in a loving way, "You know,"—after he made a couple of mistakes, he say, "Son, you got a head on you and so has a glass of beer."

HOWARD MC GHEE   I had heard Louis at the Greystone in Detroit; I snuck in a dance there one night when he was playing. He was an inspiration to me, really. I had never heard any horn sound as pretty as I heard Louis play, like high Cs, Gs and shit like that. I guess I always go for the exciting sounds, most things that a person would automatically hear. I heard him make a G. I never heard it made as comfortably or anybody else hit a G that pretty, then or since. He taught everybody. You had to listen to this cat, boy. I know I learned "Basin Street." It was probably the first thing I ever knew. One of his famous records—"West End Blues"—I heard that, I says, "Goddamn, this is bad." He made that intro. I didn't know a guy could play horn like that; I didn't know nobody who could play horn like that. Only thing I'd ever heard was church singing. That's about the only thing I liked, I guess, was to hear people get into it when they were singing. All the other horns that I heard didn't impress me much. In fact, I don't know whether I did hear a Dixieland band originally.

❖❖

Armstrong's introduction to "West End Blues" has, in its magnificence, certain phraseology that prefigures bebop. Charlie Parker liked it well enough to quote a portion of it during a solo on one of his own blues, "Visa" *(Bird at St. Nick's)*. Then there is Armstrong's introduction on "Struttin' with Some Barbecue" with the big band on Decca; its melody and rhythmic contours contain a bebop feeling.

❖❖

EDDIE BAREFIELD   What do you think about "Laughin' Louie?" Did you remember that record? It was way advanced for Louie's time—that was *way* ahead of its time.

And then he did "West End Blues," which was more in keepin'. But "Laughin' Louie" was really way ahead of his time.

❖❖

If Lester Young learned from Armstrong, he also favored C-melody saxophonist Frankie Trumbauer. Veteran musicians who go back to the 1920s feel that the move toward modernism that coalesced in the 1940s was already in motion when flappers flowered.

❖❖

RED NORVO   I don't think you suddenly woke up one day and there it was. No. Because I go back with guys like Bix and Frankie Trumbauer. In those days, I think they were harmonically and all equipped to do whatever was in the bebop era. Actually, Bix was, I know Frank was, and I know guys like Roy Bargy were. He and Tatum studied from the same teacher. Frank Trumbauer influenced everybody. But in those days the style was to play melodic; that was the style. That was the way that set it. It wasn't a technical style or anything like that, it was more of a melodic—but when it got from the big bands and started to—the big band as a band became more technical, arrangement-wise, and they got higher up on the scale, and the trumpets were doing—larger bands. I think it was just a natural outgrowth. It was bound to happen. You felt it was happening all along.

❖❖

When Benny Carter soloed on "Boppin' the Blues" with Lucky Thompson's Lucky Seven in 1947 (RCA Victor), he played some licks that he wouldn't have played before the advent of Charlie Parker.

❖❖

BENNY CARTER   I may have been unconsciously influenced by what I was hearing, because I was listening. I certainly don't know now or never did have anything against playing something I had heard if it fit. If I felt good doing it. Not that I consciously attempted to copy anyone ever, other than when I copied Frankie Trumbauer's solo on "Singin' The Blues," which was back in the '20s. There was nobody else to listen to really at that time, unless you wanted to try to play what Boyd Senter was playing. But what Frankie did was very interesting to me, and that's probably the greatest reason I wanted to play a saxophone. Of course, at first I wanted to play trumpet because of my cousin [Cuban Bennett] and Bubber Miley, who lived in our neighborhood and I knew quite well.

EDDIE BAREFIELD I had been playing with this band around Minneapolis for about three months. Finally a fellow named Clarence Johnson, who was a piano player—he had got a job up in a hotel up in Bismarck, North Dakota, for the winter at the Spencer Hotel—took me and "Snake," the trumpet player, Roy White; and the banjo player, Landers; and he had a drummer from St. Paul. It was five pieces, we went up to Bismarck.

Well, this was fifty-five below zero weather up there that winter. This hotel we played in, the Spencer, was right on the corner. And then they had an annex where we stayed, and we didn't have to go outdoors. We only played two hours a day. That was from six to eight for the dinner hour, and that's all we had to do. And the job paid thirty dollars a week. In this annex, where we were stationed, Lester Young's father had his family band. Lester Young and his little brother Lee, who wasn't big enough to play then but they'd dress him in a tuxedo and he would conduct that band.

Irma, his sister, was a saxophone player; and his mother played the piano; and his father played tenor. Lester was playin' alto. But he was learnin' to play then. I had my records, my Frankie Trumbauer records, and I used to play them. One day, I hadn't met him yet, and I heard a knock on the door, and he opened the door. "I'm Lester Young," he says. "I heard those saxophones," he says. "Who is that playin' saxophone?" I said, "Frankie Trumbauer." He says, "Do you mind if I listen?" "Come in." So he came in, and we met. He started to borrow these records. He used to tell me that he had an old beat-up alto, but one of these days, when he learned how to read good, his father was gonna buy him a new Selmer. We became good friends then, and he used to come over every time he got a chance when they were out. This was in '27. We stayed over through into '28, through the winter. And that next spring we left Bismarck.

LESTER YOUNG I had a decision between Frankie Trumbauer and Jimmy Dorsey, you dig, and I wasn't sure which way I wanted to go. I'd buy me all those records, and I'd play one by Jimmy Dorsey and one by Trumbauer, you dig? I didn't know nothing about Hawk then, and they were the only ones telling a story I liked to hear.

Bud Freeman?! We're nice friends . . . but influence, ladedehump-tedorebebop. . . . Did you ever hear him [Trumbauer] play "Singin' the Blues?" That tricked me right then, and that's where I went.

BUDD JOHNSON I think he [Young] hadn't been playing tenor too long then. That must have been, oh . . . '28 or '29 or something like that. I don't think he'd been playing tenor much longer then that 'cause my brother [Keg Johnson] used to work with him. When my brother left Kansas City, he went to Minneapolis, and he was working with Grant Moore, Eli Rice, and all those bands out there. And he went, and he told me, "Say, man, there's a cat out here, he plays a lot of tenor, he sounds something like you." He said, "But this cat can really play, his name is Lester Young." I hadn't heard him, 'cause he never hit like Kansas City or nothing. He was out in Minneapolis with his family and he played out there. I probably would have run across him, but I had quit traveling up through the Dakotas then.

BENNY CARTER   I did hear Lester Young in 1932 in Minneapolis. He was playing alto. He had not yet gone to a tenor. And I have told many people that, had they heard Lester Young play alto at that time, they would have heard a lot of what Bird was doing. Believe me. They would have. Taking nothing away from Bird really, because I think he was fantastic in all these years since he came on the scene. His things still hold up beautifully, and it's still a joy to listen to. But Lester had a different conception than he was blowing later on tenor. He had so much of it covered and, of course, you heard him play clarinet, which was still another kind of approach.

LESTER YOUNG   I was playing alto, and they had this evil old cat with a nice, beautiful background—mother and father and a whole lot of bread and like that, you know—so every time we'd get a job . . . this was in Salinas, Kansas, so every time we'd go see him, we'd be waiting ninety years to get us to work while he fixed his face, you know, so I told the bossman—his name was Art Bronson. So I said, "Listen, why do we have to go through this? You go and buy me a tenor saxophone, and I'll play, and we'd be straight then."

So he worked with the music store and we got straight, and we split. That was it for me. The first time I heard it. Because the alto was a little too high.

❖❖

For some people Lester Young's tenor was a little too high. The same kind of thinking colored a similar attitude, later on, toward Parker.

❖❖

RED CALLENDER   A lot of the older guys that couldn't cope with it found all sorts of excuses to put it down. They used to say the Bird's tone was bad, they said Lester's tone was bad; they were used to the Coleman Hawkins and the Ben Webster big, lusty sound. They weren't ready on the top of the sound thing.

❖❖

In Minneapolis, when Young would finish work at 2:00 a.m., he would listen to Count Basie's radio broadcast from Kansas City, where it was only 1:00 a.m. He didn't care for the tenor player and wired Basie those sentiments and that he was available whenever. Basie responded with the fare.

One night in Kansas City, while he was playing with Basie, he went by Fletcher Henderson's job to check out Coleman Hawkins. As Hawkins wasn't there, Lester played his book, before dashing back to his own gig with Basie. Soon afterward, Hawkins left Henderson for the Continent, and Fletcher sent for Lester to replace him. It was an unhappy experience.

❖❖

LESTER YOUNG   It wasn't for me. They were whispering on me, everytime I played. I can't make that. I couldn't take that. . . . Fletcher's wife [Leora Meoux Henderson] she took me down to the basement and played one of those old wind-up record players, and she'd say, "Lester, can't you play like this?" Coleman Hawkins records. But I mean, "Can't you hear this? Can't you get with that?"

You dig? I split! Every morning that chick would wake me up at nine o'clock to teach me to play like Coleman Hawkins. And she played trumpet herself—circus trumpet! I'm gone!

❖❖

Young returned to the Basie band and, beginning with his incandescent solos on "Lady Be Good" and "Shoe Shine Boy" (*The Lester Young Story, Volume I*—Columbia 33502) announced to an audience-at-large that there was a new zephyr blowing into jazz. The ones who listened the hardest were the young musicians of the next generation.

❖❖

JOHNNY GRIFFIN   Prez was the trunk of the swing tree. The Basie arrangements sound dated. When Prez plays his solo it sounds like *now*. Bird just took that to another degree. His involvement with time . . . He expanded the language.

❖❖

Dexter Gordon, who became one of the important transmitters and converters of Young's message, was already strongly influenced by the time he joined Lionel Hampton.

❖❖

DEXTER GORDON   I joined Hamp Christmas '40, and I'd already been listening to Prez for three or four years, so that was the direction; I was already into that. It came like a bolt out of the blue to me. And I readily identified with his ideas and concepts and so forth. That was just automatic. "That's it." Like that.

❖❖

The first time he heard Basie and Young in person was in 1939 at the Paramount Theatre in Los Angeles.

❖❖

DEXTER GORDON   It was the first time they'd been to California—in those days that was a major trip. Lammar Wright, Jr., and I ditched school that day to catch the first show, which I think was at eleven in the morning. They opened with "Clap Hands Here Comes Charlie," and Lester came out soloing—and he was just fantastic. I really loved the man. He was melodic, rhythmic, had that bittersweet approach. And, of course, in his pre-Army days he had such a zest for living. It felt so good to hear him play.

❖❖

Another young California tenor saxophonist, two years Gordon's junior, also latched on to Lester.

❖❖

ZOOT SIMS   You remember the early Bird records with Jay Mc Shann, sounds like Prez a little. He loved Prez, you gotta love Prez anyway; you know the way Bird played, gotta love Prez. I really jumped on Prez in '43 when I was on the road with Sonny Dunham. Earl Swope would say, "Listen to this." Prez on a Basie record.

I heard Prez before, but I really got on him then. Really realized.

❖❖

In those days you could go into private listening booths in record stores. You would ask for particular records and could spend quite a bit of time just listening. Sims did just that in many towns when he was with Dunham. By the time he joined Woody Herman in 1947, he was carrying a big stack of 78s with him on the road. Everybody used to come to his room to listen, particularly to the Basie records that featured Young.

❖❖

ZOOT SIMS   Before '43, of course, I heard the Basie records, and I always liked Prez, but I was kind of hooked up on Coleman Hawkins and Ben Webster. And my brother used to get—everytime a record came out, we'd go right up to L.A. and buy it. I still love Ben, of course.

❖❖

At that time Prez was so different that when people heard him, when musicians heard him, they really got hung up with what he was doing because he *was* different and in another direction.

❖❖

ZOOT SIMS   Right. I fell in love with his sound eventually, then the melodic quality. It was refreshing; it really was. And, of course, his sense of time rubbed off. I never really quoted Prez in my playing, but you don't have to quote somebody to be influenced.

❖❖

Sims fell in love with the sound and did have the sound. So did a lot of other people who just dug that sound. It came out differently in different players. But there was a whole legion of players. Maybe to the untutored ear, they all sounded the same. I know people used to say, "Oh you can't tell the difference between Stan Getz and Zoot Sims," when they were first on Woody Herman's band. Anyone that was really listening could. The analogy I always use is that it's just like a friend calling you on the telephone.

You know who it is immediately. It's the same thing when you hear a musician play. We used to put the tone arm on the record and know who it was from the first phrase, the first sounds.

❖❖

ART PEPPER   The first time I heard Prez was Basie's band. I just loved him immediately. The things that he did. All those things that he did with Basie's band—"Taxi War Dance"—and that [singing]—you know that one—he's got that break [singing] ["Easy Does It"]. Well, that one thing is just like, that's my whole inspiration of black music, that's music, that was music to me for years. It still is. Just that thing. Man, he comes in after that break, and he's just floating after that. I used to go over to Zoot's garage, where he lived with his parents, and he used to play that for me, and I just loved it, and he knew all of Prez's solos, every one by heart—every solo. And that was my main influence.

❖❖

It wasn't only saxophonists who tuned into Lester Young but musicians of all instruments.

❖❖

JOE NEWMAN   Back at Alabama State, Prez was really the person who excited most young players. We knew of Coleman Hawkins particularly because of his "Body and Soul" record, and this was really his vehicle for getting to young musicians, and it was also a good composition. Well, it was different from what you had been listening to most of the time. But then Count Basie was on the scene, and Lester Young had a very flamboyant style. I mean it was smooth, it was easy, and it flowed so freely that he excited me. I liked Herschel Evans a lot, and I had great admiration and respect for his ability—of course I never knew him—but Lester Young was really the one who excited me.

❖❖

Prez was truly an exciting player. He has been widely celebrated for the mellow, tender, thoughtful swinging he contributed to the late '30s-early '40s Billie Holiday recordings—whether an obligato or a short, pithy solo—but he could also take one note and swing you into bad health. The way he actuates the Basie band on "Every Tub" is but a hint of his rhythmic impetus. It was at jam sessions that he would really stretch out, using his many resources to be interesting at great length.

❖❖

JOHNNY CARISI   When Lester Young left Basie, which was around '41 or something like that, he and a drummer named Harold West [Doc West] and a marvelous trumpet player named Shad Collins would show up at the Vanguard a lot with a little group, and you never heard such . . . and Lester was one of the guys, that to this day, I could stand to play twelve choruses of something. You know no matter who they are. He was one guy that could always, just when you think he had done it, he would, like, back off a little bit, he would goof and then descend on you again, only more so than before, get everybody crazy, man. That times everybody put their horns down, and Lester would just play—seriously, ten, twelve, fourteen choruses. And nobody else did that. They took their two or three, and that was it.

TRUMMY YOUNG   Meantime I played a lot of little jazz things with Prez around there. A lot of jam sessions. I never did really record with Prez. I'm sorry I never got a chance to record with him, but we played a lot of little jam sessions, and he used to encourage me a lot, you know. He used to tell me, "Hey, Baby! I like that!" Prez was a sweet player. He didn't like nothing harsh. Harsh talk or harsh playing or nothing. He just liked nice, pretty things all the time. He even swung pretty. You see this is the secret about Prez to me. When he swung, it was always . . . I don't care how harsh you were playing. He swung pretty. Oh, he could play so much. You don't get him in a jam session. He's the king of sessions, man. To me. He could play fifty choruses . . .

❖❖

One thinks of Ralph Ellison's description of "Halley Richardson's shoeshine parlor in Oklahoma City—where I first heard Lester Young jamming in a shine chair, his head thrown back, his horn even then outthrust, his feet working on the footrests . . ."

Something of what Prez was about when he was wearing his session clothes can be heard not in his concert recordings—these came later in his career when his playing attitudes had changed—but in a studio-made "I Got Rhythm" from December 1943 with a group led by Dicky Wells. It originally was issued on a Signature 12-inch 78, with more playing room than the usual 10-inch 78. Prez plays a chorus between Bill Coleman's trumpet and Wells's trombone. Then he takes four uninterrupted choruses—except for some verbal exhortations by Wells—that tell us something about the Prezian modus operandi of getting into gear. You're left exhilarated but with the feeling that he is just really revving up. The last issue of this adrenal-aid is *Classic Tenors* (Doctor Jazz).

A lot of people have said that Charlie Christian was influenced by Prez: that he didn't play the same way before and after he heard Prez.

❖❖

DEXTER GORDON   I wouldn't be a bit surprised. You know I'm not a Charlie Christian authority, but come to think of it, he did play lines something like Prez. Things like [hums] that kind of . . . I mean he wasn't playing guitar at that time as other people were playing guitar. What he was doing was different and probably—also, he was from that territory. I mean the Southwest.

RED CALLENDER   Charlie Christian, Lester Young, and Bird. I think they all influenced each other. You notice their approach to a song was different. Prior to that when a guy would take a chorus on a song and get to the release, or the bridge, they never did really analyze those things, they'd skate through; but starting with Charlie Christian, he really dug the interrelated chords leading in and out of a bridge—turnbacks. Charlie Parker, Charlie Christian, Lester Young, and Dizzy Gillespie, they had a steady flow through there.

JAMES MOODY   I used to remember that tune "Savoy" *["Stompin' At the Savoy".]* They used to play it, and I remember Charlie Christian would be playing on it, and he'd start playing, and on the outside of it he would just be going along slowly, and as soon as he came to the difficult part, the bridge, he would tear it up, he would dive in. Now I know that was intentional, it was beautiful. So I would think that Charlie Christian was really at this time, I can see now, more, that he was really involved with the chord construction.

MILT HINTON   And then I remember that night we got off in Dallas, Texas, and we went to a little ballroom at Thomas and Hall, and there was a cat playin' up there, and they said, "I want you to hear this cat," and it was Charlie Christian. And it was a "spider" mike—he didn't have any amplification—and I remember us all crowdin' around him to listen, and there he was cookin' away with this nonelectrified guitar with a "spider" microphone, trying to hold it down. Keep it stable with rubber bands, or something like that.

MARY LOU WILLIAMS   I got him to join Benny Goodman. He wouldn't have left for anybody else. John Hammond and everybody, they tried to get him out. Fantastic. The world doesn't know how fantastic he was. When he was out on the road when I was with Kirk, I was in New York at the Dewey Square Hotel. We'd go into the basement, where the rats were running around and with the piano that was so dirty I had to wash my hands when I went upstairs. We'd sit down in the basement and play from eleven in the morning, please believe me, until twelve at night. I didn't have a piano upstairs, and we couldn't bring that one upstairs because it would have fallen apart. And Charlie Christian would eat ice cream. He'd look me up whenever he came into town, and we'd sit there and play.

Now nobody knows his ability, and when I told Benny Goodman he almost fainted. I said, "You're playing the classics you didn't know he could play." I'd take a break, like run upstairs and cook something and bring it down, or else run to the store and get ice cream. Charlie Christian would be playing "Rhapsody in Blue" and all these heavy classical things. I wrote a couple of things with him and one I never did finish. I have sixteen bars of it. It's beautiful.

EDDIE BAREFIELD   Oh, I knew Charlie Christian in Oklahoma City. I mean, he used to come over when we went there with Bennie Moten. He used to come and take guitar lessons from Eddie Durham.

BIDDY FLEET   Eddie, to me, was one of the early boys, but I heard Eddie way before I had heard of Christian because Eddie told me of a boy that was from Oklahoma City that was playing guitar and had it electrified, and I thought to myself, "Well, yeah," but my ears were full of Eddie Lang, and there was another guy that was considered great at that time on guitar—Bernard Addison—by the way, he's a "homey," too.

It was a man in a band told me that there was a guitar player out there that played guitar like a horn. Well, the first thing came into my mind is, "What has he got?" I thought about the piano, with all them pipes running from each note. I figured he had something hooked up from the neck of the guitar that he blows through. When he say horn I thought of blowing. I wasn't thinking of the sound that he played. Later I find out that he played the guitar—he picked it the way everyone else do—but it was the way he went over the neck. I got to know Christian, and we were in several sessions, but Christian was one of the few early ones to do that. Later, many did.

What Charlie played is what the kids today call "soul." Charlie played without musical knowledge how he felt. What the boys have today is a bit of what Christian had then. The Eastern boys tried to hook up some chords and get a harmony pattern, where Christian got a one-note pattern that fitted the harmony chords, which said more as a solo man.

JAY MC SHANN   Yes, Charlie came by one night when I just had a duo. I hadn't been in Kansas City very long. He'd been with Alphonso Trent in North Dakota. He came through Kansas City, and he came by Wolf's Buffet and that's where I was playing. That was at 18th and Vine. He came in, and he got his axe and set up and played. We were supposed to be through playing about one or two o'clock, but we played till about seven, eight o'clock that morning. We just stayed there. All the musicians in town was coming by. I guess we had about a 15-piece band before it was over with. He really broke up the house that night, and he stayed right on through. That was the first time I'd ever heard him blow.

BARNEY KESSEL   Almost all of the black musicians that I played with, at that time [1937], had all known Charlie Christian and had already heard him. And they were trying to tell me, in a way, not necessarily to play like him, but when I would play a solo they would say, "Play like a horn." I did not know that they meant to play a melodic, single-note line, to try and play and sound like a tenor saxophone or a trumpet. I recall my very earliest, feeble efforts were to play either chords, like a ukulele, or to play single notes, but I would tremolo it as though it was a mandolin. They would say, no, play like a horn. I didn't know what they meant. Finally, when I did hear Charlie Christian it had an enormous impact on me. That was on records. The first record I heard—the recording with the Benny Goodman sextet, "Soft Winds"—even on that record he really didn't have any solos. He had little figures that he played, but I heard already that attack and sound. His style was very reminiscent of Lester Young to me. And then I could see what they were talking about. I was much moved, and that became a very great and long-lasting influence.

I met him later. I did a story for *Guitar Player* magazine that is in two episodes that I wrote about meeting him. Two running issues, and it's in there in great detail. But the thing that had an enormous impact on me was meeting him for three days. He came back to Oklahoma City, and I was playing with a college band, going to high school—at a place called the Oklahoma Club in Oklahoma City. I was playing that night with this band. I had a lot of solos to play. I'd even taken off some Benny Goodman sextet arrangements for a little group within this big band to play. And while we were there, a black waiter that was there said to me, "I'm going to tell Charlie Christian about you." He said, "I think he'd like to know that there is a white boy around here playing jazz." I put it out of my mind, because, first of all, I figured that he didn't know Charlie Christian and, second, where would he tell him and what would it mean? But within an hour, Charlie Christian was standing in front of the bandstand. He had called him up and he came down there. I was sixteen.

It would be like young girls meeting the Beatles, I think—the impact—because he was home—it was during the period when Benny Goodman broke his band up because Benny had a slipped disc. During that time Charlie Christian went back to Oklahoma on a leave of absence, and he was standing there. I was just flabbergasted, and the bandleader asked him to sit in, and he sat in and played on my guitar. After it was over, we drove around. The impact was this: As a kid of sixteen, I used to stop certain professional musicians. If Tommy Dorsey's band came through or Henry Busse, or whoever it was, I would ask them questions. And almost all of them ignored me—they wouldn't give me the time of day—and Charlie Christian was very nice, very kind. He was not a terribly literate person, he spoke in grunts. He spoke in very short phrases, and he was not a philosopher or had any kind of phenomenal esoteric wisdom, he was just a tremendous jazz musician. But he spoke in short phrases, and you'd almost have to piece it together as to what it meant. We jammed together for three days. That was one of the impacts. People of less stature were not that nice.

❖❖

Christian and Jimmy Blanton are often mentioned in the same breath. Each died in his early twenties of tuberculosis in 1942, but not before changing the guitar and the bass, and the face of jazz.

Blanton did not visit Minton's with the same degree of frequency as Christian. Therefore he did not have as direct a hand in the actual development of modern jazz through those after-hours sessions. However, the recordings he made with Ellington, particularly the piano-bass duets, influenced every bassist within earshot. So many bassists in the mid-'40s were carrying those Victor 78s of the Ellington-Blanton duets around with them.

❖❖

MILT HINTON   Ben [Webster] always had the bass player in a band as his friend. In Cab's band it was me; and in Duke's, Jimmy Blanton became his pal. Ivie Anderson discovered Jimmy in St. Louis and recommended him to Duke. He was amazing. He revolutionized bass playing, and Duke was just the man to know how to use his talent. Nobody had ever showed off a bass player before. Bass players just sat back and supported. But Duke came up with "Plucked Again" and "Pitter Panther Patter" and spotlighted him on the band numbers and so on. Ben called me up and said, "You gotta hear this kid."

I remember we met backstage at the Apollo in New York, where our bands came together every now and then. Ben was always in trouble, drinking and getting broke. I was trying to be conservative, and I would try to hold onto my money. Ben would come and get money from my wife Mona. Now Blanton, though he was a kid, was very secure. He didn't smoke or drink, and he saved his money even when he hung out with Ben.

One time I got broke and needed some money, and I said to Ben, "Look, you owe me a lot of money, and now you've got to give me something." I met him on the corner with Jimmy. I can remember it as though it was yesterday—Ben called him "Bear" and Blanton called Ben "Bull." He said to Blanton, "Bear, you got any money? I need a couple of cows to give Fomp." ("Fomp" was my nickname in Cab's band; a cow was one hundred dollars, a calf was fifty dollars.) Blanton reached in his watch pocket and pulled out a roll of fifty-dollar bills. He peeled off four and gave them to me.

Blanton was a weak kid. He might get on the bus soaking wet after a gig and drive two or three hundred miles like that while his clothes dried on him. Eventually he got tuberculosis, and of course we had no penicillin or sulfa drugs then. The only treatment was to go to bed and rest. So he got sick in California. The reason I know this is Duke was closing there, and we were the next band to come into the ballroom where he'd been. Ben said to me, "Bear's pretty sick. We gotta leave him in a rest home here. Please go out and see him." I said, "Don't worry, I'll be there." It was way out of town, but I went every other day, had to hire a car to get me there. He had a lovely room, but he was twenty-two years old, at the peak of his career, and his band was going off and leaving him. He's from Tennessee, and he don't have a friend in California, and his poor heart was broken. So every night when we broadcast, Chu Berry and I would sit down and scratch out a little tune, and we'd play it and dedicate it to him on the air. Then when I'd go out to see him—he'd had his radio by his bed—we'd sit down and he'd tell me about the chords. "Hey, you used a D flat ninth there, you should use this." But he was getting weaker and weaker. You could see the loneliness of it took away his strength and will to live, and he died.

RED CALLENDER   Blanton was my idol and also a friend. I used to carry my bass around for him to play it. Take him all over town. He'd never sleep. I'd sit up and listen to him play all night.

AL MC KIBBON   Blanton had twisted my head around sideways . . .

ROY ELDRIDGE   In the early '40s, I used to have the band at Kelly's Stables with Kenny Clarke, Ted Sturgis, Kenny Kersey, and John Collins. Charlie Christian and Jimmy Blanton used to stop by and sit in, and one night they swung so much I felt so good I had to stop playing.

JOE NEWMAN   For a trumpet player, Roy Eldridge was it. So much so that I pasted one of his photographs, a small one, on the bell of my trumpet. And every time I blew I looked at it. Well, I used to also, while I was at Alabama State, listen to him coming from the Roseland Ballroom.

HOWARD MC GHEE   I heard Roy when they [Fletcher Henderson's band] came to the Grand Terrace in Chicago. I think that was in '35—'35 or '36 or something like that. He played "Christopher Columbus" with Chu [Berry]. Then I heard him at the Three Deuces—that's when I really got a chance to hear him play, I mean more than just a chorus and eight bars, or sixteen bars. The band at the Three Deuces was a small band; he really had to play. So he really inspired me to play, but then he quit playing. I mean he quit thinking as far as I'm concerned. He's always been a hell of a trumpet player; I think his peak was with Krupa with "Rockin' Chair"—I think that was his best solo—that and "Let Me Off Uptown."

Roy told me one time, we were going downtown—I think we were going on a Jazz Philharmonic tour, I think it was in '47, '48—he told me, "You don't like that [bebop] do you?" and I said, "I know you're not going to like me for saying it, but I like it." I said, "I like the way Charlie Parker plays, the way Dizzy plays, I can't help but like that." He was trying to get me on his side. I couldn't go for that, even though he was my idol a long time ago.

We accidentally bumped into each other after Louis died. I said, "Well, Roy, that make you Pops now!" and he said, "Don't say that, don't say that, I'm not Pops, I'm not Pops!" I say "I know you not, you Roy Eldridge but you're the oldest one out here, that's all, it makes you Pops." "Oh no, don't call me Pops, don't call me Pops!" I say, "All right, okay." From then on every time he sees me he's kind of leery, he don't know what I might say to him. Sy Oliver told me how he was in his youth. He used to chase after them trumpet players, outblow everybody. So Dizzy caught up with him and shook him up, and he went haywire so he didn't play no more "Rockin' Chair" and shit. I thought that was one of the prettiest trumpet solos I'd ever heard.

❖❖

When historians simplify the development of the trumpet, three names—Armstrong, Eldridge, and Gillespie—are offered in that order. Where Gillespie came directly from Eldridge, Roy did not descend in quite that way from Louis. First he admired Rex Stewart, who was playing in brother Joe Eldridge's band. Roy was ten or eleven years old, and Rex would show him breaks.

❖❖

ROY ELDRIDGE   I liked "the nice, clean sound" that Red Nichols was getting for a trumpet in those days. I was doing all right playing in that style until I got to St. Louis. Every Sunday, five trumpet players came down and tore me apart. I was about sixteen, and I was playing smooth. They played with a guttural kind of sound. They were more or less on a Louis Armstrong kick, the way Louis used to play but more guttural. I was playing what could be called cool then, and I wasn't familiar with that other style. I couldn't understand how they got around to playing like that—the lip vibrato, trills, and the like. Some of the names of those trumpet players in St. Louis were Dewey Jackson, Baby James, "Cookie," and "Big Ham."

❖❖

Later on, Eldridge ran into another trumpeter in Milwaukee.

❖❖

ROY ELDRIDGE   That town was where Jabbo Smith caught me one night and turned me every way but loose . . . he wore me out before that night was through. He knew a lot of music, and he knew changes.

❖❖

And, as Benny Carter has said, Eldridge knew Cuban Bennett.

❖❖

ROY ELDRIDGE   He was playing around New York in the '20s and was one of the first cats I ever heard play the right changes. He was really making his changes in those days. You could call him one of the first of the moderns—he mostly gigged around. He wouldn't hold a steady job; he drank a lot. And he never made any records. He was a great trumpet player. He played more like a saxophone did. You see, the saxophone then, or some of them, would run changes, would run through all the passing chords and things, and then do a little turn-around. Like they might play six bars, and in the seventh would start going into the release and then the eighth would be all set up for the second eight . . . I listened to Coleman Hawkins and Benny Carter and be stunned. I didn't know the right names for anything at first, but I knew what knocked me out . . . Changes, man, I dug . . .

When I first came to New York, I thought more of speed than of the melody. I had to play everything fast and double fast. I couldn't stand still—all my ballads had to be double time. I was fresh. I was full of ideas. Augmented chords. Ninths. . . . Also, I was playing fine saxophone on the trumpet. Trying to hold notes longer than they should be held, trying to get a sound which I couldn't and shouldn't get. When I discovered that a trumpet has a sound all its own, and a way of playing all its own, then I began to play.

❖❖

Eldridge first heard Armstrong on record in 1927 when he ran into clarinetist Matty Matlock in an Omaha, Nebraska, music store. Matlock played "Wild Man Blues" and "Gully Low" for Roy. Years later (1951) in France, Eldridge recorded "Wild Man Blues," "Skip the Gutter," and "Fireworks"—Armstrong features—with pianist Claude Bolling.

It wasn't until 1932, however, when Eldridge heard Armstrong in person at New York's Lafayette Theatre, that Roy really was affected by Louis. A building solo on "Chinatown" that climaxed on a high F delivered the message.

❖❖

ROY ELDRIDGE   I started to feel that if I could combine speed with melodic development while continuing to build, to tell a story, I could create something musical of my own.

DEXTER GORDON   I dug Roy Eldridge—I still do. I used to get almost the same thing listening to Roy as I did listening to Lester—the same "story" feeling.

❖❖

Musicians do not exist in the vacuum of their own instrumental category. Trumpeters listen to saxophonists and vice versa. And sometimes they double.

❖❖

BENNY CARTER   I studied saxophone. I never took any clarinet lessons. I just picked that up. I played trumpet first, or I attempted to play trumpet first for three days. Then I took it back and changed it for a saxophone. So I played trumpet later really.

Doc Cheatham was the one who really encouraged me to play trumpet. He was playing in my band, and I wanted to play trumpet, but I was afraid that it might mess up my chops for the saxophone, and he assured me that it wouldn't because he had played saxophone before and the only reason that he wasn't playing it now was that he didn't have time to divide the thing between the two instruments. I could certainly understand what he meant at the time. But he encouraged me to really take up the trumpet, and he helped me quite a lot.

❖❖

And then there was Art Tatum. He turned everyone around. For instance, there was a night in Toledo when the Fletcher Henderson band went to hear him.

❖❖

REX STEWART   Coleman Hawkins was so taken by Tatum's playing that he immediately starting creating another style for himself, based on what he heard Tatum play that night—and forever after dropped his slap-tongue style.

BUDD JOHNSON   Don Byas used to learn Art Tatum's solos and play them on his alto. That was way before he became anything—he was living in California at that time. This developed a terrific technique for him because trying to copy some of Art Tatum's solos in truly difficult—especially for a horn.

RED NORVO   I adored Tatum. The first time I heard Tatum was in the early '30s. Roy Bargy used to tell us about him in Chicago, and Earl Hines was at the Grand Terrace—'30s—1930 I guess it was. Somebody has always got somebody who can play greater, and we'd say, "Oh, yeah. Yeah." So we got to Detroit, and one night Roy came around and said, "You want to go to Cleveland tonight?" I said, "Why?" He said, "Ask Mildred. [Bailey] I also asked Andy Secrest. I want you to hear this piano player." So we went over and just made the ten o'clock show. But we were just thrilled to death with him. You can imagine. We became great friends after that. But I think harmonically he affected a lot of people, I don't want to mention names, but all of them have told me that he affected them harmonically, and I think emotionally he could do most anything he wanted to do on the piano.

BUDDY DEFRANCO   I would say from the mid '40s to the late '40s my major influence was Charlie Parker. Before that, my influence was Benny Goodman, Artie Shaw, and Art Tatum. Of course, Art Tatum you could not emulate because he did so damn much, you know—harmonically, at least. And I think Art Tatum and Jimmy Jones were really the first pianists I heard with a turnaround and chord progressions and harmonic development—modern harmonic development. Art Tatum is another world and one of the biggest musical worlds of all time. And, there again, I had occasion to play Art Tatum records to a young rock group in my area where I live, and they were absolutely overwhelmed! They just could not believe one man could play so much piano and with such harmonic development—including my son, who is now nineteen. I recently had him listen to Art Tatum records, and he fell off the chair. And this is the effect that such a great musician has. And there again, I remember reading reviews about Art Tatum in the '30s and somebody criticized him for having too much technique—a showoff—cocktail piano, you know? All sorts of things. But if you really stop and listen to what Art Tatum was doing *harmonically*—not only technically—he was the greatest of all time. I consider the record I made with Tatum as one of the greatest *experiences* of my time. But there again, I was not really feeling well. Now, I'm not going to cop out. This is really no excuse . . . But I really should not have done that session. Only because I wanted to be better prepared. To measure up to the challenge because playing with Art Tatum is like chasing a train and never catching it, see? I knew one thing: you're never going to outdazzle Art Tatum because he has it all. There's no question about it. But, to me, it was among the greatest experiences of my whole life—if for no other reason than to sit in that studio and watch him play and watch what he did. And also try to get in with him. It was absolutely a thrill.

JIMMY ROWLES   I started memorizing Teddy Wilson's solos, and I got so I could try to cover him, not the way he did, but I tried and I just thought he was . . . I still do. Such a gentleman—after I got to know him finally. And then I started hanging out with Art, and he showed me . . .

Art lived in L.A., and when he was in L.A.—the first time I met Art I was petrified. I was playing at a place on 7th and Vermont, playing solo piano, and there was nobody in the place. The owner liked me, and Art had played there before. I was up there on the dais where the piano was. Pinpoint spot. Can't play shit. I'm just starting, trying to get into it. Nobody there, and I heard the front door open and close, and there was silence. I got the funniest feeling. I was scared. And I'm telling you the truth. The guy who owned the joint, Tiny Eddington—he was a good guy—and I got scared. I just ended what I was doing and got off real quick and went and sat down in the corner. It was dark down there. You couldn't see. I knew there was somebody sitting there. Tiny was talking, and he calls me and introduces me to Art. Then I went, later, I went to up on 8th where Art was playing and I sat real close and watched him. Whewww! And he had a chauffeur. You know he couldn't see very well. He took me under his wing. Some kind of a *wing*. So I'd be sitting down there at Tiny Eddington's playing—they called it the Latin Quarter, the name of the joint—and here comes the goddamn chauffeur. Art *wants* you. Tiny would say, "Get out of here and go with him." So I'd go. Sit in the car. We'd pick up Art and we'd go. And I was staring over Art's shoulder all night. One time I went for three days without sleeping with that son-of-a-bitch, and he never stopped playing, and he didn't eat. Bourbon and beer. Boiler-fucking-makers. Later on I finally overcame my fear of

playing in front of him. He would say, "Play" and I'd say, "No, I . . ."
And he'd say, "Play." So I finally, slowly but surely, overcame my fear.
Well, I'll play my little simple shit. He loved to hear everybody play.
Loved everybody. He was outta sight. I used to follow him around like
a puppy. But he showed me a lot of shit. "Wait a minute, play that
again. Do that one more time." "What's that?" "That shit you just did."
And he'd go through it again another way. By the time you got through
with him—after ten hours—something had seeped in, but you didn't
know what it was because it was too complicated.

❖❖

Art Tatum was one of the people who was way ahead of his time—
harmonically—and who led into that next period.

❖❖

JIMMY ROWLES   If it hadn't been for him it never would have happened,
I don't think. He was ahead of his time because he influenced so many
pianists. He was the heaviest.

When I got out of the Army, when I came back to work with Woody
[1946], the first thing I did was to check into the Taft Hotel—took a
shower and went down to 52nd Street, and I walked—the first place
I walked into Art Tatum was playing. The place was almost empty,
and there were some people at the bar. So I went to the bar and got
a drink and sat down in the dark. It was just too much. When he finally got through he went over the service counter, and they gave him
his double shot and his beer, and I walked up to him. I said, "Art,
when you gonna play my tune?" Without a second warning, he turned
around and said, "When did you get out?" Just like that. He knew my
voice immediately. And we started talking. I hadn't seen him for three
and a half years. And he went up and played my tune for me. We sat
down and talked together.

BILLY TAYLOR   The first time Tatum came to New York he was exposed
to the great stride pianists like James P. Johnson and Willie "The Lion"
Smith and all the "kings of the hill," if you will, in that style. And they
really wiped him out that first time. James P. Johnson just did him in.
So he went back home—he was nineteen—and worked on a lot of stuff.
When he came back, he had all his stuff together. One of the reasons
he played a classical piece [Massenet's "Elegie"] is because there was a
pianist named Donald Lambert whose gimmick was to play classical
pieces in stride style. So this was his way of saying, "Okay. Try *this*
one." And he played it about four times as fast as Lambert, and he
played a lot more interesting harmonies, and he did all kinds of jux-
tapositions of melodic streams—playing a half-tone higher in his right
hand than he was in his left hand, things like that.

❖❖

With the changes in harmonic perceptions, the rhythmic contours
of the solo line also began to undergo alteration and, with this, so

did the approach to the basic pulse. Until rhythm sections for-
mulated a style compatible with the changes there was bound to
be an inhibiting clash.

❖❖

BUDD JOHNSON   We didn't really have the new sound in the Earl Hines
band. 'Cause we started to do a little bit of it, after we heard Dizzy.
The cats said, "Oh man, that's it," and they wanted to play like that,
so we'd write some of the passages and pick up on it.

Of course he wasn't doing too much playing *that* way then. Because,
I mean, like you're limited. For instance I was beginning with Sy
Oliver—Red Oliver—and Sy likes [sings back beat on two and four];
that's all he likes. And when I get up to play my solo, I can't do a
thing. You either wind up honking or . . . I imagine when Dizzy was
with Cab, it would be very difficult for him to play that progressive
music against the background he had because they didn't play that
way—they had a very great band, but they didn't play that way. What
I'm tryin' to say is it's hard to push one style against another style. A
modern cat comes in with just a plain ordinary group, and they play
none of the changes that he's playing, and the drummer ain't dropping a whole lot of bombs like he's been used to hearing, and it's gotta
mess with him. He can't really play his thing.

BARNEY KESSEL   I think of Sid Catlett as being the last of the swing drummers. Max Roach, to me, is the first bebop drummer. Kenny Clarke
was the bridge.

SHELLY MANNE   Big Sid and Klook* were the first ones to move away from
your accepted traditional way of playing by using more accents on the
bass drum. More work on the ride cymbals and things like that. And
more independent work with the left hand. Up to that point, the
drummers were more straight ahead. 'Cause I heard Jo Jones—who
was a big influence—only in Basie's band. I only heard him in a big
band context. And of course I always used to follow Davey Tough
around. I listened to Davey. But Davey wasn't that same kind of
drummer. He was a different type of drummer.

Davey was very adjustable. He was very flexible that way. He could
play with Bud Freeman one night at the Brick Club and go down and
play with Woody Herman the next night with the new Herd, which
was very modern then, and really drive the band. But he had that the
permanent, well, the permanent things that drummers have to have.
I mean the most predominant thing is that they have to swing. I feel
if a drummer could swing, he can play with anybody. It doesn't matter, whether he's playing with Art Hodes or Ornette Coleman. But I
heard the change starting to happen, and naturally Max (Roach) took

---

*Kenny Clarke's nickname, short for Klook-a-mop after his offbeat drum accents.

it—at first there was Sid, then I heard Klook, and then Specs Powell got to be very syncopated in his time playing. And then I started to hear Max, and that was another whole area of playing. They all—the influences were running around. Everybody was infuencing everybody else. Stan Levey was really a direct offshoot of Max's playing.

KENNY CLARKE We worshipped Big Sid. He told me, "You're really doing things with that bass drum."

BUDD JOHNSON Big Sid now, of course Big Sid could fit with anybody. I mean he was just a great smooth, beautiful drummer. I preferred him over Cozy [Cole]. Cozy to me was an older man who played the rudiments. Instead of like coming from here, he would say, "I'll make a five stroke and a seven stroke and an eight stroke rolled together and I'll make [imitates drums]." I'd like to hear a guy go after something and make a mistake sometimes. That's excitement too. Not just be too perfect. 'Cause Big Sid was something else. He was just a beautiful drummer. And he had the touch. He had the sound. But Kenny Clarke, he's the first cat I ever heard play those kind of drums. And I had heard Kenny. The first time I heard Kenny we played a battle of music with Edgar Hayes in Dayton, Ohio. And they washed us off the stand 'cause Kenny was dropping bombs and blowing then, and this was back—probably I had been with Earl maybe a year. You would call anything past '35 late. About '36. But I'm sayin' all that to say this: that the drums played a great part in creating the guy's style, because it has an influence on him. If a cat is saying [imitates drummer], you're liable to say [imitates horn]. You'll fall behind it and fit with him, and actually you're really creating together. You say, "Yeah, let's keep that in." And you start doing this. All of it helps. But if a drummer's just sayin' [imitates another drumming style, just keeping the time], then you really got to go get it, but it's very difficult for a guy to play. So anyway this transition all came through, I would say, the drums.

KENNY CLARKE I arrived in New York during the winter of 1935, and at that time I was the youngest drummer in the city. [Thelonious] Monk was still in school, Benny Harris and others were in college. At night, I worked with musicians who were older than I was, but during the day I felt really alone. I started playing with Sonny White, Benny Harris, and Monk after school hours. Finally I founded a trio with my brother Frank, who played bass—he's dead; he was assassinated in 1949—and a guitarist. I played vibraphone and drums. The trio became famous and known. I had offers from John Kirby because at that time in New York nobody played the vibraphone.

Frank and I started working on the problem of the rhythm section in 1931. We worked a long time to find out how the rhythm men should "play together." At that time, drummers played "dig coal": they beat the snare drum like miners digging for coal. The bass players, including my brother, didn't like that. When Cozy Cole played, he rarely hit his cymbal—five or six times a night. My brother liked Jimmy Blanton a lot, and he thought that this style should be kept up by a light drummer who let the bassline be heard. That's how I started experimenting with the continuous cymbal line.

❖❖

After the Clarke trio's job ran out, Frank got them a job at the Black Cat in Greenwich Village.

❖❖

KENNY CLARKE   He told Lonnie Simmons, the bandleader, about me, so Lonnie hires me. So there was Freddie Green, Lonnie Simmons, Frank Clarke, Bobby Moore, who was the little trumpet player who played "Out the Window" with Basie. He was working with us. So, like, we had trumpet, tenor, piano, bass, and guitar. That was our band. And what a band that was. Lonnie and Freddie Green were raised together in South Carolina. Fats Atkins from Philadelphia was the pianist. Count Basie got his style from Fats Atkins. That's where Basie got it. Because Basie played like James P. Johnson.

What happened is that the rhythm section was so fantastic until everybody used to come in and jam at the Black Cat. Benny Goodman, Harry James, Basie, Lionel [Hampton], because I had vibraphones. And everyone used to come there and jam. The boss's name was Frankel, and Frankel used to keep Benny Goodman, used to keep us there 'til nine o'clock in the morning.

AL HALL   I remember one night, Prez and Benny Goodman jamming on "Honeysuckle Rose" for forty-five minutes, switching horns.

KENNY CLARKE   And Harry James used to come right by the sock cymbal with his trumpet and blow into the sock cymbal. In 1936. And Basie used to come all the time with Benny and jam with us. And that's when he got the idea, the way the rhythm section was jumping, he just took Freddie right out. I imagine if Jo [Jones] hadn't been with the band I would have joined the band, too.

In the latter part of 1936 I went with Edgar Hayes's band. It was the next best after Jimmie Lunceford's. That was the school. That was the university for me. I had started writing then—with Joe Garland and Rudy Powell and all those guys in the band. They just taught me everything. And I used to write for the band—"The Goona Goo," tunes like that. I used to make arrangements on that.

And I used to copy Ray Mc Kinley. I used to buy all his records. I never was a soloist. I thought it was stupid. I always thought drum solos were very stupid. So I always concentrated on accompaniment. I thought that was the most important thing. That was my basic function as a drummer, to accompany, so I always stuck with that. And I think that's why a lot of the musicians liked me so much, because I never show off and always think about them first. So, Ray gave me the idea to play something, some kind of solo. So I started copying his things and playing them, little eight-bar phrases and things like that. I'd fit them. That's when I started the style of playing along with the brass and making things like fill-in holes, as we call it.

❖❖

Later these accents became known colloquially as "bombs."

❖❖

KENNY CLARKE But nobody understood it. They thought I was crazy. They said, "Oh, that little guy is crazy. He's always breaking up the tempo." So there it was. But I stuck to it. I liked it so I wasn't about to change something that I had found. And I really had a flair with that. So I stuck with it, on out.

❖❖

After touring Europe with Hayes and returning to the U.S., Clarke left the band in 1938 and, after a stint with Claude Hopkins, wound up with Teddy Hill. The ideas that had been "in the back of my head" from the Hayes days came to the fore in 'Hill's band.

❖❖

KENNY CLARKE That's where the whole thing happened. Because Dizzy understood being a rhythmical musician. All kinds of rhythms fascinated him. I used to write out little things, and Dizzy was right behind me. I would hand them back to him. I'd say, "Hey, Diz, how do you think this would sound?" He'd say, "Well, try it."

So I began to play with my foot and my left hand, and with the cymbal, because everyone says you can play the sock cymbal like this, and I say there has to be a better way, because if I play the sock cymbal, then I can't use my left hand. I had to find a way to use it, so I changed over to the top cymbal, which gave me the freedom of my left hand. See, because Jo was cramped. And I used to watch him. I used to follow Basie all over, to find out the advantage of playing the sock cymbal with the right hand like that, and I traveled all over the country with Basie. I'd just get on the bus and go. Freddie and Basie would see that I had something to eat and a place to stay, so I never worried. Sometimes Jo would say, "Well, I'm not working tonight. Kenny, take my place." When I would play in Jo's place, I would try to understand exactly—but I guess he had played that way so long that he had it quite undercover, exactly what he wanted to do. But what he was doing had no bearing at all on what I wanted to do. Jo Jones played long passages on the Charleston,* but not with the cymbal. One day, a guy asked me, "Why don't you play like Jo Jones?" I told him that I didn't like that. I wanted to be free with my two hands. To play

*Two syncopated notes, one falling on the first beat of the bar and the other between the weak second beat and the strong third beat.

on the Charleston, you have to cross your arms. The left hand is then blocked. I thought that if I played the cymbal with the right hand it would first of all be light, and secondly, my left hand would be free.

So I started playing this way and freeing my left hand. My idea was to never leave your left hand idle. Because if people look up, and they see me playing with one hand, and this hand isn't doing anything, it's like a one-handed piano player. So I began to work on it, to coordinate my left hand with my right foot and my right hand and my left foot. Because rinky-dink, bang, I had the sock cymbal over here, and the left hand was the bass drum, so I figured, I talked to Diz about it, and he said, "That's a perfect combination. Now you have the whole thing working."

Well, I never expected to—for things to turn out the way they did as far as modern drumming is concerned. I never—it just happened sort of accidentally, because what really brought the whole thing about, we were playing a real fast tune once—"Old Man River," I think we were playing, with Teddy—and the tempo was too fast to play four beats to the measure, so I began to cut the time up, you know, but to keep the same rhythm going, so I had to do it with my hand, because my feet just—my foot just wouldn't do it. So I started doing it with my hand, and then every once in a while I would kind of lift myself with my foot, to kind of boot myself into it, and that made the whole thing move. So I began to work on that. I said, "Gee, I got out of that." When it was over, I said, "Good God, was that ever hard." So then I began to think, you know, and say, "Well, you know it worked." It worked, and nobody said anything, so it came out right. So that must be the way to do it. Because I think if I hadn't been able to do it, it would have been stiff. It wouldn't have worked.

The trombone—Henry Woode, Jimmy Woode's uncle—was Teddy Hill's right hand man at that time. He hated that way of playing. He hated it so much that I got fired. He said, "Kenny keeps breaking up the time. Why doesn't he keep four beats on the bass drum?" So then I began to argue with them about the fact that, if you are playing, the tempo should be in your head, don't depend on me. Depend on yourself, because if you're playing music, the tempo that you're playing in is in your head. It's in your mind, or either it's no use of your being here, if you're depending on somebody to keep the tempo for you. You keep your tempo yourself. Because you can play the music without anything, alone. You can play your part.

I didn't care. I was young. I could play the way I wanted to play. I got fired for playing that way, but I kept on playing. A month later, Woode left Teddy, and Teddy rehired me! He liked my playing! He told me, "You're playing some hip things." Diz was thrilled to see me come back. I played a long time with Diz, from 1938 to 1942. Then I left for the Army, and during my absence, Dizzy, who plays the drums well, taught all the other drummers my way of playing. He would say to them: "You have to do it like Klook. Do something with your left hand, anything, but you have to do something!" When I got out of the service, I noticed that in New York, like in Chicago, all the drummers played like me. Dizzy was the one who showed them, as Max Roach informed me. That style was adopted by all the young players, and it is still strong today.

❖❖

Down in Cheraw, South Carolina, during the middle '30s, a teen-aged Dizzy Gillespie would go next door to Mrs. Harrington's house and listen to "Saturday Session at the Savoy" on her radio. It was Teddy Hill's band, and although he didn't know the names of the soloists he knew he liked them very much—tenor saxophonist Chu Berry and trumpeter Roy Eldridge.

When did Gillespie first begin hearing those advanced chordal inversions that became a characteristic of bebop?

❖❖

DIZZY GILLESPIE   Oh, way back when I was with Teddy Hill. My playing is documented; if you listen to me playing with the Teddy Hill band in 1937, you'll hear them then. At that stage I sounded like Roy, and when I was with Cab [Calloway] I still sounded like Roy Eldridge. But each musician is based on someone who went before, and eventually you get enough of your own things in your playing, and you get a style of your own. You always will hear Roy Eldridge in my playing, but my main influence came from Charlie Parker. Coleman Hawkins influenced me too. I was influenced by many, really.

MILT HINTON   So we came to New York. We opened the Cotton Club in 1936 downtown, at 48th and Broadway—that's when we opened. I never played the Cotton Club uptown—played downtown. We opened that club when I came in the band in 1936—with Cab. We took six months to get into New York, and Ben Webster was in the band, and he was my idol. He took me with him, because Ben was one of the few jazz musicians in Cab Calloway's band that went around in towns like Pittsburgh and went up on Wylie Avenue and went in the clubs and would jam with the guys. And it was his policy always to take his bass player along, because we had been rehearsing all afternoon in the theaters, and I knew his tunes and his changes. So when he got sharp and impeccable as he always was, he would say, "Come on go with me," and we'd go in a club, and of course we got in there and we would blow, and be invited to blow, and of course the booze was free, and if you wanted a chicken sandwich, it was also on the house after you blew—and you got to meet the nicest chicks. 'Cause now you're exposed. And so I hung with Ben, and when we got to New York in 1936, Ben had spoken to Duke—told Duke he sure wanted to play. Because there was no solos. Cab hadn't gotten to the era of solos, letting instrumentalists play. He was just all Cab Calloway and hi-de-ho's.

It was just a showcase for him, and we just sat there. We kept our-selves together academically by rehearsing ourselves, because he didn't care. All he was concerned with was that we play this music, and it was all hi-de-hos—"Minnie the Moocher," and "Smokey Joe," and "Reefer Man" and what not. And Ben was very unhappy because he only got eight bars every now and then. So he had spoken to Duke, and Duke had told him, well, "Cab is my brother band, and I love you, and I wish I could have you, but I couldn't take anybody out of Cab Callo-way's band, 'cause this is my brother band." But bein' as chic and ma-neuvering man that Duke was, he said, "But, if you didn't have a job, I would have to give you a job."

So, of course this stuck in Ben's mind, and he began saving his money and buying some new clothes so that he could quit Cab—get him a little bankroll, and he could quit Cab. Which, of course, he did before '36. He was in Cleveland at the Trianon Ballroom and said, "Hey man I'm gonna split." Cab had this thing—everybody left was okay, but you had to replace yourself with somebody qualified, because Cab didn't know, and he took Ben's word, since he and Ben were friends, and said, "Well, who do you recommend?" So Ben said, "Well, Fletcher is in the Grand Terrace, and Chu Berry is with him, and he's an excel-lent player." So Cab said, "Okay, let's get him." So Ben called Chicago, and Chu came home to the Trianon Ballroom, sat in the band with Ben, and Ben showed him the book, and then Ben split. Went back to Chicago, knowin' that Duke was booked in some club in Chicago. And so Ben is straight—he's got his bankroll. He's got his togs, and he's got Cab replaced with a good saxophone player because Fletcher wasn't paying but thirty-five dollars a week, and Cab was paying one hundred dollars a week or more, which was absolutely fantastic. Tre-mendous money. This was before '36, so there was no income tax. You had ninety-nine dollars of your money. The union took a dollar tax; you got ninety-nine dollars. Get a great room for six dollars, you could get a great meal for fifty cents, so it was *quite* adequate, and I figured when I got in the band I'd be rich in about six months. So Ben left, went to Chicago, and sure enough Duke showed up in no time at all, bein' booked in Chicago, and Ben says, "I don't have a job." And, of course, Duke hired him.

Dizzy took Doc Cheatham's place in the band. Doc Cheatham got sick and took a vacation, and Dizzy came in, and, of course, he was so modern that there was just no place for Doc Cheatham to get back. Diz came in the band after Ben [Webster], and Diz was of the same type of guy that Ben was. He wanted to experiment like Ben experi-mented and took me with him, so I was happy to have somebody like Diz come in. He had been with Teddy Hill and had been to Europe and was playing some new innovations instead of just a straight chorus—screaming brass with the added sixes, we used to say. So Dizzy wanted somebody to blow with. A bass is more portable—you can't take a drum up on the roof, but you can take a bass player. This was the down-town Cotton Club—after 1937, and Dizzy would take me up on the roof and, of course, Dizzy had been into the new innovation of changes, using the flatted fifths and what not. Dizzy would take me up there to blow with him, and he would show me the hip changes—substitution chords as we call 'em—and so I was very happy 'cause I'm learning now. I'm progressing from where Ben left off and when Ben left off; Chu was straight down the middle—he played his riffs, and he knew his thing, and he was a musician's musician. He didn't have to prac-tice. He was a great sportsman—football and baseball—and he went around to jam sessions, of course, but he didn't call me in a corner, but Dizzy would say, "Hey, come on upstairs." And Dizzy would show me a new change.

And then I lived uptown, and of course, Dizzy was livin' uptown. Lorraine, his wife, was dancin' at the Apollo Theater, and supportin' Dizzy, 'cause Dizzy, until he got with Cab, was starvin' to death. There wasn't nothin' happening. And Lorraine was the one who was keepin' everything together, dancin' with that number-one chorus at the Apollo Theater. And Minton's was open, and I lived right across the street from Minton's, so Dizzy would say to me, "Look, when we go up to Minton's tonight, 'cause I want to show you some new changes, 'cause a lot of cats coming in and these cats are a drag. They just get in and they blow and they get up and don't know what the hell they're doin', so let's change the changes to "I Got Rhythm," and we'll play B-flat to D-flat to G-flat to F—we'll change the changes around, and tonight when we go in there, I won't say anything—I'll just stomp off and you'll go through these changes with me and we'll blow, and these cats don't know the changes and they can't get in."

So, really it was like isolation, what we were tryin' to do, to isolate everybody—white and black—who had a horn, who would come up to Minton's and buy a beer and figure they could sit in. And Cab had the Cab Jivers with Chu Berry and Danny Barker, Cozy Cole and I, and Dizzy would show me a very hip solo to play, on certain things. That's how that cuttin' thing went with Diz, which was in Hartford,* years later; and it was Jonah [Jones] that did it, and he just walked away. I don't want to prefer to say that Jonah didn't admit it, but when it was all over, Jonah walked off the bandstand, and Cab accused Dizzy, and Jonah was back in the bandroom. He didn't even hear it. Proba-bly if he had heard it he would have said, "Fess, I did it," and I'm sure he knows later, now. But the big thing was that Cab didn't know that Dizzy didn't do it, and it was the first time he *didn't* do something. He was always wrong, and, of course, he stood up for his rights and, of course, the altercation occurred.

*During a theater stage show, Calloway accused Gillespie of throwing a spitball. They scuffled, later backstage and Dizzy cut Cab on his posterior with a knife.

NEAL HEFTI   Bands would come to town [Omaha]; we'd see Basie in town, and I was impressed by Harry Edison and Buck Clayton, being a trumpet player. And I would say I was impressed by Dizzy Gillespie when he was with Cab Calloway. I was impressed by those three trumpet players of the people I saw in person. 'Cause sometimes other bands would play in town that I really wanted to see, but maybe I didn't have the money to see them. I thought that Harry Edison and Dizzy Gillespie were the most unique of the trumpet players I heard.

I heard Dizzy as a completely different soloist from anyone. As a matter of fact, I sort of strangely enough associated him with Ziggy Elman. I thought he sort of sounded like a Ziggy Elman type to me. Because maybe up until that time, maybe Ziggy Elman was the most different trumpet player I ever heard. Like maybe Dizzy Gillespie even sounded Jewish like Ziggy Elman in "And the Angels Sing," and those kinds of things he was doing with Tommy Dorsey. That he had sort of that ethnic flavor to his playing, and maybe Dizzy Gillespie had that too. I don't know.

BENNY CARTER   I met Dizzy first with Teddy Hill's band, later with Cab Calloway's band, when I returned from Europe. And then he played with me for a short period when I headed a sextet. Leonard [Feather] called it a John Kirby style outfit. I guess that's the thing, because we had Jimmy Hamilton on clarinet and myself on alto and Dizzy on trumpet. The instrumentation was certainly the same. By this time I heard him—he had sort of gotten out of the Roy Eldridge influence. He was coming out from under anyway, and certainly there was something of his own evolving from it. But it was quite definite that he had something quite different to say. It must have been later than '41, because I left New York in September '42 on my way to California, and I arrived in California in November. So I lived in New York during that period. The only flak I can remember getting was from Irving Alexander at the Famous Door. He didn't care for me to let Dizzy play too many solos. He thought it was kind of mysterious music. But I ignored that, and Dizzy played, and I think Irving started listening a little more closely and realizing that it did have more validity than he had at first thought.

❖❖

It was while Gillespie was with Carter that he wrote and first played "Interlude," which became known as "A Night in Tunisia" when it was named by Earl Hines at the time Dizzy was with the pianist's band.

❖❖

FRANKIE SOCOLOW   I heard Diz quite a bit before I ever heard Bird. And since the first time I ever heard Diz I was convinced he was just the greatest trumpet player in the world. I don't know, that was my man. I heard him with Cab. And I would follow Diz. I remember I used to see him on 52nd Street. He worked with Benny Carter for quite a while at Kelly's Stables. I was there every night. Art Tatum was on piano as a single. And the Nat Cole Trio.

He was already into the new thing, and it was so wild hearing somebody like that. You knew something new was happening. You knew it. The way he played his changes; the way his whole conception was set apart from what was happening.

❖❖

BILLY ECKSTINE   I knew Diz from here [New York]. And we used to hang out every time I'd come to town. I met Diz when he was with Cab Calloway. No, I even met him before that. I met Diz when he was with Lucky Millinder. And we used to hang out together, and Roy—of course, Eldridge—was from my home, and when I first met Diz he was playing like Roy, and then you could see him gradually getting away into things of his own, some of those early records of Diz's with Cab Calloway like "Pickin' the Cabbage." You could see him beginning to move a little bit away into his own thing built on chord progressions. Because Diz at that particular time, when he was off the bandstand, he was at a piano constantly. And when we all lived in 2040 7th Avenue, and Diz lived right up over me and Shadow [Wilson], we were all right in—well, Christ, it was a musician's building, and Diz had an old upright piano in his house, and it was a constant upstairs sitting at the piano and working out things.

❖❖

While Gillespie, in New York, was developing his ideas, Charlie Parker, in Kansas City, was finding his path toward the eventual meeting of their minds.

❖❖

BUDD JOHNSON   Bird admired Prez a lot, but Bird really came from Buster Smith. Because when I was a kid Buster Smith was playing like that then. Way before Bird was ever born. In Dallas, Texas. We used to go by a joint, and they called us—we were little cats, we had our little band. And they used to say, "Here comes the "gnat liver," the young blood, "gnat liver." We were so little, little cats. And we would come up and play around. Buster played the hell out of the clarinet and the alto. He played that loping style. Now we got Tommy Douglas out of Topeka, Kansas, and put him with George E. Lee's band. He was a little angel. Played very good clarinet and saxophone. He could blow; he didn't have that style but he could blow. He would just blow good jazz and was a very good saxophone player. Fine saxophone player.

We used to rehearse in George E. Lee's mother's house on Euclid Avenue in Kansas City. Bird had to be around eleven or no more than twelve years old. I didn't know him at that time, but I did see the little cats playin' stickball, and they used to come and peek through the window when we would be rehearsin'. So long after that, the Three Businessmen of Rhythm, who were dancers—I forget all the names of the guys—and Bird was together one day when we were working working the Apollo Theatre and when I came, we were talkin'. Bird said, "Yeah, you don't remember me, but we"—these dancers and Bird—"were the kids that was playin' stickball out in the street and used to come and peep in the window when you were rehearsin'." And I said, "Was that you?" They all grew up together. Went to school together in Kansas City. They weren't working together. I think Bird was just on his own at that time, because we had been tryin' to get him with Earl's band before I left. It all really started cause Billy Eckstine used to tell me a long time before, he said, "Man, I heard a little saxophone player named Charlie Parker; you got to hear this guy play." Benny Carter was the big thing on alto. He said, "Man, this cat will outplay Benny Carter." I said, "You've got to be kidding." So right around 1939 or late '38 we tried to get Bird in the band. We were in Detroit at the Paradise Theater, and Bird came by. Between the shows we'd go down to our dressing room, and he would play for us. I said, "What? This cat is unbelievable." So we all started to try to write along these veins. I never heard "Cherokee" played that way before. He ate it up. Earl wanted to hire him, but he wasn't too sure whether he thought he would like to play in that band. So he turned it down. But we sure wanted him in the band then.

IDREES SULIEMAN   I was with the Carolina Cotton Pickers doing one-nighters for four years. We stopped in Kansas City in 1941, and I met Bird blowing every night at the Kentucky Club. They'd start at four o'clock after the other clubs closed and go, sometimes, to twelve noon.

I didn't recognize it because there was an alto player we had named Porter Kilbert. So, for us, Porter was the world's best. Because he could do the same thing, too. He had a photographic memory. Play arrangements, and he could play all the solos. We heard about Charlie Parker, and finally when we got to Kansas City, everyone in the band was waiting to see what would happen. So the first night we played, Charlie Parker was there listening to Porter. So we said, "Yeah. He's getting the message."

When we finished they had this jam session, and they both were really blowing. When it was over we said, "We're still with Porter. Porter don't have nothing to worry about."

But Porter said, "Yeah, but he threw in something different, man." So we said, "It's different, yeah, but you played everything he played." And he said, "Yeah, but he thought of it first."

❖ ❖

Kilbert, who later played in Benny Carter's band recorded with Coleman Hawkins for Sonora in 1946. ("Bean and the Boys" and "I Mean You" were reissued on a Prestige LP bearing the same title as the first song.)

❖ ❖

IDREES SULIEMAN   On records they never really got what he could do because he was a cat that, after he played a lot of choruses, he went into
another thing. But he didn't have Bird's strong sound.

When we left Kansas City we went to someplace in South Carolina,
and after the job we went in to eat, and there was this nickelodeon.
Every time they put a nickel in they'd play Jay McShann [sings Bird's
solo from "Sepian Bounce".] So Porter said, "That's him!" So we said,
"Who?" "That's the alto player." So we kept listening, and by the time
we left that night, we *knew*. When Porter got home he played the solo,
too, and we made him play it over and over. That was the first time I
really understood Bird.

JAY MC SHANN   I came to Kansas City in the year of 1937, and I thought
I'd heard all the musicians in town. So I happened to be passing by a
club, and Bird happened to be sitting in at this club playing. You know
they used to pipe the music outside. So I was gonna go on home, but
I heard a different sound, and I went in there, and Bird was playing.
I never met him before. I asked him, "Man, I thought I knew all the
cats here, but I haven't met you. Where are you from?" He says, "I'm
from Kansas City, but I've been out of town with George E. Lee's band.
We've been down in the Ozarks."

He said it was very hard to get musicians to go down to the Ozarks.
So he said, "I wanted to woodshed* so I went down to the Ozarks
with George E. Lee." I said, "Well, you sound different from any cat
I've heard here in town." He said, "I guess that comes from the
woodshedding that I did."

❖❖

It's amazing but the small-band records McShann made at a radio station in Witchita that have come to light in recent years, are
like a missing link for a lot of people because you can really hear
more strongly than ever how Bird had listened very hard to Prez
and from that developed his own style.

❖❖

JAY MC SHANN   Well, yes, he loved Prez, and he also loved Buster Smith.
In fact, he played in Buster's band, and I think that was something
that had quite an influence on Bird. He had a lot of respect for Buster.
Buster, I always felt was a man that never knew how much he could
do. Buster had it, but you would have to make him play. And so many
people never had the chance to hear him play clarinet. To me, Buster's
one of the greatest clarinet players in the world. We used to feature
him, and we'd have to make him play, and also on the alto we'd have
to make him play. He'd play one chorus and put his horn down, and
we'd have to make him keep going. After his glasses began to drop
down, then you knew he was gonna play.

❖❖

*Practice—from going off by oneself to the woodshed for intensive, private practice.

The Kansas City style that has been talked about so much over the years has a distinctive feeling. When you say Kansas City you are actually referring to the whole Southwest and a particular kind of player.

❖❖

JAY MC SHANN   They play jazz. What they do is definitely based on jazz. They play the blues; they play boogie woogie, and they swing. And that's about as close as I can get to it. The cats, they *did* believe in swinging. If it didn't swing, it didn't say nothing. Because there's been a lot of very good groups that played really great stuff, technical stuff, but a lot of times it would get so technical in many cases that you ceased to pat your foot. Well, we feel like if you didn't pat your foot, you wasn't swinging. It's always kind of nice to look around when you're playing to look around at the tables or see someone patting their foot or people moving to the sounds on the floor and so forth like that. They're giving expressions of what they hear, what they're listening to.

BENNY BAILEY   A place I particularly enjoyed visiting was Kansas City, Charlie Parker's hometown. There were so many good musicians there that K.C. had an aura, an atmosphere very conducive to playing. I can't really explain it, but it was all very loose and happy-go-lucky, and I could see where Bird had benefited from it when he was young. There was a mixture of blues, country music, and jazz which all added up to that special flavor that Charlie Parker had. His music was deeply rooted in the blues, even hillbilly music, it was *all* there in his playing.

JAY MC SHANN   Bird always did swing—I always say that. But I think be-bop—you know how people put a name on this or that. Bebop, I always felt they was trying to show how technical they could be. They're showing technique and so forth, so consequently when you're gonna do that, then you get away from the swinging bit. They said Bird played bebop, but Bird could still swing. I've heard a lot of guys play bebop, but they wasn't swinging. They was playing a lot of technical stuff, but they didn't swing. Bird could play anything because, primarily, Bird was the greatest blues player in the world, and I still hang onto that. Bird played the blues. And if you don't believe he played the blues, you let him pick out what we used to call a "sweet tune" or ballad, as they say, and Bird played blues on a ballad.

MOSE ALLISON   A lot of Bird's figures are right out of gospel and traditional Negro music. Bird, to me, was like a blues player caught in the age of anxiety. The blues were pretty basic to him.

JACKIE MC LEAN   This is one music, man! It's one music that started out with plantation hollers. Bird's blues things [vocalizes a Parker line]—those were field hollers that somebody sang a different way in slavery.

GUS JOHNSON   Coming up with McShann, he had a very good band. And we had Charlie Parker, Gene Ramey, and myself. We had a guitar player named—they called him Lucky—Leonard Enois. And he was a great guitar player, too. He passed away years ago. But we had a darned good rhythm section in that band.

JAY MC SHANN   Lucky could play. And the thing about what we did—unless he was doing a solo, we had him to cut it off [his amplification] and just play while we could feel it, where it could be felt in the rhythm section. But then he also did some very nice solos, and he had a good feel, a good feeling going. Yes, even with his rhythm he was effective.

❖❖

Another guitarist was Efferge Ware, whom Charlie Parker worked out with in George E. Lee's band. As the story is told, Bird worked on hearing chords with him.

❖❖

JAY MC SHANN   Well I met Efferge and was around Efferge. I never had the pleasure of playing with Efferge, though. But Efferge was quite a serious musician. He took the guitar seriously. I never was too much acquainted with him during the time probably when he and Bird and those guys was working out. I wasn't up on that too much. And then later Efferge played with another big band after he left George Lee's band. He played with Harlan Leonard. I know that Bird and Efferge was in that band together. Bird played with my small band and played with the big band.

❖❖

McShann had a big band at the time, but it was a smaller unit, that cut some records at a radio station in Wichita, late in 1940.

❖❖

JAY MC SHANN   I had just organized the big band and, in fact, I would always pull out five pieces, maybe four, six, or something like that out of the big band, and we'd do a thing. Even when the big band would play maybe four, five tunes, I'd just pull these other guys, just bring 'em out to the front, and we'd do things with a smaller group—things that we'd gotten together just for kicks. That's how this happened. We used to go out to Witchita University. You know how the guys fool around and have a lot of fun out there. That's how that happened. This guy Pete Armstrong, and Fred Higginson, they all of a sudden decided, "Well, look, let's go down to the radio station, and we'll just do some stuff." So that's what we did. I just picked out four, five guys that was on then, and we went on down there, did that and thought nothing about it and just forgot about it.

GUS JOHNSON   We made the radio date. And on top of that, we didn't get paid for it. Not even the radio date. They just asked us to come by and—that was a live broadcast. I even had a picture of myself, the same night, on drums. Because I had a tweed suit, and I never will forget that because I lost it. Right after that. That was a good date, too. But I even hate to talk about that date because we didn't get paid for it.

When Bird was playing with McShann and before then, I think I liked his playing better. He changed after he came back to New York, but the way he was playing before, I loved it much better. This was during the time when we first made the records, too. I liked his playing then. Very much. I liked it after, too. But there was just a little bit difference in his playing, and bop came in as it was, and everybody thought that they had to play like Bird. One of those things. That Bird was playing just anything. But when Bird played, he knew what he was doing because he could go through the keys, from A to G, and that's what he used to do all the time. You know, we'd have jam sessions, chromatic right on up. Start at one note and keep right on half-step—each half-step each time. And most of the musicians couldn't do that. But Bird could. That's the reason I liked Mc Shann's band at the time. Because, really, we didn't care much about anybody.

We came to New York, and we were afraid because, one thing, we got there late. And Lucky Millinder was on the stand at the time, and he had to play till we got there. And we got there about—almost eleven that night, and we were supposed to have been there at five that evening. The cars broke down, and that's was why we were late. But we got there and just stayed on one tempo—one of them jump tempos—and blew Lucky Millinder off the stage. Get Panama [Francis] to tell you about that because he was with Lucky at that time. And it was really a great band they had. So we had the floor just jumping up and down. Like that. Which the floor had springs in it, I found out afterwards. It really did. The dance floor had springs underneath, so when they would start dancing, well, it would just go up and down. That was a great time then. I loved it.

JAY MC SHANN   During the time when the big band was in its height, we never got a chance to record what we really wanted to record because we did have a great book. We had a fantastic book. We never got a chance to record but very little of that stuff because the record companies were in business to sell records. As Dave Kapp told me in Dallas, "Listen." We came out with stuff like *Yardbird Suite* with the big band, and he says, "Listen, I can not sell that. Now we've wasted three hours here. You all played a lot of stuff which is good, but I can't sell it. I want something that I can sell."

Had I been smart, had the money, I would have had them take off fifteen or twenty of those tunes and just held them. But I didn't have the money in those days, and things were pretty tight. So he asks us, "Can you do any blues?" We said, "Yes." We did a blues. "Do a boogie?" We did a boogie. He said, "Do me one more blues, and I'll take one of those other tunes." Then we did "Hootie Blues," so then he accepted "Swingmatism." That's how we got "Swingmatism" on there and on the next session we did "Jump the Blues" ["The Jumpin' Blues] and some other stuff.

❖ ❖

There's a story that Charlie Parker got his name "Yardbird" because of a chicken that was killed on the way to some gig.

❖ ❖

JAY MC SHANN   People don't want to believe it, but it is true. We used to go up to the University of Nebraska and play dates up there—you know, "Big Red," the games, after the games, and so forth. We were on our way up there this particular time, and you know how it is traveling on the highway, you run into, you be traveling along and these chickens all run out on the highway. So some of the chickens run out on the highway. So this guy ran over a chicken. So Bird told him, he says, "Hey, Pat, back this car up and pick up that yardbird there. You just ran over a yardbird." So sure enough Pat backed the car up, and Charlie got out and got the chicken—took a chicken on into Lincoln with him. During those times we would find private homes where we would stay. So at the private home where you stayed he went in and asked this lady, he told her, "Miss, we ran over the yardbird on our way here, just a little ways out of here, and he's still warm, and I wonder if you could cook him for me?" She said, "Yes." So she did. And from then on we started calling him "Yardbird." Some called him Bird; some called him Yardbird. And he did like chicken.

We traveled in three, maybe four cars. The guys was young, and they enjoyed it, they had a lot of fun. The young cats are always into something. Bird's word was "a chicken ain't nothing but a yardbird," so that just gave us the idea. So every time we referred to him, we referred to him like that.

They did a lot of jamming. You know how guys always—they go out and maybe after they get through with the gig they're not satisfied—they want to go find out what's happening here and there and see what's going on. Maybe there are some cats across town getting together. They seek those places out. You'd see Bird with his horn in his arm, in the sack. Wherever he was all he had to do was just put it down, pull it out of the sack, and just start blowing.

In the Kansas City clubs we'd always have someone singing like Joe Turner or some girl singing. Back then in those days when the chicks would sing the cats would put the bread on the end of the table. The chicks would sing, and while they were singing they'd pick up that bread.*

Bird played with the small group. Then he told me, "I want to just go to New York and look at New York." That's when he left the group. In '39 he went into Chicago, came to New York. He used to tell me

*not with their hands

how he'd stand on the corner, look up at the sign at the Savoy Ball-room and all that stuff, and he was just digging New York, period.

❖❖

In his travels around the city, Parker met a guitarist.

❖❖

BIDDY FLEET   There were some good readers in those days, but only first men and third men. Horns I'm talking about now. Second could skate. He could get by, but first men had to read to carry the section. Now the third man playing the third part any note would sometime—if it's not hit too often—would be accepted because all breaks or solos and what not he would get. But actually, the musicians in the big-band days—every one of them—had an ear and a head for the sounds, and they could tell from what you're doing what he's supposed to do. With or without the music. We've had many a new man come in and sit down, and we didn't know whether they could read or not. Sat in the section and played the parts. Well, I as a guitarist, I'm not in a section now. Many times the guys would ask me in a session—jam session—do you know so and so and so? I say, "No, but play it." They say, "Why play it if you don't know it?" I say, "Then I will know it." And, when it was over, "Man, I thought you said you didn't know it." I said, "But I could tell from what you all were doing what I was supposed to do." Experience told me what to do. And there was more of that in the old musicians—the jazz big band musicians—than the guys with the college degrees. I worked with many of them with those college degrees. Knew any thing you wanted to know about music but could half play their instrument.

And there's another thing that happened in the big band days. When a man hit a note according to the tune he played—I talked on the horns more than my instrument because I learned from the horns. I heard chords from the horns. (Yes, I studied a few banjo chords, and I learned to read and to play the notes and all, but that didn't tell me anything, harmony-wise.) When the band hit, no matter what the sound was, or what the tune or the key, every chord man, piano or guitar, or to go back before to the banjo days, he knew what to do. And take him out of the band and sit him in the studio and give him a sheet—the violin sheet or the clarinet sheet or something to play by himself—he's stuck. And that followed most of the rhythm section—bass, guitar, drums, and piano. Most of those guys worked as a section. Because we used to call the horns—the brass—the other band. We called the saxophones the other band. We did that mostly because in rehearsal the reeds would be over here rehearsing, but the reeds are playing five or six times; trombones and trumpets would be over here working on their thing; the rhythm section would be here working on our thing; and when we get it together we would bring it all in, and the whole band could blow.

You can always hear something—I'm speaking about chord men,

now. As I told Bird—when I was doing the thing with Bird—"I don't know the name of these chords I'm making, man, but they go together. If you follow 'em you'll come out at the same place you would if you were just making a plain C, F, G, B-flat, like that. These chords have no names, as far as I'm concerned, but the body—the one, three, five, I can follow and associate it with what I'm using, and they'll come out. These altered notes is saying something because I'd heard tunes in the past that had no-name chords and they gave a fair-name chord like, say make an E-flat 7th add D. Or make a C 7th and add A. You know, they wouldn't say, "Make C 15th." An A to the 13th would be a pretty big name.

Years ago, when Duke first made "Solitude," I'll never forget because I read the little sheets, and it was D-flat—five flats. And he had a plain D-flat major was the chord, by name, you was to make. But the melody was C, which made today's chord knowledge a major seventh. That halftone lower from the octave. But they didn't call it a major seventh then. We just called it a plain D-flat. Well, I'm making D-flat, but the melody is a halftone lower than my tonic. I didn't know the name. The name wasn't on my music. And from that time on, I started associating the added notes to name chords that we knew about. When I say we, I'm speaking about all chord men knew the same thing. Nobody knew any names until later years—the raised ninths, flat fives, double augmented elevenths came out, and you'd be doubling your hand up trying to make 'em and all because they had names, and they were put in guitar books, and it was considered a usable chord and moveable—a guitar instructor would say "immoveable." You can form it but you can't move it. It's impractical and all that sort of junk where harmony tells a different story. It'll have another name or a voice so that you'd have to be an octopus to form it.

Well, Bird would come in at the after-hours club—Clark Monroe's Uptown House. Not only Bird; all the musicans come in there. Kenny Clarke and Kenny Kersey and all the guys because there's where I met Freddie Green, the Basie guitarist, and, by the way, he willed me that job. But he's still there because he used to tell me, "You play like a rhythm guitar." He didn't know I'd had that big-band experience in the back and to play a definite beat and make big, fat chords with body enough for a horn or a band to balance 'em. You'll find many guitarists today—many good ones—who'll run all over the neck—who'll do "Kitten on the Keys" backwards, but try to play anything with him and he won't give you support. It won't be there.

But, getting back to Bird, I had my little gig up at the Chili House, and it was a nice little place where the musicians would drop by. I used four pieces. But you know what happens on a three- or four-piece gig. When the guys find out, before the night's over you've got ten. It wasn't a name place. The name spots were Minton's and Monroe's and places like that. So I got to know Bird—because he'd come in the place and

would put his horn over in the corner and wouldn't play unless someone made him play, ask him to play. Something happend between him
and McShann the first time, and he left the band. He went back to
McShann, later, but this was '39. Because in '39, he and McShann
had had some trouble, and he had hit New York and left the band. I
never saw Bird nodding out, but he used to come out in the spotlight
in raggedy clothes.

I don't know—I never found out from Bird what was happening
with him, union-wise. But a lot of times unions caused you to keep
leaving town and doing things, and you don't want to tell people because you don't want them to know that you're nonunion. But, so far,
I don't think that Bird had union trouble. I think Bird was like many
other musicians—myself at one time—didn't like the sounds and the
money. We did not compare the pay. We put the art above the commercial side. Some say it's a commercial thing. Some say it's an artistical
thing. What happens is a guy sitting up playing some sounds that he's
tired of hearing. You don't care what the salary is. You're looking for
another place to play. Many times, we would go where there was no
money and sit up and jam all night, free, with the right group, rather
than to play and be paid with certain groups or certain places.

So, after Bird played down to Monroe's several times, the musicians
came 'round there, and they couldn't figure what Bird was doing, because they had their minds set on Johnny Hodges, Benny Carter, and
Red Rudy (Rudy Williams), who was with the Savoy Sultans, then, these
was the top alto men. And they even had Earl Bostic as one of the
great alto men. There was a lot of guys who played an awful lot of
horn. But, they were playing the *right* horn. They were playing right
changes and doing a beautiful job at it. What Bird did, Bird played
the right changes and, where they would go from one chord to another, Bird played that in-between. And *that* made his playing sound
different. Bird, to me, just had a slight edge on the other guys from
the way he felt and Bird was a good musician.

There's a lot of people know a lot but just can't execute it. Bird was
able to do—I used to run changes from the middle of "Cherokee"—
"Cherokee" seems to have been the tune, the release, the channel, the
middle of "Cherokee," they had many names—was the part that used
to catch most of them because it was moving in half-steps and the different keys. A lot of the greats had pet keys as well as pet tempos.
And you put 'em in another key or another tempo, they're in trouble.
When I say the greats, I'm talking about *name* greats. However, I'm
excluding Tatum, Bird, Diz, and several more who made no difference about the keys. But there were some more greats, but they played
in the original key. You should hear horn players saying, "Man, put
it in the original!" 'Cause they're in trouble in the key you're in. But
another guy'll say it makes no difference.

Hawkins is in there, too, because, while I think of it, I was put on the bill with Hawk down at Kelly's Stables, and Hawk came in a few minutes later than hitting time, so everybody's on the stand ready to hit. Hawk pulled out his horn and opened up on "Embraceable You," long meter, B-natural, which is a rough key for horn players. I don't know what the original key is but I know it wasn't B-natural. And he started blowing so it was—either you could or you couldn't.

As Diz said many a time, the purpose of those changes and different keys is to separate the sheep from the goats—is to get them no-players out of your way. And I found that a good way to do it is to put it in a key or a tempo or play it in such a way that they don't know what's going on. If and when they *do* know what's going on, they become one of you. A commune brother.

Let me tell you what happened after we got Bird playing. Got him playing and a few of the musicians—Kenny Kersey dug him and—oh, many did. Lips Page used to be there every night, then. And Lips knew how he sounded from before. It seems like Lips came from out that way some place. But, anyway, Bird liked my playing, and it wasn't because I played that much. Lot of guitar players was playing more guitar than I. But the voicing of my chords had a theme within themselves. You could call a tune, and I'd voice my chords in such a way that I'd play the original chords to the tune, and I'd invert 'em every one, two, three, or four beats so that the top notes of my inversions would be another tune. It would not be the melody to the tune I'm playing, yet the chords, foundation-wise, is the chords to the tune. And Bird had a big ear, And he listened. He say, "Biddy! Do that again.!" So, after I found out what he meant—I wasn't lucking on it. I had it set under my fingers. I can do it today, too. I can get in a spot and play the name to any tune and invert 'em to first, third, second, or fourth inversions, which I'm getting a different top note everytime, which is a theme within itself, but still I'm making the foundation name chord to the tune I'm playing, whatever it may be. And he heard that, he said, "Yea-a-a-h!"

Vic Dickenson used to come in there, too. Vic and Jabbo [Smith], Bird, myself, and there was somebody else used to come in there—musicians I'm talking about—and we'd be playing but we'd actually be rehearsing 'cause we'd be improvising.

After I had played up to Jimmy's Chicken Shack and heard Vic, and we got to be buddies, Vic would come down. Vic, Bird, Jabbo, and myself, and we would be playing around, mostly, as I told you, with "Cherokee." And we'd play other tunes. That's when Bird, I think now, found out that he could run the altered notes that I was using—I had only inverted the chords in order to keep a beat going. I didn't want to hold the same formation for four beats. I would make it move. The names, in spots, moved, but the sound remained until a new foundation name took place in the tune. Well, I played that way, and I found out, later, through Freddie Green, that that was one of his secrets in

Basie's rhythm section. He didn't hold one formation and beat four or eight times. He was moving. Moving and carried a beautiful theme with a punch, with a body of chords, which meant Basie could leave the piano.

After that I was on the gig with Bird with the Banjo Burney band. However, my past experience had told me when leaders—I might say this because it might help to explain what I'm going to say: some leaders, not all, in those days you played and they got a story at the end of the night—there's no money. They found a thousand things to tell you, but you went home with no money. Banjo Burney was famous for taking your money, but I had heard it in the past. The way we used to do was take all the first parts. That crippled the band. So I took all of Burney's music, because we were playing at a place on 7th Avenue—the name of the place was Dicky Wells—and Bernie had a way of taking certain guys' money and give 'em a story. So I took all of the music, all the first parts. You just don't go and take them because then you find a way to get a part in case. If it turned out all right then you would leave them there. If they don't turn out all right, you're not going to show up no more and the band can't play certain tunes because you have all the first parts. The next thing, the bands in those days didn't use special types of uniforms. They used street clothes, suits. We would join bands in order to get a new suit. After you joined them, you get your suit and cut out. Another band, the Bill Baldwin band, we had tuxedos, and we'd have the silk taken off the lapel and make suits out of them. There was a lot of tricks.

Bird kept gigging with different ones, but he was just satisfied with a lot of—the reasons I'm saying this is when you're broke, and I spell that Broke with a capital letter, it don't make no difference who it is or how well they play; you, I thought, would be after a piece of money. Money or no money, Bird didn't stay with anybody long that wasn't saying too much, music-wise, and if he had to leave broke, he would.

JAY MC SHANN   Bird came on back to Kansas City. That's when he started playing with Harlan Leonard's band. We had a battle of bands one night. So after the battle of bands, Bird came over and said, "I like the way you cats blow. I want to get with you cats." I said, "Well, all right, just go on and give your notice and whatever it is, come on in whenever you're ready." So that's what he did. We came to New York in '41. The big band was hardly a year old, or maybe a year old. We played the Savoy Ballroom. We had a lot of fun in the Savoy.

HOWARD MC GHEE   Oh, I heard Bird, it was in '42. I was with Charlie Barnet. We were playing at the Adams theater in Newark. We came off the show, and I turned on the radio just like I did, and all of a sudden I heard this horn jump through there. Bird, playing "Cherokee," with McShann broadcasting—from the Savoy; when I heard this cat play,

I said, "Who in the hell is that? I ain't heard nobody play like *that.*" Of all the alto players I knew—I knew everybody—I didn't know anybody who played like what was comin' through the radio. So everybody shut up, everybody sittin' there. We just listened till it was over with, then we heard the guy say it was at the Savoy, so that night, the whole band, we all went to the Savoy to hear this horn player, what this cat was playin'.

I knew Jay McShann 'cause he's from Muskogee, Oklahoma, so I asked him, "Jay, did you play that tune broadcast that features that alto player?" And he said, "Oh, Charlie Parker." So he called him down front, and he blew the shit out of them, everybody standing with their mouth wide open, "Aaah?" But he was into it. They said he was here before, but I never seen him before, and I never heard him till I heard him jam on "Cherokee," and, boy, he was some alto player, wow! He shattered the whole band. We all come unglued, running off at the mouth, and then next time we heard them notes everybody shut up. Nobody said "Be quiet." Everybody just shut up. Chubby [Jackson] was crazy about him.

CHUBBY JACKSON   We didn't know it was "Cherokee" either. That's so dumb because that brings a funny story back to me. I'd been with Barnet, and our theme song was "Cherokee." We played it nine thousand times a week, and I remember after I left Charlie I went in to sit in somewhere and they said, "Let's play 'Cherokee,'" and I didn't know the changes. That really did it to me—terrible.

JAY MC SHANN   I used to get the biggest kick out of Benny Webster, you know. Benny, he's quite a comical guy. He was down on 52nd Street telling the saxophone players, "You guys better go up at that Savoy and go to school—there's some young cat up there named Charlie Parker, and nobody knows what he's doing." He said, "All you guys had better go to school." Anyway, it was right funny as Ben says it. He would come up there, and he would hide in a corner where nobody could see him and hide and listen. The next thing he knew all these guys was running into each other. They was finding a place to hide and listen, and he says, "Hey, man, what are you doing here?" "Well, what are you doing?" Oh he tells that story, but we got the biggest kick out of that.

❖❖

"Cherokee" was another arrangment Mc Shann never recorded.

❖❖

JAY MC SHANN   No, we didn't, unfortunately. That was quite an arrangement. That was a Skip Hall arrangement. When we were in Dallas, Bird went down at Abe and Pappy's, and he heard Jimmy Forrest blowing. He came by and woke me up that night, "Hey, man, there's a cat down here, I think we need this cat." I said, "Who is he?" He

says, "Jimmy Forrest." He says, "Come on, I'll take you down there."
So I took him on down; we listened to Jimmy blow. We asked Jimmy,
"Can you travel?" He says, "Yeah." "When can you leave?" "Whenever
you're ready to leave." "So we'll leave tomorrow." That's what we did.
I can't think of the name of the band he was with. You know how
they'd hire guys in those days—a good man's in town, and they'd snatch
him. So you never knew who had the band.

Yeah, Jimmy could blow, and the funniest thing—we were speaking
about that "Cherokee." Back in those days Bird would blow everything there is to blow, but this was the way that we had the arrangement set up. Right after Bird got through blowing, Jimmy would follow up. Jimmy Forrest would break the house up. But the people just
never was hip to all this stuff that Bird had done, and I couldn't understand what the people was thinking about. But it really wasn't that
hard to understand, because Forrest was blowing good, too, but he
was also a showman; he had a thing going along with it. And the people went with it for that—as far as breaking up the house.

❖❖

Then there was trumpeter Buddy Anderson. There are only a few
short solos on some of those records, but everybody has talked
about him, too, as being influential.

❖❖

JAY MC SHANN   Buddy was quite influential. He just never received—Buddy
was sickly, but he had it. He just didn't have the chops to do everything that he knew. He had it together. Dizzy, the time when Diz used
to come to Kansas City with Cab Calloway, he would go down and get
Diz, and he says, "Come on, son, get your horn, I'm gonna take you
over to the hotel, in my room." And they would go there. That was
Diz's man. Yeah.

❖❖

And, of course, Buddy is the one who introduced Bird and Dizzy
in Kansas City.

❖❖

JAY MC SHANN   Cats don't get together now like they used to then. All good
musicians wanted to be around good musicians. What you detected in
a cat, you recognized it, and if he recognized something in you, he
recognized it, and then you also recognized each other. You had respect for each other. He respected you, you respected him, that's as
close as I can get. They all had enormous respect for each other.

❖❖

Miles Davis has talked of Sonny Stitt coming through St. Louis in
1942* with the Tiny Bradshaw band and sounding much like he
did when he made his first recordings a few years later. According to Sonny, he had not yet heard the Parker solos with Mc-

*Stitt says 1943 or maybe late 1942.

Shann on Decca. The following year, when Stitt was nineteen and had heard Parker on record, he met Bird.

❖❖

SONNY STITT   I picked him out of a crowd of people. I said, "That's him." He had a blue coat on with six white buttons, an alto saxophone in one hand, and a handful of benzedrine in the other. And he had dark glasses on. We went down to the Gypsy Tea Room, as I remember. And I knew Chauncey Downs. He was a bandleader in the Midwest. They were arch rivals, and they hated each other. I don't know why. But Chauncey and I were from Michigan. I was from Saginaw, and he was from Flint.

I got into Kansas City with Tiny Bradshaw, and I had two over-seers, "Heavy" Smith and Earl "Fox" Walker. They were my "fathers." We stayed next to the union. I threw my bag in there and took my saxophone down there and walked—and they followed me. They sure did, and looked after me 'cause I was crazy anyhow. And I went there at 18th and Vine. That's where it is. And I saw this dude come out. I said, "Are you Charlie Parker?" He showed me that gold tooth of his and said, "Yes, I'm Charlie Parker. I'm *Charles* Parker." You know, very dignified and all that stuff. "Who're you?"

I said, "I'm Sonny *Stitt*." And he said, "Well, let's go down to the Tea Room and play some." And we went down and played, with a piano player. That's all we had. And he said, "You sound too much like *me!*" And I said, "Well, you sound too much like *me!*" So we started going through a thing and Chauncey came in the joint, and Bird said, "Let's cut out." But he was a great man. I loved him.

« 3 »

Minton's and Monroe's

Although it was bubbling up in many places, the new music began to crystallize in New York, particularly at a couple of places in Harlem—Monroe's Uptown House and Minton's Playhouse. At the time Charlie Parker was playing with Jay McShann at the Savoy Ballroom in 1941, he was also playing again after hours at Clark Monroe's Uptown House.

❖❖

CHARLIE PARKER   At Monroe's I heard sessions with a pianist named Allen Tinney; I'd listen to trumpet men like Lips Page, Roy, Dizzy, and Charlie Shavers outblowing each other all night long. And Don Byas was there, playing everything there was to be played. I heard a trumpet man named Vic Coulson playing things I'd never heard. Vic had the regular band at Monroe's, with George Treadwell also on trumpet and a tenor man named Pritchett. That was the kind of music that caused me to quit McShann and stay in New York.

ALLEN TINNEY   The first meeting with Bird? Well, he was playing with Jay McShann. He came down, and he sat in with us. And he dug what we were doing. He said, "Man"—we didn't know we were going to be saying "Man" about him!—"Man, what are you guys playing?" So he sat in, and we played "Cherokee" and things like that, and we had already developed a "Tea for Two" thing in the middle—the 2-5-1 thing—and he dug this, and right away he started in fitting into what we were doing. And before you knew it, when I came out of the Army he was famous, just like that. He could really get over his instrument, I knew that. And he had a lot of feeling when he was awake. He slept a lot, real heavily. And a guy named Earl Bostic used to come in and watch him. You know it's like gunslingers, and one night they hooked up. I don't really know who won because it was too tremendous, but Bostic had been scouting him, and they really hooked up, and it was tremendous.

HAL SINGER   I was working with Don Byas on 52nd Street in 1944 or '45. There was a club uptown called the Heat Wave. I think it was on 145th Street. They had jam sessions on Sunday afternoons—sometimes with regular groups or just invite people—and they made up the band on arrival.

I was there with Don Byas's group on this particular Sunday. It was not his regular group that played in the Three Deuces. Charlie Parker was the headliner. Don's group played a set, and then Parker played a set. Earl Bostic sat in with us, so it was three Oklahoma boys—Don, Bostic, and me.

Then for the jam session Bird called "Cherokee." The two horns were Bird and Bostic. Both of them were great and had a great feeling towards each other. There was a great admiration for each other's drive and technique.

❖❖

At the time, Max Roach was one of the young, up-and-coming musicians who went to "school" at the jam sessions.

❖❖

MAX ROACH   In the church they'd have all kinds of activities for children. Actually I started dealing with music in the church—piano and trumpet before I started dealing with the drums. But you know the community was just fraught with music. You could walk down the street; you heard people singing, you heard people playin'. Duke Ellington says a wonderful thing about a Harlem airshaft. An airshaft was a dumbwaiter. You open up your airshaft, and you heard people singing and playing saxophone. You know it was just in the air at that particular time. When I recognized that I was doing something a little different was when I was about fifteen or sixteen. We used to jam in Brooklyn, and Cecil Payne came running into a little joint that we were jammin' in. He said, "Man, I knew that was you, a half a block before I got to the club." And so you say how do you tell when somebody does something different? I know that Lester Young and Jo Jones and Count Basie were when they came from Kansas City, and Jo Jones was playing broken rhythms and things like that—the way he dealt with the instrument, the way Lester dealt with his. I guess that was one period in all of our young lives when we realized there was change. Of course Coleman Hawkins also was an integral part of that. Charlie Parker came up. Then later we were working what they called "black and white" clubs—downtown. During that period you worked in all-white clubs in New York City from nine to three, and then went uptown to the after-hours spots, and you worked from four to eight. That's when I met Bud Powell and Al Tinney and all those people. And we became friends and started workin' together, playin' together, jammin' together.

KENNY CLARKE   One evening at Monroe's, Max gave us a very strange demonstration. He was playing and whistling at the same time; whatever was going through his mind, and he seemed not to care very much about what Parker was doing. He was using brushes, and when I asked him why he wasn't using sticks, he replied, "Because I haven't learned that yet."

After that evening he came to Minton's and began practicing in the style we were trying to develop. He seemed very happy at this encounter. He was already playing whatever he felt like because he was so gifted with a fantastic left hand.

MAX ROACH   And we started forming a camaraderie. Of course, there was Harold West and all those wonderful folks up to Minton's when we got old enough to go to those places. And of course Monk was around at that time. There was so much activity in New York and that particular period musically speaking. You just don't pinpoint one . . .

You know we had to play shows. Charlie Parker came to town—was with Jay McShann. He came down to the 78th Street Taproom, where we were working. In those days you worked seven nights a week. And then you worked six weeks straight and had a week off, a seventh week. You didn't have a night off. So we were working from nine to three downtown at Georgie Jay's 78th Street Taproom. Then we'd pack up our gear and run uptown to the Uptown House, and we worked from four til eight, seven days a week. That was a good opportunity for a person to play and develop his horn and things like that.

ALLEN TINNEY   My gosh, that's right, that was the 78th Street Taproom. And Charlie Parker, too, was in the band. Man, I forgot all about that. In fact, Monroe took the band there. He was directing it à la Leonard Bernstein.

MAX ROACH   But I think that what was more significant to the development of the music—people talk about change and who did this and who did that. Well, the war had a great deal to do with what went on because during that '40s period the government had leveled a 20 percent tax on all entertainment, excepting instrumental playing. That meant that if an operator had a singer or a tap dancer, or even if there were public dancing in a room, he'd have to charge that extra 20 percent on top of the usual tax there that existed during that period. You know, city tax, state tax, federal tax, alcohol tax, and buy his stock and pay for his help and pay for his music and other things. It was just prohibitive. So the only artists who were outside that perimeter the club would take a chance on, as I remember, were people like Billie Holiday—singers. But anyway, the sole source of entertainment was just instrumental work—instrumental playing. And so the best instrumentalists were the ones who got the gigs. Art Tatum. So most of the musicians worked harder developing themselves so that they could get jobs. So I think the war had more to do with the change than any individual pressure's effort like, "I'm gonna change this." It's the society. That 20 percent tax was the most important thing because of all this instrumental playing. And that period produced the kind of instrumentalists that we know, that produced the Charlie Parkers, these people. You know you *had* to be an exceptional instrumentalist in order to garner any kind of job. That's what it was. And there were good musicians who did not go to that Army.

When Bird came to New York, he freelanced; he left the band. We were all freelancers. Everybody was around New York, working wherever we may and this and that and the other. And bandleaders at that time were usually guys who owned the clubs, in some instances uptown. Clark Monroe was a dancer. Monroe could get some jobs, and we were the musicians. There was a lot of freedom.

ALLEN TINNEY   I started professionally when I was nineteen, and I can remember because I was with a Broadway show, a song-and-dance type thing—my brother, sister, and I were all into theater for dancing and what not, and I went to Monroe's Uptown House when I was nineteen and I played and the owner, Clark Monroe, said, "Hey, kid, do you want a job here?" And I said, "You already have a piano player." And he said, "No, we did have a piano player." So I started working; I think it was three dollars a night, something like that. But that was back in either '38 or '39, one of those years.

It was a trio. It was a guy called Ebenezer Paul who played bass, and by the way, he played bass with his chin, really going through theatrics. Ebenezer Paul played drums, also, very loudly, and then there was a guy called "Popeye" that played trumpet—muted—and this consisted of a trio, but his sound, this guy Popeye's sound, still lives, or it did at a time when Miles Davis started playing. It took me back when I heard Miles. I said, "Jeez, that sounds like Popeye and Benny Harris"—Benny Harris the same way. And when I heard—I came out of the Army and heard "How High the Moon"—and I said, "Oh, man, great, Benny Harris made it." The guy said, "Benny Harris. That ain't Benny Harris, that's Miles Davis," and I said, "Miles who?" because I didn't know him, I'd just come out of the Army.

I probably played at Monroe's about 1940 or '41, I'd say, just about that time, because I went into the Army in '43.

DEXTER GORDON   I started hearing new things, I guess, about '41. I heard Bird that year. Heard him at the Savoy—with McShann, and which wasn't really that—sounded good—but he wasn't really fully developed at that particular period. And then I heard a little bit of Diz, too. Then I'd met Benny Harris in New York. I was hearing it gradually here and there. I mean not in an organized band or even with all the cats playing that kind of style in a group or something. I heard a little bit at Monroe's old place, Monroe's Uptown House, when Vic Coulson, and the cat that married Sarah Vaughan—George Treadwell. They had a little group uptown in Monroe's, two trumpets. Vic played like Benny Harris or something like that—that kind of stuff. That's what I remember. Played beautiful. And it fit that room. Sometimes I'd go over there and hear those cats. It was like '41, '42, when I first started getting around a little bit.

ALLEN TINNEY   Roy came in—Roy Eldridge and Hot Lips Page were very influential on Victor Coulson and George Treadwell. Very much so. Victor was a cornet player, a cornetist. He played beautifully, and in fact, he took the band over after I left Monroe's Uptown House. Very dapper little guy. When I saw him a few years later when I got out of the Army, I couldn't believe it. He had become a wino. . . . Did you hear Fats Navarro? That was Victor Coulson before Fats Navarro. These young guys like that influenced a lot of those guys that became famous, became great, like I said Benny Harris. But Victor Coulson played I would say similar to—well, Fats Navarro played similar to Victor Coulson, if you want to make a comparison on that.

BUDD JOHNSON   I understand that he was playing that way before Dizzy. He was great—and he would take all the caps off his valves, and he just played on the stems. He didn't like valve caps. He liked the feeling of the stems—I don't see why, but maybe he felt it was faster for him. But anyway, him and, of course, Joe Guy, and Monk, and all were at Minton's.

AL HAIG   Vic was in the Coleman Hawkins band when I heard him, and he fitted that band very neatly. So therefore I don't know how he would be taken out of that environment. I never heard him with a different rhythm section. He was a very low-key, understated type of trumpet player. He didn't have a lot of range, I don't think. His playing was rather impeccable in a way. He did what he wanted to do. He played a little bit like beginning Miles.

❖❖

Dizzy Gillespie has mentioned Dud Bascomb's influence on Fats Navarro. Fats's fellow Floridian, Idrees Sulieman (known as Leonard Graham when he was playing on 52nd Street in the '40s), confirms this and also points out that Miles Davis admired Bascomb, too.

❖❖

IDREES SULIEMAN   I met Miles [Davis] when he was fifteen and I was seventeen. We met because of Dud Bascomb. Everyone thought it was Erskine Hawkins playing the solos on the records, but my father told me, "It's not Erskine. It's a little trumpet player on cornet." My father booked bands in Florida. He brought Cab [Calloway] to Florida. Louis Armstrong came to the house when I was a kid.

Fats [Navarro] and I left home together. We were good friends. And the night I left home was the Monday after Easter, in '41. J. J. [Johnson] was with Fats in Snookum Russell's band, and we had a big jam session in Orlando, the three of us. In Snookum Russell's band, Fats used to play the same solos that Dud Bascomb played with Erskine Hawkins's band, and I was playing those same solos with the Carolina Cotton Pickers, and when I got to St. Louis, they said, "We got a trumpet player here playing with George Hudson's band that plays all of Dud Bascomb's solos." It was Miles. [On his Prestige quintet recording of "The Theme," Davis quotes from Bascomb's "Tuxedo Junction" solo.]

❖ ❖

Monroe's lured musicians from all over. Some came across the Brooklyn Bridge.

❖ ❖

ALLEN TINNEY   Ray Abrams, Cecil Payne—a lot of these guys were from Brooklyn also, and it was like a school. They all used to come in and sit in and jam, and we put a band together. Our favorite bands were Duke Ellington and Count Basie, and we would take things that they had already recorded, and we would try to do something else with them. All of a sudden people started coming down to the club, like Charlie Shavers and Dizzy and Charlie—Charlie Parker—was with us at the time. He left Jay McShann—him and, what's the singer's name, Al Hibbler? They both left McShann to stay in New York with Monroe's Uptown House. And we heard different things happening among each other. Everybody contributed something. I believe that changed the scene because musicians from all the big bands—I would say maybe Glenn Miller's, Harry James's band—I met Corky Corcoran down there at Monroe's Uptown also and most of the bands that had the big ensembles—they would all come down after work, and they would sit in, or either they would sit and say, "What the heck are these guys playing?" because it was different. The job started, like say, three in the morning, and we went until seven or eight o'clock.

CECIL PAYNE   Max used to come and tell us about Bird playing, and then we went over—after hours—to the Uptown House. It could be '42 or '43. I remember Ben Webster coming in there. He was raving about Bird. And Bird was standing up playing chorus after chorus of "Cherokee." And the place got raided—the same night we was in there. When they raided the place—at that time I was working at the Navy Yard in the daytime. Me and this—I forget the musician's name—we went out to get some kind of soda, coffee across the street, and when we came back, the police had locked up with our horns in there. We had to go to the police station next day to claim our horns. And we were so young, we didn't know if they were going to lock us up or not. "What were you doing in there?" But when we told them and gave them identification, they let us have our instruments back.

ALLEN TINNEY   Christian came down too. He came every night and used to sit right in front of me. There was a small baby grand piano. Christian used to sit his mike right down there, and Jimmy Blanton was there, Ben Webster—man, with that kind of company how can you be in arrears. I was like a student. These guys were into it so deep. Like Don Byas. Don Byas would request a tune. He'd say, "Hey, Al, let's play this" or "let's play that." Then he'd say, "Let's go through the keys," and I'd say, "Are you crazy?" "C'mon man," and we would try certain tunes in every key, and this got me sorta familiar with the instrument to say the least. And then there was a guy they called Scotty.

DEXTER GORDON   I'll tell you something, though. There was a tenor player around Minton's named Kermit Scott—he's in San Francisco now— and he's where Jaws [Eddie "Lockjaw" Davis] is coming from.

ALLEN TINNEY   Scotty was a heavy influence also. But everybody was trying to sound like Coleman [Hawkins] at the time. Lester was a new thing. He was a new influence, and I believe he inspired Bird more than— everybody comes from somebody. A lot of people really contributed. It wasn't just something you turn the page, and it was there. You had to go through several pages, which is like several people to really bring to a point. Dizzy used to just come in because he was with Cab Calloway at the time. He thought like we did. He came from the same thinking thing that we were into, and, as a result, he used to come down all the time and sit in after finishing playing with Cab, and so did Charlie Shavers who was working with John Kirby, I believe, at the time. Joe Guy was a big-timer. We were just like kids starting out, except for Charlie Christian and a couple of them. Joe Guy was going with Billie Holiday at the time. He used to sit in with us, too, because he had that same type of thing going. He used to love to play the changes and whatnot.

TRUMMY YOUNG   Now, I didn't see Bird again until I got to New York, and Bird came in later. I was around New York with Lunceford in the '30s, and Bird came in later. But I knew Monk. I knew Monk. Kenny Clarke and I used to jam a lot together. Well, Kenny turned me on to these guys. This was at Monroe's Uptown House in New York, and we hung around. And this was when Lady Day [Billie Holiday] was just getting her break, too, down there. Buck Clayton and a bunch of us, the guys from Basie, we'd hang around down there and play. It was nothing but a coalbin. And from there on, we started going down to Minton's, and this was because of Teddy Hill; he was running it.

KENNY CLARKE   At that time we were not used to hearing a trio play for hours, and if I chose Joe Guy it's because he was an old-timer of Teddy Hill's orchestra.

At the time I felt it was very good. When Teddy left his orchestra, mainly because he didn't like impresarios and agencies, he thought that he owed us something. By taking the organization of Minton's into his own hands he thought he could help some of the musicians and asked me to hire Joe Guy.

EDDIE BAREFIELD   They used to have the sessions at Minton's. I was in the house band up there. It was me and Thelonious Monk and Nick Fenton and Harold West and Klook sometimes—Kenny Clarke. I was playing clarinet in the house group. Just four pieces, but it always ended up to six or seven or nine or ten.

KENNY CLARKE   As our quartet—Guy, Thelonious Monk, and Nick Fenton—did not have a saxophonist, Charlie Parker would often come to eat chicken on Teddy Hill's bill and gave us an idea that he knew what to do. He was playing at the Apollo with Jay McShann at the time. He already was fabulous. Personally, I've never heard him play badly.

TRUMMY YOUNG   The guys liked Teddy. They say, "Let's give Teddy a break." So they started going down there, jamming. But, it got out of hand down there, see. Twenty or thirty guys would come to jam and one rhythm section. The guys would say, "Let's do something to trick these guys." So Dizzy had an apartment around on Seventh Avenue, and we all hung around there because Lorraine used to cook. And they started working on different chord progressions to keep these guys out of there. And they wouldn't tell 'em what tune it was. It might be "I Got Rhythm," but the chord progressions would be different. They did it to run these guys off there. And they used a lot of technique with it.

JOE NEWMAN   That was a good atmosphere. The people that came in there really came in to hear music. In spite of whatever else they might be involved in and all, these guys, actually, they made their reputation. Ben Webster was one of the guys that frequented Minton's, and there used to be a lot of musicians that would come up and want to blow, and they were not really up to par with these guys. I was frightened to get up there really. I really was, man. I never did, really. And guys would get up there, and they didn't blow well. So in order to keep guys like this from getting on the stand, they'd call keys. They'd say, okay, "You want to play so and so?" So the guys would put it in a key maybe like an F-sharp or something, anything where the fingering doesn't lay right on the horn. Everything you touch, it's not that, it's something else. And if you don't really know your instrument and know the theory of music, you just don't play it. Every note you touch is wrong. You can't really hear those keys like that.

BUDD JOHNSON   As I remember, once Prez walked into Minton's, and Ben, and they were gonna jam with the group. Of course the guys tested them out, their knowledge, and they started to play Monk's tunes, and they didn't know which way the tune was going because it was so different from anything they had played before. It was a lot of fun because the guys were anxious to learn—nobody put them down—and they were very happy to sit in and try to do this and catch these sounds.

❖❖

The big bandleaders like Goodman and Shaw used to frequent Minton's, and they would play for them at times like that rather than use the new chords. But these were some younger white musicians who were into the new music and actively sought it out. There would be more of them shortly, but when Johnny Carisi began hanging out in Harlem he was an advance guardsman.

❖❖

JOHNNY CARISI   I joined the union, 1939. I guess I must have been about seventeen. At that point I was living in Queens—Jamaica. I moved to Jamaica when I was about fifteen. I had lived there earlier when I was younger, much younger. I lived in Connecticut and Westchester and then from Westchester we came back to Jamaica. In Connecticut my teenage brothers were asked to take me along with them. Their friend's* family owned a record store. So they had access to all the sides—Louis, Bix. I didn't know what I was hearing but it sunk in. Later, in high school, when I took up the trumpet, I was able to amaze my schoolmates by saying, "I know that," and singing an Armstrong solo. By then, by the time I was eighteen, I'd been playing school things with the football bands, which were brass bands, in the orchestra and playing local proms, playing stock arrangements. Somehow or other I had the idea I could play jazz. At first the kind of jazz exposure that I got was Nick's. Even before [Bobby] Hackett, with Hackett, too, but before Hackett there was Georgie Brunies, Sharkey Bonano, guys like this. And I went that way, with the collective, and I knew all those tunes with the trios. And I didn't know all of them, but I learned a lot of them. I already knew about Louis so that was an easy connection to make with the Dixieland, I guess, until I heard Roy Eldridge. Then I started spending much more time uptown. I was somewhere between eighteen and nineteen. That was 1940 and '41. And right up until I went in the Army, which was '43—'41 up till '43 I would say.

I went on the road with obscure bands. Later on I played with Thornhill. I played with Barnet. I played with Elliot Lawrence, and I played with Ray McKinley. That chronology I can't keep straight because some of it was before the Army and some of it was after. And I was in the Miller band in the Air Force. But already George Simon

*Roger Brousso, later a partner in the Half Note when it was on West 54th Street.

and a couple of those guys knew me. As a matter of fact, that's how I got into the Miller band—recommendation. They got me somehow after my basic training, got me out. But by that time I had already been hanging out at Monroe's uptown and Dickie Wells's and Minton's.

It was still a time when you would see a lot of whites in Harlem, especially at Monroe's and Dickie Wells's and the late-hour places. I even went to some of these people's houses in cellars, where I heard like Art Tatum and Teddy Wilson playing all night. But they'd serve you coffee cups with booze in them or even food, in somebody's house. But this was after Minton's and Dickie Wells's, which were clubs, would close. But sometimes they'd stay open. But if you'd leave at three or four o'clock, you'd find one of these other places. I can remember going up with Don Byas—a bunch of people, a mixed group. Actually at that time, having achieved rather little technique, and feeling as I did about jazz at that point—now, somewhere in the long year, of course, I ran into a little cat, Benny Harris. And by that time I had gotten into this Roy thing. And incidentally, it's funny how the divisions suddenly become aware. Whereas at one time I was welcome in all those Dixieland joints, I remember going to Eddie Condon's once, and he threw me out. I was playing too "uptown." I didn't play that Chicago kind of thing, and he really ridiculed me, really put me away. And the guys in the band were very embarrassed. He wouldn't leave me alone. But he was that smart kind of person, bullshit-type thing that figured with his bad, bad guitar playing. Although Hackett always dug me.

I remember playing for Hackett on New Year's Eve. I went to a New Year's gig—it was a club date; it was real club date playing that I didn't really know about at that time. I could go and play a jazz thing. And I got on this date, and these cats were nonplussed. They didn't know what to do with me, so they said, "You better go home, man." I failed. I flunked out. And I got a little juiced somewhere, and I remember I had carried some weeds in a bag. And I remember I went through one of these bar turnstiles [subway] going back into town. And I didn't want to go home. It was New Year's Eve, so I went to Nick's, and I got there, and Hackett was drunk and he said, "Come on, John, play for me." So I finished the rest of the evening for him, which kind of saved me.

But somewhere I had met Benny Harris. We were sitting in somewhere together, maybe in the Village, because the Vanguard was a big sessioning place. He heard me playing, and he said, "Goddamn, you sound like Roy, but you never heard Diz, I guess." And he got up and played [imitates horn], and I said, "What's that?" "Diz does that. There's another guy, there's two of them." And he mentioned Charlie Parker. As things turned out later on at Minton's, I got to blow with all these cats, starting first of all with Charlie Christian, who used to leave his amp and stuff there. And the guys that worked there who were all into Diz and Bird. Kenny Clarke was there at a certain period. But

Monk seemed to have been there all the time. I don't hardly remember anybody but Monk. And here I was into this new thing, I was cutting my teeth on Monk and didn't really know who I was listening to. I dug it. What the hell was the clanking sound? What? With the raunchy intervals.

He don't hardly sound any different now than he did then. I don't think he was any more technique, which is almost non-existent. He doesn't have any, just for what he does he has. He used to kind of skidder-over, like an ice skater over an Art Tatum-like run; he never really made the whole thing, but he made the shape of it and the time. There was no problem about that. Notes, that's another story, and fingers I'm sure—well, I'm not sure, but I think that he probably never learned how to finger pianistically correctly. So he made his own way. But it was quite an influence. And then I started bringing cats up there that never—Kai Winding and a couple of guys like that. And if they'd meet me after a long time, somebody would say, "See this guy, he's the first guy that took me up to Minton's."

But there was places downtown that I used to blow with Roy. There was a joint on 52nd Street, a bottle club that was open for a while, upstairs, over the House of Chan, you know that corner between 7th and Broadway. And you'd go upstairs, and everyone, all kinds of people, used to come up. And I used to get into these things with Roy. We talk about it now. He says, "You were a little kid, and I was a pretty snotty young cat," because he would do things. Well, I remember one time Joe Guy—we had a love-hate kind of thing—he grabbed me by the lapels. He said, "You ofay cats come up and you steal all our shit." It was like half mad, and at the same time it was like really a tribute. He was like saying, "You're doing it."

HOWARD MC GHEE   When I came here with Andy [Kirk], about '42, we were down in Loew's State, and Dizzy came down with Kelly.* Kelly was a trombone player; he was with Erskine Hawkins's band. So he brought Dizzy down to hear me; I heard Dizzy in Detroit, but I didn't know who he was. He was with Cab, but I didn't know who he was. I just saw him, and he didn't impress me because he wasn't Louis Armstrong, he wasn't Roy Eldridge. But in '42 they came down and invited me up to Minton's, so I came for the music, to hear what was goin' on. That's when I met Curly Russell, Monk, Kenny Clarke, John Simmons, Charlie Christian. But I knew Charlie from Oklahoma; so I used to go up there, and I heard what they were playing. Don Byas, he was up there, Prez used to come up. That's when I heard what they were doing, but I knew when they started to fool around that I had already heard that, and I knew about it, but I wasn't using it on the solo because I used it a couple of times, and I heard the band used

*Ted Kelly, later with Dizzy's big band.

to flinch, like that don't sound like what they was used to hearin'. All they'd been used to was the same old chords, but then I started writing, using it in voicings with the band to educate Andy's ear to hearing that sound, and from then on I could play it. I remember Fats [Navarro] used to sit up there and fool around, using flat ninths and raised ninths, flatted fives, and fourths, and playin' in fourths. Some of the themes were based on the chord structure, so if you didn't play that, you didn't keep on playing. Dizzy wrote "Bebop"; the release is [demonstrates]. That's right on the changes. If you played anything else there, you wrong. "Salt Peanuts" the same thing, "I Got Rhythm" changes; the melodies is on the chords. I used to use a flatted five on, say, even "Perdido" that we did on "Jazz at the Philharmonic." The chords are to the "I Got Rhythm" changes, and the release, I used to play the E-flat at the top [demonstrates]; the trumpet players out in California would say, "What's that supposed to be?" I said, "Well, if you can't hear it, ain't no use in me tellin' you about it. You'll hear it one of these days." Even Ernie Royal didn't know what it was about. He said, "That note ain't in the chord." I said, "I know." But it *is* in the chord. He just didn't know where it is.

❖❖

The musicians who embraced the new music really became involved in it. There was an enthusiasm, something special in the way young musicians responded to it.

❖❖

HOWARD MC GHEE   To me it was like a relief. Before that most of the solos were like [demonstrates]; you hear the same all over. I used to hear a lot of trumpet players; all of 'em would want to play that; they copied after Louis. I heard Louis play that, and ain't nobody play that any prettier than he did, or any higher than he did, so it was a relief to me to hear somebody doing something different, to say, "Now I don't have to stick to that dat-dat-da-da-da." When I first heard Roy, he was a relief getting away from Louis; I listened to him that way. When I came here to New York and found that the guys were doing everything—they were playing more notes—it was a relief because even at the time Jimmy Forrest was with Andy's band, I used to tell him, "You're staying too traditional. You ought to come and hang out with Don Byas and learn to play, 'cause you got a good sound and everything. I said learnin's not gonna stop you from just playin'." But he was playin' more like the old traditional and I got him out of that. We had another tenor player named Ed Loving that was with Andy Kirk. He used to have three tenor players in the band—J. D. King, Jimmy Forrest, and Ed Loving—but Ed Loving was playin' 'cause he used to hang out with Fats [Navarro] all the time. Everytime the band wasn't doin' nothin' they'd be up at Minton's playin'. I noticed him, that he was thinking the right thing, so I go onto Jimmy Forrest about that.

So Jimmy started hangin' out with the two over there. He was just a natural player anyway.

❖❖

Before McGhee was with Kirk, where he made his first major splash with "McGhee Special," he had been with Lionel Hampton, joining him from a job at the Club Congo in Detroit, where Howard had been leading a band in late 1940 and early '41.

❖❖

HOWARD MC GHEE   This was in the last part of '40, the first part of '41, I went with Hampton in the summer of '41, but I only stayed with him about four weeks because Gladys weren't giving him enough bread. I was making seventy bucks a week at the Congo Club in Detroit. I was at home, no problem, and writing for the shows and everything, and I figured if I go to Hampton I'll be doing that much better. I went out there, and we worked three nights, and he was paying ten dollars a night, and you had to pay your rent and food out of that. I said, "What's the matter with you; you crazy or something?" I'm leaving a good job and coming with this band, regardless of how well they on their way. And I dug Hampton. I found out what Hampton wanted out of music, and I didn't like that either, 'cause he wanted me 'n' Ernie [Royal] to be hitting high F's and G's on every end of every song, and I said, "Ain't no use in workin' for his cat 'cause he's gonna blow my lip out!" I said, "Lemme get the hell outta here." So I told him I was going back home to Detroit, and I did. And the same day I got home I got a telegram from Andy. So I called him; he told me what he was paying me, so I decided to go with him, but I was going back to the Congo.

I had Wardell [Gray], Al McKibbon, Kelly Martin; a lot of trumpet players—Edwin Youngblood—he's in Pittsburgh now—in Detroit, he was the upcoming young trumpet player. We were a good band. That band was swingin'; we played at the shows and we had the big names comin' in, all the cats that didn't have bands. They didn't expect us— we had no name, nobody knew none of us, but we were playin'! So Hamp said, "Oh, man, you gotta join my band, we on our way." When I found out about his money, that canceled all that in New York. Shit, I ain't goin' to New York *broke*. What good is that gonna do, goin' with a band and goin' to work every night—that's when he first had his band, and we had a helluva band. I really did miss the band, and there was Ernie Royal, Dexter Gordon, Karl George, Joe Newman—but I didn't enjoy playing no high F's and G's and F-sharps and Hampton would hold the chord till you turned blue in the face.

JOE NEWMAN   I was with Hamp from the later part of 1940 to December 1943. My last engagement with Hamp was in the Famous Door when it was over the House of Chan. That was a revival of the Famous Door.

Cat Anderson was in the band at the time. I had become ill. I had a bad cold, a flu, whatever it was at the time, and I didn't go to work that night, and early in the morning, after Basie's band—they were playing at the Lincoln Hotel—Jo Jones knocked on my door. I was staying at the Braddock Hotel, and he came and says, "I want you to work tomorrow night with the band. Think you could make it?" And I said, "Yes," because actually Basie was the band I'd always thought about playing with. There was really no other band that I really wanted to play with but Basie, outside of Lionel Hampton and, the attraction there was that Jacquet was in the band, Dexter Gordon. One of the things I'll always remember with Hamp's band was at the Paradise in Detroit. Dexter was always coming late. He'd come in at the last minute, and we were playing this tune he was supposed to play on. There was no Dexter, and just as it got to his solo, he walked out on the wings with his horn, man, like Prez, man, blowing away, man, and broke it up. Because that was a hell of a thing for those people. They didn't expect it, and we fell out, and they fell out, too. And Hamp was— normally he would have been angry—but he couldn't be angry because it broke it up.

We also had Marshal Royal and Illinois Jacquet, Vernon Alley. It was loaded generally. Before I went in the band, Lee Young was the drummer, but then when I went in, Shadow Wilson was. That's where I met Shadow. And Sir Charles Thompson was the piano player. Anyway, the war became a reality, and it was very difficult for bands to travel at that time. By the way, I was with Hamp's band at the Brooklyn Strand when Roosevelt went on the air and declared war—Pearl Harbor. During that day we were playing, Maxine Sullivan was on the bill. I remember just like yesterday.

Well, we traveled, most of the time. No matter where we stayed, it didn't matter, you just left some of your belongings in. We went all through the South. All out West and places like you wouldn't even know existed. All of the Dakotas. I haven't been to South Dakota since that time. I remember we played Spokane, Washington, and we stayed at this lady's house who raised rabbits, and we had rabbit for breakfast, rabbit for dinner. And at that point in my life I'd never eaten domesticated rabbits; I'd always eaten wild rabbits. They were tame enough that you didn't have that real wild taste to it. I remember this morning when we woke up, she put this rabbit on the table, and it was so tender and this was strange to me. I asked her, "Gee, how do you cook this?" and she says, "Oh, just regular." She said, "I raise them myself," and I looked out there and I saw all these white rabbits, and I being so accustomed to them being pets, it really made me sick. I just couldn't think of eating it. The next day was the day we went to Boise, Idaho. We went to an Army camp and they met us at the train station and the reason for that, as I started to mention earlier, during the war, it became very difficult to get buses. They were used for everything. So bands had to travel by train and you'd get off in some chitlin' switch town and have to wait four to six hours for your connection to get to another town. That meant we had no place to sleep but the railroad station. And it would be cold. This is when I remembered the remark that this guy could sleep standing up. I actually did that. There was no place to sit, and there were bags thrown all over the place, and I'd have to lean up against this wall, and I went to sleep. And I was so surprised when I woke up and found that I was standing up there. I knew I'd been asleep—but we'd have to make all these trips like that

Naturally, big bands were flourishing then, but you kept hearing about Roy Eldridge, and then he finally went with Gene Krupa's band, and then we got to New York and there was Dizzy Gillespie and Charlie Parker. I remember Charlie Parker came to the Savoy Ballroom with Jay McShann's band, and Jacquet and Dexter were on tenor saxophones with us and Ray Perry on alto. It was a musical night. When I was with Jacquet's band, it was Ray Perry, J. J. Johnson, Shadow Wilson, Leo Parker, Al Lucas, I think maybe John Malachi. But Ray Perry, he started fooling around with heroin. He didn't really take care of himself like he had been, so his hair got longer, and he had these John L. Lewis eyebrows, very heavy eyebrows. He was always a little hip-type guy, those gestures. I remember we played down South in this tobacco warehouse—the place would be packed, thousands of people, that's the way they came out in these size towns. So Ray Perry, the minute he walked up to the microphone with this violin, he'd stick it up on his chin, one guy one time called, "Why there's Zeke." So this name stuck with him 'cause he sorta really looked like somebody you might call Zeke—to the way he was dressed and everything. His pants were baggy, but the minute he put that bow on the violin, like all of that left and he had the crowd with him. He was really like Charlie Parker on that violin at that time.

The only record I know of him is with Lionel Hampton with the sextet. That wasn't even a shadow of what the man really was. Now Charlie Parker—at the time Ray Perry was really great—wanted him to come with him, when he took that string group out, but Jacquet paid him more money than they offered him, to keep him. So consequently it was a bad decision because unfortunately there's no record of what he actually did. Just a few people know about him.

❖ ❖

The big bands were to die later but they were still breathing strongly and, alongside the burgeoning small groups were breeding grounds for the new music. Charlie Barnet, a scion of a wealthy family who dashed his parents' ambition for him to become a corporation lawyer by leading his own band on a transatlantic liner at age sixteen, was always noted for his swinging (in all ways) outfits. His was one of the most integrated of all the white bands, and his open admiration for Ellington and other black bands did not result in a pale imitation but in a healthy jazz expression. That he was a leader who enjoyed himself and did not deny his men a good time is exemplified by Jean Bach's account of an engagement in the late '50s, long after Barnet no longer led a band on a regular basis.

❖❖

JEAN BACH   Did you see Charlie Barnet, the last band he had here, with Nat Pierce on it and Willie Smith and all those great people at Basin Street East [in early 1967]? It ran about a one or two week engagement, and Nat pulled it all together, but they imported gorgeous people from the coast. Barnet sat on a barstool in front of the band, and he said, "Now where's the waiter for this section?" What waiter for the bandstand section? He said, "Right here, for this table." So the waiter came over, and he said, "Okay, now what are you drinking? You're drinking Scotch? What are you drinking? Scotch here, scotch. All right, the whole rhythm section, scotch." Then one guy said he wanted rye or something, and he said, "Oh, an exotic drinker over there. All right, bring that." So now they're all drinking on the bandstand. He's ordered them drinks and I figured how's the guy going to have a drink, hold his trombone, smoke his cigarettes, do all the things? But the music was just divine.

❖❖

In the early 1940s Barnet had all kind of stars in his band—Howard McGhee, Oscar Pettiford, Chubby Jackson, Trummy Young, and Buddy DeFranco, to name but a few.

❖❖

HOWARD MC GHEE   I was working with Andy Kirk at Tic-Toc in Boston, the one that got burned down, and Andy Gibson, the arranger for Charlie, came over and heard the band and heard me, and he went back and told Charlie 'bout me playin' high notes, 'cause Charlie was always looking for a high-note trumpet player. So when Andy told him that I was starring up there at the Tic-Toc, he told Andy to ask me would I be interested in joining the band. So I said, "Yeah, of course. For money I'd go with King Kong." So that's how I got in the band. He thought I was a singer, which I was, but not the kind of singer that *he* was looking for. He wanted somebody to sing like Peanuts Holland. I didn't sing that way. I said, "I can sing like June Richmond in Andy Kirk's band, but I didn't sing that kind of shit—real scat-singing. But anyway he hired me and put me in the band, and after I got in there and hit the high notes, then he was satisfied, but he hired Peanuts back just to do the singing, since I wasn't thinking about doing that. He had me singin', "Miss Jaxson, I want some fine barbecue," and shit. I didn't like that no way! I said, "I don't like singin' that kind of shit!"

    Charlie Shavers heard me, when I first came into the theater, I did "Oh, Miss Jaxson". So Charlie Shavers never let me forget it. Every-

time he see me, he say, "Maggie, you got that barbecue?" I say, "You
dirty . . ." Oh, I hated that thing. He knew I didn't like it from the
way I was singin'. Anyway, we used to laugh about it. So, that's when
I joined Barnet—in '42. I was with him for about six months, an' he
fired everybody. He said, "Everybody fired!" I called up Andy [Kirk].
I thought Charlie was serious about the situation, but he was drunk.
Lena Horne had been up to the theater, the Apollo, and they'd been
ballin' and drinkin' all day and most of that night. He was drunker
than a hoot-owl, so he turned around and said, "The whole band is
fired. You don't sound like Duke no way." Okay, so it don't sound like
Duke; so I called up Andy. Barnet didn't have the music that Duke
had—shit. You got to have the music that sound like what Duke plays
to make it sound like that. We never had nothin' that—all the shit that
he was doin' was either done by Andy [Gibson] or some other cats,
Billy May, some of the other arrangers that were writing for him.
How're you goin' to sound like Duke?

But anyway, the next morning Kurt Bloom called and says, "You
know Charlie didn't mean that." I said, "Oh, yes he did, I heard him!
He said everybody's fired, so I got me a job!" So he said, "Well, no,
man, you know, Charlie gets drunk like that, he do that all the time."
So I said, "Yeah, well he don't get drunk and fire me." So I told him
if he wanted me to come back it was going to cost him fifty bucks a
week. He gave it to me. But the next time he got drunk, he said,
"Everybody fired except McGhee!" He wasn't *that* drunk, so I say, "Uh-
huh." But that was funny.

Oh, Charlie was all right. We used to go gamblin' then. He used to
throw away twenty, thirty thousand dollars. They wouldn't give me a
ten-dollar raise. I said, "You jive!" But he was a nice cat. We had a lot
of fun together, but I had to quit. After I seen him throw away all
that kind of money, I said, "Now, man, you can give me a ten-dollar
raise!" "No, no, no." He said, "I can't do that, all this is money I'm
just spendin', this ain't really my money." I said, "Whose money is it?
I don't see nobody else spendin' somebody else's money!" But he
wouldn't give me a raise. That son-of-a-bitch wouldn't give me a raise,
'cause I hit him for a fifty-dollar raise when he fired the whole band.
But he wouldn't give me a ten-dollar raise, and we'd go out gamblin'
every night with him, and he'd like me to go in, 'cause when I'd shoot
the dice, he'd win money. He wouldn't give me a ten-dollar raise, so I
quit. Then I went back to Andy's band, 'cause I was featured trumpet
player, and I could write anything I wanted to.

TRUMMY YOUNG   Meantime, I played with Barnet for a while. And, incidentally, Woody Herman's first Herd, he got all those guys out of
Barnet's band. Barnet wouldn't keep a band but so long. When the
band got popular, he broke it up because he said it was interfering
with his pleasure. People would call him about business, and he said,

"Aw, this thing is interfering with my pleasure." He would break the band up. So, he broke up this band. Chubby Jackson, Ralph Burns, myself, and—what the trumpet player's married to Frances [Wayne], the vocalist? Neal Hefti. We were all on that band. And Al Killian. What a band that was, man! Serge [Chaloff] . . . I think . . . No, Serge was on the other band I was in. He was on Raeburn's band with me. You get mixed up when you play with so many. But, it was a good band that Barnet had. The trombones was Eddie Bert, myself, and a kid named Ollie Wilson. And Oscar [Pettiford] was on that band. We had two basses. Oscar and Chubby Jackson. Howard McGhee was in that band. Paulie Cohen. Oscar and Chubby used to lay down their basses and do a dance together. It was the funniest thing you ever saw in your life, man! Oh, boy. I had a lot of fun on that band. It was a good band.

MILT HINTON   When we went to Minneapolis, Minnesota, there was Oscar Pettiford, and all of his brothers there. And I went over to St. Paul, right across from Minneapolis. Twin cities. In St. Paul, there was this black Elk's Club, and Oscar was playin' over there with his brother Ira. But there was one that played tenor that was absolutely unbelievable. And I remember his sister played drums 'cause bein' in the rhythm section I had eyes for *her*. Oscar was playing bass, and Ira was play-ing—one of them was playing trumpet, and one of them was playing tenor. The one playing tenor impressed us most, other than Oscar. He was playin' tenor like that very hard, rough Coleman Hawkins of that era—the big, reedy, hard sound with a lot of notes and he sounded magnificent.

❖❖

The members of the Doc Pettiford orchestra did a lot of dou-bling—and tripling. Ira Pettiford played trumpet, guitar, and bass; Alonzo played trumpet, later on, with Lionel Hampton; Harry, who played all the reeds, is probably the tenorman Hinton re-members; and sister Margie has been mentioned as a saxophonist by Oscar. Another sister, Leontine, played piano, reeds, and did most of the arranging.

❖❖

MILT HINTON   I went back to the Orpheum Theater in Minneapolis, and I'm ravin' about Oscar Pettiford, and I'd invited Oscar to come over, backstage, 'cause in the rehearsal hall I wanted the guys to hear him. So Oscar came over for all of us to hear, and I called all the guys up includin' Cab up to hear him, and he was so amazed. Cab wanted to fire me right on the spot and hire Oscar, and he would have fired me 'cept that Oscar wasn't ready to leave, and he was havin' too much fun. And Cab seein' the potential and hearing everybody ravin'—and his only criteria was if the guys rave, he must be good. And so Chu and Doc Cheatham and Keg Johnson were all ravin', includin' me—*I* brought him over. So there goes my gig right out the window! [laughter]. Course, it didn't happen that way, and later Oscar went with Barnet.

CHUBBY JACKSON I discovered Oscar Pettiford in Barnet's band; I don't mean that as an idle boast. We were in Minneapolis, and there was some political thing going on in the theater that gave us about three hours off between shows. Somebody said, "There's a young guy in town, and his whole family's playing over at the same club; the Pettiford family."

   I went over, and I heard this furious soloist, and I got together with him and found out that he didn't read but that he had a marvelous feeling for the bass. I went back to Charlie and said, "Hey, this is not out of school because I do recall that at one time Duke Ellington had two bass players, and I think it might be a very wild idea musically and theatrically to have the two of us do a bass number out front. It might be wild and, frankly, I might learn something." It was quite an adventure for me because Oscar was a very difficult person to get together with, especially when he got into Charlie's band. There were quite a lot of pressures that he'd never been under before. He got into the early drinking habits and would constantly tell off the saxophones, that they weren't together, or he'd stop playing, or if we were playing in a theater he would walk offstage or sit down when an act was on because that was my job—"department" bass player. I did have a certain amount of fun with him, but all of a sudden there was a very obvious sense of competition between the two of us. But the period I did spend with him my left hand did improve. I always had a pretty fast feeling on the bass, but I found some areas that he showed me, so I have really nothing to say about Oscar except that he was great. He and I didn't have the same time; his was way on top like Walter Page used to be, and mine was more in the middle; if anything it was underneath and then it graduated right square into it. But Oscar always was pulling the band. So there was a time lapse between us, and I think we were together maybe about a year or so, and then he disappeared into 52nd Street.

HOWARD MC GHEE I got him the job with Barnet. We were goin' to play Minneapolis, the R.K.O. theater in Minneapolis, and I told Charlie, "There's a bass player over there." I had met him when I was with Harriet Calloway's band; they went off and left us stranded. It was in Grand Forks, Minnesota, so I came down through Minneapolis and met the Pettiford family. I got a job workin' in St. Paul, in one of those little jive joints—drums, trumpet, and a piano. We made good tips— about forty-five dollars in tips a night. That was good in those days, plus we got a dollar and a half a night from the club. Oscar and I and Alonzo, the younger brother—he was a trumpet player—we all started hanging out together. We were about the same age, and I didn't know anything about the after-hours spots there in Minneapolis, and they come and get me and take me over, and we'd go in and jam all night. So Oscar and I got to be good friends. So when Charlie [Barnet] was up, I said, "There's a hell of a bass player out there, man. I'd say we should give him a job. We could use him, 'cause he can play!" So he said, "You want to introduce me to him?" I said, "Yeah, I'll have him come down to the theater and you can talk to him."

I got in touch with Oscar and brought him down to the theater. Chubby had his bass in the back there, Oscar went and picked it up [demonstrates a run], and Charlie looked at him, he said, "Oh yeah, yeah, yeah, he know what he's doin'!" And Chubby came out and saw Oscar, and he said, "Don't touch my bass! Don't touch my bass!" Charlie say, "It's all right," and he said, "Play something." Now Oscar played "Body and Soul." I went and sat down at the piano and played the chords for him, and Charlie said, "Yeah, you hired. You can start on the next show. You got the tuxedo?" He gave him money and said, "Go buy you a tuxedo and come on and join the band." Hired him right on the spot.

He made Chubby awful nervous though. They got an act together, the two of them. Did you see them? We used to call them "salt and pepper" 'cause they would sing a little bit, then they would dance a little bit, and they played the bass. But Pettiford played so much bass, he turned Chubby into a nervous wreck. When he couldn't make it he told Charlie that he was gonna have to fire Oscar, 'cause his nerves just wouldn't stand it. So he let Oscar go, and Oscar came on in to New York and stayed. He didn't have nothin' to worry about, as good as he played bass. He just come right on in here and went right to work.

BUDDY DE FRANCO   But the most enjoyable, in terms of *fun* fun, plus one of the greatest bands I ever worked with, was Charlie Barnet. And the reason for that was Charlie himself. He was not only a swinger—musically, as well as in the other sense of the word. He just loved to live, and he hasn't changed a bit! I don't know how much he practiced his horn. Not very much, because he was having a good time, but he had a feeling on the instrument, and he had a feeling—course he loved Duke Ellington, and he loved the Duke Ellington style—but, he had a feeling in his heart, and he had a happy thing about everything in the band. The band rarely rehearsed. Practically never rehearsed, really. That was one of the best bands in the whole business.

Gil Evans, believe it or not, brought in several arrangements to Charlie Barnet's band when I was on the band, which included people like Al Killian, Pete Candoli, Joe Triscari, Trummy Young, Oscar Pettiford, Chubby Jackson, Ralph Burns, Peanuts Holland, Howard

McGhee, Neal Hefti—you could go on and on with Charlie Barnet's personnel, right? All heavy players in this business, past and present.

One thing that stayed in my mind was "Buster's Last Stand" by Gil Evans. And, I guess, to me, Charlie would stand out as the real bright, happy times. Along with Basie. Those two years were the real happy playing times for me of my career, that I can think of.

There's a problem with [Charlie's] being termed "wild." You get the kind of reputation you don't really deserve because one of the nicest guys, and still is—he happens to be one of my closest friends—is Charlie Barnet. Everybody has a different idea of what is wild and what is crazy. Charlie was never the kind of guy who would do anything rotten to his players. And the guys in the band—he treated us all marvelously, and we had a picnic.

HOWARD MC GHEE   Earl Hines went to Philadelphia to play at the ballroom, some ballroom. Dizzy and Bird were with Earl. That was the band that didn't record. We were all in Philly together. That's how I got to really know Bird. We were all living at the same hotel. I got to talk with him and get to know him. We used to sit there and put a cup mute in our horns and blow at the hotel all night. There wasn't nobody but the band staying there anyway. It was like the Showboat in Philly. So that's how I really got to know Bird, and I found out that he was doin' some funny things with his life. We had a ball in Philly. We were about three weeks in the theater and then a couple of one-nighters. Me and Bird got together; we got to be good friends.

❖ ❖

The Hines band, circa 1942–1943, is one of the great unrecorded organizations in jazz history. The recording ban enforced by the American Federation of Musicians imposed a heavy silence in the studios but there were many transcriptions of radio broadcasts, for instance, that are still surfacing today; many rare and beautiful nights from that period. But no one has come up with any Hines performances when Parker and Gillespie were aboard.

Budd Johnson, who played with Hines until Parker took his place, was involved with many of the bands—as player and arranger—in which the music changed. The Hines band was a connection to the Billy Eckstine band of 1944 and the activities of Gillespie and Parker on 52nd Street in that year and for several years thereafter.

❖ ❖

BUDD JOHNSON   I first came to New York in 1934. I was here for just a little while then. I came here with Reuben Reeves,* primarily as a third trumpet player in his band. I used to play a little trumpet and then

*trumpet player earlier with Cab Calloway.

double on the saxophone. We were on the bill with W. C. Handy and J. Rosamund Johnson at the Alhambra Theater. We did a weekend in New York and stayed around for a little while. Then we went to Baltimore, and then that's where the manager ran off with all of the money. We got stranded in Baltimore. That's where the band broke up and I kept a few cats and I—Roy Eldridge and McKinney's Cotton Pickers came in town, and we used to go jam in a place called the Moonglow all the time. This was on Pennsylvania Avenue.

It was a nightclub. Rubel Blakely* was emcee. This was back in 1934, before I joined Earl Hines. So Roy said, "Well, man, we've been playing in here every night, and we oughta to make the man give us a bottle of whiskey." It was a nonunion place. So Roy said, "Man, why don't you go down to the union and tell them to talk to this cat and take this job and unionize this place." So I spoke to the secretary of the union and whatnot and talked to the man and we—people had begun to like us, because we'd come in there and jam all the time—so the man let me put a band in there and they unionized the job, 'cause it was nonunion musicians in there. I was just working there to save up enough money to get back to Chicago, and it took—I lived in Baltimore for about six months—took me about six months to save up enough money to get back to Chicago, and I did. Then I got married, and right after that I went with Earl. May the 10th, 1935, and I won't forget it, because this was when they had that bad accident, and Cecil Irwin got killed outright, and I had been going by the Terrace sitting in the band, and when Cecil wanted to take off and do some writing, I would work in his place. At intermission, all the band would leave the stand, Earl would be up there on the piano, I'd take my horn, I'd get up there and play with him. So when Cecil got killed, naturally they knew I could read the book, so they sent for me. That's the reason I wouldn't forget that date.

We took Freddie [Webster]. We put Freddie in the band. Freddie, Tadd Dameron—he was included in that. Tadd Dameron and Freddie were in high school together. Tadd Dameron, one of his first arrangements I brought in and played it in Earl's band. It was "Sweet Georgia Brown." And the first guy we took out of Cleveland was Peewee—the trumpet player Peewee Jackson. Harry Jackson was his real name. He was a very good trumpet player. And then he pulled our coats to Freddie, and we got Freddie. Freddie was never quite the trumpet player that Peewee was, but he had that big sound, and he used to play pretty. And he fit in the band very good, because in those days we loved to have the variety, and not everybody tryin' to play the same style. So Freddie would play the big sound and the pretty things, and Peewee would play the bop-type a26ngs. And we had Gail Brock-

---

*later a vocalist with Lionel Hampton.

man as the first trumpet. You remember an arrangement we played, "Yellow Fire?" Well that's him on trumpet. Peewee. Harry Jackson.

He never drank or smoked or anything with the guys on the band. He finally wound up drinkin' a little bit, but I don't know what caused Peewee's death because by this time I was away from it.

LEON WASHINGTON   He stole a milk truck in Cleveland at five o'clock in the morning and drove it around the streets in a respectable neighborhood, blowing taps and bugles, waking people up. There were big headlines: GABRIEL BLOWS HIS HORN! The police got him. He got sick after that and finally died. He was drinking two fifths of wine a day.

❖❖

Jackson also solos on "Southside," "The Father Jumps," "Swingin' On C" and "Windy City Jive," the latter also at one time described as a Webster vehicle. In fact, "Windy City Jive" features both Jackson and Tommy Enoch.

❖❖

BENNY BAILEY   Another influence around Cleveland was a cat called Tommy Enoch who came from Pittsburgh. He was in the Earl Hines band in the late thirties, and his style really got to me. He had that buzz like Roy Eldridge, but it was his own style and very unique. I asked some fellows from back home about this guy, and it seems he's given up playing and works in a factory. He got caught up in narcotics like so many other musicians in those days, but I'll never forget what his playing meant to me. He had a beautiful way of improvising on the chords which I hadn't heard before, and I think if there was anyone I sounded like, it was him. Oh, this cat was beautiful. He used to play in a nightclub for a floor show. And after the floor show, they would play dance music, but very hip arrangements. I think they had a trumpet and tenor, I believe, maybe a trombone or so, very small group. And Tadd Dameron wrote some of the arrangements. This was early '40s, '41.

When I was growing up, I dug Louis Armstrong but, I was lucky 'cause I could go in either direction. I liked listening to Louis Armstrong, Roy Eldridge, but Diz was completely new. The first time I ever heard him it was like a shock. It was in Cleveland when they had a jam session. About two or three bands were in town at the same time . . . Probably Eckstine and Cootie Williams was in town. Bud Powell and Eddie Vinson, who was then playing fantastic alto in the style of Charlie Parker, were playing with Cootie Williams. And Tadd Dameron happened to be in town. Everybody was in town. So they had a jam session at the hotel, the Majestic Hotel. And all the cats were up and just listening. They played all day and all night. So at first I started listening, and I says, "What's happening here?" I thought Dizzy was missing notes—you know, the style, the bebop style, "ba—de bop," you know. But after a while, I began to get very fascinated with it.

One trumpeter named Hubert Kidd influenced my playing quite a lot around this time. He came from a musical family billed as "The Kidd Brothers." They were a good band but never became famous and played just around the Cleveland area, but Hubert was a real virtuoso on the trumpet. In the session at the Majestic, at one point they were playing "Indiana" pretty fast, and Hubert sat in with them and sounded pretty good too. Now that's really saying something because Dizzy was at his real peak then, and there's this cat with enough nerve to not only take his horn out but to play it too.

Freddie Webster, who was with Jimmie Lunceford in the late thirties, was an even greater influence on my style.

IDREES SULIEMAN   I left the Carolina Cotton Pickers to join Earl Hines and came to New York. Every night we'd be at Minton's. I met Dizzy at this time. Freddie Webster was the trumpet sound. I had heard him with Lunceford in Indianapolis when I was with the Cotton Pickers. He played "Yesterdays," and that sound really struck me. So after that the cats began to say, "You sound like Freddie." Everyone would say that. I wasn't doing it intentionally. And then I ended up working with him at the Zanzibar with Sabby Lewis's big band.

Sabby Lewis had a small group in Boston, so for New York he had to add some more musicians. We were rehearsing at Nola's Studio, and they brought Freddie Webster for the job. But Freddie said to him, "Okay, you have to announce my name. You have to give me a spot to play on the radio, and a lot of money," and Sabby couldn't pay it. So he told Sabby, "I'm really not too interested in the gig," 'cause Freddie was like that.

We were playing this tune, and I got up and played this solo, and he came over and said, "Hey, man, you sound like me,"* and because of that he took the job, and we got to be very good friends. Every day we'd hang out together. I was honored that he took the job because of me. He was a beautiful cat until some trouble between him and his wife.

I took a solo on a record with Ella Fitzgerald—"No Sense"—and someone in *Down Beat* wrote: "There's no doubt that it's Freddie Webster." That was a nice compliment.

BENNY BAILEY   Freddie was from Cleveland originally but not when I was around. He made a few records, a couple with Sarah Vaughan, "If You Could See Me Now" and "My Kind of Love," but the recordings were not too good, and it's difficult to tell from them just how beau-

---

*Listen to Sulieman's lead work on Clifford's Brown's recordings with Tadd Dameron's band.

tiful his sound was. In my opinion he had the most wonderful sound of any trumpet player I've ever heard. It was sheer beauty which no one can ever know unless they've heard him play in person. I'm sure Miles was very much influenced by him also. During Miles's early formative days, they shared an apartment in New York, and Freddie, being more experienced, was sort of schooling Miles. I happen to know for instance that on the recording of "Billie's Bounce," which Miles made with Charlie Parker, his solo was exactly the one Freddie played for this particular blues. Evidently Miles said he was nervous on the date and couldn't think of anything to play, so he did Freddie's solo note for note.

CHARLIE ROUSE But all the trumpet players got a little bit of that thing from Freddie Webster. Freddie wasn't like a soloist that'd be running everything, but that sound Freddie had. And that includes Dizzy and all of them—tried to get that sound of his. Freddie would hit one note, man, and it would fill up a whole stadium, whole theater. But they all, far as that sound, they were all trying to get—Fats [Navarro] was articulate where Miles, at that time, had his little style, but Miles wasn't recognized as a trumpet player. He wss trying to find his thing. 'Cause Miles would never have been a trumpet player, as far as the sound of the trumpet, when you put him in with Fats and Freddie Webster. He wasn't that type of trumpet, but he was a stylist. Freddie was a big influence, man. Dizzy and all of them, from Fats on down. 'Cause he had a trumpet sound, and he would hit a note and expand it. It would get, like some cats say, "Baaaaaa." Well he would say, "BAAAAAAAAA," and it would go like that. Freddie was a nice cat—to me. We'd hang out a lot together. During that time everybody was—their lifestyle was music. He was always talking about music. He was a very hip dresser, wore colorful things. But he wasn't a boisterous cat. Wasn't loud or anything. He was working with Jimmie Lunceford a lot. He was a quiet sort of guy, like Fats. He was in that kind of temperament. Quiet. They all would hang out together. Max [Roach] and Freddie and all. It was like a little clique. It's a pity that he didn't record a lot man. 'Cause he died very young. I think he was working with Stitt . . . he was out there with Stitt.

❖❖

Webster had departed the Hines band in the fall of 1941, and in the winter of '42 Enoch was replaced by Maurice "Shorty" McConnell, who was featured on "Second Balcony Jump" and "Stormy Monday Blues."

❖❖

BUDD JOHNSON We got with Shorty with a later band. And he played "Stormy Monday." A funny thing happened with Shorty. We sent for Shorty—nobody even knew Shorty couldn't read—and we had our rehearsal, and Shorty couldn't get out of the first bar. So I got, oh, five joints from this cat, took Shorty upstairs and started to teach him how to read music. And we stuck with it. We didn't fire him. And you know, he came on through fine.

After Dizzy and Bird got together, that put the icing on the cake. Diz and Bird came to the band after I left. But then I still wrote a few charts for the band. Like "Air Mail Special." Actually you tried to write like the cats were playing, which was kind of hard because then you have to get the overall voicings to produce the sound. Dizzy could write. He was starting to write for Boyd Raeburn and bands like that. And actually you would take something somebody played and really make something out of it.

I never will forget the time that Teddy Wilson wrote the arrangement of "Shine" for Earl Hines. And for the trumpets he transcribed Louis's solo in four-part harmony, and it was the rave of New York. That's the thing they came to New York with and tore up the Savoy.

❖ ❖

Johnson had been instrumental in Billy Eckstine joining Hines, and later, the two of them were responsible for the modernists coming into the band.

❖ ❖

BUDD JOHNSON   When we were all with Earl's band, the progressive style of music, 'cause most of the guys of the new music that came in Earl's band were the guys that I brought in the band because they were all buddies, like Dizzy, Bird.

SHELLY MANNE   The first time I heard Bird was in Earl Hines's band, in the section. This was when he had Sarah [Vaughan] on the band, Billy Eckstine, Shadow Wilson—such a great band. They played the Masonic Temple in downtown Manhattan. Bird played quite a few solos that night. That's when I first became aware of him. But it's funny like with most musics, there's a lot of talk among young musicians. Just like there is now with the rock musicians. They all know who the "in" guys are, even though they're not accepted as great stars publicly or by the critics.

BILLY TAYLOR   When I was living in Washington, D.C., Charlie Parker and Dizzy were with Earl Hines, and little Benny Harris, who had lived in Washington, came through with the band, and he was telling everybody about these two guys that were coming out with what really were extensions of Roy, and other people that we were familiar with; and at the particular time that he was saying these things he was playing some lines himself that were really quite different from the Roy Eldridge, Louis Armstrong, or Shad Collins, and those kinds of things, quite different, very attractive things, funny little twists in them and really demanding a much clearer knowledge of harmony to make the proper kind of phrasing, and so Benny Harris was for me one of the first people who pointed a finger at this. I was aware of changes my-self, just as a pianist, because Tatum, the kinds of things he did were basically, well, Tatum on the piano, Hawk on the tenor saxophone, Ellington with the orchestra were doing the things that later became really formalized in the bebop context, in terms of harmonic exten-sions and melodic extensions, and really the kinds of rhythms that were first found in the Ellington band. When I first came to New York, I was playing a four-note chord in my left hand, and an octave—either just a plain octave or a four-note chord made in octaves—with my right hand. Everybody but Ben Webster objected to this. They'd say, "You're in my way. I can't hear. You're in the wrong part of the piano. Play down in the bass like Basie or Ellington," for accompaniment. That wasn't what I heard. I had been playing with guitars and other things. I was playing locked hands 'cause I like that, but I didn't want to sound like Milt Buckner, whom I admire tremendously, but this was another kind of approach to it, and I heard Ellington do something like this, and I liked it, and it worked, so I began to do that, and I found that it got me out of the way of the bass player.

So instead of being down here where the bass player was then, I was up in the middle of the piano, and up in the treble and the bass player was very audible, and Ellington, I guess, was really the first one to zero in on it. Basie did it, but Ellington really put the bass out there; if you listen to even his early records, you've got a clear picture of the top and the bottom, of the melody and the bass line with all this other stuff filling in, very classical in terms of orientation. But Basie did a little differently with Jo Jones on drums 'cause Jo is a strong drum-mer, so he did a lot of things that accented what he was doing. But Sonny Greer, who was not that strong of a drummer, but who had his own flair for doing things, colors and all, was also out of the way, so that all of the weight of the rhythm section, that really became for-malized once again in bebop, was with Billy Taylor, the bass player, and Jimmy Blanton and Junior Raglin, also strong bass players; so they really came in with that concept, and they became another kind of thing.

So between late 1936 and 1941, there is a period that I call pre-bop, 'cause it's not really swing, nor was it bebop, but it had all of the in-gredients being kind of formalized by various people, like Clyde Hart, Sid Catlett, Jo Jones, and other people. When I first really embraced bop, it was—I had, of course, become aware of Parker and Gillespie, prior to coming to New York, but I was very much into Tatum and that kind of thing. I used to have some knock-down, drag-out argu-ments with Bud Powell, because I'd run into him frequently at Min-ton's and other places. This was in '44.

I came here in '44, and when I got here I worked with Ben Webster at the Deuces, and the whole transition was really being formalized then beacuse this was just prior to Dizzy Gillespie opening at the Onyx with the first bop band downtown. And, yet, Ben Webster and Ike

Quebec and a lot of guys were playing. Ben was always at Minton's, and so he knew—even though he didn't play bebop per se—he knew all the lines, and he played a lot of things, and a lot of his compositions reflected his awareness of what was happening. He was a very big booster of what the guys were doing, and then I guess Jo Jones was so secure in his own style (Hawkins and guys like that) that he just didn't choose to make that abrupt a change over from what he was most comfortable doing and what other guys were doing; but Hawk got not only Monk to play piano with him, but he had Don Byas in his front line for a long time at the Downbeat, and it was really fantastic to hear Don playing all of those things that really weren't bebop, but they were an extension of what Hawk had done which was, in the first analysis, closer to what Bird was doing than most of us realized at the time. The lines were long. They were four bars, eight bars, depending on what he was doing, but really long lines in terms of melodic development and they were very harmonically oriented.

Bud [Powell] was totally responsive to Charlie Parker. He wanted to make the piano sound like Charlie Parker, and he did. It really had that kind of rhythmic and almost tonal quality in his early work. I had great difficulty with that because I wanted to play pianistically and all of the things.

AL HAIG   Bud's playing was so completely perfect and so highly stylized in that idiom. He outbirded Bird and he outdizzied Dizzy. And here he was, playing on a percussive instrument, a plectrum instrument, not a front-line instrument, and at times outdoing any of them.

ALLEN TINNEY   We used to hang out. We were like three hoods—there was me, Bud Powell, and a little guy that came here with Helen Humes, Gerald Wiggins. He was the speed king. He could play fast. He still does, and then Bud was more or less quite heavy, very dynamic in his playing, and I believe I was a little of both. We used to walk into different clubs, just the three of us, like three hoods. The minute a piano player would spot us he'd think, "God, there goes my job." But we weren't really after a job, we just wanted to get the guy. And one of us would get whoever it was. We'd all sit down and play.

I caught Bud at a time when he was—could have been obnoxious at times, but with me he was all right. We were friendly, and his mother would ask me to take care of him because he was a little bit on the alcohol. But he was into music so deep that there was really nothing else that mattered. He was just that type of person.

KENNY CLARKE   Monk wrote for Bud. All his music was written for Bud Powell. All this piano music, he deliberately wrote for Bud because he figured Bud was the only one who could play it. He wrote for Bud just like a composer writes for a singer. And when you hear Bud play Monk's music, then you really hear something.

❖ ❖

Along with his Parker, Gillespie, and Monk influences, Powell also was moved by Tatum.

❖ ❖

BILLY TAYLOR   He was aware of him but Tatum didn't enter his consciousness until later when he began to work with Mary Lou Williams and became more interested in the sound of the piano. Mary Lou Williams took Monk and Bud up to her house and really worked with them because she's such a sensitive person that she said, "Look, I mean, you guys play too well not to make the piano sound any more pianistic than it does when you play." She made them both more aware of touch. And you could hear the difference in the early Powell records and the later Powell records in terms of just the touch. You can hear the same with Monk, when Monk was recording for Blue Note and labels like that—it was one touch. And then later he began to record for other labels, it just wasn't the change in sound, he changed. And you could hear a more pianistic approach. This was, in my opinion, a result of his close association with Mary Lou. That was '49, almost '50.

Tom Tilghman used to have Monday sessions with his piano players, and the attraction was that Tatum was a friend of his and Tatum would come up almost every Monday. And all of the piano players showed up, but Tatum wouldn't show up until after the gig or whatever. But all the piano players were there from about ten o'clock at night playing for one another. Marlowe Morris, who was one of the closest in terms of style to Art in those days, never recorded like that on piano, and many people just knew him as an organist and had no concept that in feeling, in technique, he was perhaps the closest to Art, stylistically. He didn't play like that with any kind of rhythm section— he played another style. With Sid Catlett, for instance, he worked with Sid a lot, and he played very spare, almost like Monk, in some of the things he did.

The first time I ever heard Monk, he was playing much more like Art than what he later became. When I heard him, with Hawk and other people, it was like another guy. I mean he was doing all those things before. And he was playing all these things, but I was accustomed to hearing him play tenths and other things—three-fingered runs like Tatum. I mean he didn't phrase it like Tatum, but you could tell that that was the influence. And the touch was so different. But there were so many pianists around that bridged that particular gap. Billy Kyle was primarily known for the Earl Hines kind of inspired style of his, yet Billy had a lot of those kind of phrases that were like pre-bop. It was not quite bop yet. But in his style you could hear the phrase ending on the off-beat, and other kinds of things like that. And he had quite an influence on Bud Powell, too.

ALLEN TINNEY   I liked Billy Kyle also—the style of Fatha Hines, with the one finger hitting at the bass theme and then hitting something else, so I had already heard that particular type of thing.

BILLY TAYLOR   Mary Lou Williams is probably one of the best examples of someone who made the transitions of style from ragtime—from early ragtime. She played for Jelly Roll Morton, who put her down. She worked with, and played for, James P. [Johnson] and Fats [Waller]. And she was, of course, influenced by their work as well as Earl Hines. She not only composed and played in all of the styles, boogie-woogie and all those things, but she is a walking encyclopedia of what literally the styles were about. I heard the Scott Joplin presentation at Lincoln Center, when they had Bill Bolcom and several other pianists to play the Joplin works, and they all played them very well—they read the music, and they gave it the kind of loving attention it should get—but Mary Lou Williams was the only one who improvised on it. She was so secure with the music, she just said, "Yeah, it goes like this." And she went on and wailed on it. The critics didn't understand that. They said she really didn't learn the piece. She knew the piece from before and not only was secure enough to improvise on it, but it became Mary Lou playing Scott Joplin, which any jazz musician knows it's supposed to be. But she plays authentic stride, authentic boogie-woogie, absolutely authentic ragtime and, of course, was in this pre-bop thing by— I think it was 1937 or '38 she wrote the "Zodiac Suite"* which had all of those intervals, and that whole number that later became formalized in Dizzy's and Bird's work, but she had it all because the piano was the obvious thing. I mean all that was in front of you—the altered chords and the melodies that resulted from it. And, so she was quite a person in that regard.

MARY LOU WILLIAMS   My inspiration was Jack Howard, a man that isn't well known in musical circles. He used to bang so hard on the keys. He was from Atlanta, Georgia. He played boogie-woogie kind of style and ragtime. That was my inspiration. The next inspiration I heard Earl Hines, and then the next inspiration was Fats Waller, and the greatest inspiration was Buck Washington that played piano with Buck and Bubbles. He was as great as he was when he was around Chu Berry and the rest. He showed me a run that Art Tatum stole from me. He said to me, "When you're around Art Tatum and Count Basie, don't play this run."

And I forgot; I was hanging out with Art Tatum in Cleveland, and I played it, and Art Tatum said, "What is that, Lou? Play it again." So I did, and from that day on that's his famous run up and down the

*recorded for Asch in 1945.

piano. Buck had showed it to me, and naturally I wouldn't sound as great as Tatum playing it with his technique.

❖❖

It is interesting to trace the last eight bars of the second chorus of Williams's arrangement of "Walkin' and Swingin'" (recorded with Andy Kirk in 1936) into the modern period. Al Haig recorded it as "Opus Caprice"; Sonny Stitt as "Symphony Hall Swing"; and Monk as the renowned "Rhythm-a-ning." Nowhere does Mary Lou receive credit of any kind.

❖❖

MARY LOU WILLIAMS   We were inseparable: Monk, Bud Powell, and I. We were always together every day, for a long time. You know another thing, you remember that old thing I wrote, "Steppin' Pretty?" It was about the third composition that I wrote before Andy [Kirk] showed me really how to arrange. I heard a bop tune of that—"Steppin' Pretty"—and I just heard it this year [1977]. I don't know what it was called. There was something else that was written from "Cloudy"—you know the old, "Days are cloudy, nights are cloudy, since you went away." And "Blues in the Night" was written from a clarinet thing I did in, I think it was "Little Joe from Chicago"; and "What's Your Story, Morning Glory?" became "Black Coffee."

In Kansas City, we'd jam all night until seven or eight in the morning and then we'd go to somebody's house or speakeasy. There would be a piano there, and the musicians would have their girlfriends with them, and they're a little tired, and they're resting up for another session. I'd sit there and play modern harmonies and things that came to me, just as modern as what you hear now. It would seem that they'd come out of the sky. They'd be sitting there with their girlfriends and stuff, and I'd play all kinds of weird chords and things, just anything on the piano, and they were amazed about it. After awhile it became so that after I'd start an arrangement they would copy certain things. Or like if it was a club I was playing in, while I'm playing I may play something that's never been played before in the strain of a lick.

❖❖

In her apartment, during the late '40s, Mary Lou was again inspirational.

❖❖

MARY LOU WILLIAMS   Sometimes Tadd Dameron would get stuck with his arrangements, and he'd say, "Come on and play something, Lou," and he'd know while I was creating it would push him off again. And Bud Powell used to come to the house. Of course, Erroll Garner never needed help because he found that 4/4 here. The piano was over there, and I was in the back room. He says, "I've got it. Now I don't have to worry with the rhythm section." He ran in the back and said, "Come and listen to this," and I said, "I heard it."

You see, Andy used to sit down and take ideas of mine. It seemed during my early period—sixteen and eighteen, nineteen, twenty years old—I was full of ideas, new things, all the time and that made musicians hang out with me, take me out on jam sessions. It seemed to inspire them, and whenever I created—I never listened to radio, TV, or anything—I'd just go out and maybe drive a car, and if I didn't have a car I'd borrow one, and go out where there were flowers or water and sit there and start to write. You see, I don't need a piano. It would slow me up. I just get to the piano to find out if I made any mistakes or how it's going to flow.

❖ ❖

Another arranger, whose "Puddin' Head Serenade" was recorded by Kirk in 1936—twenty-nine days after "Walkin' and Swingin'—" was pianist Clyde Hart.

❖ ❖

TRUMMY YOUNG   And one other guy I really loved back in those days—he and I used to get together quite often on things, just the two of us—was Clyde Hart. He was one of my dear friends. When he first got sick—well, a lot of guys thought he was crazy because he wore rubbers all the time over his shoes. But I know why he wore them. He had lung trouble, and he figured it might rain, and he didn't want to get his feet wet. I had a little room on 44th Street. I wasn't married then. And he used to come by there. Every time I got a new record or something, he'd come and listen to it. I remember when I first got Stravinsky's *Firebird,* and I was playing it, and he loved it so much. He used to come up, and I'd put it on and go to the bathroom, shave, do whatever I wanted to do, and he'd just sit there and listen to it. I got very close with him. Budd [Johnson], Ben Webster, and myself, I think we were some of the closest guys to Clyde. We were concerned about his health, and we worried about him, and I used to always check with Edna, his wife, about how he was feeling, and things of this sort. Three or four of us were very close 'cause we knew his condition and we worried about him. . . . He was one of the *writers* who knew what to do back there with the new things that were coming out. He knew.

OSCAR PETTIFORD   All of us were thinking about the new style, trying to get used to playing it. Clyde was the only pianist that could play those things without any trouble. In fact, he was the first to play the modern-style left hand. He told me as long as I was playing that much bass he didn't need to play rhythm in the left hand, and he could just use it to establish chord changes.

BUDD JOHNSON   Clyde was one beautiful musician that had a great ear. I'll give you an example why he picked up on it so easily. Back in the old days, when I was in Kansas City, Clyde Hart came to Kansas City, and he was working with a band called Jap Allen. Now we used to go into restaurant, order some food, and Clyde would get to the new jukebox and put on . . . you know, they had a lot of McKinney Cotton Pickers records on there. He would sit down there and put a few nickels into that jukebox and be writing while he's waiting for the food and eat. Then he'd sit around and write a little more. I'll tell you how great his ear was. This guy was takin' off the record note for note, solos and all—every note that McKinney Cotton Pickers played on the record. And one day, the McKinney Cotton Pickers came into Kansas City and played a battle of music with Jap Allen's band. Don Redman was with the McKinney's Cotton Pickers at that time. They had been out in Buffalo, New York, and all around, on their way, and their whole library had been stolen, and when they heard Jap Allen's band playing all of their music, they thought they had their music, and they called the police. But Clyde Hart, with his ears, had sat down and wrote, note for note, all of their music off the records. And that's the way Jap Allen's band played. Ben Webster was with Jap Allen's band at that time. He had been blowing some of Prince Robinson's solos. Prince Robinson, who was a great saxophone player, was the threat to Hawkins at the time. Everybody was saying, "Wait a minute. Who is this cat? Damn, you sound almost as good as Coleman Hawkins." Anyway, this is how great Clyde was. He could catch onto anything. In nothing flat he would have it. And that's when Clyde and I wrote this "Bu-Dee-Daht" together.*

We used to write a lot together. Clyde and I. I would say, "Come on Clyde, let's do this music now, we got to . . ." 'Cause I used to peddle arrangements. So Clyde said, "Okay." So I'd come back, maybe if I'd sell two arrangments. I might come back with 250 bucks, and I would give Clyde one hundred and a quarter, and I would take my hundred, and he says, "Oh no, no, no, don't give me all that money." I say, "What do you mean, man, you earned it." He said, "Uh, uh. I don't need that much money." He say, "Don't give me that." I say, "What are you talkin' about?" He say, "Give me twenty-five dollars, you keep the rest." Well, you know what it was? Clyde knew that he wasn't gonna live long.

He had been in the hospital with tuberculosis, and he told me once he had seen death. That he had seen death, and he had to get out of that hospital. Him and Alex Hill was in the hospital at the same time. He said he had seen death, and he was gonna never go back in there. So he never went for his check-ups or anything. And his wife used to beg me, "See if you could get Clyde to go back to the hospital." Ah, no. He would never ride on the subway. He would take a cab if it cost fifty dollars, and he would buy him a $2.50 cigar, smoke the best and drink the best whiskey. He said, "I'm gonna live out my days."

❖❖

*The Apollo record date with Coleman Hawkins.

Clyde Hart died on March 19, 1945. *The Encyclopedia of Jazz* lists his birth year as 1910 so he was either thirty-four or thirty-five when he passed.

❖❖

BUDD JOHNSON   Anyway, he knew. See, Clyde was an atheist. He didn't believe in God and all of that and—Charlie Shavers was just like him. Charlie knew he was gonna die, and he just kept throwing that stuff in him. But back in 1929, '30, '31, Clyde Hart had a great musical head on him. He had been to school. He had talent then. I mean he was sharp. He was a great arranger then. He was just one of those rare geniuses. But then he always looked the same. He looked as old then as he did later in years. I mean he had that look.

❖❖

If Clyde Hart had lived there is a likelihood he would have made a further transition towards bop piano with the right hand.

❖❖

BILLY TAYLOR   He was very sensitive and he had a lot more technique than his records would indicate. I remember one night up at Tom Tilghman's place—the Hollywood Bar on 7th Avenue in Harlem. Art Tatum sat down and showed about seven or eight piano players how to play a break that he had recorded in "Battery Bounce," one of his early records. And somebody asked him, "How did you do that?" And he said, "It's just this." And he played it. He played it two or three times, and the only guy that got it the first time around was Clyde Hart. And Clyde didn't use all that technique normally. You don't hear it on the records. But he had tremendous facility, and he was a well-rounded musician. He could play other styles. He could do a lot of things, and I found out that time and on several other occasions where I heard him up at Tom Tilghman's.

But there were a lot of other people who didn't live in New York who had a great deal of impact on Bird and Dizzy when they would go to different towns. There was a musician whose nickname was "Georgetown." I don't know his real name. John Malachi and some of the guys who've been in Washington since would know, but he was such a phenomenal trumpet player that whenever Roy [Eldridge] would be in town, he would look him up. He said: "That's the guy I'm looking for," and he played in this style. It wasn't swing. It was beyond swing, approaching bop. There were a couple of saxophonists in D.C. There was a piano player named Toby Walker who did this. There was another pianist who since died—Toby's dead, too—but this pianist was the accompanist for the Ink Spots. He came out of the Army, and he just couldn't get into the jazz scene so he took a job with the Ink Spots. He never really got back into the jazz thing. His name was Harold Francis, and when I was coming up, he and Toby Walker were the baddest piano players in town. Everybody aspired to do what they did and the only way I can describe it is that Harold had, on all levels, a much more aggressive approach to Teddy Wilson and Art Tatum. It had harmonies that I associate more with Tatum because they were further evolved but he had a touch kinda like Teddy, so he and Julius Pogue* and a lot of other guys were influential. Frank Wess and the baritone player, Leo Parker, and Charlie Rouse—all of these guys came up aware of this Washington contingent, and all of the guys knew Benny Harris and liked these little things he was doing and did things based on those things. And so on the whole, during that entire period I was most aware of the Washington contingent, but there was a contingent in Detroit.

❖❖

Hank Jones was from Pontiac, but he left the Detroit area early. Then in New York he heard Al Haig and Bud Powell.

❖❖

HANK JONES   When I first got to New York, one of the first groups I heard was the Dizzy Gillespie-Charlie Parker group. Al Haig was the pianist at the time. Now I understand that he and Bud Powell alternated with the group, as did Max Roach and Stan Levey on drums.

But during the initial period when I first came to New York, Al Haig was the pianist. His style of playing was quite a departure from what I had previously been trying to play, which was more oriented towards the Teddy Wilson school with hints of Art Tatum, only hints, faint hints. It was a different style. That style—as I look back on it—I suppose the style came about mainly because these pianists rarely, if ever, played solo. I think they played with groups, and with groups it was not necessary for them to use a lot of left hand, with the moving tenths that most solos of the day utilized—pianists like Art Tatum, Fats Waller, Teddy Wilson. But these pianists all worked with groups. And the bassists in those groups took care of the bass hand, or the left hand, or the bass support for the horns and, when the piano was playing a solo, for the piano as well. So it wasn't necessary for the piano to carry a full, fleshed-out sort of bass style. It didn't occur to me at the time. In retrospect it seems that's probably what happened. But Al was the first of the New York pianists that I heard—later on, of course, Bud Powell. And I don't recall any other at the moment, but these two made quite an impression on me. First Al and then Bud.

At first the style seemed quite complicated, mainly because I wasn't familiar with the background harmonic changes that the style was superimposed upon. Whatever we call the "line," it's always based on the harmonic changes underneath, and these changes were completely new to me. The chords themselves weren't new but the placement of the chords, and the progressions, and the way they were used. And, of course, the melodies that were built on these chords were all new to me. I was listening to the lines more than the harmonic background.

*A Washington, D.C., tenor saxophonist who was harmonically advanced.

When I began to consider the harmonic background everything sort of fell into place for me. As a matter of course I subconsciously started to think in that vein. It showed up later in my playing.

BILLY TAYLOR   When I first heard Hank he was working with Hot Lips Page, and he was playing what I have to call a pre-bop style because it was beyond swing harmonically and otherwise. And his touch was, even then, just gorgeous, and he had been playing with other kinds of bands. He had a really beautiful touch on the piano, and he reminded me in those days of Ellis Larkins, who had the same kind of harmonic approach. It wasn't bop, but many of the aspects of what he did were long flowing lines. And because he was a pianist, there were other things he could do rhythmically. It was very interesting style, and Hank just had a good feeling, was a great accompanist, and many of the things that he did with Lips Page and other bands were, to my ear, post-Teddy Wilson kind of things, somewhere between Clyde and Teddy. He had memorized some Art Tatum things so he had that under his fingers and he was really quite a player, even then.

There were other contingents in various cities and all of these guys played some extension of swing. I mean it was their transition period where they were beyond the heavy 4/4 and the other stuff. Whether they listened to Charlie Christian, or whether they listened to Django Reinhardt, who was a big influence on many of the concepts. Not just guitar but Django had these long lines, long lyrical lines that he did, and that became part of the guys' consciousness, too. So, there were a lot of different influences that led into guys approaching bebop. It's easy to say that out of Lester [Young] this came, out of Hawk this came, and you can certainly document that, but it wasn't that clear cut.

❖❖

Taylor moved to New York from Washington and found himself in the middle of the transition. It was one of the richest periods in jazz because you had the best of the swing players intermixing with the modernists.

❖❖

BILLY TAYLOR   One of the most exciting things that happened to me was to be on the bandstand with, say Dizzy and Ben Webster, Ike Quebec, Jack the Bear [Parker], the drummer; the bass player, it could have been any number of bass players—Charlie Drayton, John Simmons, guys that played really personal styles on the bass. But, it was really exciting because you got such a wide variety in one session. You would hear a whole gamut of things. One guy is really playing on the changes, another guy is playing all these beautiful melodies. You know, Lester Young. And just floating rubato all over the—the rhythm is Charlie Christian. He's doing something else entirely. And just the combination of those kinds of things and the fact that guys encourage the rhythm section to do other things with changes. If you're gonna play

"I Got Rhythm," I mean we've played those changes already, do something else with those changes to extend that. And, so the rhythm section was making small or large—depending on who you're playing for—differences in the harmonies. You get a guy with ears like Don Byas or Hawk or somebody like that, you could go into another direction, and you'd end up instead of the B-flat, G-minor, C-minor, F-7th change, you'd end up doing the cycle of fifths startin' on F-sharp, B, E, A, D, G, C, F and then back to the B-flat, and just that kind of thing that had been done prior to this period but weren't really dealt with on the level they're being dealt with now. And I recall listening to Clarence Profit, who wrote "Lullaby in Rhythm" and some other pieces, and who was never considered by most people more than an imitator of Fats Waller. Yet he and Art Tatum would sit down and jam, and they would jam on by playing the melody over and over. And changing the harmony, so instead of coming up with different melodies, they came up with different harmonies, and that became particularly interesting when they started off with something like "Body and Soul," which already has some changes. And harmonically this guy was just unreal and to my knowledge he never recorded in that way.

I heard him play solo, I met him in a strange way. I had come up to New York to a place called Jock's. Now, it used to be called the Yeah Man Club, and a friend of my father's was the manager. We were talkin; and he said, "Your father tells me you're a piano player," and I said, "Yeah," and he said, "Why don't you come in the back and play somethin'. I got a trio back here."

That was kinda nice so I went back there and I didn't know any of the guys by sight. This was in '38. I was just visiting. I knew who Clarence Profit was, but I had never seen him, and so my father's friend introduced me. In fact he didn't even give me the guys' names. He just said, "Fellas, I got a young player here, the son of a friend of mine, and I'd like for him to play a little bit," and the guys said, "Sure, come on." And I sat down and of all the pieces—now I hadn't noticed the sign outside—and of all the pieces I could of picked up, I picked "Lullaby in Rhythm" because it was my favorite song at the time, and I played it. I shot my best shot. I'm playing for New York musicians, so the piano player said, "Say, that's pretty nice, kid. I've got some friends who would like to hear you. We're going to take an intermission in a minute, and I'd like to take you around the corner."

I went around the corner with him, and it was in somebody's house in an apartment building, and there were five or six guys. A couple guys were playing cards, and a couple other guys were just rapping. So we went in, and he said, "Hey, I got a piano player here you guys oughta hear." And everybody looked up, and I said, "Yeah, okay," and I sat down and played "Liza" or something else, and one of the things I figured I could get my stride together and do a little solo piano, and he had led me into the lion's den because all of these guys in there was a piano player, and there was a guy named Gibby who had the damnedest left hand I ever heard in my life. I ended "Liza," and all of them played "Liza" after me, and it was quite an experience. I really don't remember all of the guys now but I do remember Gibby. These were older pianists, but they really could play in the post-ragtime style. It wasn't swing as played by Teddy Wilson or guys like that, but it was the extension of the Harlem stride thing that James P. and Fats did, because harmonically they were into more current Art Tatum.

But the style was the stride. That's what I was trying to play, for them, which was a big mistake, but I got to know several of them after when I came to New York later and I met and listened to Donald Lambert and several of the other guys. But everybody had his "crip," everybody had his particular thing. Donald Lambert would play, for example, a classical piece like "Anitra's Dance", or something like that, and he'd swing it; he'd play it in the jazz style, and other guys had particular things they'd do. Clarence Profit was just a master of substitutions as far as harmonies are concerned. You just wondered, "What is the logic of going from there to here?" But it all made sense, and I really wish someone had recorded him. I've listened to some of the re-releases on Columbia and other things, and I don't hear any of that. He used a lot of clusters, and he used a lot of things that we now associate with Tatum, and some with Monk, because he used a lot of tonal things that Monk used, and I'm sure Monk was aware of his playing because he was one of the guys that was around in Harlem.

❖❖

All of this activity was taking place within the framework of a world at war. Those who were in the service, especially the ones stationed overseas, were not aware of the changes happening in the music. But musicians, particularly those who remained in this country, managed to keep up, even though they were in uniform. And just as the service centers suddenly had top football teams, they also had first-rank bands.

❖❖

AL GREY   When I was in the service I was out at Great Lakes [Naval Training Station]. I had a lower bunk. Up over me was Osie Johnson. Every night they would have to come in and "Sssh" to get us quiet because we just had so much fun rappin' and talking about life. Man, he was something.

They had the Bachman brothers. They had Luther Henderson that has this thing with "Ain't Misbehavin" right now. And Dudley Brooks that writes out in Hollywood. They had Stack Walton on tenor, Peewee Jackson, which I felt was so great—I thought he was the greatest trumpet player. There was a lot of lively cats around Great Lakes—'cause they had Clark Terry and he was bad, and these cats, the Bachman brothers, from St. Louis, were bad. And Soupy Campbell who played a lot of years with Count Basie had completely a nonpressure system. I was so far behind till—I had been a tuba player really and just to be around them—it was just like everything to me. The bands were segregated at Great Lakes. You had the main side where Eddie Peabody had everything—all the Glenn Miller bands. He was the big man, Lieutenant Commander Peabody. We were over at what they called Camp Small. We had all these musicians there. Then I was shipped out to Boston. We had a trumpet player Charlie Young that used to be with Bird in Jay McShann's band. And that's where I really began to get a lot of learning from Charlie Young. And a guy named Henry Noyd was the trumpeter that played 'round there with Jay McShann, too. He was just a natural player. He couldn't "see"* because Benny Carter needed a trumpeter, and he just couldn't "see" but he could play very much. Henry Noyd—"Cowboy" they called him. But Charlie Young was writing music and had been around with Bird. And that's when he really made me aware of Bird. Because I had never even heard of Bird at that time.

They shipped me out—to Boston—because they had so many musicians at Great Lakes, where they shipped out one band to the islands—Guam. And then at Great Lakes they had three bands: the A band, B band, C band. And they had another trombone player—Rocks McConnell, who wrote "Sweet Slumber." He could really play the trombone. They had a lot of good trombone players out there, and I couldn't get nowhere's near to getting into all those bands. After we got up into Boston, we went to Hingham, Massachusetts, which was an ammunition depot. All the sailors there—we used to call them "stevedores," because they had come from Mississippi and Alabama and all that part of the country. Many of them couldn't read or write at all. And when they would get paid they would have to make an "X" to get their pay. I used to sit down and write letters home for some of the guys. And, in return, the letters would get home—somebody would have to write so that I could get the letter back to them.

Then we got this group together—a little sextet which won all these competitions around in New England. To be awarded, to be paid, and to get away on a leave for a week into New York City for the Major Bowes Amateur Hour. And I'll never forget that. And they'd come and get us, and we'd go to rehearsal. And we had a tremendous spot on this thing. But this was all designed by this Charlie Young. When he went home from the service he got stabbed from a domestic problem and bled to death. He got stabbed in the leg. And no one would touch him. And he just bled to death. They couldn't get him to the hospital in time. It was a terrible tragedy. Terrible thing, terrible loss.

In '42, that's when we would go in to Boston to see Coleman Hawkins with Benny Harris and Don Byas. And then I got good enough to come in and sit in with Sabby Lewis, who had a band up at the Savoy.

*read music well.

So then the government wanted to make the band lift ammunition. They got together and wrote to the president a lot about it. So then they shipped us out. I went to Grosse Hill Naval air station outside of Grosse Pointe in Detroit. Then I was around Detroit—that's when I met Tricky Sam [Nanton]. And that's when he was calling Betty Roche to the microphone. Betty Roche and his trombone—and that intrigued me so much until I used to try and figure out how he was doing these different things. They had great musicians around Detroit. They had a club that let me come in. Nobody knew my name at that time. They just knew me as the sailor boy, because we had these sailor suits on. I used to go in the clubs there. There was one called the Three Sixes, and the C&B club. You could come into Detroit every day, and you had everything free with the USO. You could go to Stroh's Beer and take it right out of the vat and put it in the trough and cool it off. Today they still have tours like that.

BIDDY FLEET   I was in Special Service, and they had a special order to take all of the musicians and the show people to give them thirteen weeks of infantry training because we were going to New Guinea to entertain the wounded soldiers behind the lines, and the Japs was taking care of everything that came over then. The colonel told us, "What you ought to do when you get an attack from behind the lines, you throw your instruments away and find a foxhole and get your carbine and get ready," because you were then on the front. He told us that this evening, and the next morning Jimmy Mundy, Irving Ashby, Willie Bryant, Rochester—I could name a bunch of stars as well as musicians, including myself—all got on sick call. Mundy was writing an arrangement for Basie's band, and he stayed in the hospital and had two tables pulled up side his bed so he could finish that arrangement. Then the Post Commander found out that, even though it was considered a great thing for the service, being in Special Service, doing shows and playing the instruments and all, he found out that we had no fighting spirit. We didn't want to go where the "bang bang" was. Especially at that time because we saw some of our friends who went over. They were coming back with one leg, one arm, like that.

JEAN BACH   Shorty's [Sherock] little band broke up because his draft number was up, and we just arranged to wind up the band. The engagement was gonna end. It was a six-week engagement in Denver, and I think they played some other dates before then. And then I was in our hotel room typing, on a typewriter which I still have, a letter home saying, "Well, I'll be coming home because Shorty is going to be drafted," and there was a knock on the door. It was about twelve noon, and he's standing out there with a bunch of flowers. He says, "You're going to have to put up with me a little while longer." They rejected him. He was the most perfect Army specimen, strong, exactly perfect character, powerful, perfect teeth, not a filling in his mouth, perfect bones, and everything, and leadership qualities, and so forth, but apparently he had been so brought down at the thought of having to go into the Army that for about six weeks he had been drinking practically a fifth of Myers's rum every night, and it was all in his blood. That stuff is really like molasses. He was drinking it when I first knew him, when he was playing with Gene Krupa. He sat down next to Gene, and Gene would be playing the drums and breathing, and all of a sudden he'd say, "Is there some rubber burning around here?" [Laughter].

JOE NEWMAN   People were really afraid, and nobody wanted to go to the Army.

When I came here for induction, I was still with Hamp's band, and I had to take a train in from somewhere in Pennsylvania and rode most of the night and got here early in the morning. And I didn't want to go to the Army. And the fad at that time would take pills and eat Benzedrine inhalers—the paper out of them. I did everything, man. I took Nembutals. My heart must be the greatest in the world. I was taking uppers and downers together, and I drank, and I stayed up for three nights in a row before I came to New York. When I got to New York I was run down. I had the piles, everything, and it looked like they were going to pass me through anyway. But finally when I talked to the psychiatrist, I told him—well, they asked me about homosexuality. I said, "Well, I don't go for it but I've had affairs with men. I do it for the money." And he said, "Tell me, how much do they get nowadays?" And I said, "I don't know how much they get but I generally take all they got." He says, "Do you want to go in the Army?" I said, "Not really, but if I have to go, I'll just go." He said, "Why wouldn't you want to go?" I said, "Well, I'm a young musician, and things are just beginning to happen for me, and I feel if I go in now, I'm going to lose a lot of it." I said, "You know Harry James?" I knew he would know Harry James. I said, "Well, I'd like to play like him." I really went off the wall. Then I started getting red marks on my chart, but before that, I think they would have passed me anyway. And I reached in that bag. I tried everything. And the minute I left there man, oh, God, my stomach hurt me. I felt like I was gonna die. I was dry. It was a dry feeling. Because I remember not long before I got to New York, I ate this last piece of paper—the Benzedrine. It was like cotton paper and, man, this paper, I never did digest this piece. And talk about praying to God, man, I prayed to God. And the only person I really knew in New York was Billie Holiday. I called up before, so she said, "Come up to my house." When I got through I went up. I said, "Well, I made it. I got rejected." And I was so sick. She called a doctor for me, and this woman cooked food, everything, for three days. She nursed me and got me straight, and I was able to go back to the band, but I thought I was gonna die, really. And I would never go through that again. I just was young and didn't know and everybody else was also doing it—drinking Coca Cola and putting Benzedrine inhalers in the Coca Cola. I'm not necessarily proud of it, but that's the way I felt, and I just wanted to stay out of the Army. It might have been the greatest thing in my life if I had gone.

❖❖

Terry Gibbs was stationed in the United States, and by the time he got to Texas he had heard the new music on 52nd Street. Allen Tinney was overseas and wasn't aware of the state of the developing art he had been so involved with before he was called to arms.

❖❖

TERRY GIBBS   Now the band I was in in Texas—I lucked out, and I was about ready to go overseas, I got all my shots, and I was with the Eighth Army Division, got everything. All of a sudden, you don't know what's happening. I got put on a train and went to Dallas. I was in Louisiana. They sent me to Dallas, and all of a sudden I found myself auditioning with a hundred other percussion players, drummers mostly, for a band they were putting together to make Army music, music for Army pictures. These were some good players. A guy, George Barati, the cello player who wound up conducting the Honolulu symphony, was one of the guys. I wound up in that band, and all we did was work two days a week, recording, and then five days off. So when I heard the music [Parker and Gillespie], and I came back, I showed it to some of the jazz players and about four of the guys, we used to get together. In fact, I wrote some tunes those days. We had a little group. And we'd play these tunes, these bebop tunes, with trumpet, tenor, and vibes. The rest of the guys, they were lazy. They would say, "What is that crap? What are you guys playin'? All that noise." Except George Barati would come over to me, and he'd say, "Listen,"—he had a Hungarian accent—he'd say, "You don't listen to them. You experiment. You play." He liked what we were doing. He was a little older than us. We were like eighteen or nineteen, he was thirty-five. And of all the guys he encouraged the shit out of us. Especially me 'cause I came back with what I heard. They'd never even heard it. No records. So about four or five out of the forty guys liked what we were doing. The other guys said, "Stop that shit. Get out!"

ALLEN TINNEY   I was coming up during the record ban, I have no proof that I ever existed even. But when I went into the Army I didn't go into music. In fact I demanded a gun. I thought if somebody is going to be shooting at me you'd better give me a rifle. So I more or less didn't get into the entertainment until the end, practically on my way to being discharged and then I went into a band. The 201st AGF band. Army Ground Forces Band. I re-upped for a short period of time. I said I'd better get my chops together. I was in Nuremburg, Germany, where the war trials were held. When I returned, I should have been surprised but I really wasn't because I had heard that the guys were doing great. But after I heard of the reputations, I didn't really want to be associated with that element because I wasn't into getting high. I was into playing. So I would more or less play with commercial groups, and I became more or less a commercial pianist. I think I had more Carmen Cavallaro records home than any other jazz pianist. I loved him, especially when I heard the soundtrack of the *Eddie Duchin Story* when he played "Brazil." That was about '46. In fact, I was in the Army with the owner of Minton's Playhouse, Teddy Hill, and we got together and we talked while we were in the Army, and after I came out of the Army I went to his place. But Minton's wasn't around when I was, earlier.

❖ ❖

Monroe's had preceded Minton's, but Teddy Hill's place was to have a much longer life. The Uptown House, under Monroe, lasted from 1936 to 1943. Then Clark, known to his friends as "The Dark Gable," moved downtown that year to run the Spotlite on 52nd Street.

❖ ❖

ALLEN TINNEY   I didn't bother with downtown. I decided that I wanted music but I didn't really want the elements that went into it.

❖ ❖

Tinney was atypical of the post-war musician. By 1945 52nd Street had become the center for the new music.

« 4 »

Fifty-Second Street

In September 1943 Dizzy Gillespie left Earl Hines. Oscar Pettiford, who had been with Charlie Barnet from January, left that
band in May. Gillespie played with Coleman Hawkins; and, for
three weeks in October, with Duke Ellington at the Capitol theatre on Broadway. Pettiford worked with Thelonious Monk at
Minton's for four months before moving down to 52nd Street's
Onyx Club with Roy Eldridge. Then Gillespie and Pettiford got
together as coleaders of what is generally acknowledged to be the
first group to formally present bebop to the general public.

❖❖

AL COHN I didn't get on the scene till I was really aware of what was happening outside of what you heard on records and stage shows. I didn't
hit it until about '44 when I met hipper musicians and started listening. I had heard Lester Young and Roy Eldridge and all the guys who
were popular, but I didn't get to really see the scene till about '44. To
hear the guys on the Street was another thing, and when I finally arrived on the Street, I guess it was the last few years. It was the few
years before that that I didn't know too much about. When I got there,
that's when Dizzy had the band with Oscar Pettiford, Don Byas. And
then Budd Johnson was on there for a while. Then there was a band
with Don and Coleman Hawkins, Benny Harris and Monk. As a matter of fact I played in the only square club on the Street for a while
which was called the 51 Club. It was opposite from the Three Deuces—
the same side of the street as the Onyx Club. And they just had a little
trio. Bob Baron was the leader, and piano players, there was revolving
piano players in and out, and tenor. We played for a couple of singers. I don't know what that club was doing there. But it was straight
. . . just a corny club. I played there a few months. And one of the
piano players was Al Haig. Before he got to play with Dizzy and Bird.
He was still in the Coast Guard, I believe. Apple cheeks. Clean-cut
young fellow. I guess he sounded like Teddy Wilson. I don't remember too well. We didn't get a chance to play a lot down there. We just
played the shows, 'cause they had dancing. But it was great 'cause I
was right on the scene there, and between sets I could go to hear all

these guys. I got to hang out on the Street a little more after that. Got to know some of the guys. I was young enough to be flexible. It wasn't the thing that it hit me over the head because it was something new. It was something new but it wasn't a dramatic thing like it was for older guys that couldn't bend with it.

BUDD JOHNSON   When I did come to New York to settle down in 1942, I joined Diz, Oscar Pettiford, Max Roach, and all those men at the Onyx Club. We really started to get into it, getting down arrangements, head arrangements, and recordings and all of that. So that's what I did. That's when it started. The Street made everybody aware of this new music. Dizzy was the theoretician to this music to my way of thinking and my knowledge, and he *was* really. It was lots and lots of fun. But some guys it didn't really influence too much—a lot of guys like Don Byas and Lucky [Thompson] and all of 'em. They stayed more in the Hawk thing, but they got the swiftness and the changes but they didn't necessarily sound in the exact style.

Dizzy tried to hum everything; he had to hum everything to everybody to get them to see what he was still talkin' about. It would be hard to explain it. It could be notated, but it was very hard to read, because cats weren't used to reading—he would be writing in double time, but the rhythm would be going [sings rhythm], so you gotta feel a double time feel against "one, two, three, four," say, and then, therefore, you're looking at sixteenth notes and sixteenth rests and thirty-second rests and all of that thing—which the cats were not used to doing—you have to kinda say, "Hey, wait a minute, let me . . ." then you gotta get the melodic structure of it, and once you heard how it goes, you say, "Oh." So he would sing [imitates Diz], and actually, that's how I think it got its name, bebop. Because he would be humming this music, and he'd say, "Ooop bop ta oop a la doo bop doo ba." So people said, "Play some more of that bebop" because he would be saying, "Bebop." And the cats would say, "Sing some more of that bebop," and actually, I think that's how it got its name, because that's the way he would have to sing it to make you get the feeling that he wanted you to play with.

I put down a lot of things for Oscar Pettiford. Actually, what they call "One Bass Hit" that was Oscar's tune. He called it "For Bass Faces Only." It's absolutely his tune, and he was the first one to play it. Oscar Pettiford contributed much to this music. Most all of those tunes that we played on 52nd Street when I worked with Diz, damned near half of them were Oscar's tunes. He was writing tunes every day. "Hey, Budd. Put this down. Put this down. Put this down." 'Cause he couldn't notate it on paper, so a lot of that happened that way. A lot of that happened with Monk. I used to put down things for Monk. That was back in the 52nd Street days. In fact, me and Monk used to hang out. We'd get a bottle of wine. I'd go over to his mother's house where he was livin' over on the West Side. I would put down things for him. Sometime he would come to my house. I was livin' on 152nd Street then. Oh, he was beautiful. He was a little bitter, because everybody was sorta getting credit, and actually I really heard Monk doin' this stuff before anybody. I don't think anybody else had the tunes. I really would put Monk before Diz from my knowledge. Of course, I wasn't in New York.

ALLEN TINNEY   When I came out of the Army, I was very hurt because Charlie Parker had become famous, Dizzy had become famous, Max had become famous, and I said to myself, "What happened to Monk?" because we were playing a lot of Monk's tunes. We used to go to an after-hours place; this was an apartment. After Monroe's would close down we would all go to this guy's apartment called Mat Maddox. This would be about nine or ten in the morning. And we'd be there until twelve or one in the afternoon playing in a little room that had a piano in it, and there was Monk, myself, and—who else now—well, Victor Coulson and George Treadwell were always there.

❖ ❖

It has been said that Monk wrote "Round Midnight" about 1939. And a lot of the tunes that he recorded much later were written in the early '40s, but nobody heard them on record.

❖ ❖

IDREES SULIEMAN   There's a funny story about "Eronel".

I wrote the first sixteen bars but I wrote it [sings]. I didn't have a middle, so Sadik Hakim put a middle on it. I played it for Miles, and he didn't like it, didn't like the middle, but we said, "No, we're keeping that."

So I took it to Monk, and Monk said [sings, changing one note]—made a mistake. I said, "That's the wrong note but play it again. Leave that note in. We'll do the writers' credits three ways."

And Monk recorded it five times and never mentioned our names at all. I saw Monk in Copenhagen and told him: "Why don't you make a statement and tell them how it really happened." See, Sadik was in love with a girl named Lenore, and he was going to name it after her, but he said, "No, that would be too way out." So we spelled the name backwards.

And Monk wrote so many tunes, so much *better,* so I can't understand why he wouldn't say it like it is. But he took the whole credit. That wasn't fair.

BUDD JOHNSON   'Cause Monk and this little guy Vic [Coulson] that used to play the trumpet were playing in that vein of Monk's. He said, "That's all right" He says, "I'm gonna let them have this, and I'm gonna find me something else." And so we used to drink this wine, and he would say "Dig this. How does this sound to you?" And he would be playing the stuff like he's playing now; he was getting on to it. I say, "Hey, that's cash." He say, "I'm gonna let them have that, and I'm gonna write me something else." But he had little tunes. You couldn't even play that style unless you played Monk's tunes because they had the chord progressions, and everybody would get with Monk and say, "Listen, what on earth are you doing here?" You'd get with the piano, and you'd try to find out the changes so you could play correctly. Then, after you got the changes, then you'd try to play maybe like a Diz. 'Cause if you learn the correct progressions, the modern progressions that they were playin' at that time, then you could play on that style. Especially if you had some good rhythm patterns of your own, it would fit, because you played the correct changes, and you got a set in the right amount of time to get it out. In other words, instead of playin' like C, C, C, C, F, you had two bars of C there. Well these cats didn't do that. In those two bars they would probably have but maybe four, six, or eight different changes. And if you were playing all of these four to six to eight different changes correctly, then you would be playing modern, because they would be the modern changes. Now all you got to do is to let a little bit of the influence, like they put a little triplets. The few little triplets or grace notes in there. And you would be playin' sort of on the style.

Instead of playin' like an eighth note triplet, which is one beat, it became an eighth note and three sixteenth notes.

Instead of saying,

you say

Instead of sayin' [sings], you say [sings]. It's just a matter of concept.

I don't think it comes from any one man, because without that rhythmic concept, and without the bass rhythms and changes, I don't think you would be able to play it because that's what Dizzy used to tell me: "If I could just get somebody to play these chords, then I could be free to play this way." And it goes a little deeper than that. You could have a great group and lose that drummer, and that group will never sound the same. So it shows you how important your drum is, 'cause he's bringing out the best in you. You feel the pulsation in what he's feeding you. And he's listening to you, and he's fitting in his style plus playing for you and with you. This just makes the whole thing. It makes you more creative. It makes him more creative. So things just start to blossom. And I think everybody—every instrument player, drummer, bass, piano, everything—helped to bring that style about, that transition. Because naturally the piano players caught on to it first and faster because they had the keyboard.

❖❖

Shortly after the debut of the Gillespie-Pettiford unit, a recording was put together on February 16, 1944, that was the first formal statement of the new music on record. The leader and featured soloist of the date was Coleman Hawkins. Budd Johnson and Clyde Hart co-authored "Bu-Dee-Daht," the piece that later made Daniel Bloom rave to us in front of Columbia Grammar School, and "Disorder at the Border"; and Dizzy contributed a milestone with his composition "Woody'n You."

❖❖

BUDD JOHNSON   When Hawk came back from Europe, he was up and down the Street, and when he heard the new music, he liked it. So Hawk said, "I'm gonna surround myself with some of the cats that are playin' it, and we're gonna make a record date." And he asked me and Clyde [Hart] to make this arrangement. We had been workin' together. And Diz. He asked Diz to make "Woody'n You." Hawk did the arrangement on "Rainbow Mist," which was "Body and Soul." He did that. And he wanted to be surrounded with the new sounds. He made that the statement. He said, "I want to see what these cats are doin'. And what better way to do it than to get them together on a record date, have them to put some of their ideas down and I'll do some of my things." And that's how it came about. Because I went by Hawk's house. I used to live just around the corner from Hawk, when he was getting this together. I don't know whether a lot of people realize that or not but he fell in love with Monk. 'Cause Hawk felt that's where it was. When he heard that playin', that piano playin' that stuff with the *changes*, he said, "This is where it is" [sings snatch of Monk's "Lady Be Good" riff*]. Hawk dug that. He said, "Well, I want that man for a piano player." He would pick up on a million things that were happening. 'Cause Hawk was always Hawk, whether it was new or not.

❖❖

Hawkins always had a very sophisticated harmonic conception. There were also others whose harmonic acumen made them receptive to the new ideas.

❖❖

BUDD JOHNSON   You know who else a little of it rubbed off on? Benny Carter. I can hear a little bit of it. Every once in a while he gets into it. You want to move along with the times. You don't want to stay in the same rut all the time. And this is what I'm tryin' to tell the kids. Sure, rock is fine. But there's some other music besides that. Listen to some of the other things. Like when we came along we listened to all kinds of music, classics, everything. If fact we had to because we had

---

*Hawkins recorded it as "Rifftide," and Monk later did it as "Hackensack," but it had its origin on a Mary Lou Williams session for Asch that included Hawkins.

the music appreciation classes in school. Then they say this is borrowed from the classics. This type of music. The sounds.

❖❖

"Woody'n You," according to Gillespie, evolved from chord progressions he had been playing for a long time. During a Coke break he was playing the piano, and the tune "popped out." He named it for Woody Herman because Herman had liked and encouraged his writing. Woody never recorded it. When Dizzy's big band did in 1947, it was called "Algo Bueno" but it is still best known by the original title.

❖❖

DIZZY GILLESPIE   "Woody'n You" came from a minor sixth chord to the dominant seventh. That's one influence of Monk. B-flat-minor sixth with a sixth as the bass to a C. A-flat-minor sixth with the sixth the bass to B-flat. It's a natural progression in fourths. From G to C is one fourth. You jump down to F, which is a fifth from C, to another fourth and then jump down a fifth to another fourth, and then the tonic, which is D-flat. And that's the key you're in.

Looking at the notes in my right hand, I discovered a counter-melody. There were two melodies in it—a melody, and a counter-melody. That's how I wrote "Woody'n You." I didn't try to express anything particular, just music, just what the chords inspired.

❖❖

Gillespie had wanted Charlie Parker for that group with Pettiford, but Bird was at home in Kansas City and later told Dizzy that he never received the telegram that had been sent requesting his presence in New York.

Bud Powell was supposed to be the pianist, but he was working with Cootie Williams at the time. Williams was legal guardian for the underage Powell and wouldn't let him go. Before George Wallington filled the piano spot, Billy Taylor was doubling between his regular job with Ben Webster at the Three Deuces and Gillespie-Pettiford at the Onyx.

❖❖

BILLY TAYLOR   That's how I lost my job with Ben, but I played with Dizzy, and he taught me many of the early bebop tunes, like the tune "Bebop"; "Night in Tunisia"; "'Round Midnight"—and some of those early ones. He just sat down at the piano and said, "These are the changes," and some of the things he had written outlines on like "Salt Peanuts," and things like that—the simpler things. But Dizzy preferred to show a piano player because he wanted certain voicings on the piano, and he said that if he wrote just C 6th, that may or may not have a ninth in it which he wanted in that particular case. And so, he would say, "This is the voicing that I like and that just does this." And much of it—much of his voicings, I'm sure—were influenced by Clyde Hart, who was out of the Tatum-Wilson school and who was a part of the newer thing coming in harmonically.

The first thing that impressed me was that the tempos were un-godly. I mean Oscar Pettiford and Max Roach were two of the strong-est rhythm players I'd ever played with at that time, and Max still is. Oscar would get annoyed if we played "Bebop" [sings introduction very rapidly]—if we played in that tempo and didn't give him a solo—now, most bass players they'd say, "Well, look, man, I've been playin' four behind you guys all these choruses. Let the drummer take it." But he said, "Look, you played on it. I'll play on it, too." Until he broke his arm, playing ball with Woody Herman, he really had just unbelievable strength in terms of playing tempos and playing tremendously fast passages on the bass violin. But everything he did, fast, slow, medium, whatever, had the extension of what Blanton did. Blanton had started this melodic approach, which was perhaps more closely related to Charlie Christian and earlier players, but Pettiford's work was plugged right into Dizzy and Bird. That's right where he was coming from; the same kind of drive, the same kind of melodic impetus that stemmed from that rhythmic security.

TRUMMY YOUNG On 52nd Street I remember getting into several fights trying to help Oscar Pettiford because it seemed like he had a nose for trouble, and guys used to look for him that weren't musicians, and I got beat up two or three times, fooling with Oscar and trying to help him. And once a bunch of sailors were going to beat him up, and Dizzy and I both got beat up trying to help him on this occasion. On the subway. Oh, Lord. I can tell you so many strange things that hap-pened. So we started watching Oscar more carefully. We'd tell him, "No. Wait in the car." We wouldn't let him run right out after work, because he would always get into something.

❖❖

Before Gillespie was to really settle in on 52nd Street, he became an important part of the newly formed Billy Eckstine orchestra. Gillespie and Pettiford had had a falling out, and while Oscar re-mained at the Onyx (with Joe Guy on trumpet and Johnny Hartz-field on tenor), Dizzy moved across the street to the Yacht Club with Budd Johnson in tow. On the same show with them was their old colleague from the Earl Hines band, Billy Eckstine, billed as X-tine, thanks to his booking agent Billy Shaw.

Eckstine's, or X-tine's, career was not exactly roaring along. It was decided that he head a big band but, at first, he and Shaw argued about the basic philosophy. Eckstine was committed to the new sounds and convinced Shaw he wanted Gillespie as his mu-sical director and Charlie Parker, working at the time with Car-roll Dickerson at the Rhumboogie in Chicago, as the leader of his reeds. In June 1944 the Billy Eckstine band was born.

❖❖

BILLY ECKSTINE It was a whole evolvement of something new, aside from the trite ways of doing things. When I started my band we got bad,

bad reports on it. Even the William Morris office, they said, "Why don't you just get a band like in the vein of the Basie band and with good vocals of yourself, and you just sell the band on your vocals and things like that." But they didn't stop to realize that I was already hooked into this thing. If you look at some of the early *downbeat* write-ups, Christ, they used to pan hell out of me. They said I kept singing, I was running all over the place and wouldn't sing the melodies, which was just a way of seeking at that particular point—you're hearing things also. Now when we all got together, when the different guys got together, I saw the reason why I wanted to sing—well, now we call it "changes" and because it was new usage.

When we recorded "Cottage for Sale" I ended it on major seventh. We had a guy in the control room named Emile Côté, who was a head of the Pet Milk Singers, as the A&R [laughs] man. When I hit that, he came out and said, "Well, I think we got a good balance on that. Now shall we go back in and do the thing?" I said, "Hey, that was it." "Oh, you're not going to end that on that note." I said, "Well, why not, it's a major seventh." Then he gave me the old cliché about Beethoven or somebody giving a lesson and a kid hit the major seventh and then left, walked off, and he had to run downstairs and resolve it. Well, I said, "I ain't gonna resolve it." Those kind of things during that era, and getting to what you've seen, it was a feeling among a nucleus at that time of younger people, of hearing something else. We didn't knock. You see that's the other thing that was so funny about the guys then. You couldn't find one guy, you take Dizzy, Bird, any of the guys that were in my original band, we never knocked nobody else's music.

My God, my band, when I started, the guy that gave me my music to get started was Basie. I went over here to the Hotel Lincoln and walked in there with Basie, and he said, "I understand you're gonna start a band," and I said, "Yeah, man, I ain't got no music." So he turns around to Henry Snodgrass and told him, "Give him the key." I went back in the back in the music trunk and just took scores of Basie's music to help me be able to play a dance. We didn't have any music. The only things that we had in our vein of things was "A Night in Tunisia" that Diz had written. As we kept doing these one-nighters, we were constantly writing. "Blue 'n Boogie" was a head arrangement. We were constantly just sitting down everywhere we'd go and have a rehearsal and putting things together on these kind of things. Little head arrangements and riffs that Diz started or Bird started. "Good Jelly Blues" and "I Stay In The Mood For You"—Budd Johnson wrote that on the same type of a thing. And the little things I wrote—"I Love The Rhythm In A Riff" and "Blowing The Blues Away," they were just more or less—we were gradually getting our music together, but when we started out we didn't knock anybody's music like that. My God, I don't think there was a time that we ever were anywhere where another band was that all our band, if we were off, was not right there listening to them. It wasn't a knock, of putting their music down in preference for ours. It was just another step, it was another step beyond. I guess, possibly the same thing happened back when Louie took his step past King Oliver, maybe, who knows. I wasn't around to pay any attention to music then, but possibly the same type of thing happened then.

Then another very important thing, too. Our music was more studied. Up until that point, you didn't have the musicianship, other than Ellington, Lunceford, like that, where you had some great schooled musicians up there on that stand. But a lot of the other bands, there were a lot of guys who couldn't read a note, even some of the first Basie band that came East. It was a head-arrangement band. When here we came on, in my band and in Earl's band, all musicians, seasoned musicians. But when we came along these were all new usages of chords, new voicings, the arrangers were hearing things, began to write. And another thing that happened, my band ruined a whole lot of musicians who had been bullshitting before. But everywhere we would go with my band, after it was together about two months, we'd look out into the audience, and the young, the real young, was out there going, "Yeah, man." It was hitting that young; it was the music of the young really, and because the young, a lot of them, were in the war in Europe, the widespread popularity never was acquired, never was achieved.

I'll never forget, though, we used to have more problems with the powers that be, the agents. Christ, that's where I had the problem. They wanted me to sing, and play "One O'Clock Jump"; the things that were famous or something of Glenn Miller's or something of Tommy Dorsey's; in other words, let the band copy other successful things and you sing. That wasn't my idea of what I wanted to do. Shit, if I wanted to do that I could have gone with—'cause after I left Earl and went back to 52nd Street, I started getting calls from certain bands, different bands like Kenton. They wanted me to come in the band as a vocalist, but I wouldn't go because I said, "Hell, if I'm gonna break up my own band, what am I gonna go with somebody else for when I couldn't make my own successful? And here's some guys who are gonna try more or less to copy what we're starting, and I'm gonna go with them? No way!"

So it was always a fight, a fight, man. Christ almighty, I'll never forget, they came down to the Riviera in St. Louis. And I was working in there with my band, and the William Morris office sent some schmuck down there to do a report on the band. He came back and said, "There's no love vein in the band." Imagine this guy gonna go dig a swinging band: "there's no love vein in the band." So when Billy Shaw, God rest his soul, whom I loved, when Billy called me—Billy believed in me—and he said, "Hey B, we're getting rapped, and this guy come back here sayin' 'There's no love vein in the band.' " I said, "Well, shit, he didn't check into it. Now me and Dizzy been goin' together for years. There's the love vein" [laughter].

Well you know what he told me to do: "Well, why don't you get a real pretty girl, with a big ass, to sing?" Didn't listen to Sass [Sarah Vaughan]. He's gonna tell me about some chick with a big ass, and here's a girl with the greatest voice that I've ever heard. He never even heard that. Well, that's the kinda shit you went through in those days and on. Man, it just got to the point—I think it discouraged a lot of people. It even carried on over into Diz's band, so Diz's band wasn't successful.

It was musically successful. So was mine. Now it's the "legendary Billy Eckstine band," and some of these same guys that are now calling it a legend rapped the shit out of me. Leonard Feather, he rapped the shit out of me. Every time we'd come in, "the band was out of tune," and the this and the that, and now it's the "legendary Billy Eckstine band."

I don't want this to appear racist, but nevertheless, it's factual. Anything that the black man originates that cannot be copied right away by his white contemporaries is stepped on. It was copied. Shit, Woody Herman, get a load of his things—"Northwest Passage." All those things were nothing but a little *bit* of the music that we were trying to play. All of those things. All they did was that. Shit, but they got the *down beat* number one band, yap, yap, yap, all of this kind of shit, but Woody better not have lit nowhere near where my band was. Nowhere. And I can say it now because it's all over and I don't have to appear egotistical, but he better not have lit anywhere where we were. And that goes for any of them, because let me show you, we would play, and the guys that were in that band will tell you one thing; we played against Jimmie Lunceford at the Brooklyn Armory. Jimmie Lunceford, big star of the thing, and we were the second band. We ate his ass up like it was something good to eat, so much to the point—I'll never forget this, Freddie Webster, God rest his soul, was with Lunceford at the time, and Freddie wrote a letter to a buddy of ours in California, and all he wrote on the letter was, "Did you hear about the battle of jazz?" He says, "Billy Eckstine," no, "B and his band, life; Jimmie Lunceford," in very small letters, "Jimmie Lunceford and us, death" [Laughter]. That's what he wrote on this thing.

Musicians—that's the other thing—young musicians would be around us like this all the time listening, and they *knew* what we were trying to do. Arrangers started hearing. The technical aspect of the music was grasped first. People who knew something about music right away said, "Hey, this is something else." It's the moldy guys that relied so much on their ear. They didn't have the ear to follow this—it's the same as this Emile Côté that heard this major seventh, he didn't hear that thing resolved where he was waiting for it to resolve. And when I said, "Here's a cottage for sale," and he didn't hear that [sings]. He didn't hear that. All he heard was "da" and he was waiting for "daa."*

*The conventional ending would be the tonic. Eckstine, like many instrumentalists of the time, ended a half step below the tonic.

That's what he's waiting for. His ear had been indoctrinated into that type of listening. But arrangers jumped on this. You'd be surprised, you know how many free arrangements I used to get? Every town I'd go into, some little young musician who's studying would bring me up an arrangement to play. He is voicing it off of the new voicings, the new thing; nine out of ten of them you couldn't use, but you could see the seeking, trying to, hearing this kind of music which used to inspire us.

And again to get back to the love thing, Diz and Sonny [Stitt], all the different guys will tell you this, that was in the band. We used to get in a town and, man, it was like the bus getting in at twelve o'clock—I wouldn't call rehearsal. The guys would go on to the hall, set up, jam, or Bird would take the reed section, sit and run through things. Just at night, the Booker Washington Hotel, there in St. Louis for Christ sake, when we was working the Riviera, the people used to move out, we'd rehearse four o'clock in the morning. Sit right in the room; the reed section would be there blowing all night. It was a love where everybody was seeking things like that, trying and learning. Sass and myself used to learn things on the piano. I'll never forget, Diz wrote an arrangement of "East of the Sun" for Sass. We worked out the ending of it [sings]. We'd work out things vocally, because every aspect of music could fit into this. There was a way to do it vocally; there was a way we heard it vocally; a way it was done instrumentally; the way it was done rhythmically: everything had a new concept to it. It wasn't just one trumpet player playing his style which was an innovative thing. Or one saxophone. There was a collective unit of the whole concept. It was the camaraderie in that band. Me and Diz, the other night at the concert,* we were breaking up laughing at different little things that we used to do in the band. We still have big laughs, any time we get together—like the other night, Sonny and all of us were up there, and I swear to Christ that you would have thought that some great comic was in. We were breaking up in there laughing, remembering incidents that happened, which then were morbid. Riding these Goddamn Jim Crow cars through the South were these dirty cracker conductors, we all sitting in the aisles and all of this bullshit, in a little car that's got eight seats, and here we getting on there with twenty guys and no room. And now we just sit laughing about it. The different incidents where a guy would say, "Hey, ain't no more room. You all sleep, stay in the baggage car," and we get back in the baggage car and open all the doors, get undressed and lay back there in the baggage car, smelling the hay and shit, traveling. But we can sit back and laugh about these kind of things now. You had to then. You'd have never gotten through it. We said the same statement the other night, Diz and I. You had to make your own fun. You *had* to make it, 'cause,

*Newport Festival Tribute to Charlie Parker in 1974.

Christ almighty, this was during the war. We couldn't get a bus because you couldn't get priority then for gasoline. So the only way, Billy Shaw worked some strings—this was '44—where if I would play for the troops, whenever I would get into the town—if there was an Army camp there—go right out and do a free show for the troops, then they would give me a priority for a bus. But I had to do a certain amount of them every week. Now, if I happened to be booked in such a place where there ain't no Army camps where we are, they look and see that I don't play no Army, they snatched the bus without even telling me. We go out one morning to get the bus, there ain't no bus. Now we got to run and grab all of this crap, look at the train schedule—and there was always an hour, and hour and one-half late, these trains in those days. You know, the troops and things. Jumping on you is the guys with their bass and amplifiers, for the book, and valets getting on these trains with this and what are you gonna do. If you can survive through that, man, you gotta make your own humor. I'm telling you, boy. And arguments, fights with soldiers and these crackers down South, and man you'd get in fights with them all the time. It drove me crazy.

And the guys still stuck it out, 'cause we'd get on the stand at night, regardless of what problem we had during the day, there's our chance to let it out. And, baby, some of the times when we've had the worst problems during the day, we'd get on the stand at night and, man, you never heard a band play like that in your life. We'd be wailing, because now's our chance to relax and do what we want to do. We were just waiting to get to that stand.

❖ ❖

There were numbers in the Eckstine book that were strictly instrumental, but there were other numbers where a blues was concocted in order to give the soloists other opportunities.

❖ ❖

BILLY ECKSTINE   I had to write some little dumb blues—dumb lyric, in order to let the band play, like "Blowing the Blues Away." I just wrote two choruses of the blues, so I can let Gene [Ammons] and Dex [Gordon] blow. "Lonesome Lover" and things like that and all of those things were just written because in those days the philosophy of this small company was, "Hey, if a man puts a nickel in the jukebox for Billy Eckstine, and he don't hear no singin', he thinks he's got the wrong record." Beautiful thinkin'. So I had to do it that way. I've had things that used to crack me up. For instance, we played at the Club Sudan that's up at 142nd and Lenox Avenue. So we used to get seasoned names like instrumentalists, trumpet players, saxophone players, and would come up and sit in and when you'd get up to take solos, you never heard anything sound that old. I mean good musicians, good players in their respective bands, and I'm going so far as the guys on Ellington's band, who used to sit in with us, like Ray Nance, and man, it didn't sound anything. It just didn't fit. Then you'd realize what a decided change in music that was, and as great as they were, it wasn't the fact that they'd *had* it, but the sound and everything that went along didn't fit; it didn't jell.

Do you know that when Art, Art Blakey, first joined us at The Plantation in St. Louis, the first night when Diz was up playing, and Art started playing shuffle and Diz stopped right in the middle of what he's been and, man, we jumped right in and said, "Man, don't play that shit, don't ever play no shuffle." And Diz was the one who started showing Art.

ART BLAKEY   I came in the band and was doing some funny stuff on the drums, trying to play shuffle rhythms, I thought. And he stopped me right in the middle of it. The band was still playing, and people were still on the floor dancing. "Blakey, what are you doing?" he said. "I don't know," I said. "Then why do you do it? If we had wanted a shuffle here, we'd hire Cozy Cole. We want you to play your drums the way *you* play them."

KENNY CLARKE   He is a drummer with a solid basis. Nobody can fill up a hole like Art Blakey. He can put more rhythm into two bars than anyone. That's difficult to do, and that's his major trump.

❖❖

Circumstances dictated that Eckstine join the instrumentalists.

❖❖

BILLY ECKSTINE   It was a funny thing, it was a lot of all different innovations that happened then. Like on the trombones. My trombonists at first were very weak. I didn't have a good trombone section. So that's why I started playing valve trombone, to play the solo on "A Night in Tunisia" because the trombone player couldn't make that D.

CHARLIE ROUSE   The first time I left Washington was to join Billy Eckstine's band. That was in the '40s. I'd say '44. Billy sent a telegram telling me they're meeting in San Antonio, Texas, and I thought he meant St. Louis, and I went straight to St. Louis [Laughter]. I replaced Tommy Crump, who used to play tenor with Earl Hines. When I was with Billy's band it was Art Blakey, Charlie Parker, Dizzy Gillespie; the early part of the band. Lucky Thompson. It was in the first part of the band. Oh, man, that was [laughter]—well, actually it scared me to death because I'd just come out of Washington and I came out of school. I graduated in '43 from Armstrong High. That's when John Malachi and Tommy Potter, they left. They broke up the band at the Crystal Caverns and went with Billy, and that's when Crump left the band during the time of the war and went into the Army. When we were playing one-nighters, and it was somewhere in the South, we left the music at the previous job we played, in another section of the state we were in. I don't know what state it was. Anyway, when we got to the gig that night we found that we had left the music. So we had to play the whole dance without the music. And Bird was playing first and Diz, and it seemed like—Billy had a big book—and don't know whether they did or not, but, to me, man, they played everything. Everything just came down, and I was scuffling, and I knew there were other cats in the band that were scuffling, but they, Dizzy and Bird, they held it right together. And Fats [Navarro] was in the band too, at the time. I remember some, how you say, dynamic nights, nights where people didn't know what they were doing or playing, but it got so, the whole—everybody was moving together. It had such a pulsation going on.

You looked forward to getting on the bandstand every night. In fact, to wake up in the daytime, 'cause usually when you wake up you go to someone else's room and they're playing. 'Cause Bird used to always, like on the grass—sit down and play. And cats around and Dizzy's clapping, or Diz is playing with him. It was like an institution sort of. Every day was like that.

BUDD JOHNSON   In 1945 we went to California. Los Angeles. And we worked in a place called the Club Plantation. We had Sarah Vaughan in the band, and Billie Holiday was part of the show. Sarah was singin' so much at that time that Billie Holiday tried to stop—tell Billy Eckstine to stop her from singing because she wanted to be the only singer in the house. Sassy was makin' it very hard for her. That was an outstanding thing. I got a big kick out of that. And another time we made the V-Disc* with Lena Horne and Sassy. I liked the band because it was kind of wild, and you were tryin' to play this new music and doing a pretty good job of it. He had a good book. And he had some great cats. The only cats that really gave him a lot of trouble was the reed section.

❖❖

Parker had left for the environs of the Street by this time, and the reed section was made up of Gene Ammons and those dubbed "The Unholy Four"—Sonny Stitt, John Jackson, Dexter Gordon, and Leo Parker.

❖❖

BUDD JOHNSON   That's why I was sent out there. Billy Shaw sent me out there to see if I could whip this band in line and make these cats make time because they were missing trains and missing gigs. The reed section, most of them, were strung out. And that's really the main reason I went out to join the band. And to get them to rehearse and improve generally. So I did a pretty good job when I went out there. And I was making a good salary whether I worked or not. Well, finally, coming back, we went into Baltimore, and after our engagement in Balti-

*Victory Discs: recordings made during the war for the Armed Forces.

more we went out to a party—me and the trombone player, Albert Outcalt, "Chippy." And we getting high. Ernie Fields was with us, by the way. We were having fun talkin' and drinking, and I heard something going on, and I looked around and Chippy had a pistol, tryin' to blow this girl's brains out 'cause she had said something. I forget whether she said something about Billy or something. So I conned Chippy out of the pistol. While I'm conning him out of the pistol, the chick ran downstairs and got the police. So when the police came into the room, I got the gun in my hand, right? I had sneaked out of the room and started down the stairs, and here comes an old guy policeman with a badge. He says, "Halt!" I say, "I got a gun, officer. Don't shoot." And they took us all to jail. So the girl told the cops that it wasn't me. But they didn't go for that. They had me anyway. So we had to pay this fine and everything. Get a lawyer. Get out, and Billy then was pretty peeved about that, so we sort of parted the ways then. That's when I left the band. Oh, we had a lot of fun.

DEXTER GORDON   There was a first-year anniversary of the band, and we were in South Carolina, and there was some special guy that booked this route, which was like Virginia, West Virginia, Carolina; he had this sewed up. So we were playing in this town—I think it was one of the big tobacco warehouses—and the band had enough rehearsal, so for some reason everybody got drunk—was out. So the guy saw that half the band was playing and the other half was out on the floor dancing with the chicks, and then they'd switch. This went on, and the promoter wigged. He said, "Goddamn, what kind of fuckin' band is this? You guys are screwy. You'll never work for me again."

There was no discipline on the stand at all. In fact Connie Wainwright, the guitar player, packed up and said, "Oh, fuck it." Halfway through, he went on home. On that particular night, too, after we left the hall, we were going back to the hotel—who was it? I think it was Leo Parker. Yeah, we waved down a cab or we walked to a cabstand. It was a white cab driver, you know, and we started getting in the cab and so and so and so and so. And this cat said, "You niggers get the fuck out of here. I don't ride no niggers in my cab," or something like that. And all of a sudden, there was an arm and a knife around this cat's neck. The cab driver. Who had him? I can't remember who. I think it was "J. J.", John Jackson. Anyway, so he huffed and puffed, blah, blah, blah. He didn't hurt him much. But, so then we split. And I don't know, somehow, we split up; there was different groups gettin' back to the hotel. So finally we get back to the hotel, and about an hour later the manager of the hotel comes up and says, "Say, I just got a call from the police. Mr. Eckstine and four or five fellas in the band are down there in the jail for disorderly conduct or something. Where's the manager, where's he staying?" I said, "Well, he's staying downtown at a hotel. So what had happened was that this cab driver had gone to the police and said there's some wild niggers on the scene. They're musicians. They're out-of-towners and they put a knife on him and da da da. So then the police came out and just happened to run into B and Jug [Gene Ammons] and others.

But every night was musical. And there were a lot of colorful characters around the band. Redcross,* of course. Yeah, there were cats all over. "Ice," the cat from D.C. Yeah it was Ice and Red. They'd hang around the band, follow the band around. They were around there so much, they were just like the band, really. "Ice Freezes Red" by Fats [Navarro] was named for them.

❖❖

If the wartime materials used in the pressing of the records prevented the true quality of the Eckstine band from coming through, those who heard it in person, especially the young musicians, were fully aware of its capabilities.

❖❖

GERRY MULLIGAN   I'd been out of town with Tommy Tucker's band for a few months as an arranger. When I was with Tucker, we were in Chicago at the Stevens Hotel for about a month and a half. It was in '45— the end of '45. And of the bands that came through town at that point to Chicago, one was Billy Eckstine's band. Diz was playing with the band. I forget who else was there. But there were guys that I had heard of like Jerry Valentine, and this one and that one. So I had obviously been aware of Diz before this. Oh, sure. Gene Ammons and Dexter Gordon. They did "Blowin' the Blues Away." Oh yeah! Well, that's one of the reasons why my job with Tommy Tucker was shortlived. I signed a three-month contract with Tommy to write two jump or three ballad arrangements a week for a hundred dollars a week. On the road! And we were in Chicago and these bands would come through town and I'd go hear 'em all. Billy Eckstine's band's jumpin'. Then Earl Hines had a terrific band. And this band and that band and the next thing you know I'd run back to the Stevens Hotel and work on some charts— my charts kept gettin' wilder and wilder. So I wrote myself right out of a job [laugh]. Tommy was very sweet about it. Funny. He said, "Gerry, you know you're a young guy and terrific and I have the greatest confidence in you. If you ever want to go into any kind of business where I can ever be a help to you, you let me know. Except the band" [laugh]. "If you want to be a bandleader, forget it." If I wanted to go into business, see, he'd gladly invest money in me anytime.

BUDD JOHNSON   But I remember when Fats Navarro first heard Diz he said, "Oh, man, that's the way I want to play. That's where it is." Bennie Green and all those cats, "Man, that's it." Fats had been with Andy

---

*Bob Redcross, at that time Eckstine's valet.

Kirk, but then when he got with Billy Eckstine's band, that's when it really hit him and was doin' his best to get with it. Dizzy was in the band then. When Dizzy left the band, then I took over as musical director, but Fats stayed. They were in the band together. So all of that rubbed off on him there, and he was struggling with it until he really got it. And he played pretty good saxophone too.

I still think Dizzy rubbed off on him. They were all—'cause Dizzy might not have started it, but he was the one that mastered it, and everybody was tryin' to play like that. Had they been able to hear that sooner, they would have been into it sooner, I'm sure. But when some of the guys started to travel East, then they started to meet up with Diz and people like that and then started to listening to things. Bird had played it before 'cause he'd been to New York before. He was in New York before me.

DEXTER GORDON   I would say that Diz was like the schoolmaster.

BUDD JOHNSON   We used to hang around up at Dizzy's at 2040 7th Avenue, and all the musicians used to come up there. Dizzy was sort of like a school also, and he used to sit down at the piano, and of course, he was playing the modern changes. You'll find Dizzy plays pretty good little piano. Instead of saying C7 C7 C7 C7 C7, he would be going to the minor seventh—G-minor 7th chord and this—and he'd go up half [a step], and I'd say, "That's real pretty, man." He did a lot. He was actually Tadd Dameron's professor. He taught Tadd everything he knew about modern arranging. Tadd lived up there. 'Cause then especially when Dizzy had the band, Dizzy would have Tadd write. And Tadd would say, "Hey, Dizzy, is this the way it goes?" Dizzy say, "No, no, no move over there. That's the way I want the changes to go, like that." And then Tadd would do it on paper, put it down on paper. But you see Tadd got the credit for all that, but actually it was really Diz. Diz was really always writing it.

❖❖

In the pieces credited to Gillespie and Gil Fuller, the latter orchestrated Gillespie's ideas.

❖❖

BUDD JOHNSON   This man has always been a mystery to me, Gil Fuller. But I know that "Manteca" and all of that, that's Dizzy. All of that's Dizzy. But Fuller, he had some knowledge, but I never saw him really make an arrangement.

I remember when we were doing this movie *Sepia Cinderella*. This was a movie made with Billy Daniels, oh a whole bunch of cats. Gil Fuller had the band. I was in the band. This had to be like around '43, something like that. So he called me up, he said, "Hey, I'm writing a movie. You want to help me do some of the work?" I said, "Yeah, I'd be glad to. So he gave me a couple of things, and he gave Elton

Hill some things. And we did all of the writing of the movie. He didn't write one song in the movie, but now he's gonna take the credit for it. But he was a sharp operator, smooth operator. I had a hard time getting my bread from this cat. I don't mind it going on tape either.

❖❖

The formalized jam session was an idea that took hold during the '40s. Milt Gabler, the owner of the Commodore Music Shop and Commodore Records, moved his Sunday afternoon bashes from recording studio locales to Jimmy Ryan's on 52nd Street in 1938–1939. Before that Harry Lim had run them at the Panther Room of the Hotel Sherman in Chicago.

❖❖

JEAN BACH   I remember Harry Lim's sessions. 'Cause I was very friendly with Harry back in the '30s. We were chums. He came to Chicago from Amsterdam, 'cause the bombs started falling in Europe, and he figured he had to get the heck out so he was going to go back to Java, and on his way he stopped off in New York, and there was a party that was given for *Life*, "Life Goes to a Party"—remember they staged these things about every half-hour. Now the ratio of stuff getting into *Life* magazine in those days was a minimum of ten to one—against you. So you would get your picture taken and get all excited, and then it wouldn't be in. They took millions of this party, and he had everybody in the world. It was just a great party. All schools of music.

❖❖

In New York Lim, who was soon to have his own record label, Keynote, ran Monday-night sessions at the Village Vanguard. Monte Kay was presenting modern sessions at Nick's in the Village but soon moved them up to Kelly's Stable on 52nd Street. Gillespie played them all. In fact, when he was living in Philadelphia in 1942, he would take the train to New York just to play the Kelly's Stable Sunday sessions. His train fare was almost equal to what he got for playing.

❖❖

RED RODNEY   It was '44. I had left Jimmy Dorsey, and I got back and I heard Dizzy Gillespie. He was living in Philly then. Working at the Downbeat* and just getting together with Charlie Parker.

He was living in New York and Philly both. His wife was in New York, and his mother was in Philly. Dizzy was just getting back into the scene, and he had some chop trouble. He had no chops at that time. He soon got them shortly after, but as I remember saying, "Wow, if this guy ever got chops, he'd be good." I didn't understand him at all, and I thought Roy Eldridge was much better.

Roy Eldridge was someone who had been with Gene Krupa and was famous. He was great. I loved him, but he wasn't any influence on me,

---

*Nat Segall's Downbeat in Philadelphia as opposed to the Downbeat on 52nd Street.

not like Harry James was. When I came home and started sitting in at the Downbeat Club, it was 'cause it was jazz, then I got interested and this was, of course, the earliest part of my career. It was very early for the bop movement. And having Dizzy Gillespie there was a tremendous influence.

Then I met Howard McGhee. He came through and worked the Downbeat for quite some time, and he was an early influence. Howard started showing me things, teaching me things and how this went to that and how this is supposed to be like that. I was very impressed with Howard's ability, because he was a very fine trumpeter; aside from being a very good jazz player. Howard was a very big influence on me in those days. I met Dizzy first, but Howard was more instrumental because he was there longer and all the time. Then he left, and Dizzy came back, so I'd have to say Howard was influencing me in Dizzy's direction.

And then Dizzy kept telling me about Charlie Parker. One Sunday he brought me up to New York and 52nd Street. I heard Bird play, and I liked to flipped. That was it. I understood it immediately. Immediately. Except harmonically, which is the thing that came to me last.

I was impressed with their technical ability. The speed. Their tremendous facility in playing their instruments. Everything. Except their harmonic ability. That I didn't understand yet, that didn't come.

Howard showed me the conception. How the music was played and the chord progressions, but harmonically I was not ready for it.

❖ ❖

One of the things that musicians started to pay attention to were turnbacks, getting in and out of the bridge. People never used to approach those things before in quite that way.

❖ ❖

RED RODNEY   And Howard was, of course, a very good musician harmonically. He's a very underrated player. Always has been. Now there are certain things about his playing that perhaps differ from many of us, but still he knows what he's doing. The turnbacks were there. I didn't understand 2-5-1—simple as that—which is really the way a turnback went. And I used my ear, which got me through a good part of it, but you need more than just your ear. I could spell the chords. If someone asked me what the G 7th was, well I'd immediately be able to spell it for you. And I even knew that G 7th went into C and why. But it didn't really make that much of an impression on my *musical* playing until years later. But I came up with that scene.

❖ ❖

Gillespie continued to be more and more of a presence and a force on 52nd Street and, hence, the New York scene. At Kelly's Stable, Nat "King" Cole had shown him the changes to "How High the

Moon." Dizzy began playing it, and it became the anthem of 52nd Street and the boppers.

❖❖

MAX ROACH   Dizzy was really the catalyst of that period. He's the man who thought about bringing in Bird to New York and told us about Oscar Pettiford. And Bird was challenging at that time, these kind of things. But I think Dizzy was really the catalyst of that period. Not taking anything away from people like Thelonious Monk, who was probably, along with Dizzy, with the harmonics, one of the innovators of the period. Dizzy was much more outgoing, and he organized bringing people forward. And he's a personality; he still is like that, of course.

JOHNNY CARISI   Diz, after playing a Sunday afternoon session at Kelly's Stables, was walking to the northeast corner of 52nd and 6th followed by a crowd of fans. When they got to the corner they gathered around Dizzy and began peppering him with questions. Most people would have split from that situation. "Where you working next?" "Are you coming to my party next Tuesday?"

Diz climbed one of those wooden telephone poles they had then, by using the metal prongs that were like steps, and when he was a body-length above the mob, fielded their questions as rapidly as they were fired.

❖❖

In that entire period and on through the '40s, the best "Swing Era" players, the soloists, were mingling with the guys who were starting to play the new music.

❖❖

JEAN BACH   Except for a terrible experience that Shorty [Sherock] had on the Street. Now Shorty was just absolutely—if you could get inside another person's shoes—so gone on Roy. Roy did that to people, and I mean he changed his whole wardrobe; he bought a car just like Roy— the LaSalle convertible, eighty-five dollars a month, and his salary with Gene [Krupa] was eighty-five a week. I mean we had to pay our expenses on the road. But anything that was like Roy. So it was very hard for him to shake himself loose because he'd been so much the sort of imaginative Dixieland person before that. You see, I met Shorty through Roy. And so he was kind of like our "flower girl" and everything. But then suddenly he didn't have a job and was just extra, and Shorty was just so thrilled to think that he could spend some time with him. He said, "Why don't you come on the road with us?" And Roy said, "Yeah, it'll be fun. I'll go and listen to the music." And he was comfortable in the car 'cause it was just like his. Shorty was driving and just took him along as his chum in the LaSalle convertible. So after they had been traveling around a bit—there were one-nighters—Gene would say, "Gee, do you think Roy would play a number and the next thing Shorty knew he had his notice. 'Cause they didn't need two of the same.

And suddenly he's sitting in on the Street, and Coleman Hawkins was terribly cordial and nice to him and gentle and appreciated the fact that he loved Roy and everything. And then Charlie Parker came in and just did that mean thing of picking tunes that he didn't know. Well, it was shattering to him. And, of course, the big tune that he didn't know was—luckily I'm so big on show tunes and I'm trying to teach him the changes—"How High the Moon." And it never happened, 'cause he had been sitting in with the greatest people since he was about eleven and suddenly there's this horrible experience, and he could tell that it was like a little game—games people play—'cause they just wanted to freeze people. But up until then there'd been this great, as you say, this spirit of camaraderie, and everybody was so darling to everybody else.

❖❖

Sherock's rejection was from the early '40s, an outgrowth of the Minton's "rulebook," but as bebop took hold on the Street, mixing of musicians became as natural as any shared, positive, human experience.

❖❖

JOE ALBANY   There was so much going on, if you were a good listener, it was easy. I could remember Shelly Manne walking down—he was in the Coast Guard, he'd broken one of his feet, he was on crutches; Rubberlegs Williams swishing about. The first time I ever met Lennie Tristano was walking down the Street. Oscar Pettiford and Benny Harris.

❖❖

The jazz clubs on 52nd Street were located between 7th and 5th Avenues. It was almost like being on a stage set. When you stepped on to it, you became part of the cast. The block between 7th and 6th was active but had nowhere near the concentration of clubs situated between 5th and 6th. Musicians went from club to club sitting in, and patrons wandered around taking advantage of this musical buffet. It was a little village unto itself.

❖❖

DEXTER GORDON   You go around the corner and it's over. Get past the White Rose.* Blank. And it was only for half a block really, yet it was fantastic. That was the life. Beamin'. Steamin'. 'Cause everything was movin—cabs, doormen. People going in and out. It was just really happening.

DON LANPHERE   In 1948 I was going to college in Chicago at Northwestern, and opportunity came up there for me to work with the Johnny

_____
*A bar on the southeast corner of 52nd and 6th Avenue.

Bothwell septet. The other horns were Johnny Howell on trumpet; Jimmy Knepper on trombone; and Bothwell on alto. And we learned to play in D-flat because that was the only place he played. Everything was in D-flat. It didn't make any difference what it was. So we had arrangements written for the four horns and rhythm section. Opportunity arose for the group to come to New York. The day I got in town I moved into the President Hotel, and we opened at the Baby Grand, right near the Apollo Theater on 125th Street. Milt Buckner was playing piano. I remember Bothwell and I as horns. There probably were other horns, but my memory does not fill in the holes. I was a junkie by this time so I came to New York as a junkie.

Coming to the job that first night Bothwell's date, Chan,* evidently liked saxophone players because she took me home that night. I moved out of the President Hotel. I also got fired from my job. But it got me to New York.

7 West 52nd Street became sort of intermission haven for all the musicians from the clubs up and down the Street because they found a place they could go, and nobody would bother them. So there would be Bird or Fats or whoever happened to be working along there. And I had opportunity to meet them through that.

About the third or fourth night on the job—even though I was fired I had two weeks notice—Chan brought Ross Russell to the job, and, as he left, he handed me a note that said, "Be at such-and-such recording studio, Friday afternoon at three o'clock," but it didn't say anything about who it was or what it was or anything. It just said, "Come here."

I showed up Friday afternoon, and when I walked in and saw people whose records I had been buying and were idol-type people to me, I got scared because I was twenty-one. Here I was walking into this, and I'm sure, as they looked at me, they determined I wasn't who they wanted on the record with them and they would do their best to get me out as rapidly as possible. So before the vocals started—it was supposed to have been a vocal date all the way—the device they were using to move me on was "Move." And they said, "Turn on the recorders," and Max [Roach] called me over and said, "We've got this tune we play called "Move," and we don't have the line written out for it so that the two of you can play it together, but we'll just let Fats [Navarro] play the line and when he's through, you can have the first chorus."

And they turned on the machines and, "Ding deling deling, dling, dling" away we went. They turned to me and smiled at the end of the line, and it wasn't the end of the line evidently. They let it run on through, and we became friends. Fats sort of, well, not fathered me, but just started taking me around to different places and introduced

---

*Chan Richardson, later to be Charlie Parker's wife, who lived at 7 West 52nd.

me to people, and we played a few times together. There was never a real close running-with-him kind of relationship, but he did come up to the room during his intermissions to "get on." I got to know him but not that well. He was after musical perfection and I think this is something he let be known to people. He worked hard at achieving this.

IDREES SULIEMAN   Fats would practice all day long. Sit in the bed with his mute and practice all day.

❖❖

Lanphere recorded for New Jazz with Navarro in 1949.

❖❖

DON LANPHERE   I wrote those lines, and I'm no longer credited for having done that. I wrote "Stop" and "Wailing Wall." "Go" didn't have a line, and "Infatuation" had no line. It was "Gone With the Wind" with a little introduction. Both "Stop" and "Wailing Wall" have been credited to him. I brought them to the date, and he read them fast. He was a quick reader. They were recorded fast. I don't know how many takes were done on them.

❖❖

One of the most exciting things about the Street was the sitting-in that was an every-night occurrence. Members of working bands would drop in on each other's bandstands. Then, there always were visiting soloists from New York's vast player pool, either the local residents, or the musicians working in the bands at the Broadway theaters and the Apollo on 125th Street.

❖❖

SHELLY MANNE   When you'd go down the Street at night, you'd go into one place and hear somebody, and play; and then you knew another set was going on someplace else, you'd go over there. You didn't even have to ask. The guys would say, "Hey, c'mon and play." It was always that kind of feeling.

FRANK ROSOLINO   I sat in with Bird and Oscar Pettiford at the Three Deuces. I was working out my card* in New York, and I used to go down to the Street. Erroll Garner was working at the Deuces, too, and he said, "Come on, man, come on. Why don't you sit in?" You're scared stiff because it's Bird, but the fact that they let me sit in was a beautiful feeling. They'd always encourage me, which I really appreciated. Makes you go forward. And I think all good musicians, basically, if there's someone shows some kind of talent, they would encourage him. Rather than say, "Make it lousy."

---

*During the waiting period for an out-of-town musician to get his membership in the local musicians' union, he could only play paying jobs on a limited basis.

SHELLY MANNE   It was beautiful because you'd play all kinds of music. I remember one night playing with Diz at the Onyx, going across the street playing with Trummy Young at the Deuces, and then sitting in with Billie Holiday at the Downbeat. And then you could go into Jimmy Ryan's if you wanted to play. It was like a history of jazz on one street, for that time.

It was really healthy for musicians. I think that possibly, even thinking about all the music that's happened since, I think that was the most creative, one of the most creative times in jazz. If you were a jazz historian you could have gone down there and seen and heard, with your own ears, the evolution of the music, right there on the street, and it all made sense.

BILLY TAYLOR   One night in particular comes to mind. Roy Eldridge had just come in from Chicago, and he hadn't played in a couple of days, so he came to sit in with Ben Webster, to just kind of get his chops together. I guess he was supposed to open either there or another club, and so he came in and was taking it very easy. I mean he hadn't played, and so he was just playing simple kinds of things. Well, Charlie Shavers was at the bar, and he hurried out to his car and got his trumpet and came in and challenged Roy very quickly, and you've never seen a guy's chops get together so quick. And then Webster, who was one of the principal instigators of things like that, was just cheering him on. I mean he would play an opening chorus and then get out of the way. And say, "Hey, you all got it." And they played fours and twos and everything. Stop time and whatever. And so that was a very exciting night because these were really two master trumpet players at the height of their powers.

Other nights similar to that would be the kind of sparks that used to fly between Don Byas and Coleman Hawkins. Don would play unbelievable choruses on "Cherokee" or some fast tune, and you would wonder, "What is Hawk going to do behind this?" And he'd come up with something that was very well worth listening to behind that. And there was that kind of surprise where at any given period someone would be invited up, and he may just be astounding. I remember there was a pianist who worked with Jackie Paris named Deryck Sampson,* and he was a dynamite player—a kid, I mean he was nineteen or twenty years old or something like that.

Then there were people like the guys that were out of the big bands that would come in from time to time, like Jimmy Crawford had left the Lunceford band and really was kind of nervous—he didn't con-

---

*He made some boogie-woogie records for the Beacon label in 1944 but he never recorded the way he was playing on the Street in '45 or '46. He died shortly after that, very young. But he had made the transition and was accomplished in the new style.

sider himself a small-band drummer. And it took a lot of cajoling and a lot of stuff from Ben to say, "Well, come on, man. You know I want you because you can do what I need." And he came in, and of course, he became a dynamite small-band, big-band, any other kind of drummer you want. It was just terrific.

The thing that I really appreciated in those days on the Street was—there's a lot been said about specific musicians leading other musicians down the garden path in terms of drugs, in terms of other bad habits. I always looked back at Sid Catlett and Jo Jones and many other musicians who were the next generation—Art [Tatum] to me, who literally stopped me going nuts.

It wasn't due to tremendous strength on my part in those days but those guys were self-appointed big brothers. On many occasions Jo Jones took me by the arm and led me out the White Rose and said, "You had enough. You have another set to play." And I'm trying to get closer to these guys who can belt 'em down all night and not feel it, and I'm trying to be one of the guys and everything, and he'd say, "Get out of here—what are you trying to do?" There was more of a camaraderie, for me, in those days. And I think for people like Hank [Jones] and for many of the guys that came in on that. I know there was for Erroll Garner; there was for many of us who came to New York around that same time. The lack of feeling of competition—each guy was pretty secure—even the younger ones were pretty secure in what they did. First it was when Erroll Garner was going to leave Slam Stewart. He gave me the job. He said, "Look, I'm going to the Coast. The job's open." I talked to Slam and got the whole book that they were playing with Slam and Doc West—Erroll Garner's and Slam's tunes, I had to learn a lot of the things that he played. He said, "This cat can handle it," and, by the same token, on many occasions guys worked in different places on the Street; one guy would be the leader, and his name would be out front, and the same group would move down the street to another club and somebody else's name would appear. 'Cause he got the gig.

❖❖

After he left Eckstine, Gillespie returned to 52nd Street. He and Parker finally got together in a small group setting in 1945, and their engagement at the Three Deuces made history. Town Hall concerts in May and June, presented by the New Jazz Foundation (Monte Kay, publicist Mal Braveman, and disc jockey Symphony Sid) made even more people aware that Bird and Diz were *the* full-fledged force in jazz.

❖❖

BARNEY KESSEL   As I listen back to all of those records—many, many groups—I feel that the rhythm sections, right down the line—that is piano, bass, drums—were the slowest to evolve. With few exceptions. I think that one of the guys that is very underrated in the bebop movement as far as his accompaniment and the way he played was Al Haig. He didn't get into this "boom-chick"; he left a clear role.

AL HAIG   The first group that I heard, I heard on an airshot, which was Dizzy Gillespie, Don Byas, Oscar Pettiford.

I had been listening to jazz, but I had been listening to people like Teddy Wilson and Art Tatum. One night, very late, I heard that particular group, which just impressed me so much at that time that I decided to find out more about the group; who Dizzy Gillespie was and so on. I happened to be in Boston at the time, and I remember the band that I was playing in, the following day I talked to somebody in the band who said, "Sure, I know Dizzy Gillespie. You can buy his records"—that first record he made with Coleman Hawkins. So I went down to the record shop, and I got those two records.

I remember the broadcast very distinctly; it was impressive. They played "A Night in Tunisia" and some other things. On first listening it was kind of rough. First of all the station didn't come in very clear. It was just the general configurations of the melodies that made it sound so different. Then when I bought the records I got into the harmonic part of it which was different, and the drummer—all parts of the group sounded different, too. They were indeed playing a different type of applied style.

Then what I wanted to do was get into New York and hear the group in person. I started learning those tunes. I came to New York, but I don't think Dizzy was working then. The group had disbanded. I got my card and permission to work, and I found myself working with Trevor Bacon.*

This was at the Elks' Rendevous. That wasn't my first experience with a mixed group because I'd been over to the Savoy Ballroom, and I'd worked over there a night or two with Rudy Williams and Bob Dorsey and I forget who else. Rudy had heard Charlie Parker. He knew what he was doing—I didn't even have an idea who Charlie Parker was because he wasn't on that original broadcast. I was working with Trevor until that group disbanded or went somewhere else. I was kind of pleased with things in general because it gave me an opportunity to at least go down to 52nd Street and hear what was going on. I really was interested in hearing Dizzy. Evenutally as I stayed in New York, Dizzy did make his appearance at the various clubs sitting in, so I used to go to the Street on the chance of hearing him. Anyway, from there I went to Tiny Grimes and—during that preceding interval I had met Dizzy at Kelly's Stable and places like that on 52nd Street, and I got to know him—"Mr. Gillespie, can I have your autograph?" I was very tentative and diffident and scared about actually even talking about music with him, and there was never enough time. So Tiny Grimes

*The vocalist, who used to be with Lucky Millinder.

must have sat in with him that night, and he said he needed a pianist, so I started working with Tiny.

One night when we were playing, Charlie Parker and Dizzy Gillespie came in with their instruments, and I thought I was going to faint. And they unpacked their instruments and came up to that bandstand. Up until that time I was very secure and hiding behind bars and people and listening and watching, but, Jesus! This was at the Spotlite. So both of them hurled themselves up on the bandstand and started playing something like "Shaw 'Nuff," which was just incredible. This was my first experience with Charlie Parker, too. It was just shocking. I was in there with our group—Eddie Nicholson and myself and Gene Ramey. But what that was in fact was an audition because when I got through—when they got through, they said, "We're forming a quintet. We'd like to have you," or "We'd like to know if you're interested in joining the group" or "We'd like to have you join the group."

It was very upsetting. But I said, "Sure." They said they'd be in touch, packed up their instruments and went out. I felt sure that I'd never hear from them, but indeed I did in a month or six weeks. That was the beginning of that quintet that went into the Three Deuces. I think we did the records about a month later.

My only criticism of the recording in general is just a basic thing, and that is, it's too bad they couldn't record it in better fidelity, better situation.

It [playing with Dizzy and Bird] was kind of frenetic at times. It was new, it was awesome, it was spectacular, it was curious. I think that I was, to be quite truthful, a bit intimidated by the front line—all this being in the context of a front-line instrument, that is, a solo-playing pianist. First of all I didn't know anything about Charlie Parker's background or where his origins musically began. I just knew a little about Dizzy. So it was kind of stunning.

I didn't hear Bud Powell until many months after I joined that group, and then I only heard him on records. As a matter of fact, it might have been more than a year before I heard him. But I heard him on those Cootie Williams records, and I was really knocked out. I suggested to Charlie and Dizzy that that was the piano player that should be in that group, not me. But I don't know where Bud was. He just didn't appear on the scene, so I just did my thing such as it was, but truthfully, I would have liked to have had a little more pre-bebop playing. It was just suddenly being in the middle of very fast company.

❖❖

At the Deuces the rhythm section was Haig, Curly Russell, and Stan Levey. For "Shaw 'Nuff," "Hot House," "Salt Peanuts," and "Lover Man," the quintessential date in May 1945, Levey was replaced by Sid Catlett. Even more instrumental in spreading the word than the Deuces gig and the Town Hall concerts was this session, along with "Groovin' High," "All the Things You Are" and "Dizzy Atmosphere," Diz and Bird dates from February and March, and the Gillespie-Dexter Gordon "Blue'n Boogie." (All of these were on the Guild label). These were the 78 rpm recordings that became instant classics among the cognoscenti.

Even before that, hip listeners latched on to the records that Parker made with Tiny Grimes and Sir Charles Thompson. New York-born Jimmy Butts was the bassist on both sessions. As a young journalist he had a job on a newspaper that paid him fifteen dollars a week. He bought a bass and got a gig for fifteen dollars a night. He played with Doc Sausage's Tramp Band—it had washboard, kazoo, maracas—and in 1940–1941 worked with drummer Chris Columbus at the Elk's Rendevous and the Savoy and Golden Gate ballrooms. In 1944 he was with guitarist Tiny Grimes.

❖❖

JIMMY BUTTS   I was working on the Street with Tiny Grimes at the Spotlite, then into the Downbeat. Then Tiny got the date from Lubinsky for Savoy. It was *his* date, but the way it turned out it became Charlie Parker's date with Tiny Grimes. Bird used to sit in with us, and that's when Tiny decided to use him. "He'd be good for what we want to do," he said.

Bird used to come in and run some of the numbers down, sometimes even after the club closed.

I liked Bird. He used to call me, "Jimmy Butts, Jimmy Butts" [imitates Parker's deep, booming voice]. He knew I used to write—*down beat, Esquire,* the black press. I remember one time he said, "It's a shame. I got a chance to make a lot of money, and all I need is fifty dollars to get in the union."

So I went around to my agency at the newspaper. "I think we ought to get the fifty dollars up and let him have it." So they looked at me and laughed. I couldn't understand it. They knew he was hung up. I didn't know he was hung up. "Butts, don't you know what's happening?" They never bothered to tell me so I just assumed that that's what was really happening.

The Apollo date [September 4, 1945] with Sir Charles Thompson took place at four or five o'clock in the morning. Bird and Dexter [Gordon] were nodding. I knew what pot was, but I didn't know about hard stuff. Dexter would come out of his nod and say, "I'm tired. It's early in the morning," and I said, "Yeah, I know what you mean. I just came in from Atlantic City." Later I found out all these guys were hooked.

❖❖

"Blue'n Boogie" preceded the date with Sir Charles by seven months.

❖❖

DEXTER GORDON   Dix asked me one night on the Street if I wanted to make a date. I think I was working on the Street that night. Anyway, I was there. This was about four o'clock, something like that in the morning. I don't even remember the studio, except it was in midtown, and I was never there again. I think we made four sides. Somehow, I only know of two.

❖ ❖

Discographies had listed a *Groovin' High** that was cut but never released.

The practice in those days was to record late. It worked well because the musicians were not going through long LP sessions. They were making four tunes. All evening they had it in their minds that they would be recording later on, and they would be mentally up for it. Today when a jazz musician tapes an LP, it is akin to embarking on a voyage.

❖ ❖

DEXTER GORDON   You'd just come off work and walk around the corner to the studio. You're already warm anyway. You played all night. Now it's a whole thing. They always expect you to do it in one day on the session. That's it. Whereas with pop groups, they take months, six months to do an album. What a difference. It's amazing jazz musicians can do that. "Now! Today! Quick!"

❖ ❖

Not only were the Parker-Gillespie Guilds immediately influential in the inner circle of New York, but wherever perceptive musicians and laymen gathered they were played with holy dedication. In the year of their release they found their way into the hands of a noted French jazz critic.

❖ ❖

CHARLES DELAUNAY   Once they heard about these records, musicians would start coming at eight o'clock in the morning to hear them. Django Reinhardt, Stephane Grappelli, Alex Combelle. Django would still have his pajama top on. Musicians would come any time of the day or night to hear them.

❖ ❖

In California it was the same.

❖ ❖

RED CALLENDER   We used to play those records—we'd get in a room and live with them all night. It was unbelievable. Something from outer space.

CHARLES DELAUNAY   Hughes Panassie was in the south of France. He heard about the records and wrote to me to send them to him. I couldn't because the musicians were bringing new musicians every day. If I could

---

*Actually the Gillespie-Gordon *Groovin' High* had been released but in a very limited number. One turned up in 1975, courtesy of a California collector, M. D. Zemanek, and is included in Gillespie's *Development of An American Artist* (The Smithsonian Collection R004).

have gotten other copies I would have sent them to him. I needed new copies myself as mine were turning white from being played so much.

RED CALLENDER   Yeh, we actually wore records out, wore the grooves out. When I heard Charlie and Dizzy together, I couldn't believe it.

❖❖

Delaunay claims that if Panassie had been in Paris, rather than in the south of France, and heard the Guilds immediately, he would have embraced bebop. (Instead he headed the opposition which led to severe factionalism in French jazz circles.) But critics in the United States who severely opposed bebop had access to the records, and they still didn't see the light.

Musicians' minds, however, were constantly being illuminated by the recordings that, for the most part, were coming out of the 52nd Street experience. The 78s of 1944 and 1945 had a direct, galvanizing effect.

❖❖

AL COHN   When I first met Socolow and those guys, I was listening to mostly Lester Young, Count Basie, and I liked Benny Goodman's band. Especially always Lester, Charlie Christian, Cootie [Williams] and Georgie [Auld]. And then that's when we started picking up on Bird. "Red Cross" with Tiny Grimes. Those recordings around then. And the ones with Rubberlegs. Well those we were listening to then. And you know we used to play them by the hour. And fall out every time. "Wowww! Listen to that!" "Disorder At the Border"—those records were big then. "Woody'n You." Well, we were right on top of that.

TRUMMY YOUNG   Well, the original "Good Bait," I was fortunate enough to have been on that band. And I knew Tadd Dameron a long time. He wrote for Lunceford. You probably don't know that. Way back! Before he left Ohio. In fact, Tadd was the one instrumental in getting Snooky Young and Gerald Wilson to come with Lunceford. He had a band, there. He had Scatman Crothers in the band. He had Scat singing and everything, and Snooky and Gerald—a wonderful little band. And Tadd had written "Good Bait" way back then. And this is the thirties, man! So anyway they came to New York, I told Diz and them, say, "There's a guy around here writes some beautiful things." And he started getting on the scene, playing with guys. And be brought this "Good Bait," and we did it, man. Everybody enjoyed that record. And that's the same date we did Dizzy's original solo on "Can't Get Started." That background on "Can't Get Started," every band in the world that plays "Can't Get Started" plays that. That was Don Byas's background. He taught it to me, and the tenor and the trombone have always been one of the most lovely blends you can find in music. Especially if the two guys play easy and try to get a good controlled tone. And we did this under Dizzy, and Dizzy came and kissed us for that background, playing that background behind him. That tune can come and go but that will be here. That will be here. The introduction and all, that's Dizzy's. He wrote the little intro and ending, but we did the whole thing. And that ending of Dizzy's—Dizzy says, "Can you imagine? They got me that time!" It was such a beautiful ending he did on that.

❖ ❖

It later became Gillespie's introduction for "Round Midnight."

❖ ❖

TRUMMY YOUNG   Dizzy was beautiful because he didn't realize at that time that he was helping a lot of guys. But he was. He was helping because Dizzy was helped a lot. Guys like Benny Carter helped all of us—Dizzy and all the rest of us. This was way back. I remember when Dizzy was playing with Edgar Hayes, man, on a little old job, and Dizzy used to say, "I got to get somewhere where I can blow my trumpet—where I can open up!" He liked Edgar, 'cause Edgar was a nice guy. Edgar would let him play anything he wanted, but they didn't think in the same vein, and that made it a little hard for him. I've always admired Dizzy. He's for real. He's not a phony in any way—there's not a phony bone.

When Bird moved in on it, it was a whole different thing altogether when he came in, because he thought differently. And you could tell he did an awful lot of woodshedding because nobody can play that good. But his thinking was different from all the guys I had been around previously. And some of the things he played, I had heard Diz play a few of the things. I think—this is my opinion, I could be wrong—I think they really complemented one another. I think Diz got some things from Bird, and Bird got some things from Diz. But, every time they got on the stand, it was competitive. The two of them. They had blood in their eyes every time. They loved one another. But they would try to extend each other to make a move. And to me it was a thrilling thing. But they loved one another. And now Bird, he didn't write music. But every time he thought of something, he'd come around to Diz to write it down. So, Lorraine said he used to knock on the door at six and seven in the morning, and "Bam! Bam!," trying to get in to play something. So, she'd tell him, "No! No! Don't let him in here. He can't . . ." So Diz would sit at his piano, and Bird would play it out in the hall, and Diz would write it down. Diz'll tell you these stories, himself. It was amazing. But Bird had such a prolific mind. You could play a song, and he could play a counter melody to it right away without even—not even think about it. And we got to admiring the guy, we really did. But, we were afraid of him hurting himself all the time because we knew where he was and how he stood, but . . . Bird had a good heart, but he never had a chance to prove it, really, because he was in need all the time. He wanted what he needed all the time,

Budd Johnson at the time he was with George E. Lee's band in Kansas City, 1928. (Courtesy of Budd Johnson.)

Benny Goodman Sextet, 1939. Left to right: Lionel Hampton, Artie Bernstein, Goodman, Nick Fatool, Charlie Christian, Johnny Guarnieri. (Courtesy of the Institute of Jazz Studies.)

Art Tatum Trio, circa 1944. Tiny Grimes, guitar; Slam Stewart, bass. (Courtesy of The Institute of Jazz Studies.)

Trombonist Al Grey, flanked by trumpeters Charlie Young and Cowboy Noyd, with Navy group in Massachusetts, 1942. (Courtesy of Al Grey.)

Jimmy Butts, Dexter Gordon, Buck Clayton, J.C. Heard, Danny Barker, and Charlie Parker at Sir Charles Thompson's Apollo recording session, New York City, September 4, 1945. (Courtesy Jimmy Butts.)

Dizzy Gillespie, Tadd Dameron, Mary Lou Williams, and Jack Teagarden, at Williams's apartment, 1947. (William P. Gottlieb/E. J. G. Collection)

Thelonious Monk, 1947. (William P. Gottlieb/E. J. G. Collection)

Coleman Hawkins and Miles Davis at the Three Deuces, New York City, 1947. (William P. Gottlieb/E. J. G. Collection)

Howard McGhee and Miles Davis, Nola Studios, New York City, 1947. (William P. Gottlieb/E. J. G. Collection)

Shelly Manne. (William P. Gottlieb/E. J. G. Collection)

George Wallington, Curly Russell, Red Rodney, Tiny Kahn, Earl Swope, Teddy Reig (partially obscured), and Serge Chaloff at Chaloff recording date for Savoy, New York City, March 5, 1947. (Courtesy Institute of Jazz Studies.)

Terry Gibbs, Harry Biss, and Bill De Arango, Three Deuces, New York City. (William P. Gottlieb/E. J. G. Collection)

Dial *Bebop Jazz* album cover, 1946. (Author's collection)

Henry Jerome Band at Child's Paramount Restaurant, New York City, late 1945 or early 1946. Front row, left to right: Al Young (Epstein), Nate Peterson, Bill Vitale, Ray Turner, Evan Aiken. Middle row: Jerry Dorn, Moe Sadwick. Back row: Jerome, Jack Eagle, Normie Faye. (Courtesy of Henry Jerome.)

Dizzy Gillespie Orchestra at Downbeat, New York City, 1947. Left to right: Gillespie, Joe Harris, James Moody, Howard Johnson, John Brown, and Joe Gayles. (William P. Gottlieb/E. J. G. Collection)

Charlie Parker and Kai Winding at Royal Roost, New York City, 1948. (Herman Leonard)

Boyd Raeburn Orchestra at Vanity Fair, New York City, 1947. The clarinetist and the saxophonist at lower right, from left to right, are Buddy De Franco and Frankie Socolow. (William P. Gottlieb/E. J. G. Collection)

Fats Navarro, Charlie Rouse, and Nelson Boyd at Tadd Dameron Blue Note recording date, New York City, September 26, 1947. (William P. Gottlieb/E. J. G. Collection)

Lee Konitz, third saxophone from the left, with Claude Thornhill Orchestra, 1947. (William P. Gottlieb/E. J. G. Collection)

Al Cohn, Tiny Kahn, and Johnny Mandel with Elliot Lawrence at piano, circa 1952. (Author's collection)

so everybody had to go when he wanted it. But this is how I saw those things develop.

❖❖

In the 52nd Street period Young made dates with Dizzy and Bird under his name and with Rubberlegs Williams for Continental.

❖❖

TRUMMY YOUNG   One thing is vivid in my mind. The one we did with Rubberlegs. You've heard this story many times, but I've heard it a lot of different ways, really, from what actually happened. I was right there. And Diz will probably tell you this. Well, it was—I think it was a very early morning date, like four o'clock or something like that. I'm not sure . . . Teddy Reig was in the booth, and we had gone down a couple of tunes that he was doing. Clyde Hart made little skeleton arrangements on these things. So we just ran over them lightly. We never did do much rehearsing on recording dates. Most of them were on the spur of the moment. But we had a skeleton usually that we'd go over. We all had coffee. Black coffee. Now, Bird took a thermos thing—that Benzedrine inhaler before they outlawed it—and he put it in one of the cups. And we had about six cups or seven, eight cups of coffee lined up. Now Rubberlegs was already drunk. There was a liquor that came out in those days called "Joe Louis." It was the baddest liquor you ever seen in your life. It was cheap and real bad. It would give you the worst headache if you'd fool with it. But it would make you real drunk. I didn't bother with it. But Rubberlegs had a whole fifth of it—the stopper off the bottle, the cork off—and he was drinking it. So, after a while, he say he want some coffee, so he grabbed any coffee there. Well, he made a mistake and grabbed Bird's coffee with this Benzedrine inhaler in it. And he drank the whole damn thing and he told us, "This is the damn bitterest coffee I ever seen in my life!" So he put it down.

And Bird, in the meantime, was fooling with his reed over there. So, Bird came over and grabbed the coffee he thought was his and drank it. So Bird told us about ten minutes later, he say, "Damn! This is the first time this Benzedrine inhaler has never worked!" He say, "My constitution is getting terrible," and said, "that ain't doing nothing for me." The meantime, we were going over some things with Rubber, and he was getting—sweating more and more and getting madder and madder. So we were going over "That's the Blues," and Dizzy was playing some flatted fifths behind him on the chorus. Rubberlegs had never heard anything like this, some modern changes. Well, Rubberlegs stopped the band. And he called everybody "Miss." "Miss Dizzy." He says, "Miss Gillespie, if you play another one of them bad notes, I'm gonna beat your brains out." And it was hot in there so he says, "Cut out them lights!" So Teddy Reig turned out the lights, and he was getting like a raving maniac, so he told Teddy Reig, "I'll come in there and bust out all the glass out of that window!" So we all were getting kinda frightened then 'cause this guy was getting crazy. So we got through a few of the tunes—I don't know what the hell they sounded like. But he was singing, I remember, "What's the Matter Now?" And he got to screaming on that thing something like an ungodly scream like I never heard before. We got through some—I don't know how many of those sides ever came out but it was a classic date 'cause . . . The guys was glad to get him out of there finally when they did, and after he left, we got to do some things like "Seventh Avenue," which I sang, and a few of those things. We did a song I wrote, "Sorta Kinda" . . . It was so pretty what Bird and Diz played. That's a tune I want to do again. I haven't done it since then because I don't feel right doing it because it's never gonna sound like that again. I'll tell you that right now. But, I'm just going to do it because some people have asked me to do it. But these are the scenes that I came up through. I know we were all hungry all the time. And Dizzy's wife used to cook. Lorraine. And she'd cook a big pot of beans. We didn't have a lot of money, either. We'd chip in and buy things and we'd all go over there and eat.

❖❖

In the period where Young came out of the big bands and began working with the small groups in New York, the new music exerted an influence on his playing.

❖❖

TRUMMY YOUNG   It affected it. It's bound to affect it. I played things that I didn't realize I was playing a lot of times because it was an influence from the guys that I played with. But I never did deviate too much from my original style. But you incorporated certain things. Without changing the style. You don't even know you're doing it. If you play with a guy like Dizzy and a guy like Bird, you're bound to pick up a few things—automatically. You don't realize you're picking 'em up. And every once in a while you hear a guy say, "Hey! Trummy! I didn't know you played modern things!" I say, "I don't". He'll say, "Well, listen to this." And he'll play something that I just without thinking—unconsciously—played because it's so imbedded in my mind from hearing it with these guys.

❖❖

In 1952 Young joined Louis Armstrong's All Stars. And, in effect, left the modern movement.

❖❖

TRUMMY YOUNG   What I loved about Louis was he was melodic. I've always been a melodic guy; I've always loved melodic things. I've never been a guy that played a lot of exercises and things of this sort, but I've always been a melodic player. Now, I've looked at various styles of playing. Now, Bird, with all the playing he did, it was melodic. Stop and think of that. With all the things he played, it was always melodic. He never did get so far away till you'd say, "Well, what in the heck is he doing?" It never got to that extent.

❖❖

The point is that those musicians coming out of the previous era, with a background in the other music, retained certain things and then they added to it. Although they were running chord changes, they still were melody players, too.

When you talk about recordings that came out of 52nd Street you cannot forget Coleman Hawkins' original version of "Body and Soul," done at a time when Hawk was in residence at the old Kelly's Stable on 51st Street. He used to use it as a closer. The 1939 Bluebird record became a saxophone benchmark and made "Body and Soul" a testing ground for aspiring tenorists.

❖❖

COLEMAN HAWKINS   Everybody, including Chu Berry, said I was playing wrong notes. A lot of people didn't know about flatted fifths and augmented changes . . ."

❖❖

Although he never once really stated the melody directly, Hawkins's ability to convey a mood made this unlikely candidate for wide appeal a popular as well as an artistic success. The new melodies he improvised retained the essence of the song, so the public was entranced; the intricacies of his imagination captured the hipper listeners; the feeling got everyone.

❖❖

SHELLY MANNE   Hazel Scott and I—we were almost twins in our birthdates, we were born the same day, the same year, we're almost the same time, so we got to know each other in New York 'cause we were both just kids, and Hazel and I,—we had a date to go and hear Coleman Hawkins's record "Body and Soul." We went to the session and sat on the piano bench listening.

❖❖

And four years later he recorded "The Man I Love" and "Sweet Lorraine" with Hawk, Eddie Heywood, and Oscar Pettiford.

❖❖

SHELLY MANNE   I was nervous to be playing with anyone of Coleman Hawkins's stature. But I was confident with Eddie and Oscar because we had been playing together on a lot of different sessions. But of the dates and sessions in New York I—oh, yeah, a session we did on Manor with Rubberlegs Williams. There was a big band: Clyde Hart, Dizzy, Serge Chaloff, Al Casey. I remember we all came in, we sat down to play, and nobody had written anything. So we ran out in the hall, and Dizzy and Clyde Hart started writing charts. And to make it easier, they got Rubberlegs Williams, so the band backed him singing the blues 'cause it was easy to do. That was a funny scene at that time. Nobody had any arrangement for a band. Weird.

❖❖

When someone couldn't go to the Street, sometimes the Street came to him.

❖❖

ZOOT SIMS   I was in the Army. I was in San Antonio, Texas, working in this club, this black nightclub, and the Billy Taylor trio came through with Doc West, Harold West, on drums. So we hung out. They left, they went back to New York and, being in Texas, I could get all the "shit"* I wanted, and I used to send him "shit," and he'd send me records. And I got "Hot House" and "Bebop" and all that; the first records, "Groovin' High."

I heard about these cats. Naturally, I heard of Dizzy, but Bird I didn't know much about. I saw Dizzy during the war, before I went in the army, with Cab [Calloway] once. But anyway, he sent me all these records, and I was really flabbergasted. I really didn't know what to . . . Jesus, the way they were playing their horns and this music. This was '45, I guess. There I was on the desert. I started by just going out and jamming at this club. And they loved me and they hired me for weekends, and I even made a movie with this band. Don Albert, who was a trumpet player, was the owner and the bandleader. Don Albert's Keyhole was the name of the club. And we had a little Filipino alto player who's in the movie also—played good. But anyway, that's the period when I heard Bird, Diz, and all that.

I can honestly say I never disliked those records, any of them. It was just so different. I was amazed at what they were doing. But I couldn't dislike it 'cause it was so musical.

❖❖

Not everyone reacted so positively. For some, the first hearing of Parker, Gillespie et al. was traumatic.

❖❖

ART PEPPER   I spent all my time in the Army in Europe, in England; we transported prisoners from London to Paris and things like that. This was in 1944–1945—the end of '44 and the beginning of '45—and then I came out of the Army the end of '46, and when I came out, I didn't know anything about what was happening over here. Over there it was still what was happening when I left, it was still going on over there. I got home, a friend of mine came by and said, "I want you to hear these records." He had two records, and one he had was with Sonny Stitt and Dizzy—"Oop Bop Sh'Bam" and "That's Earl, Brother."

That record was the first one I heard, and I said, "Oh my God," and I just got sick. I remember I got sick to my stomach. I just couldn't believe it. And then the next record I heard was, I think it was "Salt

---

*marijuana.

Peanuts," and that other real fast one—it was "Shaw 'Nuff," That thing was so fast because I had never heard anything like that. I said, "My God, nothing can be like that," and then when I heard it—the guy did it purposely, he said, "Now dig this." This was after—he was playing a game with me—Sonny Stitt was first, and that just made me ill, and then when I heard Bird I just got deathly sick. I couldn't stand anymore, and he was going to play something else, and I said, "No, no, I can't stand it. I can't listen to any more." That was all I could stand. I couldn't listen to any more at that moment. And that was my introduction. I went right from there to there—just like that. It was too much of a shock. No preparation, no nothing. I didn't even . . . I hadn't even heard of it before. Didn't know the word "bebop"— nothing. I came right from overseas and I must have been sheltered somewhere because I'd never heard the word. Isn't that weird?

❖❖

In Cuba, a man who a few years later would come to the United States and write bop arrangements for of all people, Benny Goodman, was also taken aback.

❖❖

CHICO O'FARRILL   A friend of ours came to New York, it must have been in '45, and he took back some records. He took back "Salt Peanuts" and also the big band, I think, "Things to Come." And this fellow, Manole Saavedra, we had jam sessions and so forth, and when we heard these records, frankly I was shocked. I said, "If this is the shape of things to come, how in the hell am I going to cut it?" And it was such a new thing, because here we were confronted for the first time with phrases that wouldn't be symmetrical in the sense that string-music phrasing was symmetrical. Here we were confronted with phrases that were asymmetrical. They would come in into any part of the phrase they felt like, and, at first, also the changes threw us off completely because it was a complete new harmonic—not new, but we'll say unusual harmonic concept that was so alien to what we had been doing. To us it was such a drastic change that I think anything that came afterwards wasn't as drastic as that particular first step from swing to bop. I think in a sense bop probably marks the real cut-off point of the old concept of swinging. I don't mean in the sense of swinging— we were still swinging—but the concept of the square structure of the music as to this new particular way of playing and writing.

I was playing trumpet at that time. I used to play in big bands in Havana, and at first I sounded almost like Harry James; that was the thing to do. First it was Bunny Berigan and then Harry James, and then I got very much into the kick of Bobby Hackett thing. I even got myself a cornet when they published this arrangement of—what was that thing he played on that was beautiful with Glenn Miller—"Rhapsody in Blue." I bought myself a cornet just to sound like Bobby Hackett. Frankly, for some time I was lost. However, people want to investigate, people want to find out, and we started listening to the records, and we started getting more into it, and I would say in about a year or two I was really starting to get into it, and I even started to write bop-oriented arrangements. By 1946, I think it was, we had a big band at the Montmartre nightclub in Havana, and it was a dream band. We had the best jazz musicians in Havana. It lasted only six months. It was too good to last. We had two or three arrangers in that band. By this time we were really into it, and I wrote some things that even today, I think if I heard them, I think I would be proud of them.

❖❖

Perhaps if Pepper and O'Farrill had heard the Comet recordings by Red Norvo and His Selected Sextet as their introduction to Parker and Gillespie, their indoctrination into modern jazz might have been smoother.

❖❖

JIMMY ROWLES   When I was first starting to listen to records—I bought Hawkins and I remember those Decca records, "What Harlem Is To Me," those kind of things, and I heard that big deep sound. Chu Berry, he was a gas, I loved him. I always went for the saxophone players. But then there were the trumpet players—Ray Nance, Shorty Baker, Freddie Webster. I met Diz when I was with Woody [Herman], just before I went into the Army, he wrote a couple of arrangements for the band.

The end of '42 into '43—because I went in the Army in '43, June, and I was working with Woody when I went into the Army—we had a couple of his charts, and Woody was just starting to change and getting away from the old shit, and Dave Matthews was writing a lot of stuff for him. And then I went into the Army. I wound up in Salt Lake City at Fort Douglas, and one day I went down to the record shop, and the lady told me that she had something that I might be interested in, "Congo Blues." That's the first time I ever heard Charlie Parker. I had never heard of Charlie Parker, and I heard "Congo Blues," and I said, "Who is that? Give me that." And she said, "There's another one." I said, "I'll take them both." So I started listening to that. That started to change my life. Shit, that's where it should go, that's it. He's pushing past Prez. There was a lot of Prez in it. Well, Kansas City's Kansas City. It's a funny thing about K.C., they all have that influence. So I started picking up on him, and then I used to get my radio and catch him long distance from Hollywood—I was still in the Army.

They didn't know what in the fuck he was doing. They didn't even know what Dizzy was doing, except that Dizzy was a fantastic trumpet player. I can see those dummies sitting there and saying, "Gee, he's terrific, but who is that guy?" He was a bitch— still is. I just picked up on Bird. I started absorbing him as much as I could. Much more than

I did Diz because he's a saxophone player. I swallowed him up, and I started buying all the records, memorizing solos.

❖❖

Vibist Norvo's Selected Sextet included Flip Phillips, tenor; Teddy Wilson, piano; Slam Stewart, bass; J. C. Heard or Specs Powell, drums; Gillespie and Parker. It was a time when Dizzy and Bird were becoming more well known but were being put down by many critics. These recordings changed a lot of people's minds.

❖❖

RED NORVO   Charlie—I knew him in Kansas City before he came east—I know him when they used to kick him out of the clubs. One time I was working at the Muehlebach Hotel, and Tatum called me. He was in town because he didn't fly, and he had a stopover on the train. He said, "I'll meet you at the Kentucky Club."* So somebody who worked at the club told us, "You remember that kid they used to kick out of here?" This must have been three or four years later. He said, "He's playing good!" Then I saw him again when he was with Hines. So when he came to New York we got together, and I always liked him, and we were friendly. A lot of people were putting him down. I didn't think that was right. He came with something that should have been heard. They called me for the record date, and I was doing so many dates around New York. Not necessarily jazz dates, but just dates. In this date—well, it was from Cleveland. A guy called me one morning. We were at the Paramount, and he said, "I'd like for you to do a record date." I said, "I don't want to do these dates." I didn't feel like working hard. He said he'd really like me to handle the date because, "I've always liked the way you handled the big bands." I said, "Let me get who I want and let me play what I want and I'll do the date." He said, "Okay, I'll let you know." So I forgot about it. I fluffed him off, and that's it. Two weeks later a guy called me, the same time—eight in the morning—and said, "This is such and such," and I said, "Yeah." I couldn't remember anything about it, so to speak. He said that he was the guy who had talked to me a couple of weeks ago about a record date. He said, "Okay, go and get who you want and do it." He said, "But we want to make four 12-inch sides." So I got ahold of the guys. We had no music, and I think Charlie had been down to Philadelphia on a concert. Flip was doing something. But we all met about nine in the morning. Everybody was tired and relaxed. I guess that's got something to do with it. Of course, we ruined a lot of takes. When you're tired like that, you forget to come in and all. And there wasn't tape then. You couldn't splice it or anything.

❖❖

*A club where they had Monday morning 4:00 A.M. sessions called "spook breakfasts" because "spooks" or "ghosts" stayed up all night.

This date made logical to some people, who previously hadn't understood, the connection, the evolution of the music.

❖❖

RED NORVO   I think it changed a lot of people. I think it changed a lot of things. Later, I began to realize the effect it was having. I didn't really know how strong it was going to be. Actually after we got through with that date, I thought, "I'll never be a leader again." It was such a nerve-wracking experience. Charlie wasn't necessarily regimented to discipline. He'd do anything to please me, I know. But when we got swinging, and he and Dizzy would just like forget, forget to come in or something. I think Ross [Russell] put out all the bad takes and everything.*

I noticed that the effect that it ought to have when I was with Benny [Goodman] when we were at the Paramount, and the records were out. Mike Bryan brought them in, and I had a machine, and everybody was coming out and keeping me playing those things. I finally just let all the guys in the band take the machine and the records. And that thing was going all the time.

I'm not sure that Benny liked it or disliked it. He was noncommittal, but being such good friends I thought, "Well that's normal," because I think that you have to hear . . . he was honest with himself, which was the thing I respect in all people as far as music is concerned. Then as the time went by and the months have gone by, as we went around the country with Benny, I noticed more people asking me about these records. Like, we'd get to Chicago—the Chicago Theatre—and the musicians coming back, or we'd see them in the club, and they'd be saying, "I got those records," and they'd start talking about it. Even the critics, if you know what I mean. So I began to realize that maybe there was a measurable that showed the progress or that styles are not limited to the result necessarily. You could still get a good result with a variety of styles. And the same context, too.

After it became the record of the year and I was with Benny Goodman, we were playing the 400 Club, and I ran into Charlie Parker on the street. We said hello, and we were laughing about something, and I said, "We have a pretty good record." He said, "Yeah, that turned out pretty good." He was happy with it. I said, "Okay, as it turned out good and the pay was good, what can I do for you?" And he said, "Get me in to hear Benny." I said, "You got it." So we were at the 400 Club, and the headwaiter—he used to work on 52nd Street, he was later at Basin Street East—Sidney. So I said to Sid, "Charlie Parker wants to hear Benny." "He's got the best table in the house," he said. And he sat right there, and he loved it. He'd never heard Benny in person, or a lot of the guys in the band, that way—and it was a good

*A later LP issue of the entire session that includes incomplete takes.

band. We had Gozzo, Faso, Mucci, and Best, and [laughs] that was a pretty good parlay there.*

BARNEY KESSEL   I didn't really work with people, or hear people trying to play like Charlie Parker and Dizzy Gillespie. I didn't hear it as sort of an introduction to it. The first thing I heard was them. The first bebop record I ever heard was "Disorder At The Border." And I must say that the first time I ever heard Charlie Parker, I did not like it. People raved about it. I also heard Dizzy and liked it very much, and I heard these 12-inch records that Red Norvo made. I was with Roy Eldridge when we both heard "Congo Blues" for the first time and Roy was really stunned, amazed. But at that time I found the arrangements—the epitome of it is the song called "Bebop" itself—very erratic, as was "Things to Come"† with Dizzy's big band. But many of the early things that were not of the California style—where it just floated along—many of these were very fast tempo and erratic, very syncopated. Bud Powell tunes. All these things. It seemed to be very harsh to me. I didn't get it and didn't like it. He sounded out of tune to me, and the tone sounded harsh, very harsh. I really didn't like it too much. I was very slow on the uptake. Very slow. But I remember being in California, and he was there with Dizzy Gillespie playing there, and he made some records for Ross Russell on Dial, and I remember buying those records, even though I did not like them, and one day it's just like a mist lifted and I could see what it was, but it had its good and bad points. From the minute I began to like it and began to understand what he was doing, I did not like my playing because I wanted to articulate that way and didn't know how. I found myself really fully locked into the Swing Era. I was a practitioner of, and exponent of, the Swing Era who had gotten the insight to assess and see what was going on in bebop.

Even to want to buy these records and listen—and really I had to change my own playing. I can't begin to tell you what a blow it was to my ego, for me to have to be my own teacher, to start revising my own way of playing because I didn't like the way I played. I realized that I could continue playing the way that I played, and it would have much merit within the swing idiom, but I wanted to move into this other thing, and moving into this other thing—I was almost like a babe in the wood because I didn't have that kind of technique at that time.

And the thing that I did have all the time, and that Dodo [Marmarosa]‡ had, the thing that we both had and that I liked very much was the same kind of inquisitiveness that Charlie Christian and the people

*Goodman's trumpet section: Conrad Gozzo, Tony Faso, Louis Mucci, and Johnny Best.
†"Things to Come" is actually the big-band version of "Bebop."
‡Kessel was in Artie Shaw's band at the time with Marmarosa.

that were playing at Minton's had—to take certain standard tunes but to find different notes and then make up original songs that would fit the chords. And be able to play things that didn't sound just like improvisation that's diatonic in nature in the Swing Era, where everything is sort of scale-wise. There was that desire to do that.

FRANKIE SOCOLOW   You had to evolve into it actually. In other words, if you were playing a certain way before, you just don't press a button and play another way. In fact I went through a period in my life where I played a certain way and wanted to play the other way. And for a while I couldn't play my way or any other way. Not well the other way. And it's just in knowing something you have to evolve into by listening to and constantly playing, and it's a wild thing. It hung up a lot of people, that music.

❖ ❖

Coming out of the big bands, Gillespie has always leaned in that direction. If it had been economically feasible he probably would have been at the head of an orchestra through more of his career. After the success of the quintet with Parker, Dizzy, backed by his manager, Billy Shaw, decided to form a big band. Kenny (then Kinney, short for McKinley) Dorham was among the trumpets, Charlie Rouse was on tenor saxophone, and Max Roach was the drummer. Parker remained on 52nd Street with his own group at the Spotlite, while Dizzy took his new band on a Southern tour in a revue titled "Hepsations of 1945." The show included the Nicholas Brothers as featured dancers, comedians Patterson and Jackson, and vocalist June Eckstine (Billy's wife).

Bebop had started to receive a share of recognition and popularity, and Shaw through that to tour the South and introduce Gillespie and his music to the black audience there would help to further the music and advance Diz as a personality. Dizzy had been informed that the band and acts would be doing a series of concerts, but it turned out to be a ballroom tour instead. This was unfortunate, for the rural Southern blacks were blues-oriented and unable to adapt their dancing to the fast tempi of the bop repertoire. In a word, the Gillespie band bombed.

❖ ❖

CHARLIE ROUSE   I stayed in B's band for about six months. That's when Jug joined the band. Jug took my place. I left the band in Chicago and went to Milwaukee, Lucky Thompson and myself. I didn't want to come back home. We worked around in taverns and stuff. And then I got stranded there so I had to work in a department store to get some bread to come back home. But at the time I left the band, Diz was leaving Billy's band to form his band, and he told me that when he formed the band he was gonna send for me. So I stayed in Milwaukee for about two, three, four to five months, and then I came back to Washington, and Diz called me. Diz was really like a teacher. He handles the band like a—Diz is very rhythmical. When he's in front of the band, if it's Max [Roach] or if it's Art [Blakey] or anyone, he'd do different things, and they'd catch it as he does it—he'd do it rhythmically on the beat. He would always have an interplay with the rhythm section, all the time. But he was a perfectionist. If you're supposed to make A and you make A-flat, he didn't want to hear none of that.

I almost got killed on that Southern tour. Catastrophe almost. I was very fortunate, though. They were young cats in the band. In the South at the time, you could buy guns, so everybody was buying guns—shooting guns. So one particular night—I think it was in Atlanta, it was in Georgia somewhere. It was Patterson and Jackson. They had a little valet, and this guy had bought a gun, and he was playing with it, clicking it all around. It was loaded, and he clicked it at me, close, and it so happened the safety latch was on, and it just clicked and clicked, and he was laughing, and then he clicked it again, like that, and it went off. Well, I was scared to death. That was a pretty weird trip, the first Southern trip. They wasn't ready for it because it was a new thing all over, even in New York at the time, 'cause the thing was changing. Then when we went down there the Billy Shaw Agency was trying to promote Dizzy's band, and they just took the "bebop" band down there [laughter], and the people didn't know nothing about that bebop shit. After that tour I don't think Dizzy did a tour down there. Not for a long time [laughter].

« 5 »

California

A year later Gillespie would reform the big band and keep it together into early 1950. But in late 1945, it was back to the small-group format. Bird and Dizzy were reunited and left for California in December to play an engagement at Billy Berg's in Hollywood. Al Haig was the pianist, with Milt Jackson on vibes; Ray Brown, bass; and Stan Levey, drums. When Parker's attendance at the club became erratic, Gillespie was forced to hire Lucky Thompson to insure two horns in the front line.

The reception that Gillespie and Parker received from the public in California wasn't much better than Dizzy's big band got in the South. The difference here was the musicians, who had heard the New York recordings, came to hear their new idols in the flesh. These were the young musicians, but the older, established musicians such as Art Tatum and Benny Carter, came too, as did the Hollywood celebrity crowd. The music, however, was misunderstood in the main. The people were used to the vocals of Slim Gaillard and Harry "The Hipster" Gibson. Although Parker and Gillespie recorded with Gaillard (the famous *Slim's Jam* on Savoy) and were presented on Rudy Vallee's national radio show by Gibson, their audience and the people who came to hear Gaillard and Gibson were not reconciled. Opening night was big, but as the week went on the crowds diminished, and the hip minority did not order drinks often enough to make the cash register ring with any consistency.

❖❖

RED CALLENDER   They didn't really understand it. It was a little above them. They were used to hearing pop melodies turned into jazz. But these guys took popular songs and wrote another line above the harmony. That's what "Groovin' High" was, "Whispering." Ray Brown had three strings on his bass. I took him an A-string.

❖❖

It wasn't that Los Angeles did not have jazz precedents going back to Freddie Keppard and Kid Ory, when those New Orleans jazzmen traveled to California in the early 1900's. Keppard went out in 1912 to join bassist Bill Johnson's Original Creole Ragtime Band; Ory left New Orleans for Los Angeles in 1919 and spent the next five years in California before joining King Oliver in Chicago. By 1929 he had returned to the West and was based there until he moved to Hawaii in 1966. When Bird and Dizzy came to Los Angeles, Ory's kind of jazz was more popular than theirs with the average Angeleno jazz fan.

Of course, jazz was represented by styles between New Orleans and bop in the many clubs of Los Angeles. The hub of the nightlife in the black community was Central Avenue, with clubs like the Alabam (it had been started as the Apex in the '20s by drummer Curtis Mosby), Lovejoy's, and the Down Beat. And then there were the Hollywood clubs such as the Swing Club and the Streets of Paris.

❖❖

ZOOT SIMS   I was working with Sid Catlett at the Streets of Paris in 1944 when I went in the Army. It was downstairs, a nice-looking club. I was young and thrilled, and nobody bothered us. I wish I could play with him again. He was a great drummer, great man. We had Marlowe Morris, John Simmons, so it was a good trio. I was with Benny Goodman at 20th Century Fox making a movie called *Sweet and Low Down*, and Benny broke the band up after that. He backed a little band with Bill Harris and Ernie Figueroa and myself, and we came back to Cafe Society Uptown. We had Specs Powell on drums. And Specs Powell got ill and Big Sid filled in for him. Ben Webster was with Big Sid and he left and Sid asked me if I wanted to go to California. California was my home, and this gig was ending anyway, so it was perfect for me. We took the train. That was fun, too, taking the train with those guys, with Sid.

When I got out of the Army, I went with Benny for a short tour. We got back to New York, and we did the 400 Club, and we were doing the Mobil Gas show on the radio. That ended soon, and I went back. Then I spent part of '46 and all of '47 hangin' out with that Gene Roland band, and Stan Getz was out there and Don Lamond. That was a funny gig. It was a Mexican ballroom [Pontrelli's]. East Side L.A. It was Mexicans, and we'd play Mexican stocks. We'd play their music, which we didn't mind doing. I didn't mind it, but then we'd slip in our own music, and they didn't mind it, so it worked out fine. And I used to take two street cars to get there. One street car and then a transfer. Now that was a nice period, 'cause Herbie [Steward] was on the gigs, Stan Getz, Jimmy Giuffre.

There was one place, every Tuesday night in Chinatown, this was like a steady gig. 'Cause we didn't get paid, but we'd get a big meal.

And nobody bugged us either. We just played. Jammed. There was a Wagon Wheel, and there was a lot of places. A lot of them were on the outskirts. There really was a lot of places at that time. You never had no problem, like a Monday night, you'd know where to go, certain clubs. Sunday afternoon. Either that or at home.

I met Dexter [Gordon] very early in my life, during the 40s. I remember sitting in with him when I was really young, I used to go to Central Avenue and play all night long to six in the morning. And speaking about prejudice and all that stuff and all that problem, I think I was fifteen years old, fourteen or fifteen, and if they saw you with a horn, nobody bothered you—a kind of respect. Everything was fine. That was a great period for me because I played all night. 'Cause I never got up to school, but that was my school anyway, and I learned an awful lot. And to this day, every time I hear an-out-of-tune upright and a guitar playing, electric guitar playin' the blues, it does something to me. L.A. was really jumpin' then, it was nice. Lovejoys, I used to go there a lot. Honey Murphy's. In '46 when I got out of the Army, I saw Bird uptown L.A. somewhere, some joint, I don't know the name, I don't remember the name of it. I was amazed. I never heard a saxophone played that way before, that's all. I was amazed. He played so beautiful, his tone was, everything, and he still had that Kansas City blues.

BENNY BAILEY   When I went to the Coast and I got a chance to hear Miles and Bird, I had a chance to really get into it and hear Bird, the real source of everything. Mostly I was just listening to the radio. We didn't buy any records at all. My old man had a lot of Fats Waller records and things we'd always listen to all the time. Oh, yeah, we had a group, and we were trying to play like Louis Jordan—because it was very simple. We had a sorta quintet, and we would copy the arrangements and copy the solos, exactly. It was a lot of fun. Then I started playing with Scatman [Crothers].

❖❖

Then Bailey left Cleveland and went to California.

❖❖

BENNY BAILEY   I'm glad I went there 'cause I got a chance to meet Miles and Tommy Turrentine, Benny Carter. It was really happening; everything was happening. Dexter, Illinois Jacquet, and music everyplace. After the gig folded with Scatman, I started livin' on the unemployment compensation—twenty-five dollars a week and *makin'* it! We'd go on and play all the time; Hampton Hawes, all the cats were out there. Yeah, when I see Dex now, we always go back to those days. Maggie [Howard McGhee] was very popular out there at that time. He was a very mature trumpet player. He had his own group, nice arrangements and everything, good jobs and much easier to understand than, say, Dizzy at that time. He was playing modern but more for the people to understand; more melodic I would say.

There were sessions every night at a place called the Casablanca. And it would always be late, like twelve o'clock at night these sessions would start. Yeah, every night, practically. But actually what the cats would do was try to find out where Bird was gonna be any particular night, and everybody would try to be there. And either play or just listen. They had a session at Billy Berg's every Sunday, sort of a matinee. That was a lot of fun. They paid these other guys very little bread. But whatever it was, it helped. And anybody could play. They paid the first musicians that got there. Actually maybe about fifteen musicians, something like that. Art Tatum was out there, too, at that time. So you could just listen to music all the time, all over the place.

It was a big city, but the scene was pretty small. All the musicians knew each other, jazz musicians. And I remember there was very little enmity in those days. Everybody was very friendly 'cause everybody was tryin' to learn the same thing actually. It was a very nice time.

I had met Teddy Edwards who was with Howard [McGhee] in Frisco when I was with Scatman. We came from Frisco to L.A. and worked a place in Hollywood. So the band broke up. Scatman had only a combo—alto, trumpet, and he was playing guitar and drums. So after that broke up I guess I started hangin' out. Teddy and I used to visit each other every day anyway, and talk about music. So I guess Teddy got this record date going. We never got our money for the records. The record company folded up, but I mean that was a very nice date. It was no problems at all. It went very fast, so we did the whole thing in two or three hours.

❖ ❖

Originally done for the Rex label, the eight sides can now be found on *Central Avenue Breakdown, Volume 2* (Onyx 215).

There were many independent companies that emerged at the end of the war. If they signed a royalty agreement with the union—an agreement the major labels were still hassling over with American Federation of Musicians—they were in business. By the end of 1945, more than 350 recording directors—and their brothers—were AFM approved. Howard McGhee met two of those brothers—the Biharis. There was a date of McGhee's of which I never could get a good copy: "Intersection"—"Mop-Mop"—"Lifestream." The pressings were all bad, off-center.

HOWARD MC GHEE   That was Modern Records. He didn't know anybody. Man, this guy was the luckiest cat in the world. He came to me when I first quit Hawk. He had three hundred dollars and a pressing machine, one pressing machine. Jules Bihari came to me and said, "How about doin' a date?" I said, "Are you gonna pay me for the date?" and he said, "If we can get four sides out we might make enough money to continue to keep the thing." So we get a blues date, like me an' Teddy [Edwards] and Hadda Brooks. Anyway it was a blues date. This guy *made* it from that. Those records sold, and next thing I know he was callin' me back, and we did the "11:45 Swing" thing, and they sold, and he did another date, with Pearl Taylor or somebody. There were some other titles like "Mad Hype" that he put out again under a different name. That way he kept from accounting to me for the royalties. They were all doin' it back then. We did a thing at Long Beach.* Ralph Bass sold it to Black and White and didn't pay us. I saw him in Chicago; he was workin' for Chess records, I said, "Man, have you ever felt it in your heart to ever pay me for those dates?" He said, "Well, I'll tell you what I'm gonna do. I can't give you any money right now, but I'll put you on some dates, help you make some money." That was his out to getting out of that. What can you say? Everybody's out there trying to scalp a nickel. But they wouldn't even let Jules Bihari near the plant no more. They got him completely out of it. He was somethin', boy. I come back out there, after I won the *downbeat* poll, to see him and said, "I know you owe me some money." He said, "Yeah, we got some money here for you!" He gave me eighty-nine bucks, out of all those songs. We had original tunes and blues and everything, and he gave me eighty-nine bucks.

❖❖

McGhee first went to California with Coleman Hawkins in 1945.

❖❖

HOWARD MC GHEE   I did only work with Hawk for about two months,† that's all. I was with Georgie Auld's band. I quit his band 'cause the bread vanished . . . and Georgie Auld stranded me in St. Louis. He paid the band, but he didn't pay me! He said that he'd send it to the union, but the union ain't got no record of him sending any money there for me. So I went to the Downbeat Club in Philly for two or three weeks. Then I came to New York, and Pettiford said, "Hawk's looking for a trumpet player and you workin' with anybody?" I said, "No." So he took me around to the Three Deuces, and Hawk said, "You want to sit in and we see what you sound like?" And I said, "Hawk, sit in, what you mean by that? Sit in?" So he [Oscar] says, "Well, he want to know whether you can play." And I said, "Well, you talk to him. I ain't sittin' in." So Hawk said, "O.K. We're going to rehearse tomorrow. We got a record date coming up. Rehearse with us, so I can see what you sound like." And I said, "Yeah, that's all right, I ain't playin' for nothin'. You supposed to pay me somethin' to play." He said, "Yeah, well, we'll rehearse tomorrow." So I went down to rehearse, and went in the studio and did "Beanstalking," "Ready For Love" . . .

❖❖

*Junior Jazz at the Auditorium.
†November 1944 to March 1945 according to *The Encyclopedia of Jazz*.

The pianist on the date, Sir Charles (Thompson), was credited with writing "Ladies Lullaby" and "Sportsman's Hop."

❖❖

HOWARD MC GHEE I gave "Sportsman's Hop" to Sir Charles 'cause I couldn't put a release to it. Mc an' Pettiford used to play that with Charlie Barnet's band. We were short of a tune, so I said, "If you can put a release to this, when we record it we'll split it up." We worked at the Three Deuces for about three weeks before we went to Buffalo for two weeks; then we played Chicago for about two nights; and we went out to California. And after he left California, I quit the band. He stayed up there eight weeks. But he pulled some shit over a tune. I respected Hawk; I admired him, respected him, loved him, took from the way he played.

When we went to record for Capital, Dave Dexter brought Red Nichols to play this session; Hawk ran down a tune that he wants to play. They ran down "Fine and Dandy." That was the name of the tune, but Hawk had a different chart.* We'd been playing this thing already. When Red Nichols started to play, he couldn't read that. He was in the wrong setting. He definitely wasn't in the right—so Pettiford started laughing. When he laughed, I couldn't help but laugh, 'cause he did sound funny tryin' to play this thing. So that burned Dave Dexter up. He was madder than a son-of-a-bitch, 'cause his man can't cut the thing.

Hawk calls me to come on and play the thing so we can record it and get it over with. So I go in, and I play it, 'cause we'd been playin' it all the time. It wasn't that hard really, but it wasn't his thing. Hawk liked to stuff in all those little things. He didn't know anything like that. He didn't have the slightest idea. Then he tells me, "If I were you I wouldn't feel bad 'cause that's some hard music." I said, "Well, I don't feel bad 'cause I can play it. I been playin' it every night, so it ain't no problem with me." He thought he was makin' me feel good. But I was mad at Dave Dexter 'cause they didn't tell Hawk that Dave wanted Red on the gig. He should've told me not to come.

That was a helluva band, we knew we had a helluva band, and Hawk knew it. And everybody else was sayin', "The band is somethin' else." We were getting letters from everywhere: "When are y'all comin' back this way? Where are you going next?" Like I say, when they found out that I'd cut out and Sir Charles cut out and Pettiford cut out, wasn't nobody left but Hawk and Denzil Best; and Denzil got engaged with somebody else. Yeah the records were good. The band was good. We weren't the hippest; we weren't no Charlie Parker, but we was good.

Out in California everybody thought I was a California boy. When we first got out there, we played a dance in Long Beach California,

*"Too Much of a Good Thing."

and Norman Granz came down to hire Hawk to play a concert, but when he heard me he says, "Oh, yeah, I could use another trumpet player, too, so you wanna make the date too?" I says, "Well, yeah, what's happenin'? He says, "Well the job pay thirty-five dollars." And I said, "Why not, I'm not working that night." He didn't put Hawk and me together. They put me an' Joe Guy and Willie Smith an' Illinois and Charlie Ventura. They put us together. Then Hawk did his thing by himself. So it didn't bother me none. If that's what he wanted to do, that's what he would do. No, he did have me play "Stuffy" with him on the thing.

❖❖

That was the first *Jazz at the Philharmonic* album to be released. "How High the Moon" helped launch Granz's whole series of such records.

❖❖

HOWARD MC GHEE   When that record come out everybody just took it for granted—See, Dizzy was in New York and I was in California, so they said I was a California boy—answer to Dizzy. Me an' Dizzy had been tight. We'd been with Billy Eckstine together. I'd learned his tunes, and he'd learned mine. We'd been playin', hangin' out together and everything. They just took it for granted that I was a California boy. Everywhere I went, "Hey, man! There's the California cat! Hey, man! How's California?" And I only lived there in '45–'46; I came back in to New York in '47. And everybody still, *today,* they still ask me, "When did you get back from the Coast?" I say, "Oh, I've been livin' in New York since 1947! I don't live in California!" They say, "Oh, I thought you lived in California!" I say, "No." In fact when Dizzy came out there with his group, me an' Dizzy were broadcasting at the same time. He was comin' from Billy Berg's and I was comin' from Streets of Paris. The audience didn't know who to listen to 'cause they was for me, but Dizzy was from New York. They hadn't heard him, but they used to tell me, "I won't turn away from you!" I said, "Man, listen to everybody. Don't be worryin' like that. Dizzy and I are friends. Ain't no enemies there!"

The musicians out there hated us, man. They thought we were bringin' somethin' there to destroy their kingdom. They hated it, Kid Ory an' them, they hated me! Oh, boy! We went in this joint to work. After we played the first set, Kid Ory stormed out of there. "I *will* not play with this kind of music." But the people didn't give a damn. They wasn't like that. I once read a write-up that said people walked out after every group. That's bullshit! They just stayed there and listened, to see what was going on. They wasn't objectin'. But it was Kid Ory, he said, "Nooo."

We had the same band. Teddy Edwards, J.D. King, Vernon Biddle, Bob Kesterson, and Roy Porter; we just went out and played just like we'd been playin' in L.A. But we invaded the Dixieland domain, the Jade Room. They couldn't stand for that. Huh, that was somethin'.

❖❖

When McGhee states "the musicians out there hated us," he does not mean the younger musicians. One of these was William "Sonny" Criss. When he was growing up in Memphis, he heard Charlie Parker on a Jay McShann record.

❖❖

SONNY CRISS   We had those records at home in Memphis years ago. The first time I ever tried to put anything down on paper was one of Bird's tunes when he was with McShann. I loved his playing, but I didn't know who he was. I had no way of finding out. I had only been playin' then about a year and a half, two years at the most. But it was easy for me to hear everybody, because it was in my home. I heard it all day long. Once in a while I used to go to the theater—Beale Street, the Palace Theater, everybody came through there. And then there was another place where I used to go hang out at night. I couldn't get in, so I'd go around the back through the windows—an auditorium. This is where I'd hear Basie and Duke. The first person that I heard that really did shake me up before I heard Charlie Parker, or anybody—I don't know if you ever heard of him—his name was Hank O'Day. He was an alto player in Memphis. Very famous in Memphis. Very strange-looking man. With a head about so big. But he had a kind of sound that I had never heard before. Very beautiful and very powerful, very strong. Even today, I haven't heard that kind of sound that he had. And he was my first teacher.

❖❖

When he was sixteen (he was born in 1927), Criss's family moved to Los Angeles.

❖❖

SONNY CRISS   Then I went to high school. My parents wanted me to go to a better school. We lived in Watts at the time. So I used to travel on the red car from Watts to the West Side, which was the long way to go to a mixed school. It was supposed to be a better school. And it was good for me, in one sense, because I got kind of a foundation, a harmonic foundation there that I didn't have. But soon I discovered the best *band* in town was in the ghetto, so I left and went to that school, which was Jefferson.

I met Hamp Hawes when I went to the first school. And that's where we formed the band. A little group with Hampton Hawes and Buddy Woodson and Big Jay McNeely. Big Jay could play for a while. Something happened. Money got to him. Then when I transferred, Chuck Thompson was playing drums in the band in the other school. Sweet Pea [Leroy Robinson], the alto player, was in that band. He played with Roy Porter and recorded with the Roy Porter big band.

Sweet Pea was part of that. Also at that time, Eric [Dolphy] was a part of that band. About that time I met Teddy [Edwards]. Teddy was workin' with Roy Milton. Down on 1st Street in Little Chinatown. And there was a little high-school group that we had with Hamp and the other guys. We were workin' around clubs. And the better clubs, too, at the time. Even while we was goin' to school. And shortly after that I met Howard McGhee.

Before that it was just a small group of musicians that were really into it. Very small group. The opposition from the older musicians was tremendous. 'Cause they couldn't hear it. Not only did they not like us, buty they didn't like Bird. 'Cause they would say things like, "Oh, he's playing wrong notes. He's playing out of tune. He's got the worst tone in the world." So anybody that was tryin' to go along the same line was dead. And I remember people sayin' to me that I was crazy to try and play music like that. My mother had gone to Chicago. I had heard about the new records but I couldn't get them. So I told her to look for them, and she found them. She brought "Congo Blues," "Bebop," and several others. When I heard those records just like my mind was popped. I didn't think about any other musician but Bird. I didn't have the slightest idea what he was doing, but I felt it. Before that I was listening to a lot of different alto players: Cleanhead [Vinson], Louis Jordan, Johnny Hodges, Benny Carter—all the established players. Everybody. Pete Brown. I liked everybody. Till I heard Bird; it was all over.

The first organized small group that I heard was Coleman Hawkins when McGhee came out here. They played at the Streets of Paris on Hollywood Boulevard, near Highland. Do you know the Pickwick bookstore? Streets of Paris was right across the street. There were clubs all over town and lots of sessions. Ready to session all night long. Every night there was a different session some place. And everybody at that time was trying to outplay everybody else. Wardell [Gray] was on the scene. Dexter [Gordon] was on the scene.

Now this was just prior to the end of the war and just after the end of the war. So that brought about change. Social climbing. People had money for one thing. A lot of the men were gone, so a lot of people were kind of adventuring, seeking out places. I remember being stopped by the police, and I had a joint in my pocket. They searched me, and they saw it, and they didn't know what the hell it was [laughter]. During those days there was a lot of hustling, a lot of pimps, a lot of dope dealers, a lot of gangsters. Los Angeles, I guess, like any other town, was kind of wide open because it was during the war; a lot of people coming in from the South, going into defense plants. There was new money. People hadn't had that kind of money before. They were spending it. I think that had a great deal to do with the atmosphere. There were people that were kind of adventurous, seekers. And there always are a group of people like that. And they just kinda found the music. Found out where the musicians were. There was never a lack of an audience, if you were in the right place. Especially after it got started around '45, '46.

❖❖

Blacks and whites were mixing then, and the police didn't like that. A mixed group—it didn't even have to be a man and a woman—was likely to be stopped.

❖❖

SONNY CRISS I remember in those days, if I came to visit you and you were living someplace like this,* and you had a party or jam session that lasted all night or something—if I happened to be unfortunate enough to be here when daybreak came, I'd have to stay until it got dark again. Los Angeles was a very, very provincial town at that time.

People that were really interested in the music and lived in Hollywood, they had to be very careful, because their neighbors would complain. What are all those black people doing here? What's all the noise? And all that kind of stuff. So it was kind of a trip. Goin' back, going from Hollywood back through the South Side, you had to be very careful. 'Cause if you and I were riding together, we'd get stopped.

There were many nights when I played above my head. Way above my head. And I think you know what I mean by that. That happened with a lot of musicians because the competition was so stiff, and we were having so much fun. And it was such an *in* thing. The audience were special people. They were artists, writers, actors, and so forth. They were very into the music. They inspired all the musicians to play their asses off.

❖❖

Criss participated in some of the concerts popularized by Norman Granz and Gene Norman. A series of 78s came out on the Bop label. Each side had a different musician soloing.

❖❖

SONNY CRISS That was from something on Central Avenue. And that was recorded, actually, during the record ban. I can't remember who the promoter was, but he hired all the musicians. The concert was held at the Elks with Barney Kessel, Dexter and Wardell, Trummy Young, Howard McGhee, and the trumpet player that played with Duke Ellington that died out here. High-note specialist.

❖❖

(Al Killian, who was murdered by his psychopathic landlord. He was on a lot of sessions in those days. Hamp Hawes played in the concert, too. They were on jukeboxes in black bars, and they would be listed on the box according to the soloist featured on the particular side.)

❖❖

*interview done at Leonard Feather's house in North Hollywood.

SONNY CRISS   You know how it was done? I can't remember who did that.*
This was during the record ban, a guy brought a tape recorder. Or
some kind of recorder.† It was hidden under the stage. And this is
what really started the musicians to frown on people bringing recorders around, because prior to that, if somebody wanted to bring a
recorder and record us, fine. But after that everybody really became
very, very conscious of that kind of thing. 'Cause nobody got paid for
that.

❖❖

The majority of this concert, recorded at the Elk's Hall on July 6,
1947, has been issued under the names of Dexter Gordon and
Wardell Gray on *The Hunt* (Savoy SJL2222). Other selections appear on Dexter Gordon's *Long Tall Dexter* (Savoy SJL 2211); and
Black California, Volume 2 (Savoy SJL 2215).

❖❖

Before Criss heard Parker in person, Bird had made a tremendous impression on him.

❖❖

SONNY CRISS   The impact that it made on me from just listening to the
recordings was so great. That was fantastic. And that probably is one
of the reasons why I didn't get involved more with big bands. And I
think it was an instinct, something that just came. I feel, even today I
feel like you're part of the establishment in big bands. Part of an as-
sembly line and they restrict you. It's not really my thing.

❖❖

Quite naturally, Criss sought out Parker.

❖❖

SONNY CRISS   That really was quite a scene. I went lookin' for him. They
were livin' on 1st Street. Diz and the whole band. I met one of the
musicians coming out of the hotel, and I asked him about Bird. I went
to the desk. They told me what room. Then I knocked on the door.
No answer. Then I knocked. I was really determined. I was still at
school. No answer. So I wouldn't give up. I just kept knocking because they had told me he was there. And finally he peeked out of the
peep hole. I told him who I was, and he let me in. At the time I had
one of those little Fords with a rumble seat in the back. Canvas top.
We used to ride all over L.A. He loved driving a car. But I was slick
enough not to let him have it by himself. He was notorious for not
returning things.

I was workin' at a place across the street from the Lincoln Theater.
Sammy Yates, Gene Montgomery, and a lot of people. He and Prez
used to come and jam with us all the time. It was outa sight. I think

---

* Ralph Bass.
† two portable disc cutters.

during this time was the only advice that Bird ever gave me about playing, because I would become so excited when he would come in and we'd play difficult things. I remember one night I was playing— he had played and I played behind him—and I was really trying hard. He said to me, "Don't think. Quit thinkin." That's the only thing he ever told me about playing. He was very strange, in the sense that I never knew him to tell another saxophone player how to do anything. Now maybe he did with some people, but he never told me anything. During that whole time that I knew him, that was only thing that he ever said.

But they gave Bird a bad time out here. They really did give him a bad time. I think the thing that I enjoyed most, other than the jam sessions, was the band that McGhee had. That was four saxophones and one trumpet. And that band was never recorded—Teddy Edwards, Gene Montgomery, Bird, and myself. Roy Porter; a bass player named Dingbod [Bob Kesterson]; sometimes Joe Albany, at the Club Finale. That was a mean band. Whew! The way Bird could play first alto, I've never heard anything like that since. That was an education in itself. The way he phrased. At the time I don't think he was too happy because the band was billed as Howard McGhee's band, and I don't think he liked that too much.

That was during the period when Bird was about to crack up. He was doing a lot of strange things. Like dropping ten or twelve bennies at once. Which is unbelievable. He'd be up for four or five days. Of course the music was unbelievable.

I gave a good account of myself. At least most of the people that remember those days say that I did. I think that I did. I remember some nights, though, that he played things that none of us thought were possible to play. He was going through some changes, and this is when he really began to be treated pretty shabbily. I guess he was trying to kick at that time too. Bennies and alcohol. And his nervous system was shot. He didn't know what the hell he was doing. I think then after that, right after that, he went to Camarillo. When he came out of the hospital he was fat, sounding good, sounding beautiful, and he went back to New York. I don't think he stayed here too long.

❖❖

When the Gillespie group went back to New York in early February of 1946, after having closed at Billy Berg's, Parker remained in California. He played at a club in downtown L.A. fronting a combo with Miles Davis, Joe Albany, Addison Farmer, and Chuck Thompson. The area, called "Little Tokyo," was then devoid of Japanese-Americans, who were then residing, due to a wartime edict of the government, at the Santa Anita racetrack, which had been converted into an internment camp. So the Finale Club, a bring-your-own-bottle club with "membership" cards, opened in a meeting room of an office building. Its proprietor was dancer Foster Johnson, an ex-vaudevillian who would get up and hoof with the band when the spirit hit.

Festivities at the Finale Club began at midnight, and it quickly became the focal point for all the young musicians, drawn by the magnet that was Bird. When the police noticed the happenings at the Finale they pressured Johnson for a weekly "contribution." Johnson quietly closed the club.

The high cost of heroin in L.A.—as opposed to the New York prices—had been a source of trouble to Parker from the outset of his California stay. Now "horse" was not only expensive but it was in short supply. Bird's personal connection, "Moose the Mooche," had been busted. Bird was living in a reconverted garage. The panic was on.

❖ ❖

HOWARD MC GHEE   I hadn't seen him for a while until he came out to California with Dizzy. He was very unhappy with Dizzy 'cause he didn't like the way Dizzy acted on the stage. He said Dizzy was a Tom. This is just Dizzy, period. He wasn't Tommin' but Bird thought that he was, which was a drag because they had a good group. Plus then he'd get to be bearing on me 'cause, even though he was with Dizzy he'd come to me wanting to borrow my money all the time. I went for it a couple of times, I said, "Yeah, I know you foolin' around with that shit." I know it costs three times as much out there as it does in New York, so I could understand it. That's how we got to be friends, so he'd come by. Then, after he quit Dizzy, quit down at Billy Berg's, I should say, he had a group at the Club Finale first. I think I went up to San Francisco with my group playin' at the Backstage Club. Bird got the gig with Foster Johnson at the Finale Club. When I came back to Los Angeles, Bird was uptight. He was really out there. He had no money. He was living in a horrible place. I knew he had made some records for Ross Russell, so I went and saw Ross and said, "Look, man, I want you to do something for this guy. You've recorded him, you've got him under contract, and he's going around like tomorrow is the end." In the garage. He was *always up*. I went there five o'clock in the morning, he was up. I went over twelve o'clock during the day, he was up. I'd go eight o'clock in the morning, he was up. Every time I went over there he was up. I said, "Damn, when this guy sleep?" He was taking Benzedrine and all that stuff.

But he was always reading and learning. He was a very educated man. He could talk about—my car was goofing off and I said, "Damn! I'm going to take this thing to the garage," and he said, "It ain't nothin' but such-and-such," and he got out there, and he went around the motor, and he fixed the damn thing! He knew all about the motor and what caused it to run and all that shit. He educated me to a lot of things because I'd go and keep him company. I know he's over there by himself; he wasn't interested in girls. Nothing they could do for him. He was outta sight. We used to sit up and listen to *Firebird Suite* and *Rite of Spring*. He hipped me to Stravinsky. 'Cause I wasn't listening to that. I was listening to arrangers and bands. I wasn't paying much attention to this real serious side of music, but he educated me to that fact and made me listen to it. And I got to learn Bartok and Wagner and all those guys.

Bird was a remarkable cat. He could reach back and get things out of his mind that the average guy never even think of again. You hear something in 1918, how the hell are you gonna remember it today? He could. He could reach right back and play it. "Remember this, Maggie?" And he'd play it for me. I'd say "Goddamn, man, I ain't heard that in . . ." But he was a hell of a musician. We played the Finale— the other guy closed it, the guy closed it but Bird didn't have no gig. Me an' Dot [McGhee's wife, Dorothy] had decided to open it up and use it as a bottle club. You bring your own bottle, and you just sell set- ups and admission. And, man, the joint used to stay loaded every night. We got Bird to feel pretty good. It lasted about three months, and that's pretty good for Los Angeles. In Los Angeles they don't give a shit about no jazz, especially that new jazz. But I had a good-soundin' band. I had four saxes with Bird playin' lead. I tried to get every son- of-a-bitch and his brother out there to record that band.

Man, the joint used to stay packed; before we even get into the joint, the joint was loaded. I talked: I went to Modern Records; I went to Norman Granz, Aladdin Records—every son-of-a-bitch out there that had records—Black and White. I said, "Man, I got a band out here I want you to record," and they said, "Naw, we want you to make some blues." I said, "Aw, I don't want to hear that." The band was sounding so great! For Los Angeles they was raisin' hell, man. Like I told you, they don't come hear *nobody* play no *music*. But, man, they were loaded in there *every night*. I tried to get Jules Bihari to record, and he wouldn't do it. "You making everything else, you may as well do this. This is something that will sell for years to come." He said, "No, I want you and Pearl Taylor to make records." 'cause for down South they make them Southern records. They sell down there regardless of what it is. I talked with Ross [Russell]. I said, "Ross, you ought to get the band." He said, "No, I can't afford the four saxes, just you and Bird." He wouldn't even come by to hear the band when the joint was loaded every night. He wouldn't even come by to hear it. But it was a helluva band. We had Roy Porter and Bob Kesterson; the piano player, I can't remember his name.

We tried to do a record date; that's the one that he cracked up on, just at that time. That's why I went to Ross and said, "We'd better do something, 'cause this cat is uptight." We had to close the club, 'cause without him there ain't no name that don't mean nothin' anyway. He said, "O.K." So he set up the date. But Bird couldn't find nobody with some shit, and he was tryin' to make it off of alcohol and he couldn't do it.

He was on everything. I had him for Christmas dinner. I had a whole pile of reefer and cocaine and everything, and this M———F—— did up everything; cleaned my reefer, took all the reefer and left the seeds and the twigs. I said, "Dirty son-of-a-bitch!" I got up to roll me a joint for Christmas, and there ain't no pot! Nothin' but sticks and seeds. He took a whole pound of pot. I said, "All right, this is what I asked for, dealin' with Bird. I know I should know him by now." I said, "I'll give him a snort of cocaine," and that was gone. And the whiskey—I found about that much whiskey left.

Oh, man, he could take some—he really could. I seen him take a handful of benzedrine like that. I don't know how his sytem stood it. Look like it would stop his heart. Any other man, it would. I know a lot of cats just tried to act like him, and they was found layin' on the side of the road somewhere, fuckin' with shit like Bird was. Little alto player, I don't know his name, from out of Chicago, he was gonna be like Bird, and he came to play a dance. He followed Bird around. Two days later he was dead. But he saw Bird do it. He'd see Bird fill up the thing, and he'd put up another one and put it in there, and Bird take a handful of bennies. Bird was takin' bennies and everything else to go with it. A lot of cats didn't know that. Bird had a counteract in a sense when he was takin' Benzedrine, 'cause morphine had a tendency to put you to sleep, but the Benzedrine keep your eyes open, keeps you alert so that your mind is still goin'. I think that helped Bird live longer than he would have takin' all the drugs that he was takin'. I saw him take some drugs, man. He told me, "Maggie, don't you ever get that." I said, "Yeah." I didn't. I saw him goin' through that shit, I said, "Shit, I don't need that!"

But I come in an' got stoned. I come right into New York and got stoned, and I didn't even dig it. I didn't even dig on gettin' strung out. 'Cause the cat come and say, "Let's get high, man!" First I thought it was cocaine, and it *was* cocaine, when we first started snortin' co-caine, so the cat said you mix cocaine and horse together, and you sniff the two. On the third day I woke up sick as a dog, I said, "What's the matter with me, I don't feel good!" So about an hour later, this cat come by, he said, "All you need is another snort. Take a snort of cocaine, man." So I did, but it was horse. Then the next day I was *really* sick. I said, "Oh, boy!" Then *I* went lookin' for *him*. And he tell me, "I ain't got none, but the cat got some." I said, "Listen he done strung me out. He ain't got none, but the cat upstairs. I gotta buy it." Dirty cats—they used to come down to Birdland all the time. They used to give you shit, try to get you strung out. So I can understand what Bird was goin' through. He just couldn't find nobody to cop from. When the time come for him to go to the studio, he couldn't play. He tried; his nerves wouldn't stand it. He couldn't keep his horn in one place long enough to play it. But he played the shit out of "Lover Man" as far as I'm concerned. That shit is one of the prettiest solos, even knowing how sick he was. I was right there watchin him, how his horn was turnin' around, and he was twistin' around and jumpin' up in the air and all this, but he played the shit out of that. The one I didn't think he did so good on is "The Gypsy."

But *Lover Man* he played the shit out of. And he got mad at Ross for puttin' it out. He come back and made another one,* but the other one was more impressive, because he wasn't playing as many notes, and it was prettier. He didn't have the strength or the stamina to run through the horn. He was just barely getting the sound out, but I thought it was beautiful like a son-of-a-bitch. That night, he walked out of the hotel with no clothes on, that's how high—they took him to Camarillo. But he was all right. I went out to the hospital to see him. They give him a shot of dope. He was cool. "Damn! Maggie, get me outta here!!" I said, "No, baby, you in trouble now. They caught you, they got you in on criminal charges."

JOE ALBANY   So when Bird was in Camarillo, they popped me in Camarillo, too, for some reason. And when I got there, I'm in what they call "receiving," and I see this cat walk by, and he's fat but looks like Bird anyway. So I say, "Hey, Bird" and he says, "Joe," so he comes around and talks to the guard—apparently he was all through his whatever he got, treatment or what. He laid a couple of dollars on me, some Sucrets, some chocolates, cigarettes. He said, "I'll see you whenever you get in my population, son." But then the next day or so they go to check the x-rays which are for tubercular, so I think, "What am I doing here? I've got a chick out there." So I go out, put my clothes on, and go over the barbed-wire fence and split. It may have been a chance to tighten with Bird.

HOWARD MC GHEE   You know the psychiatrist that was taking care of him commited suicide after Bird left there. He couldn't figure out how this guy could be like that. He figured he was a dumb stud, just didn't know no better, and Bird wasn't a dummy [laughs]. Bird used to tell me, "I got this cat goin' around in circles." I say, "What you doin' to him, Bird?" He said, "This fool don't know nothin'. He comes from Vienna. He supposed to be a psychiatrist. I know more than he does." I say, "You gotta be messin' with somebody, right?"

But he was out there, and they brought him down off the drugs, gradually brought him down, so when he came out, he didn't need it, but his capacity, his mind was the same, 'cause on the first night he got out we opened at the Hi-De-Ho Club. Ross and I went out to get him a suit, bought him a new horn. He picked up the horn and hit

*for Clef in 1951, reissued on Verve.

the highest note and run to the lowest note. He hadn't even touched a horn. He just picked it up and run down through the horn. He said, "That's good enough," put the horn in the case an' I kept the horn 'cause we were scared he'd—we didn't know what he was going to do. So he went on home and got sharp and come on to work that night and lined up eight doubles at the bar. He said, "Gimme eight doubles." The bartender looked at him like he was crazy, and he says, "Well, who's with ya?" He said, "This is for me!" He say, "I'll tell you what, if you drink 'em, I'll give 'em to ya." So he said, "Line 'em up!" An' he drank every one of 'em, went up on the bandstand and played like a champ. The bartender looked at him and said, "I don't believe it! I don't believe a guy can do this!"

We had Hamp Hawes then. Hamp saw him do it. So the next night Hamp come back sayin', "Gimme eight doubles!" Now he gonna play like Bird. He figures he's strong, shit. He drank them eight doubles, and before the set was halfway through, we had to take him downstairs and lay him out, because he was out, he didn't know *nothin'* was goin' on. And we got him enough to vomit so he would vomit up some of that stuff. He stayed down there all night. He didn't play nothin'. Me an' Bird had to play piano all night.

❖❖

Then came the "Relaxin' At Camarillo" date.

❖❖

HOWARD MC GHEE   We're supposed to be going to rehearsal, rehearse the tunes, so I go to pick up Bird, blow on the horn, sit out there waitin' . . . I said, "I gotta go see . . ." I don't like leavin' my car back there with my horns and everything . . . Los Angeles wasn't *that* safe, so I went to the front door and rang the bell, rang the bell, I called, "Hey, Bird!" I heard him say "Yeah!" I said, "Well, come on! We gotta go!" He said, "Yeah, you gotta come up here though!" So I go back to the car and get my horns and go in the house, and Bird's layin' in the tub, writin' music. That's the way he wrote "Relaxin' at Camarillo," right in the bathtub. An' he give me about twelve bars, an' he say, "You write this out for the band." So I said, "Well, come on, let's go, and I'll write it out when I get out there." So I finally got him dressed, and we went on out to rehearsal. The following week, when I wrote out this thing, "Relaxin' at Camarillo," nobody had an idea what that was 'cause the rhythmic thing was so different. I said, "What's the tempo, Bird?" He said, "'Bout like that [taps off]." I said, "O.K. Everybody get their parts ready. O.K. Let's go!" An' he kicked it off, an' wasn't nobody playin' but him! I said, "Jiminy!" I was lookin' at the part, too, an' I wrote it down for the guys. I said, "Wait a minute, we gotta get to this, we can't figure this out!" We took it real slow until we could play it. Boy, he had it. He said, "When you all get it, then call me." He went out, and got him a bottle of whiskey, and he was sittin' out in the car gettin' drunk, when we finally did get it together.

So the next day we made it, and he played the shit out of it. In fact, he played the hell out of everything, he sounded so good, I was so amazed to see him be back 'cause we thought he might die, if they had taken him off a little too fast, like Billie Holiday. 'Cause we didn't think of Billie Holiday then, but when they cut her off, she just went like that. We didn't know whether Bird was comin' back. We sure was glad he was back. Man, it was such a pleasure to go to work with Bird, and such a horrible thought, too: After he gets through playin' what are you going to play? I used to be listenin' to him—he's havin' a ball—and all of a sudden that dawn on me, "Now you gotta follow him. What you gonna play?" Then you had to go in your brain, try to rack yourself. I couldn't wait to get to work, and I hated to be on the gig.

BARNEY KESSEL   I jammed in different places with Charlie Parker a lot. In fact, once he carried my amplifier into the club from my car. You know, we never sat around and talked. I never saw him except on the bandstand. I really think I had my hands full just trying to learn the music. And I was doing a lot of studio work. During the day. When they were jamming at night, I had already finished a whole day's work, working in the studios.

I remember he wrote out the melodies to these things like "Relaxin' at Camarillo," which were hard to read for me. They were very syncopated. I was not the reader that I finally developed into, and it was difficult, and they were written on sort of a very coarse-grained paper, like when we were little kids going to school they would have Big Chief tablet paper. If you made one erasure, and you take the whole page, and it makes a very black mark. It's just cheap pulp paper. And this manuscript paper was like that, and he wrote in a very hard leaded pencil, so you could hardly see it, and if the light hit it a certain way you would swear that there was not a mark on that paper. I remember that one of the things—not only could I not read it, except with great difficulty, I had trouble seeing the notes on the page. I recall that really in truth the mixture of that date, not everybody was really into bebop. I don't know why. At that particular time, for some reason, I recall, when Dodo [Marmarosa] played, he played a boom-chick rhythm, which is just the opposite—he never ever did that—*that* time he did it. It wasn't the appropriate thing for that, nor did he ever do that before or after that.*

JIMMY ROWLES   I was in L.A., and Don Lamond came to me and was flipping. He said, "I've got a record date with Bird." And he did that record—I think he did four sides. And Don was so happy.

BARNEY KESSEL   I recall on one of the tunes—I don't know what it was—Charlie Parker asked him [Lamond] to play a four-measure drum break to start. And he played this thing, and I recall that on one of these

*Marmarosa had, on "Slim's Jam" with Slim Gaillard.

tunes, when he finished, no one knew where to come in. They asked him to do it again, he did it again, and he did it differently, and they still didn't know. Finally, he did it, and they came in. But it ended up that every time he was absolutely right, and he wasn't trying to be far out; it reminded me of Elvin Jones today; it was very creative and very different and right. It's just that we were used to hearing more of a tap-dance approach—but he was right. He just played an introduction, and we, being used to not counting, but rather to just pick up the traditional metric feel of a typical rhythmic drum solo, we did not bother to count. As a result it went right by us, and we didn't come in right.

❖❖

Then there was a song called "Carvin' the Bird" on that date. Later Kessel did it with Stan Hasselgard as "Swedish Pastry." Now it is credited to Howard McGhee but then, with Hasselgard on Capital, it was credited to Kessel.

BARNEY KESSEL   I think what that was, was one of several times in my life where I seemed to get a wave of inspiration, and I wrote a song, only, embarrassingly, to find out later that it's already been written. What has happened is this is latent in my head. It wasn't exactly the same, but I do recall it started out that way—note for note.

I remember his song. But it was not an intentional lift. I never knew the source of that until just now. It's one of those things where you think you're hearing something for the first time in your own mind, and it's something that's stayed with you, and you've long forgotten the incident or the source or where it came from.

RED CALLENDER   I had met Bird in New York—'39—and I guess I just happened to be there when he first came into town, and naturally he upset everybody who was aware of what was going on. Then I saw him again. I saw the good side of Bird, I guess, most of the time because he had been out in Camarillo, and we did "Relaxin' at Camarillo," and that was right after he got out. Bird was a quiet type. I thought of Bird as an intellectual. When he was straight he could really carry on some deep conversations and had some great philosophy, but he was just sick. They'd harass these guys and put them in jail, and they should have put them in a hospital. He only hurt himself, nobody else.

❖❖

A week before the "Relaxin' at Camarillo" date, Dial Records did a recording session with Parker that included a vocalist.

❖❖

ROSS RUSSELL   Charlie told me he wanted to use an unknown singer he discovered working in a club on Central Avenue. The singer's name was Earl Coleman, and he sang like Eckstine . . . I knew that any singer would ruin the instrumental date [the "Camarillo" session]. I offered Charlie an alternative. Why not do a separate date, featuring Coleman with a small, intimate group? Charlie swallowed the bait. I immediately made a deal with Erroll Garner to provide a rhythm section.

Earl Coleman struggled for two hours to complete acceptable takes on two vocals, "Dark Shadows" and "This Is Always." I didn't like them, although they were better than I realized. After the last take of "Dark Shadows," Earl was unable to sing another note and retired to the sidelines. Then, in an incredible half-hour, without preparation of any kind, Charlie invented two new tunes, "Bird's Nest," based on "I Got Rhythm," and "Cool Blues," and reeled off seven takes in thirty minutes.

EARL COLEMAN   The legendary session, huh? What was that, February 19th, 1947? Well, the real story, contrary to what you might read in the book*—I don't know what Mr. Russell had in mind when he was writing this. I guess we all want money. But the book isn't accurate, I'm sorry to say. It's far from accurate. I was never so disappointed in a human being in my whole life. I was very naive. I thought this was a man, like I find people who care about people. He had a little record store,† a little toilet, off on Hollywood Boulevard, and somehow he met Bird, and somebody told him, and he was smart enough to listen. I went by his shop six months prior to that February date and asked him about doing a record date. He said, "Billy Eckstine could walk in here if he wanted to, I wouldn't record him. Or Sarah Vaughan, because singers don't go with bop." I said, "Okay, I see." So case closed.

But Bird and I had been tight since the Kansas City days, and Bird had encouraged me to go and get that job with Earl Hines. He said, "They're auditioning guys now, look like fifteen or twenty a day. They're down to wearing the collar and parting their hair, trying to look like the guy [Eckstine]." He said, "I've heard so many cats trying to sing like B, it's pathetic. You are the only cat I've heard that I know, that I dig." Those were some pretty big shoes to fill. I was just a kid and inexperienced, but in the back of my mind I was saying, "You're right, I'm the only one." Because I had just studied the band and I had the experience for it, I got the gig.

Bird and I go further back than that. About 1943. I met him before I went with McShann. I was singing at the Chez Paree in Kansas City. There was a place—it was an old demolished building, right next door to the Booker T. Hotel, where all the bands would check in and I was lucky enough to be desk clerk at the time because *all* the bands used to come through there. I met Prez there for the first time. And they used to go out—right next door to the Booker T. was this vacant lot, and it was part of the foundation of the building, and the cats used to sit out there until the wee hours of the morning and cut it up, and some would blow their horns out there. And Bird used to sit out there in the morning because he used to come in to the club, I noticed, every time I would go in the club. I was so young I couldn't hang around in the club. I'd get somebody to come down and watch the desk for me about ten to ten o'clock. Then I'd split on over to the club. And on my way in the club I would see this same guy sitting in the back. Yeah, right by the door. Because when I finished my set, and split out of the club, he would split out with me. He would always talk to me and tell me that he liked the way I sounded and the potential that he thought I had. So somehow he mentioned Earl Hines, but I ended up with McShann first.

Hibbler had gone to join Duke. Yeah, that's the way it happened. And so they were rehearsing at the musician's union, and so I went by and made a rehearsal, and I sang, and they offered me the gig, and I split out the next day with them, and finally Bird rejoined us in Chicago for a minute or so. He had been all over because he had been playing tenor with Earl Hines. And so he came back with the band for a minute because he and John Jackson, they used to split the first parts up. And then he used to play eight, and John would play eight, like on those records, a couple of those records—I forget which ones they were—that's *two* saxophones. That's John and Bird. A lot of people think it's just Bird. But John Jackson was a demon. And he knew where that thing was coming from then. He was aware of it. "Egg Foo Young," we called him. He looked a little Oriental. J.J.—we also called him— was a guy who could just play his horn and be happy—leave him alone. Later for fame and fortune. That's all he wanted to do.

Anyway, Bird and I meet in California again, and Bird has a nervous breakdown, and I went with Howard McGhee one day to see him, and he was sitting on the beach. He was feeling good. He was in a good frame of mind and playing his butt off. They let him play his horn. Just sitting out by the Pacific. And he turned to me and looked at me for about five minutes, and he smiled and started to laugh in that way of his and said, "I'm going to do something for you, man. I'm going to record you, and you're going to make a record that's going to be so big, as long as you live you'll always be remembered, and even after you're gone." So I looked at him. I thought this guy is just putting me on or just being nice because—But I was still shook by it because I end up getting the job with Earl Hines. I thought about it, but then I threw it out of my mind. Finally one day, I go home and they say, "There's some record company been calling you all day. Ross Russell." I thought, "Ross Russell? What would he want me for? He don't want no singers." And then it dawned. I said, "Bird's home."

Somehow I ran into him at the Bird in the Basket that night. He gets out of the cab with June Christy on his arm just as I walk up, and he said, "I'm looking for you. We're going to record next week." I said, "We are?" He said, "Yeah." In fact where we rehearsed for "This Is

Always" was around the corner from the Basket, at Lester Young's house. Contrary to stories you've heard about Prez, Prez was a pretty smart man, an individual. Prez had a beautiful home, but he built his home with the idea in mind for cats who didn't have much money, who couldn't afford to pay much rent—maybe couldn't pay any at all, but if they had something on the ball Prez would not leave them out-doors. That's what that house was built for. So Bird went in the Bas-ket and, naturally, wiped everybody out, because it was a different Bird than we had heard six months ago. He had all this beautiful tone and things. And he called me up to sing, and I sang.

Like the next day, Ross Russell called me, and he wanted to know if I sang bop. I said, "No." Anyway, he wanted to hear something, and I told Bird about it, and he said, "Makes no difference. You're not auditioning because you're on the date." Ross wanted to know when he could hear us. So I got Erroll Garner to play for me. So, anyway, I take him around there, and I ask Erroll, "Would you play a tune for me, so this guy can hear what I sound like?" He said, "Yeah." So I said, "You know "This Is Always.'" He said, "I heard it. Sing it." So I started singing it, and, as Erroll always did, he went right on and played it. And Erroll, Red Callender, and Harold West had been rehearsing a trio—they were trying to get a trio together —and so naturally, Red kept one of his basses there, and Harold West kept his drums set up there.

Harold West was a heck of a cook. Down to pies and salads. So as we started going over the tune Red came in and pulled his bass out and started playing with us. Next thing Harold West came in with his apron on and everything. He pulled the apron aside and sat down on the drums and starts playing. So Bird smiled and told Ross to go get his horn. And Bird said, "Uh, huh! We're going to do the date intact, just like this." Ross said, "You sure about that?" He said, "Yeah, I'm sure." Then he said, "Earl, you got another tune?" And Ross turned black, purple. I came up with "Dark Shadows" and this man, when we get to the studio that day, contrary to what he says in the book, I wasn't even frightened. The only thing that ran through my mind was, "You're on this thing with genius. This is the big time. Forget about what the public knows. This is the big time, here. So let's be in tune, let's get this done, let's do it. That's all I have in mind.

Shifty Henry was a bass player. That wasn't his heavy stick. His big-gest stick was writing ditties. He wrote "Dark Shadows," and he brought it to me. He was very talented. He would listen at somebody saying something. Some of the funniest things. Like Elvis Presley—he wrote his big hit, "Jailhouse Rock." Shifty was a comical cat. He would walk down the street with a bow in his hand, and the chicks would say, "Are you with the band?" And Shifty would say, "Yes, I'm with the band. We're at the Masonic Temple tonight." One of those type of cats. Beautiful cat, though. But, anyway, when we got in the studio, they called me up first because Ross had in mind to "get rid of him quick." So I went right in and did one take on "This Is Always," which was a master. Evidently, because they're selling it now. And we decided to do another one, and I did another one. Bam, that was over, and we walked right through "Dark Shadows," did four takes on that, mainly for balance. We had so much time—that's when Erroll Garner did the trio things—"Pastel"—they had time to do all that. Because in the book he says that *I* took up all the time, and when they did finally get something that was passable, "poor Earl's voice was completely shot and he had to retire to the sidelines." I was what? Nineteen or twenty* then, you know. Could you imagine me getting tired? I don't get tired singing now. The more I sing, the more I can. Everybody knew that was a lie because they had so much time. They did trio sides, and then they did "Cool Blues" and "Bird's Nest," and also we had time to listen at a young man, who I introduced to Bird, who was destined to carry the message on and Bird dug him so much that Bird made them cut off the records and everything and listen at this man playing—he was playing alto then. That young man was John Coltrane.

He was out there with King Kolax playing first alto. And that day—that was the day he made up his mind to switch to tenor because he and Bird left and went by my crib, and they blew from maybe ten that night until daybreak the next day. And Trane say, "I'm going to get me a tenor because this guy's been playing all there is to be played on this alto." He got the tenor, and he started. He admired Dexter [Gordon] a whole lot, so he just combined the two—Dexter and Bird. That's what happened on that date, and Ross even came out but like it broke his heart evidently. He said, "You sound pretty good." So he gave me a twenty-dollar bonus. Which made me come out with a grand total of eighty dollars for the date.

❖❖

Dial Records continued to be one of the important independents, recording Dexter Gordon twice in June. The second session included "The Chase" with Wardell Gray, a tenor-sax battle in the old tradition that Gordon and Gene Ammons had reinforced and popularized in the Billy Eckstine band. Dexter and Wardell were prominent members of the active Los Angeles jamming scene, particulary at the Bird in the Basket, also known as Jack's Basket.

❖❖

DEXTER GORDON   There'd be a lot of cats on the stand but, by the end of the session, it would wind up with Wardell and myself. "The Chase" grew out of this.

❖❖

"The Chase" proved to be a big seller, and in December, Ross Russell put Dexter together with Teddy Edwards in another bat-

*Twenty-one

tle titled "The Duel" with Jimmy Rowles, Red Callender, and Roy Porter.

❖ ❖

JIMMY ROWLES   It was the first time I'd ever played with a genuine bebop set-up. I mean the real thing because Porter had made all those records with Bird, and I didn't know what the hell I was doing. It takes time to get yourself into that shit. But we made the record date.

❖ ❖

"The Duel" also sold well, as did "Blues in Teddy's Flat," which Edwards did without Gordon. By that time Dial's canary-yellow label was one that jazz fans looked for with regularity. It was firmly entrenched in their minds by Charlie Parker.

Russell, in this book *Bird Lives!*, states that Bird left for New York a "few days" after the "Camarillo" date, which was February 26, 1947, but in the monumental photo book by Chan Parker and Francis Paudras— *From Bird With Love*—there is a picture of a letter from Russell to Chan, dated March 25, in which he says: "Bird is leaving here today for Chicago where he plays a one-nighter Easter Sunday. After that he intends to return to New York."

By April, Bird's new quintet featuring Miles Davis, Duke Jordan, Tommy Potter, and Max Roach was ensconced at the Three Deuces. Although he continued to record in Los Angeles, before the summer came Russell had shifted Dial's offices to New York. Bird was the focus, and he was back on 52nd Street.

« 6 »

Big-Band Bop

When Gillespie returned to New York from Los Angeles in February 1946 he soon set up headquarters on 52nd Street again. On the 22nd of that month he recorded four sides for the *New 52nd Street Jazz* album, assembled by Leonard Feather, with Don Byas, Milt Jackson, Al Haig, guitarist Bill DeArango, Ray Brown, and J.C. Heard. A Coleman Hawkins-headed group of all-stars did the other four numbers in the album, which, despite RCA Victor's refusal to connect with the word "bop" (hence the title), became additions to the influential recorded music of the time.

At Clark Monroe's Spotlite, Dizzy's sidemen included Jackson, Haig, and Brown, with Stan Levey on drums and Leo Parker's baritone filling the reed role. When the group recorded for Musicraft in May, Sonny Stitt's alto had replaced Parker's baritone, and Kenny Clarke was in for Levey.

Then, at the same club, came the rebirth of the Gillespie orchestra. This time, unlike the "Hepsations" edition, there was an audience for Gillespie and his music, and the big band would thrive until 1950. Before Dizzy's band was established as a vital, continuing force, however, his and Bird's innovations had had an impact on other existing bands.

In California, just prior to and during the Gillespie-Parker Los Angeles period, Benny Carter led a band in which sidemen of the new persuasion were developing. Even if the Carter scores were not in the bop mode, the soloists echoed the changes taking place at the time. The band was formed in New York, in late '42, and continued in California in November after having traveled across the country.

❖❖

BENNY CARTER   That's when I really started here and I guess I was here—I didn't leave town again—until maybe in the spring of '43 when I went on a tour with the Nat Cole Trio, Savannah Churchill, and Timmie Rogers. Let's see—I had Freddie Webster, I had Miles Davis for a while, had Max Roach.

MAX ROACH   I wanted to travel, so I joined Benny Carter's band [in 1945]. I was on 52nd Street. I wanted to see some things. They came to town and George Russell left the band. He was the drummer. I won't forget that 'cause when I joined the band, from that point I was with it, straight till when I came back to New York to work with Dizzy and Charlie.

BENNY CARTER   We had J.J. Johnson whom we picked up in Indianapolis, I think in September or October of '42, and we were on our way to California. He joined the band immediately and left with us.

EARL COLEMAN   I ended up with Benny Carter. And I got J.J. the job. He was washing dishes, and I had to almost hit him over the head and drag him out of the restaurant bodily. Because he was afraid, scared to death. We went to California. This was during World War II, the blackout time, you had to pull shades. Benny Carter was my first experience in big time things, and I went in as a valet. But I had heard J.J. in Mississippi with Snookum Russell and dig who was in the band: Fats [Navarro], Ray Brown, and Joe Harris.

BENNY CARTER   If J.J. was washing dishes, he was probably maybe in between gigs, because I understood that he was playing with Snookum Russell. All I knew was that this young man came in with a trombone, and we invited him because we were told that he was really something else, and as soon as I heard him I was, wow, greatly impressed, and I was glad that I could get him to go with us.

EARL COLEMAN   I remember when we did drag J.J. on up there, Benny Carter said, "Go ahead, man, play something." And he's sweating and scared to death. Man, he turned "Body and Soul" inside out. This guy called Harold Mitchell*—did you ever hear of Harold Mitchell? Dangerous! And he was playing, but somehow he just got disillusioned. "Big Mitch." He used to be with Tiny Bradshaw. I had already seen him with Tiny Bradshaw. So he was in the band; George Treadwell was in the band. Chiefy Salaam. And that night after Benny told him J.J. was hired, and they calmed him down, there was so much love around him, he finally relaxed. Then they started talking about Diz. That was the first time I heard about Diz. But I was listening at Harold Mitchell doubling up the things. I heard Clark Terry playing that kind of thing with Eddie Randall's band when I had been in Mounds, Illinois, with Ernie Fields's band. Freddie Webster he played some lead.

*trumpeter from Newark, New Jersey.

Yes he did certainly, sure. That big fat sound of his. There was only one Freddie Webster sound, just as there was one Clifford Brown thing.

❖ ❖

Art Pepper was only eighteen years old when he played in Benny Carter's band.

❖ ❖

ART PEPPER   When I was in Benny Carter's band, I was with Freddie Webster, and we roomed together a lot. He had the greatest, the most huge sound, and down low it was just gigantic. I never heard anybody who had a sound that big down low. He was just a little cat, too. He always carried a loaded gun with him in his pocket, always—never without it. And I remember we were in Salt Lake City, with Benny Carter's band, and we lived out of town a little ways, out on the outskirts with a black family—my first wife, myself, and Freddie and his wife lived with this black family, a big house, and the only way we could get home after the gig was by cab, and so I would wait for the cab, and Freddie would hide, and the cab would come and stop, and I would go to get in the cab, and I would open the door, and Freddie would come sneaking up, and he would get in, and he'd have his hand on his pocket, and the cab driver would look at him and start to say something—there was something about Freddie's eyes and where his hands were, and the guy right away could sense that he'd better not open his mouth, and he never did—but they'd give me the coldest looks in the world, and I would tell them where I wanted to go because I wanted to keep peace because Freddie would shoot the cat. I was scared to death all the time. I was a crusader at that time, really a crusader for the rights, but that's what I had to do with Freddie. He was a great cat, and we became very good friends, and he played beautifully. He was a great, great influence on me.

❖ ❖

The Carter band broke up for the same reason that many other large organizations folded.

❖ ❖

BENNY CARTER   It was definitely economics. I would like to have been able to continue with it, although I will say, at the time, I had come to Hollywood and was doing a few things here, and I felt that maybe it might be a little more lucrative for me—not that I measure everything from the term of money—but we do have to live, and the band was in very bad shape financially. I was in quite a bit of debt with it. I wasn't making any money with it, so I just thought maybe I could put it down and start again later, but I never did.

AL GREY   My first band was Benny Carter; that put me really on the West Coast. We were headin' out to California, and he stopped in St. Louis and took Miles Davis with him. Miles couldn't read, but he could play such fantastic solos, and we took him anyway. But he became hung

up out there because he would go and just practice all day long—
practice, practice, practice. We used to get worried about him because
he'd practice so much. He stayed more or less all to himself. And then
he started coming along, beginning to read because he was playing
the fourth chair with the band. That's when we had Ira Pettiford, Oscar Pettiford's brother. Max Roach came in, and Jean Starr had left
the band. Benny had a girl trumpet player named Jean Starr. And
she could really blow. And Max used to keep her all upset. We had
Percy Brice on drums after Max. When J.J. Johnson left, this is when
I had the opportunity to discover that I didn't know nothing. This was
like school because I thought I was half-way reading. But I discovered
I wasn't reading anything and didn't have no conception of phrasing
and all this was being involved in this band. Benny Carter was doing
all of that and getting down to complete finesse and playing and
everything. So it was really just like school. That's where I had to really
straighten up.

They called him King Carter. That was it. And we really used to
play up a lot of music. Miles Davis found out the same thing—that he
knew there was nothin' happening. But Bird was working at 2nd and
San Pedro, which is today—is all police area—Japanese town. Miyako
Hotel, down in the hole. We was playing with Benny Carter at the
Trianon Ballroom. We'd be off, and Bird didn't never start till around
about twelve, one at night. You just had sessions all night long and a
lot of places. That was one, and you could go on down the Strip. The
Trenier twins had the sessions down there with Oscar Moore. Eddie
Beal. Then I used to go jamming all the time at Billy Berg's in Hollywood. And Bird would be out there and Red Callender. Then Miles,
we would go over there nightly. I would be scared to pull out my horn,
but Miles would be playin'. During the meantime, Britt Woodman was
working down in another club, the Jazz Workshop, on Central there
with Charlie Mingus, Buddy Collette, Lucky Thompson, and Oscar
Bradley. They had a mean sextet there. Then Mingus branched out
from there. Then I met Teddy Edwards. He used to be on these sessions. Erroll Garner. There was so much happening. You had to learn
something. And then Mickey Rooney and Jackie Cooper and all them
guys would play drums. They'd come into these sessions. Like me, being
from the East Coast and to live in California, we got around the movie
industry and everything.

Then Benny Carter broke up the band. It was a sad day when he
broke that band up. He had started running into difficulty with the
agents and out of the clear blue sky. But Jimmie Lunceford then came
along, and he was rebuilding his band. Trummy Young had left, and
so he come and give me the role to come in and play like Trummy
Young. That was no problem because I had been listening to Trummy
Young. I had to play all of Trummy's things like he played 'em. I used
to sing "Margie" and play "Margie" like Trummy Young. I remember

it used to be really tough at first to play that ending he had. I missed them sometimes. I got to play so I could be pretty accurate with it. But every now and then—because that was the main thing; if you missed that you just blowed the whole number.

When modern jazz came in Trummy Young got into it. Like in *Annie Laurie* he played [sings]. Oh sure, he was playin' all those changes and things then. He wasn't foolin' around. Lunceford had a lot of beautiful music. I did like playin' his book. It was completely a different style from Benny Carter. Everything was played long with Benny Carter. A half-note would get its complete value. It was completely different, an exact change with me because I got into the Lunceford band [sings]. Everything was sharp, you see.

❖❖

In bebop everything was flowing in longer phrases and longer lines, and the time feeling was different.

❖❖

AL GREY   In that period, being around Miles with Benny Carter and then being around Bird, I got the feeling of many things. It seemed natural, because I was learning them right off the top. We were playin' right there. They came out with so many "black and white" books.* So many things they had—many of the changes were wrong and so there for a while, many musicians came along with the wrong changes. They just thought that it went like that because they had these black-market books. You could get 'em for like about twenty, twenty-five dollars. That messed up a whole lot of people. Because they still have them on the market today.

❖❖

One of the first bands to manifest interest in and evidence use of the new ideas was the edition of Woody Herman's band known as the "First Herd."

Herman had achieved a reputation in the '30s as "The Band That Plays the Blues." In 1943, through Dave Matthews's arranging, he began a brief "Ellington" period, even to the point of using Duke's sidemen such as Ben Webster and, in 1944, Johnny Hodges and Juan Tizol on his record dates.

In September 1944 the band that would be officially dubbed the First Herd by *Metronome* magazine's George Simon (He says, "As far back as 1939 we were referring to his band as 'The Herd.' ") began to take shape with two sides for Decca. Neal Hefti and Pete Candoli were among the trumpets; Bill Harris was on trombone; Flip Phillips on tenor saxophone; Ralph Burns was at the piano with Chubby Jackson, bass; Billy Bauer, guitar; and Dave Tough, drums.

As early as 1942 Herman recorded a Gillespie chart entitled

*fake books.

"Down Under." Another one called "Swing Shift" seems to have gone unrecorded, as did "Woody'n You," at least by the Herman band, for which it was written. Woody, for whom it was named, used it behind dancers on stage shows. It is surprising he didn't reactivate it, for after the 1944 Hawkins recording, it became a modern jazz standard.

❖❖

CHUBBY JACKSON   I guess it was in the middle of the heat of the Herman band when some of the younger soloists started to come into the band addressing ideas like Diz and Charlie Parker and those people and writers. Dizzy brought in a couple of arrangements, "Woody'n You,"* and a couple other tunes that gave the band a different flavor. There were some things that were brought in, and then the soloists started to respond more to that kind of thing. As the band started to leave the Ellington period right at that time, some of the soloists who came in were starting to fly around like Charlie and Dizzy. Neal [Hefti] started to write some of his ensembles with some of the figures that come from that early bebop thing. We were really one of the first big bands outside of Dizzy's big band that flavored bebop into the big band—different tonal quality and rhythms, and the drum feeling started changing, and that I think was really the beginning of it.

When bop first came out it was very amazing to all of us. We were used to the milky alto saxophones of Benny Carter, Willie Smith, and Johnny Hodges and more melodic-type of passages. Then the staccato concept came through with Dizzy and Bird, and at first it was a little raucous. It was cooking, but it was so strange, and it seemed that you had to play double time all the time to get any kind of a raised eyebrow from anybody. I fell in love with it, and I finally got into playing it with the big band because Neal had it down. Neal would write some beautiful things along those patterns.

WOODY HERMAN   I think one of the strongest people and most influential people by far and away was Ralph Burns, because he was so versatile. He could go in any bag and make it happen. Neal really didn't do a great deal of writing while he was in my band, but he was constantly coming up with thoughts and ideas. A lot of our things were based on heads anyway, so he was invaluable in that department. Later when Shorty [Rogers] came in he took over some of that. Neal brought in unison choruses based on bop things, early bop.

NEAL HEFTI   I'd go hear bands, like I remember well the first time I heard Dizzy Gillespie, he was playing in Omaha with Cab Calloway. I graduated in '41, so it was a couple of years before then. I started arranging in my junior year in high school, and I was arranging for like all

*Dave Tough said they called it "Yenta."

the local bands, including the Mickey Mouse bands, including the sort of hipper bands and including the commercial—well, what I mean is the production bands like the carnival bands and things of this nature. Then if you want to make swing synonymous with jazz yes, then I was into jazz, or I was into jazz with Charlie Barnet. It's all according to what we call jazz. I really didn't think of it as jazz. I thought of it as pop music you know.

If you want to call Nat Towles jazz, then I was into jazz with him. I mean, I was writing vocal ballads for the band. As soon as I got out of high school I came east with a band. I played in the Midwest when I was in high school during summer vacations, all sorts of midwestern bands. They used to call them style bands and Mickey Mouse bands. Polka bands, territory bands, and sort of carnival band. As a matter of fact, I never went to graduation exercises. I got a job to leave town a couple of days before my graduation exercises from high school, and I went to New Jersey with this band, the name of Dick Barry. And I was fired after about two—I really couldn't read that music; it was too complicated for me. It was a Mickey Mouse band, and it looks harder than it is. Just the looks of the music was just too "black"* for me. It was too many notes. So I was stranded in the East. And that was my beginning.

It's a funny thing that if I had had the money when I was stranded in New York, actually in New Jersey with this band, I would have gone back to Omaha. 'Cause sometimes good things happen when you're broke; you're forced to stay there and make do. Then I joined a band by the name of Bob Astor. Shelly Manne was in the band, and Tony Faso was playing trumpet; Ray Beller was on alto, and a guy by the name of Joe Stafford was playing tenor, and Marty Napoleon was playing piano. I won't really go through the whole band, but those are the guys that as far as I know are still in the business. I was with that band for a while. And I got into a car accident and ended up in a hospital for about four months with a broken pelvis in Summit, New Jersey.

When I got out of the hospital I joined Charlie Barnet, which I would say is my first name band. Bob Astor got me the job. He was friends with Charlie Barnet from the West Coast, and he got me the job. I guess I was with Charlie for about six to eight months. Then I came down with a very severe case of tonsilitis, and I had to go to New York and have my tonsils removed. It was then that I put in my New York union card. And during that time, I played with a little band down in Cuba for a couple of weeks. It was led by Sanford Gold. Well, it was led by a guy by the name of Les Lieber. He played sax and sort of a

*Cluttered, as in too many notes. In no way connected with black bands or jazzmen's styles.

tin whistle.* When I got out and came back from Cuba, I joined Charlie Spivak. Then I went to the Coast with Spivak, and we made a band picture.

I don't know the year, but it was a year that they introduced withholding tax, because this happened while we were doing the picture at 20th Century Fox. I would say it's about '43, late '43 or early '44, and I left him to stay in California. I joined Horace Heidt, and I stayed with Horace Heidt for just a few months and left him to join Woody Herman. I took Cappy Lewis's place who was going into the Army. Woody Herman was in Los Angeles making a picture at the time, so I joined the band then, and I would say that just about '44 somehow. Then I was with Woody Herman for about a couple of years.

I would say I got into jazz when I got into Woody Herman's band because that band was sorta jazz-oriented. They had records. It was the first band I ever joined where the musicians carried records on the road. I always had a record player, but I seemed to be the only guy that would listen to records in some of these other bands. Or it would bug people if I would play it. So every time I'd leave town, I'd leave my records and record player in storage at the Forrest Hotel, until we came back. But that band always had records on the road. I'll say that Chubby Jackson's was more like the room you went to after the job, that we all went to after the job was over or days off.

Chubby had mostly Duke Ellington records and Woody Herman records; Woody Herman discs or Charlie Barnet V-Discs. Chubby played with Barnet. Ralph Burns had played with him. I had played with him. Frances† had sung with him. So there was a lot of Charlie Barnet alumni in Woody's band. And Woody was just recording now for Decca, using Ben Webster as a soloist, so we had those released and unreleased sides to play. From Ben Webster that sort of lead us into Duke. Maybe these other guys were sort of Duke-oriented anyway because of Charlie Barnet. So it was sort of like the natural progression to listen to Duke—and I always listened to Duke in Charlie's band.

I guess my first influence was a guy by the name of Andy Gibson, who was arranging for the band at the time and—he and I were about the only ones who listened to records in Charlie's band. He used to come up to my room on the road. He wouldn't travel far with the band, but for instance if we were playing in Boston and we played a hotel in Boston—the Brunswick Hotel, I remember that one particularly— Andy would come up for a couple of days and bring an armful of arrangements for the band to play. And he would stay a couple of

*He still does at the *Jazz at Noon* businessmen's jams he has run for years in New York on Fridays.
†Frances Wayne, who became Mrs. Hefti when they were with Herman.

days, and he would sort of hang out in my room and listen to records. So as I was saying, in Woody's band, we always used to listen to records, and that's the first time I sort of got into jazz. The first time I sort of felt that I was anything remotely connected with jazz.

But anyway, when I was stranded in New York before I joined Charlie Barnet and during the time that I waited out my six-month transfer period in New York, Dizzy was playing on the Street at many of the clubs that were there. Sometimes as a leader, sometimes as a sideman. So I used to go down there quite often. Got to see him. Got to know him. Got to know all the musicians. One way I could go hear them play without paying for it, 'cause I didn't have any money anyway. I didn't drink, so I wasn't going to be able to sit at the bar. So I'd sort of hang out back in the kitchen with them. So I got to hear a lot of that.

I presumed that I started bringing those things into Woody's band that I started writing—mainly not writing, mainly on head charts. Those were where I could make those up. That was my only band that ever played any kind of what you call head charts, and that was for a reason, a strange reason. When I joined the band, everything was sorta written out, just a "Who Dat Up Dere," "Woodchopper's Ball," plain three-minute charts, pop tunes of the day and etc. If it was a solo in it, it was sorta like a solo round the melody. Very little improvisation in the band. And then guys were drafted very fast, and there were vast changes. Like you'd change personnel six or seven guys in a week. And a lot of those guys really couldn't read very well. And I will name guys like Flip Phillips, who was a good soloist, but really sort of a bad reader. And I'll say that Bill Harris was another one of those kind of guys. I almost had to teach them their part by rote. And this sort of flustered Woody. He knew they were good musicians, and there were other people in the band, too, that could read, but didn't have the re-deeming solo ability that those guys did, but they were still bad readers. So we started faking things in the jobs, and after six months of faking "Flying Home," it became a tune. We would always fake things that had easy riff possibilities to it. And when I was doing that stuff, I guess I started introducing these kind of riffs for the trumpets and things of this nature. "Caldonia" was a solo that I played in "Wood-chopper's Ball" and when we made the record, they all played it in unison.

I left the band for six months and got my union card. When Woody came back to California, I joined him in California, and then he did about a two-year swing around the country. When he came back, I lived in California. I always loved California, and I left and got my union card. After the six months, Abe Turchen, who was the manager of the band, said, "Look it, why don't you come back?" I had the card then and fine. I went back with the band, and Stravinsky was sort of like a hero to guys like myself and Pete Candoli. He was sort of like an "in" classical composer. So Pete asked me if, while I was on the Coast, I met Igor, and I said, sure, I did. I hadn't, though. And I said I did. And he said, "Oh, God." I told him, "I played him the records, and he thinks they're great." That got back to Woody, and Woody went to Lou Levy,* who was the publisher then of Stravinsky's works and a lot of Woody Herman's works, and that led it in. I think it was just my out fantasy that I had met and hung out with Igor and played him Woody Herman's records and at he became obsessed with what a great band it was, because two days after I said this, they had heard from one another. They had made contact. It might have been just my absolute child fantasy that I met God and told him that I was playing with Woody Herman, played him the records and he said, "That's great. I'd like to write something for it." He probably never even heard the band until Lou Levy got in touch with him. Who knows? I don't know.

JIMMY ROWLES   I came out of the Army March '46. The day I got my discharge, I'm out. I went home and got a jug. I made myself the biggest drink I'd ever had. Sitting there with my discharge papers. Whoom, and the phone rings, and it was Woody. "When you getting out?" "I just got out about twenty minutes ago." "Want to come back?" "Yeah." "Well, we've got to do the Carnegie Hall Concert, and we're going to play Stravinsky. So and so be in touch with you, get your ticket, come to New York, and that's it." So I went back to California. I met Gil Evans, and we took a tour around. Gil and I went down to Main Street to see Leo Watson. There's Leo up there, barefoot. No clothes on except for a pair of pants, playing the drums at the 5 and 10 on Main Street, and he's in debt so deep to the guy he can't get ahead. And he's drinking wine—leaped over the bar and kissed us both on the mouth and slobbered all over us. He was beautiful. He died in San Pedro. He was something else. I used to work with him. He was at Billy Berg's when I was working with Lester. But going back with Woody, I regretted one thing. I had to take Tony Aless's job away from him because he was playing in the band, and I was coming in, and he had to leave. I didn't feel good about that because Tony was happy. He dug the gig. It was a helluva band. All of a sudden he's through because I'm coming out. But I've got to work too. I just got through with three and a half years of shit. Well, we hung together till the end of the year. Woody had a personal problem, and he broke up the band.

❖❖

Actually Herman wanted to spend more time with his family.

❖❖

WOODY HERMAN   That was the basic reason. And I did. I stayed home for seven months. The only thing I did was a radio show with Peggy Lee

*Not the Lou Levy who played piano with Herman in 1949–1950.

and Dave Barbour. I was the male singer, Peggy was the female singer and Dave was the band leader. It was "The Electric Hour."

JIMMY ROWLES   All we were playing when he disbanded were concerts, and we were playing that Stravinsky thing. When we were in California, we made the record with Stravinsky.* I'd been practicing that thing. I thought I was right. He had one thing written for me where I was solo, and it had a thing like this, and I had to reach underneath here and go . . . I had to go [sings] doum, doum, doum, doum. And underneath it I had to go da-da-da-da-da-da. I thought I had it right. I played it with one finger. He stopped the orchestra. Comes over to the piano. Igor Stravinsky! I'm scared to death. He comes over to me and says, "My darling, I did not write that." I thought,"Jesus, what have I done? Now I'm in trouble. I'm in the shithouse again." He reached over my shoulder and said, "You're using the wrong fingering." He's up in front, man. Yet he knew. And he showed me that I'm to use two fingers. Then he said, "Do it. Now that's it." And he patted me. Then he says, "Could I have some vodka?" And [Conrad] Gozzo jumped up from the trumpet section and said, "Maestro, I will take care of you." He runs across the street and comes back with a great big glass of vodka. And Stravinsky knocked that mother off like a real Russian. And his old lady comes up and towels him and changes his shirt. And we did the record.

And on the record he had a harpist, a male harpist.† Never seen him since then. My God. He thought he was rich. He kept interrupting all the time. He was always asking questions and stuff, and he was bugging Stravinsky—we are doing a record date. Finally Stravinsky said, "Take ten." He said, "Everybody but you. You stay. I want to hear everything you have to play, right now." And he made that guy go through his whole—and he just sat there. I thought, that mother better not miss any notes—but he was a helluva harpist.

WOODY HERMAN   I was never a serious clarinetist by any stretch of the imagination. But I'll never forget how hard I struggled and sweated and made myself a gibbering idiot trying to play the Stravinsky piece. I went to fine clarinetists—people in the orchestras and so on—and asked if there was anything I could do to play this thing a little better, and they all looked at it and said, "Why, that's the hardest goddamn thing in the world." Then, I was walking down 6th Avenue one day, and I ran into Benny [Goodman] on the street, and he says, "Hey, kid, is that clarinet solo in that Stravinsky piece hard?" I said, "Benny, it's hard." "Oh," he says, "it's that hard?" I said, "It's hard but I'll get

*"Ebony Concerto" was premiered at Carnegie Hall in March 1946 and recorded on August 19, 1946 for Columbia.
†Stanley Chaloupka.

you a miniscore." They put out a little score, and I sent it over to him. I didn't see him then for maybe six months. I ran into him somewhere, in some club, and he says, "That's hard." Everybody's part was hard, but I had this so-called solo part. He wrote pure Stravinsky; it had nothing to do with a jazz band. To him the challenge was, if any, the fact that he's writing for this bastard instrumentation, and also, he did like the idea of having jazz players trying to scuffle with these parts; that's why he wrote it, so it was grotesque. He knew he couldn't pull this with guys from the Philharmonic or whatever. If he did it would turn into a big mishmash. After the very first rehearsal, at which we were all so embarrassed we were nearly crying because nobody could read, he walked over and put his arm around me and said, "Ah, what a beautiful family you have." Okay, so he was getting his jollies, I could tell that. Here we are struggling at this—then when we finally recorded it, which is a long time later, he was there and conducted and made cuts, and he won't make cuts for anybody, but he did.

He was pleased at the end. He was a beautiful man. I got to know him after that socially, because we lived not far from each other, and we spent a lot of time just sitting around, and I had some beautiful moments with the man.

JIMMY ROWLES Anyway, when the band broke up I went back to California, and when he reformed I could have gone back, but I'd had enough. I couldn't take any more—the bus trips and all that stuff. I backed off. I've worked with him since then. I still think he's one of the greatest guys I've ever worked for. We had Don Lamond and Bill Harris and Flip and Chubby, Sonny Berman, Marky [Irv Markowitz], Shorty—Sonny Berman—that was a tragedy. Did you ever hear him? Oh, boy. There is one record we made called "That's What Uncle Remus Said," and he'd play a solo on that thing. Also, "Sidewalks of Cuba."

WOODY HERMAN Sonny was one of the warmest soloists I ever had in the band. For his youth he was so mature, in his playing generally because he didn't play like a young babe. After all, he was eighteen or nineteen when he came with me, and we lost him when he was twenty-one.* He was just scratching the surface of what he was about to do.

NEAL HEFTI Sonny was my roommate up until I got married, for about the last six months of my time in the band, and whenever we'd go to New York, we would room together at the Paris Hotel in New York. We'd generally stay in New York for six months at a time. We'd play the Paramount. We'd play the Pennsylvania Hotel; we'd play the Four Hundred Club; do a couple of record dates, and do one-nighters in and out. So it was a very convenient place to live, and we weren't com-

---

* Actually, he was twenty when he joined Herman and twenty-two when he died.

pletely downtown. We could see the river. He always wanted to play solos. I used to write him a lot of solos in the band. He was major. He really was going to be very good. Had good chops, easy to be with, easy to get along with, fans liked him, people liked him. He's just one of the tragedies of this world. He was gonna get married, too. He was engaged to a girl by the name of Sylvia something, and I was engaged to Frances at the time, and we were even like talking possibilities of double weddings and this, that, and the other thing.

The band was a lot of fun. I think there was great rapport between the people in it. And none of us wanted to leave. We were always getting sort of offers from other bands for much more money than we were making with Woody, and it was always like if you left, you were a rat. You were really letting down the team. I guess I was the first one to let it down maybe when I finally left with Frances. I don't know, but we got this impression—"Oh, you're gonna leave the band, how could you do this to the band?" —with song pluggers, people come to you: "How could you do this?" I guess I didn't feel that way about hardly anything. I was never sort of brought up that if you—like a team. I was sort of brought up in an atmosphere of everybody for yourself. I'm not proud of that necessarily, and I'm not unproud of it. I'm from a very poor family. Every holiday, the charities used to come and bring us free baskets of food. There was always something of this nature. And we were self-sufficient by ten or twelve. We were sorta like buying our own clothes with money that we made doing whatever, farm work, delivering papers, playing trumpet, things of this nature. I never really had and maybe I still don't really have this team thing. I'm sort of a loner. But when I'm tired of a situation, I sort of leave it. When I feel that I can't do anything more to it. So it might be a selfish attitude. I don't know. Buy anyway, I will say that maybe I started it, but a lot of other people followed suit very fast.

Frances wanted to sing. She wanted to leave the band. See, sometimes these kind of bands, there's also dissension starts. This guy doesn't like this guy, and his wife thinks this guy is getting too many solos. I used to hear all this stuff, being a writer. I used to hear everybody's gripes about everybody else. 'Cause they'd come to me and say, "I play better than or just as good as so and so. He's getting all the solos. Why don't you write me some?" This kind of thing. I would always hear this in every band, not only that band. Basie's band, my own band, whatever. Writers always hear that.

❖❖

Just as there were to be cells of young beboppers in Philadelphia, Detroit, and Chicago, there were enclaves in New York where the music was most accessible. One borough which produced a wealth of talent was Brooklyn. In fact, there was one area, Brownsville, that had more than its share of players who made their mark in the big bands

❖❖

TERRY GIBBS   Frank Socolow was like big time for all of us 'cause he played with Boyd Raeburn's band. When he was sixteen* he was with Boyd Raeburn. That was big in our neighborhood. Also, George Handy was in our neighborhood. We got together. I got to know George, who was completely weird at the time. He was wild. Different. Just different. I did a job with George where he actually stood up and told the bandleader to go fuck himself on stage. It was a society job. The bandleader was Herb Sherry. He was playing accordion, and I was playing drums, and we were playing [sings] "Night and day, you are the one." Then he said, "You got the next one, George." And George went into—you know how George wrote, he wrote abstract for those days. He got into his Stravinsky thing, and people were dancing. So Herb Sherry says, "Play the melody." And George fluffed him off, and again he says, "Hey, they're dancing. Play the melody." And George stood up and said "Fuck you." And the whole place stopped dancing. He sat down and went back to his shit like it never happened. And Herb got scared. We went on with the tune, and we played another tune whatever, society tune and, again, when it was George's turn, he went into that Stravinsky, and Herb talked to him again, and again George said, "Hey, I told you to go fuck yourself." And Herb said, "Go home." He wouldn't go home. He went over to my vibes, and, oh, it was a scene. But George was different anyhow, of all the guys. But George has got talent. Johnny Mandel—at the same time—he was another one to come down to Socolow's basement. And guys like Normie Faye, Harry Biss.

AL COHN   I didn't know those guys. I didn't grow up around there. I didn't go to their school. I was from Crown Heights.† I didn't meet those guys 'til around '44, '45. We'd listen to records all night long. I don't really remember ever blowing down there. It was a hangout. Used to listen to records all night long and everything else. Played Monopoly.

TERRY GIBBS   We were big on Monopoly in those days. At one time, Tiny [Kahn] had the only car, and Normie Faye lived in the Bronx, and he used to come there, and Tiny at four o'clock in the morning would drive him to the Bronx and drive back. We're playing Monopoly, and the only one who hasn't got a monopoly is Tiny. And Normie had his part, the one piece he needed, and he wouldn't sell it to him. And Tiny kept saying, "Hey, man, I'll be out of the game if you don't sell it to me." "Well, the idea is to win." And Normie would always be like a little boy, and he wouldn't sell it to him. And he got out of the game. Came four o'clock, "Tiny, drive me home." Tiny says, "Take the subway." Normie said, "What are you doing? It's four o'clock." He says, "Fuck you." He says, "I'm not gonna drive in with the drunks." He

---

*Actually twenty. He was with Raeburn in 1944.
† Another Brooklyn neighborhood.

made him take a two-hour subway trip to the Bronx. He wouldn't take him home. Because he didn't have a monopoly. Everybody had a monopoly. Tiny was beautiful.

AL COHN   One interesting thing was that in addition to listening to a lot of jazz, we were listening to classical music too—Stravinsky and Bartok and some stuff that was pretty far out, even then. Schoenberg. But I was tryin' to remember the Frenchman that was in New York that Bird was studying with or wanted to study with. Varèse. Frank had a record of Varèse things then. That was '44, '45. And it wasn't new then. So we were aware of these things.

FRANKIE SOCOLOW   We would get together—if we all happened to be in town at the same time. When we were traveling with bands there were lots of times when these bands had periods of unemployment. And we'd just be in town for weeks, sometimes months, doing the best we can. We used to call it the dungeon. It was like a beacon in the night for wayward musicians. We spent an awful lot of time down there. We had a piano and a drum set and, of course, a great record collection. We were night people, and we would just listen to music all night— play a little Monopoly for a change, but always hysterical laughter, very happy kind of thing. George Handy was down there a lot. Very regular. Allen Eager used to drop down there once in a while. We played occasionally but not as much as when we were younger. Tiny used to keep us entertained quite a bit on the piano. He would just sit and play and we'd listen—and once in a while I would join him.

❖ ❖

Before Socolow's basement, there was Terry Gibbs's basement.

❖ ❖

TERRY GIBBS   Tiny and I took turns playing with the records in my cellar—in my basement. We'd take turns playing with the Basie records. Tiny and I actually lived—our windows faced each other. We grew up from six years old till I was about eighteen, till I went in the service. We were together every night. Every night. He was a prodigy. But nobody knew it. Nobody knew it only 'cause it wasn't till later on in life, because like when you're kids if you don't have good looks or you're not a good athlete or whatever it is—Tiny weighed 420 pounds when he was fifteen. He was an ape, he was that big. When I was about sixteen or seventeen, he was maybe about eighteen, seventeen or eighteen, I was gonna go in the service is when we started—sixteen we met Frank Socolow, and then that clique started. When I went in the service, Tiny and Frank got very close. And actually in Socolow's basement is where I met all the guys I never knew before. Tiny and I also met them at the same time. Al Young [Epstein], Irv Kluger . . . I could tell you some funny stories about Tiny. You know I grew up with old Jewish people who would sit around and talk Jewish or Russian. Tiny is fifteen, weighing 420 pounds. And I had a piano in the living room, an he'd just walk in my house, and all these people would be sitting there, with their backs towards him, and he'd drift over to the piano and sit there and go [imitates music]. They'd be sitting, and they'd turn around and see this ape sitting at the piano. Nobody knew what he was doing. He had no inhibitions at all. Tiny was way ahead.

The only way I could put it, Tiny would be in the same class like Johnny Mandel is right now, 'cause Tiny and Johnny had the most muscal minds of all of us. In fact when I was in the Army, and I was playing drums with the band—I was eighteen and we had the Count Basie stocks, except for two, "Rhythm Boogie" and "Jump the Blues Away," which I loved—Tiny went and bought the records, and without any musical training, copies all the parts off the records—you know the fourth trumpet part—and sent me the music. Without ever studying, he put it down on paper for me. The word genius is very hard to use because there are very few geniuses, but Tiny was that good. I'm not sure if you want to call Johnny Mandel, because he never got a chance to show it off on the horn 'cause he had no chops. He played all those beautiful notes but he missed a million notes. He missed a million because of his chops. But Johnny Mandel never played a note that wasn't pretty. Tiny, before he died, he was playing vibes, never took vibes lessons. He'd go to my vibes at the Troubadour and play a tune like "Can't Get Started." He had no technique. He would pick out notes, and I'd be ashamed to go up and follow it.

Jo Jones was the kinda drums I played. But Tiny *really* played that way. Tiny and I auditioned for about four bands, and I won them all because he couldn't play "Sing, Sing, Sing." That was the big thing. Had to play a drum solo, right. I had the thing down. Until one day, we both went to audition for a band, and all they had was Count Basie stocks, and he got the job. It really gassed me in a way, because we were kids, and you were rooting for each other. In fact he never got jealous. He helped me carry my drums to rehearsal. We'd take them in a bus. We had no cases; four million parts were falling all over. "Hold the door open. Wait a minute, I haven't got the cymbal in. I dropped the cymbal." There was no jealousy between the both of us. We really had a great relationship. We were the closest until I went into the service.

In fact Tiny introduced me—when I came home on furlough—he said, "There's something you got to hear, the new music. It's called bebop." Tiny took me down to hear Charlie Parker and Dizzy Gillespie. That's what got me back to playing vibes. They were at the Three Deuces. I came in on furlough, and he took me down. And I didn't believe what I heard. I didn't understand it. What I liked was the double-time figures. That got to me. Now that's when the record ban was on. I went the fifteen days I was in town. I was down at the clubs till four o'clock in the morning. And I went to Minton's. I was all night,

all day. I was with Tiny, and we went to listen to music. What really
sunk into my head was that Tiny knew the double-time figures. Now
I went back to Dallas—I was stationed in Dallas— and these guys, I'd
show them the new music. Now I became the hit of Dallas because
they never heard Bird and Diz. There were no records. But all the
double-time figures, they were amazed with that. I played—when I think
back now—I played all wrong notes because I didn't, I couldn't understand—it was so new, but I could hear the timings but not the notes.
It took—well, let's face it, I've been playing so long, I'm still trying to
find that "Cherokee"—to play that release for twelve choruses without
repeatin' anything. I still have—I don't care who you are. I think the
key it's in. It's because of the key. With another key the first part would
be hard and the release would be easy. Because you're not used to
playing in those keys for some reason. But Tiny was the one who really
introduced me to what they call bebop. Charlie Parker. Dizzy Gillespie.

RED RODNEY   Tiny Kahn was really a gigantic influence to all of us. Especially all the young white players who were in the big bands and still
trying to play jazz. He was such a marvelous musician. He was a dynamic drummer with great time. He didn't have great hands, great
feet, he wasn't really a showy drummer. He was just a real father time-
type drummer. And he was a self-taught arranger, piano player, and
he sang along with you while you played. You know sometimes we'd
put a mike up there and he'd sing choruses better than any musician
in the band [Georgie Auld's sextet] could play them. Tiny knew how
changes went from one to another. He was a tremendous influence on
me and many others too. But I remember what he did for me. God,
I needed him another few years [laughter].

   Prior to Georgie, Tiny and I had played around a lot of groups.
And a lot of times, did all the studio jam sessions that we'd chip in
for.

FRANKIE SOCOLOW   He was a very rare talent. Completely natural. He was
the most unstudied musician in the whole world. And yet he wrote
some excellent charts. He was a swinging drummer. A very unstudied
one. But yet a natural swinger. The drums used to look so very small
when he'd sit behind them. He was a big man. He was, at that time,
probably my closest friend. We were very tight. He really wasn't a pianist. He would just sit down and kind of noodle away in the most
illegitimate, unschooled way. But what came out was beautiful. He had
no real command of the instrument. Could only play things in certain
tempos, certain keys. He was playing vibes at the end of his career,
when he was on the Jack Sterling radio show. He played that the same
way he played the piano—hunt and peck, that kind of thing. But some
how it came out good. As an arranger, again, he was most un-

schooled, most unorthodox. But he managed to get a good sound. And swing naturally. It was a pleasure to play his charts because it laid so right for you. You really didn't even have to think how to play them. You played them naturally.

CHUBBY JACKSON   Tiny, believe it or not, with Kenny Clarke, I believe those were the two distinct changes at that time. Tiny changed it from the Buddy Rich sound, from Gene Krupa, Louis Bellson. He came in with an opposite sound, and Mel [Lewis] came in right on the heels of Tiny, every one of us knew that.

❖❖

Before they moved on to bands such as Boyd Raeburn and Georgie Auld, some of the New York jazzmen apprenticed with the band of Henry Jerome. David Allyn, who had been the vocalist with Van Alexander's band after being discharged from the Army with a Purple Heart, then moved on to sing with Jerome.

❖❖

DAVID ALLYN   I was on Henry's band, and some of the personnel was interesting. We had Stan Fishelson and Stan Levey. Johnny Mandel, Manny Fox. Let's see, Allen Jeffreys. A good back line. Good players. Incidentally we had a tenor player by the name of Lenny Garment, who today is Leonard Garment. Also, Al Greenspan, who is Alan Greenspan, the economist.

I admire Henry because he was somewhat of a loyalist in the sense that he just wouldn't give up. He wanted to have a good band, and he wasn't gonna give it up. But before he came into that "Mickey" band, he gave it a good try. He lost a lot of money. Or let's put it, he could have earned a lot of money if he didn't have that band that he wanted. But Henry wanted to have a good music band. And I think at one time, it was just Georgie Auld and Boyd's band were the only bands that were making any noise in those days. 1944.

AL COHN   After Joe Marsala, I went with Georgie Auld's band. That's where I was more exposed to a younger, hipper element. I played with him off and on till '46. Georgie's band was great experience for a lot of reasons. First of all, the band was good for a young—little rough and the guys weren't all first-rate musicians, but they were all enthusiastic, and they wanted it to be good. Georgie knew how to get a band to sound good and had good taste, good arrangements. It was a Basie-oriented band, a black-oriented band. 'Cause Georgie dug Duke too. He was funny, he played every horn different. He played alto like Hodges. Tenor like Ben [Webster], but he also tried to get a little Prez in there sometimes. But he had all these influences going. He still sounded like himself all the time. But you could tell what he was tryin' for, what he liked.

❖❖

Henry Jerome, now head of his own producing firm, was a trumpeter who at twelve years old was gigging around New England. While in high school he took four months off to play on a trans-Atlantic liner for the American Export Company. "Much more educational," he told the principal.

In the mid-'30s he brought an eight-piece band down from Connecticut. For a while he went to Juilliard, and tried to find work for the band while they parked cars at the Embassy Club in the Bronx and while waiting for the club to obtain its liquor license.

After playing at places as diverse as the Paradise Ballroom on the Grand Concourse in the Bronx, the Nut Club in the Village, and the Nevele in the "borscht belt" of the Catskill Mountains, Jerome's band ended up at Child's Paramount under the Paramount Theater on Times Square in 1940.

❖❖

HENRY JEROME   It held 1500 people—it was an enormous place. We had a ten-piece band—three brass, three, four saxes, three rhythm—and it was a commercial band. It was called Henry Jerome and His Stepping Tones. But the musicianship was kinda good, and we went from there on the air. It was our first thing on the air—on Mutual. That was '40 and '41. And then in '42 we changed to almost a four-beat kind of band and more or less the big band style, and we got a break up at the Pelham Heath Inn. In those days they had places around New York like the Log Cabin, Pelham Heath Inn, Glen Island Casino, etc., and we used to do a lot of broadcasting out of there, and we enlarged the band to five brass and four saxes and a vocalist. There we found Fran Warren in the Bronx, and we started her. I can't remember all the musicians in those days, but it was building, the musicianship and all that.

The progressive band—that was Child's. Tell you what happened. We went back there—to Child's, after this big band went '40–'43 into '44—and then I altered the sound of the band. What happened was, we were playing the Lookout House in Kentucky, and Tommy Dorsey—we were dear friends, but he was always killing me—and I had to pack him in his car one night—could hardly make it style—and he was playing the theater, and I was playing the Lookout House, and he didn't say a damned word to me, but the next day his manager propositioned half of my band. But the next time I saw Tommy he said nothing about it. In effect I had to start the whole thing over, because the whole band was ripped out. Among others, he took Sid Cooper, who was with him almost from then until the end.

It was quite a personal and physical clout to me, but I had the go-go to start again, and I hired Van Alexander who is now writing for television on the Coast. And Van and I—he did the arranging and so forth and so on—put together what we called a four-trombone band in those days, which was a little unique; it was a commercial kind of thing, but very, very good. The woodwinds did a lot of doubling—the oboe, the English horn, those kind of sounds—and I stood in front and played lead and only had one other trumpet and featured the four trombones in almost everything. It was a kind of plush sound, and in those days it was good enough to play theaters; if you played theaters you'd add a couple of trumpets. But we played the Blue Room in the Roosevelt Hotel in New Orleans; Cavalier Beach Club; Surf Club; believe it or not, the Dixie Hotel in New York here and a room called the Plantation Room. We played there; Loew's State and so forth and so on. Leonard Garment, Shorty Allen, the piano player. Johnny Mandel joined me then. He always had good ears, not great chops or anything, but he was a very nice kid, and when he joined me we went down to Virginia Beach, and he was playing trumpet. The thing was after that band went for about a year, I felt it had shortcomings because the pluses were the niceness but it didn't have enough sock into it, and I broke it up. And then Lenny Garment, who later became Nixon's attorney, who had been with me since 1943, he kept banging on my head. He was really responsible for this progressive band. He kept selling me and selling me and, "Look what's happening, Henry," and, "This is what's going to be the thing of the future."

It was at that time, the influence, it threw the whole focus—the big band scene was, if you will, the music scene, and by virtue of Dizzy and Bird playing on the Street, the whole influence suddenly started changing in the big band thing and, matter of fact, it became a bit of a—like all progressive things, using the word advisedly—a bone of contention because many, many people put it down. It "wasn't swinging," and it "wasn't moving," and it didn't "have a beat." It was because the guys were making these fantastic changes and making them between the obvious standard chord changes and actually playing the changes—that it caught ears.

I started digging it and whatnot. And I said, "All right, all right, but where are we going to get the guys and where are we going to break this thing in?" So, you have to understand, it was very unacceptable. Up to this point, I had become already, if you will, using the terminology loosely, a commercially accepted band. That if we went to a spot, the networks put us on right after the news. They loved the band. They knew it was no risk. They knew they weren't gonna get hurt. It was one of the bands at whatever level they chose to think it. But now when Lenny and I started this thing, we had no place to go because no one would play it, so I called my connections from way before. It was almost like starting all over again—at Child's and I got them to let me put it back in there—and I think it was a 14-piece band. Now we got the guys, 'cause the scale was low there, and of so many guys wanting to play this kind of music. So that's when I switched Johnny Mandel to trombone, because we couldn't get a trombone player. He said, "I can do it," and he sat and played second trombone until he built up his chops. But his ears were so good that he could do that. And believe it or not, the lead trumpet player—there's a comedian around called Fat Jack Eagle.*

We started this band and went into Child's. We had Bill Vitale, lead alto; Tiny Kahn was the drummer; Al Cohn was playing tenor and writing; and Johnny was writing. And also, believe it or not, Vitale wrote good. They dug, they lived this kind of music. They were all musicians on the Street, digging Dizzy and Bird—but no one had ever orchestrated this for a big band—so the idea was between Lenny and the three arrangers and myself, we were going to orchestrate these kinds of things for sections. It was either late '44 or early '45. If we'd have done as much business as with the musicians who came down there to dig it, we would have been rich. But no one dug it. The people didn't dig it because they couldn't dance to it, because they didn't know what the hell we were doing.

With the four-beat band we had a theme called "Night Is Gone" and then, later on, with the commercial band we used "Nice People." But when we had the progressive band the guys said to me, "Henry, we can't have this corny theme song." I said, "What do you mean, it's so corny. It's my theme song." "No, we can't have that. We have to say what it *is*." "Oh. All right." Lenny Garment, Al Cohn, Bill Vitale—they're the big spokesmen. "Well, tell you what. We'll use "Night Is Gone" for the closing theme. But for the opening theme we have to say what we are, coming on the air." "Well, if you guys feel that way."

I think it was Al who wrote the thing up. And so they'd say, "Here he is, Henry Jerome and his orchestra," and they'd go, "Pow!!! Bomp-ba-da-da, beelya, deelyop!" Like this. Well, the first time we went on the air we put the transmitter off the air. It blew the limiter at the transmitter.

And the funniest story was—we went in there and the three networks put us on—CBS, Mutual and ABC—and after the first night they all moved us back to one o'clock in the morning and then finally they dropped it altogether. And I used to play Loew's State every year, and Jesse Kaye, the booker, came down and said, "My God, what's that, Henry?" and he canceled us. No one—it was totally unacceptable. Now, maybe to musicians it was acceptable, but the public was not ready for it. The bookers wouldn't touch it with a ten-foot pole and you know how the business is—the radio networks hedged off of it. But the musicians, any musicians you speak to, say it was the start of it all.

I was the one that broke that band up—for dollar reasons only. I couldn't stand it no longer. Gerry Mulligan came in and out; he didn't want to sit there. Then I think we got a guy called—oh, Danny Bank and Evan Aiken—he was a guy from the Midwest. But the brass were

*widely seen on a television margarine commercial as "Mr. Cholesterol."

Normie Faye and Jackie Eagle and Gene Roland, and Gene also wrote—
he came in from the Kenton band. A lot of guys came over because
they wanted to play this stuff. Then, later on, Gordy Heiderich took
Tiny Kahn's place. I took Tiny as a favor to Lenny Garment. Tiny,
for all his lore about him that people of today write—who turned out
to be a most progressive and wonderful drummer—was the drummer
no one would hire. Tiny used to hang around Nola Rehearsal Studios,
and he was never considered a good band drummer. He found his
niche when this music came in, and he developed really with this band.
But he could never really get with a band—no one would use him.
The sweetest guy in the world—good-natured kind of guy and he had
great potential—but obviously it didn't come out until he started playing this kind of music. Anyway, he ended up being a great one. There
was another guy, Larry Rivers—the great painter.

We had Trummy Young—he was a sensational guy—great showman from the old Lunceford band, as you know. But what I'm telling
you is that we used black guys in those days; the color line was really
broken down more in the band business before anything. Al Greenspan, we used as a straight sax player, he's running the country now.*
He was with us about a year. He used to make the payrolls. When I
broke the band up, that's when the band all went, in total, to Boyd
Raeburn, and they flew out to San Francisco to the Mark Hopkins
Hotel. After that they went to Buddy Rich and to Woody's band. This
really was the beginning of the progressive jazz of today. It might have
been called bebop then, but this was it, and it's amazing that every
musician knew about it, and the writers never picked up on it.

The musicians were very pure-thinking. They really *were* playing
for themselves. If you remember, we were talking about narrow-
mindedness. Although this was progressive and although this was
making great strides, they didn't want to know about any other kind
of music. There was no other kind of music.

❖❖

There were only a few people from the previous period that they
respected. They were all brought up on Basie and all loved the
Basie band. They idolized Lester Young and then when Bird came
along he became their God, but they still loved Lester Young, Joe
Jones, and the whole Basie sound.

❖❖

HENRY JEROME They liked to take those kind of solos and those kind of
changes with a Basie beat. That's where the beat was in those days. I
remember the coats were down to here. They never wanted a uniform conforming to what was. It was almost the beginning of a rebellion. It was a rebellion in music really, and they also carried it through
in their life-style—the way they lived and the way they dressed. All the

*interview done during Gerald Ford administration.

bands, you know, were almost drilled—when the brass would stand up with the hats, etc. That was great, too, for what it was.

They rebelled on that. I could never make the guys in this band do that. They just wanted to prove music, and I was caught up as I told you that I had a cause, and I was fighting with them, and I was supporting them, but the world wasn't supporting me. They didn't want to know from this thing, and I finally gave it up, but it is integrated into the American scene. When I had it, it was almost an uncut version, if you will, and, as a matter of fact, if you get some of the "air checks" and you hear it, it's as modern today, this many years later, for what it was. The guys played very good. The pick-ups on the radio were awful. The engineers were indifferent to what we were trying to do, and would not raise levels for featured soloists and sections or try to get good ensemble mixes. They didn't like us, didn't relate to what we were doing.

TRUMMY YOUNG   In the meantime, I was going in and out with Norman Granz, and I was doing a few things with Benny Goodman—I made a few records with him and was doing a few things with him. And it was a fun period. And then Dizzy and I went and did some things with Boyd Raeburn. And I loved Boyd—Benny Harris and I were on that band. Diz never played a long engagement with him, but Diz did some records and a few dates. We had a hell of a band. They used to get to cooking, that band did.

DAVID ALLYN   In '45 I went over to the Boyd Raeburn band. At the New Yorker hotel. Johnny Bothwell was still in the band. I think Trummy Young had just left the band. Oscar Pettiford just left. Diz did some dates with them.

❖❖

The Apollo Theater on 125th Street used to have "Amateur Night" on Wednesdays. In the middle of the amateur night they would broadcast on WMCA. In addition to the contestants, pros who were appearing that week would also play something. Dizzy performed "Night in Tunisia" on such a broadcast with Boyd's band.

❖❖

DAVID ALLYN   I never did know who did that chart on the band.* But most of those charts were written by George "The Fox" Williams, and they had a definite—it had a signature—you knew it was George. But the band itself had a good sound. With Carl Berg and Dale Pearce back there and Tommy Allison [trumpets]; and let's see, Irv Kluger [drums]; and Joe Berisi [bass]; and Ike Carpenter was playing piano in those days. Then we went out to the Coast to the Palace Hotel, and I think

---

*It was Gillespie.

that's when we started making some history. Harry Biss came out. He toured the Coast with us. And from the Palace, George Handy started to write some things. Of course the difference between George Williams and George Handy was just fantastic. Tremendous impact on the band. I remember Tommy Dorsey walked into the Rose Room once at the Palace Hotel, and we started to play an arrangement which George had written, "Out of this World." It started way up there, and it had great effects to it. And Tommy went running out of the room holding his ears. He couldn't even listen to the third bar. He just ran. We stayed there a few months. In the meantime George was writing— he was trying to write two a week. Whether we got two a week done, I don't know, but they were getting pretty heavy. 'Cause we still had those old things—those Basie things—to rely on. And the band was really shaping up.

FRANKIE SOCOLOW   At the time it was a wonderful musical organization. It was less commercial than any band I had been with, and the arrangements were great because a lot of them were Tadd Dameron arrangements. And a couple of different guys: [Ed] Finckel, I think, from Washington, and I hadn't played a book like this before, really, and it was a most enjoyable experience. George Handy became sort of the musical director of the band after a while. And the band did try to be as musically oriented as it possibly could.

❖❖

In August 1944, when much of the band's book was destroyed by fire at Palisades Amusement Park, Duke Ellington not only sent over a score by his trombonist Juan Tizol but invested fifteen thousand dollars in Raeburn's band. Except for a brief period later, when there was a wealthy backer, Stillman Pond, the band had to get along on its bookings, so it never really made much money.

❖❖

FRANKIE SOCOLOW   But it was one of the happiest periods in life on that band. There was Tommy Allison, Johnny Mandel, Lenny Green (an alto player from Pennsylvania, good player). And, well, some very close friendships—Davey Allyn, George Handy—it was a kind of band that was lunatics. Everything was one big ball—all the time. It was a balling band. When I first joined the band, we stayed pretty much East. And then we went to Chicago. Played one of those real good hotels there. And I remember Woody's band was in town that night, and after the job we all got together. It was something else.

[Our audiences were] not really hostile, but indifferent. Except there were always a certain group that did appreciate the band, that would come down to see the band just because they thought it was very musically balanced. Boyd's band was never that great a commercial draw. In fact, there was one period when we were in San Francisco that was probably the greatest misbooking in history. Where they booked us into the Ambassador Hotel,* I think it was. Now that was a very sedate kind of hotel that only had Lawrence Welk-type bands at that time, with champagne music who would play for some kind of society-type of group, and this band opened up there, and the manager at the hotel—I remember that opening night Boyd was on the phone all night long with New York trying to get us out of there. He didn't want the job. We didn't want to be there, and they didn't want us there. But somehow we stayed our full engagement. I think it was two months.

I mean, naturally, Boyd would try his best to keep the band down. Oh, man, that was a crazy time. The band itself was in a strange position. At that time Frisco was a port of embarkation, 'cause the war was still on. So either guys were just coming back from battle or else going into battle. In either case they were very salty, especially with civilians, and, out of necessity, we had to find back alleys to go to and from the job, 'cause if we used main thoroughfares we would get killed—really. There were a couple of bits where certain guys got the shit kicked out of them. We had to be very careful. Fact as a refuge, Dave Allyn found an old deserted cemetery where we used to sit. If anybody saw this, they would know there was a band of lunatics. And they naturally would put on a schtick, you know, communicating with the dead. And everything was pretty nuts, but it's literally impossible to describe it. It's one of those things where you really had to be there to get the full flavor of what was happening.

DAVID ALLYN   It was amazing in San Francisco, the war was just ending; it was somewhat a sailor's town, port of embarkation. And they weren't sending anyone overseas at the time. They were just stagnated there in San Francisco. Piling up all around. The troops were coming in and not going out. The sailors were coming in and not going back out. And we just didn't have a chance. You know we had pegged pants and long hair. They used to call us faggots and everything else. A weird scene. And so we had to stick together. Everybody rode the same cabs and lived in the same hotel; balled the same chicks; smoked the same pot. But all of that made food for playing and thinking ensemble. Being together, it brought the band tighter together, and I think that's what it takes. And of course we were sitting on that job for about three months. By the time we got into that third month, the band was just so much a part of each other that everyone was just thinking alike. Even myself, being in the vocal chair, I still thought ensemble. Constantly would think as part of the band. And George wrote changes of key for me without modulation. I'd just go into a second half with a change of key. And I felt I was part of the band. Hal McKusick came up from Hollywood. He joined the band with George. Harry Biss left

*not the Ambassador, nor the Mark Hopkins, but the Palace.

and went back to New York. Let's see, Joe Berisi was still in the band, still Irv [Kluger] and Jack Carmen. Who was the other trombone player? Ollie Wilson. Ollie Wilson and Johnny Mandel.

Afterwards we came down to Hollywood and did some one-nighters. In and out of town on Army planes. We played one day free for the Air Force, and they would fly us for the rest of the week. We had all kinds of scenes like getting up in the air and finding there's no heaters in the plane and get caught in an air pocket. The plane being overloaded with chicks, like ex-wives or ex-old ladies or something. And some wild scenes. Dodo Marmarosa was on that band.

BUDDY DE FRANCO   Dodo was always rather eccentric. I don't know if all musicians are, but a lot of them are—in different ways. He was. But he had a great, not only technical ability, but he had a great ability to hear new things. He had a concept for grasping new ideas—playing new ideas. I would say he was more progressive in his playing when he was fifteen than later on, say, when he was around twenty-seven or twenty-eight, because mentally somewhere he lost his grip. We had an unfortunate thing when we were kids. We got beat up, both Dodo and I, in Philadelphia. And Dodo got the worst of it. We were with Gene Krupa's band. In Philadelphia, in my home town, of all things. In the subway. And Dodo was in a coma for almost twenty-four hours or maybe over twenty-four hours. I don't want to cop out for Dodo, but he has never been the same since. In other words, he began to lose his grasp.

In those days, there was an awful lot of tension between servicemen and civilians, and we had on Gene Krupa uniforms. Five sailors came over to take care of us. And they did us in. We had quite a time. They walked right over the tracks. Came over and, before I knew it, I couldn't get my arms up anymore, and then we got beat up pretty bad. The thing is that, before that, he had probably the most astute musical mind that I had ever run across, which is why I—I guess I gravitated toward most piano players. They seemed to inspire me. And also I find them more interesting than most players because they have the whole orchestra at their command. They've got the whole keyboard. And each of the piano players that I liked to play and appreciate each have their own little way of working with chords—chord progressions. Kenny Drew. Sonny Clark. Of course. And Carl Perkins was one of the greatest swing pianos of all time.

When we were with Krupa, Dodo was into, of course, like most of us, Roy Eldridge; our close friend, Art Tatum; Jimmy Jones; Stuff Smith; Lester Young; Buck Clayton; all the Basie group and the Duke Ellington group; Jimmy Blanton. These were our influences then. We had not heard Bird. We had just heard stories about him, but never really heard him in person, never really heard anything recorded by Bird.

He was always searching, always into new things. And in any band, he could pick out the solos. As I said before, a lot of things escaped me. But I was smart enough to hang on to Dodo. Because he knew. He knew. And I knew he knew.

Later on, we were all featured with Tommy Dorsey's band, and we did those V-Discs which some of my friends still have. It was Dodo, Gene Krupa, and myself. I have one of the records. That was on the Tommy Dorsey band. That's when Tommy got Gene when he got out of jail, and Gene joined the band. And then, later on, I joined.

DAVID ALLYN   Dodo was pretty wild. I remember a funny thing. In a job in Denver somewhere out in those airfields. Played the job, come into the town and sleep. And the next day the Army bus was to pick us up and take us back out to the airfield again, and I was rooming with Dodo. I was trying to get some sleep, and he was hung up making faces in the mirror. *All* night long. It came time for the call around seven o'clock to get up and down, and he was still in the mirror making faces. The bellhop come up and said, "Here's your loaf of bread." Dodo took the loaf of bread and started throwing it out the window onto the roof, feeding pigeons. So I said, "Hey, we gotta make the bus. The guy said we should be downstairs already. Let's split." He says, "I'll be right down." So we get downstairs. In the interim everybody's busy and having coffee or something. So we jump on the bus, and go out to the airfield, and Boyd says, "David, where's Dodo?" I said, "My God." "Did you check him out?" I said, "Well, gee, he said he was comin' down, but I didn't check him out downstairs. I didn't look for him there." He says, "My God, let me call. Come on, and we'll go and call. Maybe you could talk to him." So we go to a pay phone and call Dodo. And Boyd was being very kind. "Hiya, Dodo. Hi, this is Boyd. Listen, what happened? You missed the bus. You know we're out at the airfield. What do you mean you're not coming? Horses? What do you mean you want to buy horses? Dodo, would you stay there, we'll come and get you. No, no, no. You'd better come back to Hollywood with us." He said goodbye to him. He got a jeep. And Boyd and I and the driver went back to the hotel and picked him up. We finally got him on the plane, but he swore he was going to stay there and buy horses and have a lot of birds and animals, and he was just through with whole world.

Another time, Dodo was on the Artie Shaw band. They were playing this theater downtown here in Los Angeles, and the curtain was up one morning and he didn't show. So we started sending out the wires. Where's Dodo? We can't find him. They got another guy to fill in for him second show. They couldn't find Dodo. Two days later, one of the guys, tuxedo shirts and all that, was taking his laundry from the theater, going around the corner to a laundry. He walked into this Chinaman's laundry, and there Dodo was ironing in the back. He says,

"Dodo, man, what are you doing? We're looking all over for you." So the Chinese cat says, "No, no, you leave him alone, he fine. Very good handkerchief. He very good laundry man. You leave him alone. He belong here. I like him. He do good work." Dodo says, "Get the hell out of here and leave me alone." So the only thing he could think of was to call the manager of the band who knew a friend of Dodo's who Dodo related to all the time—Harry Givent—Billy Grey the comedian's brother. So anyway, this great big cat goes down there, big fat cat, and walks in and says, "Dodo, what the hell are you doing here?" And again, "You leave him alone. He good worker. Iron handkerchief very good." So Dodo says, "Wait a minute. Wait a minute." And this guy used to like to wear loud ties. So Dodo reached in his pocket, and he took out three one thousand dollar bills. And he said, "Here, buy yourself a tie." "You get your ass on that bandstand, bla, bla, bla." It was a big thing. I don't know what happened after that [laughter].

But what a player. Lyle Griffin had a record coming out here at Atomic Records called "Flight of the Vout Bug," featuring Dodo. So on a Christmas eve, they're going home, and Dodo was supposed to be in the house, and they're going to have a nice Christmas. Lyle and his chick, they go to the market and load up on groceries. They park the car, couldn't get in front of the house. They park the car a couple of houses away, and they come out and walk in front of the house, and all the furniture's out on the lawn. Lyle's a real animal kind of a cat, and he said, "What the hell you doin', Dodo? Jesus Christ!" He says, "Well, man, I had to move it out because all the furniture was bugging the sound of the piano."

That whole transition though, that period, was just wild. The more we played, the more people turned their ears away from us. Then there was also another group who kept opening their ears, very susceptible to what we were saying, like Pete Rugolo was in there making notes all the time. In the club that we played in, a place on Vine Street—I can't remember the name of the place, but it was right next to the bowling alley—and we were packing them in because we were the sound of the day. And George's arrangements were fantastic. Johnny [Mandel] had already left the band. He went over to Jimmy Dorsey, but he left a lot of charts on the band, which was great. "If I Loved You" and "How Deep Is the Ocean"—Tommy Allison played on it. A lot of great things. But it's strange, we're being turned away, we couldn't get work, and everyone else was working, I mean all the bands. It's a band business world. All but for us. People were just backing away; it was too harsh for them. They weren't used to those dissonances and the harmonies. It made us turn around and run. Speaking about being loyal, I think Boyd was the most loyal I've ever seen or heard of in the business, ever since or before. He wanted the new sound. He was willing to sacrifice bread for it. I mean bread in his mouth for it. You know the times when he could have just gotten a "Mickey" band and gone back to Chicago and worked all the time, I'm sure. But he wouldn't do that. He believed in George and Johnny's things and the new sound, and he wanted to be part of it.

George wrote him in for like bass saxophone and baritone and soprano. He wrote Boyd in just for kind of a show thing there every once in a while. Boyd wasn't a soloist. Not at all. Couldn't play at all, but he was loyal. As a matter of fact there were times when the tempo would be going along, and Boyd would get so engrossed, he'd have his arm swinging at the right tempo, but someone would ask him a question from the dancers on the floor or someone, he'd turn around, and his arms would go completely out of tempo and his foot would be tapping in another thing, completely off, but he'd be smiling and taking care of business. In other words, he would be looking the part constantly. We all had a lot of respect for him. We really did, because he was the only guy who would listen to what we had to say and say, "Well, you're right in whichever way you want to do it."

❖❖

George Handy joined the band in 1944 at the age of twenty-two. He submitted an arrangement for a vocal and Raeburn called him "the man I've been looking for."

❖❖

DAVID ALLYN   Well, they knew George's work. He had a couple of things with Alvino Rey. He wrote something for a tenor player—not Stan Kosow, but Herbie Steward. I think he wrote something about the "Stocking Horse"—yeah, the "Stocking Horse," and just one or two charts. He'd place one in one band, and it just would make so much, say so much, that people couldn't get away from the fact that George was gonna be one of the biggest things in the business. I didn't know what he's doing now, but he sure left a mark. What a talent. But he really changed the lives of a lot of people up there. You know his concept, and he's tied into Stravinsky. I really thought that he was a genius. It's a shame. If the band had been accepted a little more—record-wise, appearance-wise—I think we would have perhaps come right up to make some records that—I say record-wise meaning if we were accepted in the record business.

❖❖

The Raeburn band had recorded for Guild/Musicraft, but when it moved into its George Handy period, an affiliation was formed with Jewel, a company owned by Ben Pollack, the former drummer-leader in whose band Benny Goodman and Glenn Miller had gotten their starts in the late '20s.

❖❖

DAVID ALLYN   Now, Jewel Records I don't think had a good distribution—they couldn't have had—but if we had been with a label like Capitol or Mercury or something like that . . . but they wouldn't even hear of it. They wouldn't hear of it. And of course Ben was kind of a little guy that he wanted that thing all of himself. He wanted to make the money and the new sound. You know he'd even made remarks in the studio like, "Is it danceable?" [laughter]. Between takes George would play [hums], right, "We're in the Money," and somebody from the booth would say, "All right, cut it out, George."

Ben wanted a kind of a Benny Goodman danceable. 'Cause the ballads were too slow for Ben. Remember the thing I did, "Forgetful?" He wanted to pick up the tempo so bad on that date. Jesus Christ! You know you couldn't stop him. He kept waving his arms, and you could see it. In that control booth, like waving his arms to pick it up, and it couldn't be done, not the way George wrote it. It had no business being any faster than he wrote it. I still like it. I don't like my vibrato on it, but I like it. It did have a mood. George used the bass sax on that. He used Boyd on that. Then later he tried to say that he was just putting Boyd on, but he wasn't. And Boyd played the notes. Played them right.

That band was just too much. It really was. And then along comes somebody playing a tenor sax out of tune and hanging onto one note and, Jesus, sells a million records. A good example of how we felt, really is a pretty bad one. We played the Hollywood Bowl on a musician's outing once, a Local 47 outing. This was in '46. We were having trouble getting together and getting transportation out there. I think we needed to rent a car or something, but it was a problem, presenting a problem. We went on, and we were just about—no, we were all set up ready to go on in the field, on that field wherever the hell it was, I can't remember, near the Hollywood Bowl I think or something—but Spade Cooley comes in and they've got Cadillacs and groovy trucks, and they roll in. Gee, how it made us feel like, what are we doing—who are we trying to reach?

BUDDY DEFRANCO   Boyd Raeburn's band was one of the great bands. An unusual band. It did not make history—then. But I think it will. Johnny Richards. George Handy, Those two guys. *Unbelievable* musicians. Johnny Richards was just full of music. In fact, at one time in Raeburn's band, we were complaining about trying to play one of his arrangements in 7/8. In those times, 7/8 was really rare. I don't think anybody had done it. We said, "Oh, Johnny, we can't really feel it right." He said, "What do you mean can't feel it? I can dance to it." And he did. He proceeded to dance to 7/8 in front of the band. To show us how easy it is to feel.

AL COHN   I wasn't with Boyd's band very long. I didn't hit it off too well with Johnny Bothwell, who was the lead alto and musical director of the band. I wasn't there very long, so I really have no impressions.

The band was a good band. The guys were good. The music was good. George Handy was writing for the band then. But before they really got into the thing when George came on and Dave Allyn, it was a little before that. I did make a couple of records with them though—with Dizzy Gillespie—"Night in Tunisia," "March of the Boyds," too. Joe Megro took the solo on "Tunisia." He came from Ina Ray Hutton's band with Serge Chaloff. It was like baseball teams, trading.

❖❖

down beat, in those days, always had "Sideman Switches." You'd read that because there always would be movement of players from one band to the other with so many bands and so many places to play.

This is the environment that most young players entered and in which they began to develop as individuals. Red Rodney came out of a Boy Scout drum and bugle corps to play trumpet at thirteen. At Philadelphia's Mastbaum High School his schoolmates included fellow trumpeter Joe Wilder and Buddy DeFranco. His early idol was Harry James, but a few distinguished innovators who came to his native city turned his thinking around.

❖❖

RED RODNEY   For me, it was Harry James. Just the very beginning. That's all. I've always loved him. I still do. He's still a great, great trumpet player. I hear him every time I can in Las Vegas, which is his home. And I still think he's great. But of course he was my earliest influence, as he was most every young trumpet player's and especially young white trumpet players'.

I really became aware of jazz when I was with the name bands. To me a jazz chorus was like something—a ride, you know. You play a commercial jazz chorus, so to speak, half Dixieland, half swing. It wasn't that important. And I didn't know anything about jazz at all. When I came back to Philadelphia and joined Elliot Lawrence's orchestra, I had a studio job with Elliot Lawrence and his orchestra that was getting some recognition [Radio Station WCAU]. And there I was also becoming recognized, along with Gerry Mulligan, through Elliot. And Dizzy Gillespie and Charlie Parker's quintet started, and they were going to California to Billy Berg's.

Just at that time, Gerry Mulligan had joined Gene Krupa and recommended me to take Roy Eldridge's chair. And when they called me and asked me to take the job and said I would start at the Palladium in Hollywood, I quickly grabbed it because Dizzy Gillespie and Charlie Parker were going to Billy Berg's. They got out there a week before I did because I played with Elliot from January 1, 1945 to January 1, 1946. Then I joined Gene Krupa January 10, 1946. And needless to say, I went to Billy Berg's every night after the job at the Palladium with Krupa. But Krupa had a very good big band. It was a swingin' band. And when Gerry Mulligan came into the band as arranger,

Charlie Ventura was the tenor player and Buddy Wise, Charlie Kennedy, Don Fagerquist—good band. Mulligan started writing some of the more modern bebop figures, and Gene went along with it. He embraced it. Gene was a modern, progressive-type person who, unlike most of the big-name bandleaders of that era, decided that change was important, necessary, and right, and so we had a good band. Even Charlie Ventura, who was an established tenor star by the time we were with Gene Krupa—he was ready to go out and get his own band. Even he changed over. And you know Charlie Ventura was a great, great tenor player and, I may say, he still is. You know, we tend to dismiss him because he was sort of a Ben Webster-style tenor player and adopted some of the commercial things of bebop and at that time he was commercial himself. But he is a giant of a player. He was in that band and it changed all of us. Now I was a little ahead of the rest, because I had come up—this was my first jazz. I didn't go through the period of listening to Louis Armstrong or Lester Young or Benny or any of those. I listened to them later, after I had become fully indoctrinated with Charlie Parker, Dizzy Gillespie, and company. Then I went back and listened to the old masters. I imagine it was a funny way to do it, but I guess it doesn't matter how you do it as long as it's done.

And then I lived in New York, and Tiny Kahn, Al Cohn, Zoot Sims, Stan Getz, Allen Eager, who was a very big influence at the time, and they were into Prez. And then Dexter Gordon and Gene Ammons were offshotts of Prez. At that time, the scene was great. It was fresh. We were young. We were full of energy. And being put down by the name bandleaders that were just finishing their era made us even more arrogant about what we were doing. We belived we were right, and as youth will do it, "Why, you don't mean anything. We know what's right." Of course, youth is wasted on the young. The guy who made that statement up should be classified as a genius. Still, that was a great period in modern jazz music, because we were just getting into it.

FRANK ROSOLINO   Then there was Gene Krupa. He gave me a big break and called me Frankie Ross. My father almost disowned me. "What's a matta, you ashame of you name?" [laughter]. "Rosolino is you name?" he says, "What's Frankie Ross? I have to tell my friends the next time Frankie Ross comes up. What is this Frankie Ross stuff?" He was from the old country. Frankie Ross, the "Lemon Drop Kid."* Actually we recorded that before Woody's, but, of course, Chubby Jackson, Terry Gibbs broke it up.† Ruined my act [laughter].

---

*The reference is to Krupa's recording of George Wallington's "Lemon Drop," on which Rosolino sang a scat vocal.
†Woody Herman's version on which Chubby Jackson, Terry Gibbs, and Shorty Rogers sang the scat vocal.

BUDDY DEFRANCO   Gene Krupa was, by the way, I think, one of the major influences in music—and one of the unsung heroes in the real sense, because he had the reputation of being a wild, frantic guy and a dope fiend, and, of course, that publicity didn't—You've heard this before, but I must say I was there, in his band, in San Francisco, when he was framed. Framed. Quote. And it's as simple as that. The guy should have never been put away, never been convicted of anything. And the problem is that he was one of the most gentle people that I know. And yet, we'd go out, and some people would say, "Are you in that Gene Krupa's band? Tell me, when is he on dope? How is he? Is he weird? What does he do?" They all want this juicy stuff, and if they every met Gene, they'd be surprised that they'd meet the most mild-mannered guy in the whole business. Plus the fact that I think he really put the idea of drums, as such, on the map, as a solo idea besides being part of a group. So that was a great experience, too.

❖❖

When DeFranco was traveling with Tommy Dorsey, it was the last part of the "Big Band Era." He was constantly running into players who were getting into the new music wherever he went. Some of them were in the Dorsey band.

❖❖

BUDDY DEFRANCO   I am happy, absolutely thrilled, with the success of Supersax. I could remember back in '45 or maybe '46, Sid Cooper was playing lead alto with the Dorsey band, and Sid Cooper wrote down Charlie Parker's solos and had the section play them, and we'd go down in the basement and rehearse Charlie Parker's solos and harmony, just for our own kicks. As far back as then, he was influencing saxophone players. Tommy Dorsey never liked Charlie Parker. That's what he said. Couldn't understand bebop. Someone told him that Buddy DeFranco played bebop, and he wanted to hit him. However, Tommy stuck his head in one time while we were rehearsing this stuff, and he said, "My gosh! That's fantastic! Fantastic!! What is that?" Sid Cooper said, "*That's* Charlie Parker's solos, written for the sax section." Tommy didn't say a word—he was just so dumbfounded—and walked out. But even as early as then we were doing those sorts of things and thinking in that direction. Every big band had its group of guys that were gravitating towards the modern jazz area.

TERRY GIBBS   It was '46, when I went with Tommy Dorsey's band from Bill De Arango. I went out there. They were playing Casino Gardens. I'll never forget this. They picked me up at the train station 'cause my mother wouldn't let me fly. Forget about it, I took a train for three days, stayed out of my bird for three days, alone, in a compartment. Stayed out of it. Didn't know what I was doing at all. But it was beautiful. They picked me up at nine o'clock, rushed me out to Casino Gardens, set up my vibes and whatever they were playing—first of all,

Tommy, a trombone player, likes D-flat. That's one of the worst keys for vibes. I wasn't used to playing in that key. And it was all "I Got Rhythm" changes. At least if you had some tunes with some chord changes the key didn't mean anything. Also, the band had nothing to do with what I wanted to do in music. So I played one tune with the band which made a lot of sense. And I went up to Dave Klein. Dave Klein was the manager. I said, "Listen, I'm giving you my notice. I think I want to go home." He says, "What? You just came here." So I said, look, I told him it had nothing to do with what I was trying to do with music back in New York. So then Tommy Dorsey came over to me. He said, "I just heard you quit my band." I said, "Well, Mr. Dorsey . . . " I tried to explain. He said, "Nobody quits my band. You're fired." And I said, "Well, if I'm fired, you got to pay my way home." He said, "Oh, no. You quit my band." So I did two weeks there, and mostly I turned pages for the bass player.

But a lot of things happened while I was on that band. Louis Bellson was on the band. And Louis was great. I didn't know Louis, but since I was living alone, wherever I was staying, he thought, I should move in with him, and I moved in with him, and they were doing a movie picture with Louis Armstrong and Danny Kaye.* Tommy, Benny [Goodman], Lionel Hampton, and I forget who else and Louis and Charlie [Barnet]. And Louis [Bellson] wanted Benny to hear me play. So we stayed over after hours. Bill Miller, the guy who conducts for Frank Sinatra, was playing piano, and I forget the bassman's name, Eddie somebody, and myself and Louis. We made some tapes. In fact, it wasn't tapes, it was records, actual records we made. Discs. For Benny to hear me play. And that day he brought them, Tommy Dorsey and Benny had a fight. Tommy used to have to get up early in the morning because of the picture. And going to work late at night, he told Benny to stop doodling. He don't care, he's foggy and he's doodling. So he said, "Okay," and two seconds later, he's doodling again. So Tommy hit him, and he went home. Louis had these records, so he played them for Lionel.

Lionel heard them, and I got a call from Lionel. He said, "Hey, Gates!" He was gonna make me his protégé. I forget at what salary. "You play drums?" I said, "Yeah." He said, "Twenty vibes solos a night, and you play some drums." Then when he got with Gladys, it became nine vibe solos and nine drums. Then it became one vibe solo, and then forget about it, 'cause even though there was no competition between he and myself, because he was an established star; she didn't need any young flash around with him, so it was all drums. So I was on his payroll. Anyhow, I never played at all. He paid my ticket home, which was great. I was on Lionel's band all week, and he loved me. To this day, he always says great things about me. So he paid my way

*A Song Is Born.

home, and that was my scene with Tommy Dorsey. I lasted one-half an hour, one tune I think.

❖❖

Gibbs did find big bands that were in keeping with what he wanted to do musically, but the sphere of influence was shifting to the small combo, spearheaded by Charlie Parker.

« 7 »

The Bop Era

From the time of its full emergence as a musical force in 1945, bop had continued to elongate its lines and smooth out some of the choppier, staccato accents that were evident in the early compositions. A small but instructive example is the variance between the transitional phrases at the end of the "Ornithology" theme as recorded by Charlie Parker for Dial in early 1946, and his airshot from the Royal Roost in December 1949.

The quintet Charlie Parker put together for the Three Deuces was to stay together for about a year and a half, and when Kenny Dorham replaced Miles Davis on Christmas Eve of 1948, it was the first personnel change in a group that, through its Dial recordings and extensive touring, helped establish Bird as the most influential soloist in jazz.

Bud Powell made one recording session with Parker in 1947, but his greatest achievements were to be in the format of his own trio until mental illness forced periods of inactivity and a decline in his powers during the '50s.

Tadd Dameron became a leader of a combo—usually a quintet but often a sextet—and in 1948 he headed the house band at the Royal Roost, a new jazz club on Broadway and 48th Street. The scene was shifting away from 52nd Street, and soon there would be other large Broadway clubs such as Bop City; the Clique followed in its wake. The Clique eventually became Birdland, named for Charlie Parker, at the end of 1949.

❖❖

RED CALLENDER   Bird was like a bright burning star. If he lived to ninety he couldn't have upset the scene much more, could he?

JOE ALBANY   When Charlie was right, the melodies of his music had a rhythmic impulse built right into them. I never heard anything like that. His music danced right off the page.

AL COHN   The thing about Charlie Parker was that he was such a giant. He was so much better than everybody else. It was not like there was this guy and that guy. There was everybody else, and there was Charlie. You could take his solos, and somebody could put them down on paper and analyze them. They really had substance, creativity in the way he used changes. There wasn't anybody else doing that then. Dizzy. But Charlie Parker was really the moving force.

GERRY MULLIGAN   Bird used to invite me to play. Do you know one of the things Bird did to me at the time of that first concert?* Well he came over with Diz. They came over to the studio, 'cause Staurday afternoons we did the network show. And of all things, I wasn't playing in the band at that time. But a week before the concert was to take place, I said to the band in rehearsal one day, "Why don't one of you guys do me a favor, break a leg or something so I can play the show instead." And they all laughed ho-ho-ho, you know, what a kid. It was a kind of semipolitical job. There were a lot of cats in the band there that were merely there because it was the best job in town, and they were the best friends of such and such an officer at the union. It's all that kind of cliquish thing, which really was dreadful for the music and made for dreadful personality of the band as a whole. It was just a little peculiar. So I was a kid, and a lot of the guys—they liked me and all, and they liked my music. But they always treated me a little shitty, because Elliot was a friend of mine. Say what is this? Like being a friend of the leader. To them it's like sucking up to the leader. Oh, shit. Elliot and I were close to the same age, and we liked each other. So we hung around together. I said to the guys, "Why doesn't someone break a leg." So, Saturday morning, the day of the concert, Elliot called me up, frantic. Said, "Gerry, please, bring your tenor with you today. Frank Lewis† [one of the tenor players] tripped on his child's roller skate on the stairs and broke his wrist." Well, I get into the studio with my horn, and the guys are lookin' at me like this.

We play the afternoon network show, and Diz and Bird came by and visited, and I met Bird then, and we talked, and he said, "After the show bring your tenor over," to—what was it?—the Downbeat behind the Earle. Said, "Bring your horn back there and play." Said, "I wouldn't presume to play with you. Don't be ridiculous." He said, "Just bring your horn." Ordered me like, being very imperious.

So we played the concert, and after that we went over to the Downbeat, and I went in and put my horn in the cloak room. And Bird played, and Don Byas was there, at the Downbeat. Say, you can imag-

*A Parker-Gillespie concert in Philadelphia in 1945, also featuring the Elliot Lawrence orchestra.

† In later years Frank Lewis became the head trainer for the Philadelphia Flyers hockey team.

ine I'm going to get my horn out and play on the bandstand with Charlie Parker and Don Byas? Forget it! Plus a couple of pretty good Philadelphia guys, could tear it up pretty well. And I sounded terrific at home in the living room, but this was a little beyond me [chuckles]. And I listened for a couple of sets, and then I told Bird—because he was in his element, every inch the king and table-hopping, and everybody making a fuss over him—I went over to where he was and said, "Bird, I really enjoyed it and I'm awfully glad to have met you and all this, but I got to go now." He said, "What? you're going? Wait a minute." I said, "No." He said, "Well, you gotta play!" I said, "Bird, please! Don't put me through that. It would be too embarrassing. Forget it." He goes over to the cloak room, gets my horn, goes up to the bandstand—all of this very ostentatious. Opens the goddamned thing, gets the horn out, puts it together and says, "Here. Now. O.K. Let's play." And he made me play with him. And he was terrific because he gave me the confidence in myself that I lacked. Unfortunately for my confidence up to that point, some of the guys that I knew in Philadelphia, the attitude towards me was, "Well, man, you don't play very well. But, uh, you can *write*. What do you want to worry about playin'?" They'd like me to come around and listen to them play. But, don't bring my horn. So Bird was really the first one that ever encouraged me to play. He was always like that.

In many ways Bird was *much* older than I was because the way he had grown up. He grew up around music and around musicians. And also the accomplishment that he had done in music and on his horn. The eight years or so that he was older than I, were a tremendous eight years. Tremendous difference. At that age it is anyway, plus the experience. It was a thing which, especially with Bird coming along, there's some dividing line between something that really is music as an ideal, rather than just ordinary music. And there was something that—it's maybe the hardest thing in the world for *me* to define, and I guess in a way I try to avoid having to define it—but there are certain people that made music that is on just another level altogether. Now, in this day and age, that's *not* the most popular concept to have because, what happens to your great concepts of democracy, equality, and all the rest of it. Well, there *ain't* any in art. What makes one man so much greater than anything around him? And the greatness is contained in some kind of conception that—it's just *different*. There was a different kind of presence to Bird's music. When Bird played, it achieved some kind of response, and *everybody* responded to it. So we *know* there's something special going on, here. Prez had that, too. Specially in the context of the Basie band. It just was another element. It wasn't contained in anybody else's music. You run into that *damn* seldom in popular music. And yet there are a number of times that I have experienced that but I don't think, *ever*, as strongly as with Charlie Parker.

There was one week that I worked with Charlie at the Apollo Theatre. I worked it with the group that was based around a string band,
with some incredibly stupid string section. I think three violins, a vi-
ola, and cello. The very pedestrianness of the arrangements made the
absolute *perfect* foil for Bird. 'Cause later on guys wrote more interesting arrangements, and the things were not nearly as effective. By
the very simplicity of the arrangements, it was a better framework to
hear Bird do what he could do. He'd play a bloody *melody* and would
elevate it into something that was *art*. This was the string section plus
we had, I think, three brass and three saxophones to play the acts,
and Bird asked me to write a couple of charts. I wrote "Rocker" for
him. And the theme song that we never did ultimately record. He used
to love to do it with the strings. I did a thing called "Roundhouse"
that was based on the chords of "Out of Nowhere." At the end of the
first chorus it was in one key, I forget whether it was in E-flat and
went to G, or G and went to E-flat. But at the end of the first chorus
I'd have a four-bar break and then the key change. So Bird has got
the modulation. But he'd come *roaring* out of that first chorus, roarin',
man, and he'd start doing that curlycue thing he would do [scats two
chord changes]. O.K., say the band comes in at bar one. Well, he would
finish the modulation on the *fifth* bar. And he would take that goddamned thing, man, it just made my hair stand on end. The number
of ways he could use this idea in his head. To get to the fifth bar. "Out
of Nowhere"—that's a lovely change. If it's in G, G for two bars, then
E-flat 7th for two bars. It's a lovely, lovely thing. But, to hear him do
that as a blowing device, and to hear him use it in so many different
ways. 'Cause he loved to suspend—a thing like that—to suspend turn-
arounds and get up over the bar lines. Bird has two really famous ones
like that. One is "Night in Tunisia." But still the most impressive thing,
I think, single performance anybody ever did has got to be "Ko Ko."
That last phrase that he played is just incredible. 'Cause that's the curlycue business. It's circular, and it always keeps goin'. He keeps moving it a little later and later, and when it lights, it's always such a pleasant, satisfying surprise.

But anyway, that experience with Bird at the Apollo for a week doing
four or five shows a day, and hearing Bird, I learned more about what
I wanted from the sound of the saxophone at that point. Because he
would be blowing, and you could hear the sound bounce off the back
wall of the theater. The sound became a visual experience. You could
see that—and *big*. His sound was perfect that week. Just the tone quality itself, because a lot of times he would not spend any time with reeds
and mouthpieces, and borrow horns and all that. And sometimes it
just sounded dreadful. And I was not one of these people who said
just because it was Bird it sounded good, man. When he sounded awful, he sounded awful. And pick up a horn with a dry reed. You've
got to take care of the mechanics of any instrument, including Charlie

Parker having to do it. But that week he had it together. The mouth-piece and reed and everything was there. And that experience of hearing a sound produced on an instrument—the *big, round* quality. To hear him play these same pieces show after show, and play things *differently,* each one a gem, for an entire week. He just was incredible.

❖❖

Parker encouraged Mulligan but others, like Terry Gibbs, he in-timidated just by his being Bird.

❖❖

TERRY GIBBS   I remember hearing Miles Davis and Bird, Bud Powell and Max Roach or Stan Levey, I forget who it was. And Curly Russell. I remember that Bird—I was told by Irving Alexander* that he used to pay him by the night. He never paid him by the week 'cause Bird would never be there every night. And then he got to pay him by the set 'cause Bird would leave and go across the street and sit in and never come back. Then he got to pay him by the tune. That's how it got to be.

Later on, I was learning, and I wouldn't play in front of anyone, for I was always afraid. But Bird was watching. I got to know Bird a little before I got to know Diz. And Bird liked me. I drove him home once. Whatever it was, I drove him. In fact, I threw him out of my car once 'cause he, like, took me to 34th Street and then he wanted to go to 118th. I say, "Listen, get out of my car." I said, "I respect you on the stage." But then he wanted a quarter, and that even bugged me more. But those days I went into Georgie Auld's club.† Bird would always say, "I'm comin' to see you."

Bird always said he's gonna come sit in, but he never did. With me sor some reason, he did twice. He said, "I'm gonna come sit in with you." He did. He came down to Georgie's place, and he sat in. Every-body heard—in those days rumors got out he's coming in—and the place would be mobbed. You couldn't get in the joint. I had Harry Biss, Phil Arabia, and Louis Barrero, the bass player. Tony Scott was in the club, he's gonna sit in with us. And Tony had more nerve than anyone in those days.

My scene with Bird, I'll never forget it. I think we were playing "Out of Nowhere," and I was just really learning that tune good, see. Now every time Bird would get to the thirtieth bar of the tune, I would drop my mallet on the floor. I wasn't gonna follow him, I wasn't gonna come in after him no matter what. I'd drop my mallet, or I would go button my fly or tie my shoe. I would do somethin', fix something on my vibes, I don't know what. It got to be, he played about forty cho-ruses, so I had to do forty different things, so I wouldn't follow him. I didn't know what I was doing. Whatever I would have played would

---

*owner of the Three Deuces.
† Tin Pan Alley in the Hotel Markwell.

have been one of Bird's licks I heard anyhow and the other would have been bullshit. It got to a point, seriously, I remember this, that when I went to tie the one shoe, I untied the other one, then I had something to do when I was down there. Anything but to follow him.

❖ ❖

There were alto saxophonists who were driven to tenor by Bird, but these were more than outnumbered by the legion of his followers on alto. Some consciously tried to avoid playing like him even when they were influenced in a general way.

❖ ❖

ART PEPPER It's not like Charlie Mariano or someone like that went all Bird. I purposely tried not to play like Bird. I just made a conscious effort to not play like Bird because I didn't want to become a Bird copier and lose my thing because I heard so many guys—guys that played tenors switched to altos to play like Bird and so many alto players that had something to say on their own and they—I never ever played a Bird solo, note to note, like guys did—bought Bird books and all that, never.

We played those tunes. Like "Yardbird Suite" and "Scrapple from the Apple." And just listening to Bird I couldn't help but pick up Bird's things, but as far as being a copier of Bird, I never was. It wasn't that I didn't dig Bird. I really dug Bird, but I didn't want Bird to destroy me. I didn't want that to happen to me that I heard so many other guys do, and I got put down by a few people—they called me prejudiced because I didn't want to play exactly like Bird. Joe Maini called me that. He was a fanatic about Bird. And then some other cats that actually put me down because I didn't play identically like Bird, and I purposely tried not to because I didn't want to get caught up in that bag. I always tried to keep my thinking, as a free spirit, as myself, as an individual. I really worked at that, very hard. I more or less gave myself a pep talk that I've got to go out and play, and I couldn't ignore the new thing because I had to be modern but I had to keep me, I couldn't lose myself, and I have to approach it in that respect. And that's what I did. To have people call me prejudiced because I didn't play like Bird. Just unbelievable. I went through such incredible scenes. Until finally I went ahead and played the way I played and learned the tunes and tried to play the way I felt and learned the charts—the "heads"—to where I could blow the "heads" and then I'd blow them the way I felt.

❖ ❖

Charlie Parker was a deity to many but they knew only the musician, not the man. Dexter Gordon worked with him on 52nd Street in a band that included Miles Davis, Bud Powell, and dancer Baby Laurence at the Spotlite in 1945.

❖ ❖

DEXTER GORDON   He was it. He was such a scurvy m——f—— [laughter]. I mean, not really, but I wondered at the time, "How could this cat play so fast, at times he could be so scary," but of course that was the drugs, you know. He'd get a few dollars, and maybe you see him, maybe you don't. To us it was very new, before the fad caught on. He had a very good mind. He was aware of what was going on. Well read in music, all kinds of music. He was interested in everything. His mind was open. And very talented.

MILT HINTON   Charlie, to me, was a great philosopher. We go to be very tight. I never got to work with him, but he always came around, and we hung out at Beefsteak Charlie's. He would come backstage at the Strand Theater especially to see me. For some reason we always got into politics. Cab had one of these bands where guys were involved in things other than our music. One afternoon between sets we would play classical music. We had a record player which was in the hall, and we put a bulletin board up—"After the second show, there will be a Duke Ellington concert," and we played Duke's music. I think I was one of the instigators, and Foots Thomas was probably another one, but the machine was mine. I bought the machine, and it was one of the prides of my life. It was very expensive—it even changed records in those days. And it was the one thing that I had that I could carry with me—my records and this machine—and I could listen. I bought records, and I had cases made that I could carry 'em in. Cab had all the conveniences, but he didn't have to carry 'em with his baggage cars and all this. And when we got to the theater we would have all these records, and other guys would have their records, and we put this thing in the hallway, backstage, and after the second show, after dinner, we'd just sit there, and we'd play your records. Today, we might play Charlie Parker. Tomorrow, we might play mine, or somebody might have some Bing Crosby records, some guy was interested in classical music, and we did this thing. So Charlie would come back to see us and, for some reason, we always got into politics.

He was just hangin' in New York. This was the early '40s. He'd been with McShann, and he was doing all the other things he was doing— and all the great playin'—but he liked to talk to people, he really did, and when he was in his right mind, he would come back, and we would talk about politics and race and really deep things like the solution for blacks in America and this kind of thing.

RED RODNEY   As a player, to me, he was the most significant giant of all. He played beautifully, intellectually, low-down, dirty, funky old blues. I remember going down South with him one time, and the first day, the black promoter came over, "Now looka here, Charlie Parker, we don't want no bebop down here." Bird looked at the crowd, the dancing people, all blacks. In those days you could play—you played two gigs. You played one night for blacks, and the whites sat upstairs, and the next time for whites, and the blacks sat upstairs. And Bird said, "Don't worry about a thing, we're going to play rice-and-beans music," and he went into [imitates horn] blues, and he broke the crowd up. This crowd that was completely illiterate to jazz, the way Bird played it, he played for them his own way, and he just played beautifully. Everything he did, as a player he was without—well, he was just the greatest of all. As a person, I thought he was rather—he was very modest. He was humble. Most of the times, most of the times. There were times when he would become a little arrogant, a little nasty about— because he knew he was the best. You can't have all of this idolatry and people idolizing you and telling you how great you are without believing it. He knew it. I think he handled it better than most people would be able to handle it. However, sometimes he needed a little extra.

And he would act the part. But, in general, I don't think I know anybody that could handle all this praise and idolatry as well as Charlie Parker did. He treated me beautifully. Actually, I was like a son to him in many respects, although our ages were not that far apart. When I first joined him, I left Woody Herman, came home to New York. And Miles had left Bird—I don't really know the reason, I understand that they had some problems with each other—but anyway Miles was ready to leave and get his own band because he was contributing a great deal.

Bird came over to me and offered me the job. And, naturally I wanted it, but I said, "My God, man, there's so many people who are much more deserving than me." And I mentioned Kenny Dorham, for one, who had worked with him for a while. And Bird said, "Hey, let me be the judge of that. I want you. I think that you're the player that I want in my band." And I still thought that, "Well, gee, this is really nice and all, but he likes me personally, that's why he's doing it. I'm not worthy." And I wanted to protest more, but then I said, "How can I, man? It's a chance for me to go with the greatest." But I was so . . . I was really frightened. I didn't think I belonged. And he made me feel like I belonged. And he understood how I felt, so he did it easy. And the first night at the Three Deuces, everybody was there— Miles was there; Dizzy Gillespie was there; oh, Fats Navarro was there; everybody, sitting in the back and hearing me play the first set. The theme was so fast, and I'd been playing with a big band, and I didn't have the agility at the time. You know, playing in a big band. And I was scared to death. And Bird just brought me through beautifully, just right, to where, inside a couple of weeks, I got all the confidence in the world, and then you could tell it in my playing. I could tell it. I knew it. And everybody else would come around and tell me, "Wow." That was a great period for me. And he did that for me.

❖❖

At the same time Bird's quintet was spreading the message and entrenching bebop in the consciousness of a generation of musicians and jazz fans (and the subconscious of the American public), Dizzy Gillespie was doing the same thing with his big band. The orchestra, formed in the spring of 1946, not only endured into 1950, spreading the bop essence in the larger context, but it gave Dizzy a showcase from which he emerged not only as a brilliant musician but as a full-fledged personality.

Kenny Clarke was the first drummer in the second edition of the Gillespie big band. Through him, John Lewis entered Dizzy's domain.

❖❖

KENNY CLARKE   John Lewis and I were soldiers together in Normandy. In the Army, we formed a small band. After the war, I returned to New York. I had given my address to John, and he called me up one day. He had arrived from Albuquerque and said that he had come to New York to study. I remembered then certain arrangements that he had written for us in Normandy. Dizzy Gillespie's big band had just started a set of rehearsals that I was participating in. I told John to come and watch one of them, and to bring the arrangements we had played in the Army. He came and sat down shyly in a corner of the studio. I introduced John to Dizzy and told him that John had brought some arrangements. Dizzy stopped the rehearsal and gave the band one of John's arrangements to play. It was "Two Bass Hit," which at that time we had named "Bright Lights." When the band finished the piece, Dizzy said to John, "You're hired as arranger." That's how a long friendship began between John and me.

One night we were playing at the Apollo Theater—Monk was the band's pianist at that time—Thelonious and I got there late: the band was already set up. Milt Jackson was at the drums and John Lewis at the piano. I slipped behind the curtain and slid into Milt's place. Thelonious had to pass in front of the stage to get to the piano. The audience would see him, and that would attract Dizzy's attention. So Monk waited in the wings. Diz turned around and saw me playing. He said, "How did you get here?" I answered, "Don't worry about it. I'm here, and I'm playing." He looked in the direction of the piano and saw John. He asked me where Monk was. I said I didn't know. He went into the wings and spotted Thelonious waiting. "I'm throwing you out," he told him. That's how John Lewis became the pianist for the big band!

❖❖

In 1947 Monk began recording for Blue Note with his own groups, but his full acceptance by the jazz public was a decade away.

One who did come to public attention in the Gillespie band was tenor saxophonist James Moody. After his discharge from the Army he tried out for Dizzy's outfit.

❖❖

JAMES MOODY   We came over and went up and tried it, I think at Nola's Studios. Boy, Walter Fuller* cracked me up. He said, "When you can play louder, come over, man." And Walter knew me from before because he used to be in the YMCA in Newark, and I'd be down playing basketball. So he knew me. He didn't do it maliciously. I went back home and started working at Lloyd's Manor, a club up there, and had a nice little thing going making seven dollars a night. I'm telling you, that was good money in 1946. Then one day I came home, and my mother was smiling there with a telegram that Dave Burns had written. He sent a telegram that said, "You start with us tonight." And I went over and started with them at the Spotlite—Monk was on piano and Milt Jackson, Ray Brown, Kenny Clarke. Started, and that was it. I was with the band from then on. But it was really something to be— it was an experience to see Lester Young, see Coleman Hawkins, all these people together I'd never seen. It was a hell of an experience. Playing live and speaking to them and then getting to know them. In the band I thought Ernie Henry was a good player and also Cecil Payne, I liked the way Cecil played.†

CECIL PAYNE   Dizzy, beside being a phenomenal musician, could relate— he knew everything he played—to the chords and the changes. That's what his mind was thinking about playing. I knew he was playing great, and I could hear what he was playing, and you always figure, "One of these days I'll play like that," but you never realize that in order to play like that you have to know what you're playing. You have to relate it to the chords and the changes that you're playing, plus having the ability to be a good improviser. Now I can appreciate Dizzy better than I did at the time when I was playing in the band because now I can listen to what he's playing. It was a band that, if you made a mistake reading your music, you felt bad. Immediately. Your whole day is ruined. I don't mean miss a note even, like play something wrong or anything like that. Everybody in the band were friendly. If they weren't maybe I wasn't aware of it. When you're young you don't notice a lot of things. To me at that time it seemed as though everybody had a close relationship. Somebody had to leave the band, like Teddy would leave the band once in a while—Teddy Stewart—and they had another drummer—Joe Harris used to come in. Ray Brown left the band and that was a letdown, but they replaced him with a good musician, Al McKibbon. When Chano Pozo died, that was another thing. I think before Chano Pozo came in, Dizzy was trying to—we had a big meeting. Kenny Clarke was in the band, too. He made a trip to Europe with us. They told us we had to sell more, by moving. You have

*Gil Fuller.
†In Moody's Blue Note recordings of 1948 he used Henry, Payne, and Burns with arrangements by Fuller.

to move, you just can't sit there. I think that hit the band the worst, to tell us to be commercial, to move like that. I believe that was the turning point as far as morale. To me anyhow.

BILLY MITCHELL   In 1948 Moody left Dizzy 'cause I came here [New York] in '48, and I was with Lucky Millinder, and he was getting ready to leave Dizzy. I was telling him, "Man, at least you played with Dizzy, that's more fun than playing with Lucky Millinder." Lucky Millinder would want you to dance. That was the time when dancing was popular, and you had to do something besides just playing the saxophone. You weren't really dancing all over the floor but to get the response, dancing was all part of it. So I told him, "Man, at least you're with Dizzy, with that hip music." I would say, "I was with Lucky Millinder and Lucky Millinder wants you to dance." But he said, "Shit, Dizzy wants you to dance, too."

Yusef [Lateef] took Moody's place, and then Dizzy called me once again, I think to take Yusef's place. I forget, it was one of them. At the time I wouldn't change because I was making twenty-two dollars a night with Lucky; Dizzy wasn't paying but eighteen.

❖❖

In the summer of '47, when Bird had come back from Camarillo and was playing at the Deuces, Dizzy's big band was at the Downbeat, right next door. That was a most exciting time and continued to be.

❖❖

CECIL PAYNE   Eating watermelon and drinking whiskey. Everybody sick. Bus drivers going the wrong way. We didn't take planes in those days. We rode mostly by bus. During the time I was with Dizzy, we had thirty one-nighters in a row. That was a lot to us. That was a big thing. Bands now do 360 one-nighters, but then it was like a big thing. We would go to Chicago or something and play two weeks. New York at the Roost. We took the trip over to Sweden, the first trip. The seas were so rough, everybody's dying. Everybody was sick, and the boat felt like it was going to sink. Chano [Pozo]—he wouldn't let the nurse even give him a pill. He wanted a man nurse. After the storm was over, they found out that they had us in second or third class, and Kenny Clarke got everybody together, and we went and confronted Milt Shaw, and we had him backed up against the rail like we were going to throw him off the rail. I know he was scared to death. When we left the ship, they took us off, they had the boat come out to meet us. But they reimbursed us the money, the passengers' money, for the first class.

❖❖

The Swedish promoter, Harold Lundquist, did not pay the band properly, and it had to be bailed out by Charles Delaunay, who organized a concert in Paris. Things did not always run smoothly in the United States, either.

❖ ❖

CECIL PAYNE   Well, me and John Brown [alto saxophonist], we were like partners. We stayed together most of the time. Moody got sick in the band. That was another letdown. We went to Detroit. The El Sino club, right. The first day we got in there, everybody's tired, and we went to sleep. I don't know what happened to Moody, but somebody put something into his soda—you know, one of those inhaler things. Some people take it and stay awake. But Moody, it affected him different. He started seeing different things. And they had to take him to the hospital, and he left the band. That was demoralizing. That was one of the biggest because Moody was the soloist—the sound of him playing.

Now John Lewis was always the one who was trying to make us study more music. He'd try to get us together to learn music, which he had a little difficulty doing. Everybody wasn't ready for it at the time. They weren't ready to learn about the music that we're playing actually. Let me put it that way. He was very conscious of it, I imagine, at the time. Everybody was happy-go-lucky. John Lewis really did try but got disgusted, really disgusted. Benny Bailey was in that band, too, that went over—he stayed over. Kenny Clarke stayed over in Europe. Dizzy always took care of business and everything. I think only once—he made the job but you could tell he was juiced. A lot of fellows drank in the band, everybody drank, but everybody made time. You had to be there or your part was missing, man. It was finished.

❖ ❖

One of the Gillespie band's commercial successes was "Oopapada," with scat vocals by Dizzy and his regular vocalist, Kenny "Pancho" Hagood. The bop syllables on a blues line was written by one Babs Brown, better known as Babs Gonzales. In 1946, he formed a group called Babs' Three Bips and a Bop. It recorded for Blue Note in 1947, and "Oop Pop A Da" was done on the first session. The Gillespie version (notice the different spelling) followed and sold better than Babs's record. When he didn't see his name on the Gillespie label, he decided to sue RCA Victor.

❖ ❖

BABS GONZALES   I formed the Bips because I felt bebop needed a vocal bridge to the people. The fire was there. Bird was cooking, and Oscar Pettiford and Dizzy and them with their little group. But it wasn't reaching the people. I had been trying to do some solo work with Lucky Thompson up around New Haven—as a solo vocalist, but it was more or less a real imitation of B [Billy Eckstine], to tell you the real truth. Everybody was going behind B in those days.

In the Bips we had Tadd Dameron on piano; Pee Wee Tinney, guitar, and dancers like Baby Laurence; Art Phipps on bass. Four voices.

❖ ❖

Before Dameron, Allen Tinney was the pianist.

❖❖

ALLEN TINNEY   We've always worked together. Well, I would say more after that, but I was with a combination of Babs and my brother. Babs and I got along, but we didn't get along like my brother—him and my brother got along. My brother could get along with the devil, I believe. He was a fabulous person. He and Babs used to get along. But I dunno, I guess I just stayed out of Babs's way and wished him well, that's about all I could do. He started writing those books and putting those phonograph records out—I don't know whether I appreciated it or not.

BABS GONZALES   My two brothers and I were all Babs. Big Babs, middle-size Babs and little Babs. Both of my brothers were football players. Weighed 210 and everything—took everything from me. It used to be funny on the street over in Newark when people'd say, "Hey, Babs!" and they turn around, and my brothers would turn around, 220 pounds, and say, "Yeah, man. What's happening?"

"Gonzales" grew out of necessity and the ingenuity of a survivor.

BABS GONZALES   There was a gang in Harlem called "The Forty Thieves." They broke into cars around the Savoy. I was from Newark, and I thought, "I'm so hip and 'down.'" They left me in my *underwear* in *January*—really. I went all to California with one hundred dollars. I figured, "I can't get back. I *got* to make it."

❖❖

First, inspired by the film star Sabu, he wound turbans around his head and called himself Ram Singh. Then he got a job at the West Side Country Club in Beverly Hills, taking care of the clothes of the movie stars and directors when they came to play tennis. Two months later Errol Flynn hired him as a chauffeur. When Flynn got into trouble with an underage girl, Babs was ready to return to New York, but a burst appendix almost finished him off. In the hospital he assumed a new identity since his wallet had been taken by the cabdriver who had driven and dumped him there. He became Ricardo Gonzales to avoid "being treated as a Negro," and got a room in the Sheraton for $2.50 a night.

❖❖

BABS GONZALES   The cats didn't know where I was living—cause I wouldn't tell them—so they couldn't come and see me. One night Don Byas and Harry Edison found me, and I got put out the next morning. *C'est la vie.* J.J. Johnson and Harry Edison still call me Ricardo.

❖❖

In New York, Bob Bach, who was writing for *Metronome,* also was producing live jam sessions for WNEW radio.

❖❖

JEAN BACH   Everybody was trying to help Babs, and Dizzy and Ella said, "We've got someone for you that's the greatest. Have you ever heard bebop sung?" Bob said, "No, that's great." They said, "We'll have to get him to call you. Where're you going to be?" Bob said, "I'm in my office."

I'm sitting at my desk, like this, and he's sitting at a desk facing me in one of those chairs that leans back, and he's holding the phone, and he's listening, and a smile's going across his face, and all of a sudden he's going back in the chair like that. I thought he was going to go over backward in his springchair. These four guys are in a phone booth, and they're, what was it, "Oopy, doopy, lop-pow." And Bob said, "Well, what are you going to sing on the program?" and Babs said, "Well, I think I'll sing 'Oop-Pop-A-Da' and 'Dob Bla Bli.' "

❖❖

After the Blue Note records the Bips and a Bop began working at the Onyx Club.

❖❖

BABS GONZALES   Tony [Scott] would come and play with us every night like he had a gig. He'd be there earlier than us. So we started chipping in and giving him some bread because he still had to eat and sleep. But the man wasn't paying but for five. So we started giving him three dollars apiece at the end of the week.

❖❖

This group, with Scott and pianist Bobby Tucker (both from Morristown, New Jersey), Phipps, and drummer Roy Haynes, recorded four sides for Apollo Records.

The major record companies were also starting to recognize that bop had some commercial possibilities.

❖❖

CHARLIE VENTURA   I was signed up with RCA Victor, and the group that I had during that time was with Conte Candoli on trumpet and Bennie Green on trombone, Boots Mussulli on alto, and Jackie [Cain] and Roy [Kral], and Ed Shaughnessy on drums. RCA wanted to get it because bop was catching on as the form of music. But the average laymen, or the average listener, they thought bop was only associated with people that were on drugs, and goatees and this, and led a dirty life and that they would gear their children to stay away from the beboppers, nothing but a bunch of hopheads.

Getting back to RCA Victor, they said, "We want to use the word Bop." Then I said, trying to get it to the producer, "Amongst the people, don't let it sound like a dirty word." So that's when I said, "Bop for the People." That's how that came about. It was instrumental in wanting to, not to commercialize it, but on a big label like RCA Victor . . . During that time we were fortunate to record for these little companies like, gee, I can't think of all these names—National—and we had more freedom, but with the major companies like Coral and Decca, RCA Victor, and Columbia, they would dictate what they wanted, and if you were on a recording session you had to play—you were doing eight songs, you had to do seven songs for them, and they'd let you do a song on your own, something like that. We came out with, I thought, something fresh, utilizing the voices with the instruments and so forth.

❖❖

Jackie Cain and Roy Kral used their voices like instruments to blend with the horns. Their wordless vocalizing had a different sound than Gonzales's, which made heavy use of vowels. Jackie's and Roy's was more derived from the kind of scat that Dave Lambert and Buddy Stewart had done with Gene Krupa in 1945 ("What's This?"), and Red Rodney in 1946 ("Perdido," "Gussie G.," "Charge Account," and "A Cent and a Half").

Ventura used Stewart's voice as an instrument in his small group recordings for National in March 1947 ("Synthesis") and September 1947 ("East of Suez"). In October 1948 Cain and Kral recorded "Euphoria" with Ventura, a line based on "S'Wonderful" that also served to introduce Bennie Green, who had been with Parker and Gillespie in the Earl Hines band, to a wider audience. The Cain-Kral "I'm Forever Blowing Bubbles" from the same time became a commercial success by mixing words and scat in a kind of novelty bop. It was this type of thing, and the upsurge of the Gillespie band on its label, that led RCA Victor to sign Ventura and do the first session with him on January 6, 1949.

Meanwhile Capitol jumped into the "Bopstakes" by signing Miles Davis, Tadd Dameron, Woody Herman, Benny Goodman (having his flirtation with bebop), and Babs. Thirteen days after Ventura went into Victor's studios, Capitol recorded Gonzales with a band that included Sonny Rollins (his first record date), J.J. Johnson, and Bennie Green.

❖❖

BABS GONZALES Bennie Green had about the best tone—like there was one cat that I used to like when I was a very little boy, named Jack Jenney. There's a tone. Then there was another cat came through named Trummy Young, with tone, and then Bennie had it. He doesn't articulate as fast as Jimmy Cleveland and J.J., but the tone quality is right there all the time with Bennie Green. Capitol didn't do much promotion. They promise you the moon. Their transition into bebop was really more or less pointedly at the big names. At that time they acquired Benny Goodman and Woody Herman, and their sales and promotions went directly to these two biggest cats. And if it don't be that Miles's records was so different—for that time—this nine pieces with "Move" and "Jeru"—the melodic line they brought into it. That

did it. And I had a dictionary* out at that time. And Capitol didn't
say nothing to me. They just took the dictionary and reprinted it with
BG and Woody, like they were the big things, and way at the bottom,
in small, little print, "By the courtesy of Babs Gonzales." So I said I'd
better not sue these people because I'm suing Victor at the moment.
So I'd better cool it else I won't get heard nowhere.

❖❖

Billy Eckstine disbanded in 1947, but Woody Herman reformed
his big band in the fall of that year. This edition fully reflected
the ascendant influence of Parker and Gillespie.

❖❖

WOODY HERMAN   When we started that band then I definitely made a pitch
to get those kind of people in the band who were enthused about the
music. My timing wasn't all that good because I blew a lot of money
with that band, but musically I felt it was very successful. In the long
run I felt that what I did was the right thing to do at that point, but
I was on shaky ground, I felt, very often during that period. The general public wanted a carbon copy of what they'd heard before in '45
and '46, and they felt that I was blowing it.

JIMMY ROWLES   I could have been in that band but I turned 'em down.
I'd had enough. Freddie Otis started on piano; Gene Sargent on guitar. There's a guy that knew some songs. What a freak he was. He and
his old lady have both gone, two of my best friends. Freddie Otis is in
Glendale, works in a department store.

❖❖

Otis's bandmates used to call him "Frazier." I remember him putting the orange peels on the radiators in the hotel room so he could
get the smell of California. This was in St. Louis. That's where I
met them—the band—and there was an elaborate fruit store right
near there. They were eating pomegranates—all the Californians.
Herbie Steward.

   An important part of the new Herman band was the "Four
Brothers" sound (three tenors and a baritone) and the song of the
same name written by Jimmy Giuffre. Of course, it had been developed in Gene Roland's band at Pontrelli's Ballroom with Zoot
Sims, Stan Getz, and Steward.

❖❖

ZOOT SIMS   Woody hired that sax section, except Jimmy. 'Cause he had
Serge [Chaloff]. Herbie didn't stay too long.

JIMMY ROWLES   He gave up. He couldn't make it. They were too rough
on him. That junk and . . .

❖❖

*of jazz slang.

Steward was also a victim of the musical dilemma facing many of the young players. He was hung up between Lester Young and Charlie Parker. One of his bandmates said, at the time, "Bird shook Herbie up. He doesn't know which way to go."

❖❖

RED RODNEY   It was a great band. Every chair. It was just a tremendous orchestra, section by section. The soloists and spiritwise; the band was spirited. One great guy would leave, and another great guy would take his place and add something. We would lose something, and we would gain something.

ZOOT SIMS   Yeah, it holds up. A lot of great musicians in that band really. The brass section; the trombones; all the sections. Woody didn't know what to make of us, but [laughs] we were all young. Woody was great, really. But you know Woody's '46 band, the Wild Root Band? That was a romping band. And personalities, too. Well this band was bebop and personalities. I guess they went together. We had a different outlook. It was a turnaround for Woody. Ralph Burns did a lot for that band and even for the band we were in on. Of course Al Cohn came on the band, after about a few months, and he wrote some great things. I think the first was [hums] "The Goof and I." Which is great to this day.

It's hard to remember the public reaction, but I know one thing, that when we'd play a ballroom, Woody kept it so that people would even hardly notice it. Woody was that wise. He knew how to handle all that. In fact, being as young as we were, we all wanted to let loose, you know, and we were all kinda drug* sometimes. Sometimes the bandleader used to go home early a lot. In the old days all the bandleaders did. And the band would really romp, but looking back and seeing Woody's side of it, I think he had to do it that way. But we just slipped them in there.

❖❖

It was such a wild band. A lot of people were getting high all the time—in fact, most of the band. There were times at the Blue Note and the Capitol Theater when half the band wouldn't even be on the stand at the beginning of a show. Then they'd come straggling in.

❖❖

ZOOT SIMS   We stayed together quite a while. We didn't have any cliques, as they say, on that band. Really. I think everybody was above that. I mean you might prefer to hang out with a couple of guys, but that doesn't mean that you disliked anybody else. There was nothing like that on that band that I could remember.

*dragged, nothing to do with drugs, meaning depressed.

RED RODNEY   The musicians were so good. Yet we were so screwed up. You know it was a period of being very bugged too. We were growing up. We got very bugged for a while. Why, I'll never know, but we were. We wanted something that, I don't know, psychoneurotic is the word or psychoneurosis is the term, and we all had a good case of it. But still it was a good band. It was a lot of camaraderie in the band, friendship.

ZOOT SIMS   I was so young and frustrated at that time about music. I was kind of paranoid about my music then. Still am sometimes. I play for fun more now than I did then. Got more confidence now. I remember long trips on the bus; I could never sleep too good on a bus unless I drank a fifth, and then we used to talk. I remember one night with Bernie Glow, we were talkin' all night. I let it all out about that. He said, "You know, you're not the only one that feels that way." And that turned me around a little bit. That got me. The trumpet player, Stan Fishelson, we used to talk a lot. He was wonderful. On some of those long trips that taught me a lot, as far as my relationship with the other guys in the band. I just wanted to be accepted all the way and those talks on those long trips helped me a lot that way. But as far as everybody loving each other, there was no problem.

TERRY GIBBS   It's like a marriage. I think the hate really is love. Let me use Serge Chaloff for an example. We used to fight, 'cause Serge was so screwed up that he was demanding. "Carry this, help me," whatever it is. Serge was, like, so bad that I wanted to punch him out one time. I really was gonna kill him. And then what happens, he turns around. My ex-wife Donna was on the road. We had a little cat, and one time the cat ran out of the bus and ran under a car that was about to move. Serge was the first one out of the bus, right under the car and got the cat. So you see, that's the kind of love/hate you had. Maybe you didn't like a guy for what he did, but there was so much respect musicianship-wise. Especially on that band, because there was no dead wood at all. That you really got to love everybody. Lou Levy was my roommate. I think there was more love than hate.

LOU LEVY   I remember sitting, with the saxophone section in the bend of the piano—Al Cohn, Zoot Sims, and Sam Marowitz and Stan Getz and Serge Chaloff when these guys would stand up to play—and I'd hear all this stuff coming out. When the section would play, I would hear Al Cohn. Now I didn't know him that well, but I could hear that sound coming out of the section, that soulful sound. Then when he'd stand up to play a solo, I noticed that he didn't play as slick as Stan Getz— I'm not knocking Stan Getz's playing—but he played so beautifully and soulfully, and so melodically that he made everybody else in the band— I could tell everybody in the band liked him better than anybody else in the band. He was something else. I remember even Stan, with those cold, blue eyes of his, would look over and say, "That's it!" Needless to say, Zoot loved him and all the guys.

AL COHN   I never had anything to play on the band, so it wasn't one of my great memories. As a matter of fact, when I first started hearing Bird and Diz and all that, I was still a big band player. I liked the big bands best. Then I gradually started to want to play more with small bands. Big bands are fine, but small bands is the only way you can develop as a soloist. So that took a while for me to realize it. I think after Woody's band, I realized it. Woody didn't like the way I played. So that made it just worse. 'Cause I never could relax knowing that I didn't have him.

TERRY GIBBS   I think if anything, not with myself—yeah, even with myself—there was a bit of jealousy if one guy got a—Stan Getz on that band. See, Stan got to the audience more, and Stan was a giant player, even though Al actually, musically, could play rings around everybody at the right tempo; Al didn't know the horn as well as Stan. Woody's a smart man, and you gotta put it where it's at, who's gonna break up the audience. And Stan could play. But Al didn't know the horn as well, so he never got a chance to play. But also, when you make a record, and it hits, like "Early Autumn" hit so big, you gotta give it to the guy who's gonna get the attention. None of us got it that—I probably played more than anybody because I had the instrument. I was featured, so I got a spot; plus vibes, if you didn't know what you were doing, you could look, like a drum. So we all, nobody ever got that much to play in a big band. As much as you got to play was a chorus and a half, two choruses.

You see, if I was the leader of the band—now the big band I had had a million soloists, but I had an ensemble band. That's what I wanted out of my band. Even though I could point—the same thing. I had Richie Kamuca, Bill Perkins and Joe Maini and Charlie Kennedy and Jack Nimitz and Frank Rosolino and Conte and Stu Williamson. I had Lou Levy. I had all these guys to point to. My big thing was ensemble. I wanted that. Even though Woody had an ensemble. Woody had a hard job pointing to a guy. Who do you point to? If you want a saxophone, tenor saxophone solo, you don't know who to point to, I mean you just gotta take a man and point. And Stan Getz had the hit record, so he pointed to Stan. Zoot Sims, what a giant he was. It was hard for Woody.

For me, more than a lot of other guys, I was very lucky in a way. That I got to travel with the best band of its time. You know you're growing up with the best talent in the world. We all learned from each other. There wasn't one baddy in the whole group. There were a lot of baddies, but not musically. Serge Chaloff had a way about him. When we checked into a hotel, if he was on the ninth floor, I would go to the hundredth floor—far away, not the hundredth. If he was on the hundredth, I'd go to the ninth because I could get out of the hotel. Serge Chaloff has a way, 'cause we all know that Serge was sick those days. He'd fall asleep with a cigarette all the time and always burn a hole in the mattress. Always! In about twelve hotels. When we'd go to check out, the hotel owner—Serge always had his hair slicked down, even though he hadn't taken a bath for three years. He had his hair slicked down and when we'd check out, the manager would say, "Mr. Chaloff, you burnt a hole in your mattress and . . ." "How *dare* you. I'm the winner of the *down beat* and *Metronome* polls. How dare you?" After the conversation, the manager would always say, "I'm sorry, Mr. Chaloff," and apologize to him. Except one time when the band got on an air-pistol kick. Oscar Pettiford, I think, bought the first one, so we all bought air pistols. Serge put a telephone book against the door and was zonked out of his bird and missed the—he got three shots at the telephone book and made the biggest hole in the door you ever saw. So when he went to the check out, the guy said, "Mr. Chaloff, it'll cost you." "How *dare* you." The guy said, "Kiss my ass, how dare you. You'll pay for the door." He "how-dared" him again, a few times. Couldn't get away with it. He said, "Well, listen, if I'm gonna pay for the door, I want the door." It was twenty-four dollars. So, he paid for the door. I happen to be standing close by. "Hey, Terry," he said. "Grab this," and all of a sudden I found myself checking out. I got a valise in one hand and a door with him. We're walking out of the hotel with a door.

ZOOT SIMS   He made them take the door off and he was going to take the door with him. He went that far. He actually didn't take it with him, but you know. Another time in some town, [St. Louis] we were about four or five flights up and there was a guy waiting for a bus. And out our window, it was catty-corner sort of, and Serge was hittin' this guy with the pellets. At that distance, I don't think he could do much, but I told him, I said, "Serge you know, man, you could put this cat's eye out if he turned around," and Serge said, "Man, I don't shoot that well." That's true, and he was serious.

When Serge was cleaned up, you know, straight, he could be a delight, really, to be around, a lot of fun. He knew how to handle himself. He had that gift. He could get pretty raunchy when he was strung out, but he could also be very charming.

AL COHN   For quite a while I was in Serge's car. We weren't taking the bus. But I don't remember too much of that stuff on the bus. You know bus is a time the guys would pass around the bottle and go to sleep. I mean it was pretty tough. I remember one time, back to Serge, in his car—I don't know how we kept from being killed. Serge would always be drunk. He was quite a drinker. Everything he did, he did too much. So one time we're driving, after work. It's four o'clock in the morning, and he makes a left turn, and we're wondering why the road is so bumpy. Turned out he made a left turn onto the railroad tracks, and we're going over the ties.

❖❖

A lot of the bands had ball teams in those years. Some had started out playing hardball but most had graduated to softball by the mid-'40s. The Herman band was one of the latter.

❖❖

RED RODNEY   Musically, we cut everybody else. Any band that came near us, we were just so proud. This is Woody Herman. How could you compare with us? We went out and played baseball with other bands, and we could see by, "Wow, we're playing Woody's band," and we even beat many of them in baseball because we were such a good musical band that they were in awe of us. Of course on the baseball team, Terry Gibbs and I, we were two leading players. Earl Swope.

TERRY GIBBS   When I joined Woody Herman's band, that's when I got really tight with Al and all those guys. Zoot I didn't know till Woody's band. In fact we didn't hit it off at all because there was a baseball team, and Zoot was a shortstop, and I came on the first day, and it was practice. I was a good athlete, so I took his position, and that was the end of our relationship for a long time. He still brings it up. He says, "But I was a better hitter." Wrong, Zoot.

ZOOT SIMS   I guess he told you he took my gig away, my position. And naturally that's the first thing he always says when he sees me, "You hate me." I was the shortstop. Then I went out to the field. I played the field. Marky was pitching. Maybe Stan pitched a couple of times.

AL COHN   Our team was very good. We had some very good ballplayers. Earl Swope was outstanding. Terry Gibbs was very good. Marky Markowitz was really good. These were the stars. The outfield was Don Lamond, Zoot, and me. We had some good games. We beat Harry James, a doubleheader. Harry and Corky Corcoran showed up at the game in St. Louis Cardinal uniforms.* That was an interesting thing. I don't know what that was about. Probably the old psych out bit.

We had a few different pitchers. Marky pitched sometimes. Stan Getz pitched a few times. It was softball, you know. Zoot once made a catch where he—he's right-handed, and he was running to his left and caught it in his left hand, right. And as he caught it his hat flew off, and he caught his hat in his right hand [laughter].

I remember one time we played Les Brown's band and they beat us

*Harry James was a big Cardinal fan.

with a ringer. They had a guy that hit a home run everytime he was up. Each time to a different field. They said he was a copyist for the band [laughter].

ZOOT SIMS   Chubby [Jackson] wasn't on the band originally, you know. Like when I mentioned the difference between the '46 band and our band, well, Woody finally called Chubby up to add some zing in the band, a little life. He figured it was getting too blasé up there, so Chubby just came back from Sweden, and he met the band, I think it was Detroit. I'm almost sure it was. He came on the band with knickers. Everybody broke up. He screamed every once in a while. Woody wanted some life in the band. You know Woody's thing about the old days. In fact Bill [Harris] came to the band, too. He and Swope were the trombone soloists. They had movie stars' names for everybody in the band. Swope was Sonny Tufts. Serge was Hurd Hatfield. I was two different guys, Joseph Cotten and Charles Bickford. I think I was Bickford in the morning and Cotten at night.

❖❖

Earl Swope was not only an outstanding athlete, but he was one of the first modern trombone stylists, highly regarded by his colleagues. Born in Hagerstown, Maryland, he played in Washington, D.C., and with many name bands including Sonny Dunham, Boyd Raeburn, Georgie Auld, Buddy Rich, and Herman.

❖❖

AL COHN   The guys from Washington had their own kind of thing, too, you know. Different from anybody else. Had their own way. The way Earl played. Maybe it's just Southern. That relaxed thing that they had.

❖❖

Swope didn't sound like anyone else, although there was a feeling of Dicky Wells in his playing.

❖❖

AL COHN   The thing about Earl was, in addition to all of that, Earl was really a virtuoso on a trombone. I mean he could really play that horn. He could get around. He was one of the first cats that really could get around on the horn. This was before I heard J.J. I don't know. Jay was probably doing it then, too. But I remember hearing Earl playing duets, and he'd be reading treble clef. Be playing trumpet duets. And you know he's a whiz.

❖❖

He was an extraordinary player, because of all the modern trombonists, he didn't sound like J.J. When everyone else started sounding like J.J. he had his own.

❖❖

AL COHN   I think he was more influenced by Lester Young than by Dicky Wells. He didn't play like the slide trombone, but clean.

LOU LEVY   Earl Swope would probably be the equivalent on trombone of what Al Cohn was on tenor. Then we had Bill Harris—another great story in his own style, superb artist. Trumpet section, well, Bernie Glow, Ernie Royal, Shorty Rogers, Irv Markowitz, Red Rodney. Then we had Don Lamond, Chubby was there, and then Oscar Pettiford came in . . . and then Shelly came in. But we had superb people. Even Shadow Wilson came in for a short time. Joe Harris played a few nights. Tiny Kahn subbed one night at Boston Symphony Hall, I remember that. So many things happened. All through that . . . then we've got Mary Ann McCall, who was a great singer.

TERRY GIBBS   Oh, Oscar Pettiford. Oscar was great. In those days, you know, you go to after-hours clubs. Oscar, one time, wanted to take his own bass with him. So he took his bass. And the club got busted. Everybody is jumping out of windows. We all jumped out of windows. Except Oscar couldn't go 'cause his bass was more important than his life. It was somewhere in the Midwest. So we had to bail him out.

   Oscar, in those days, Oscar had no value of money. If he met some girl, some chick that he liked—one time he said, "I'm not takin' the bus." But he did take a taxi cab for three hundred miles, and when he got there Woody had to pay two hundred dollars to the taxi driver for Oscar Pettiford or we wouldn't have no bass player to play the job. He did it two or three times. He took a cab for ninety miles once. Once three hundred and twenty miles. Or we had no bass player. If Oscar—not only just a chick—if Oscar met somebody to hang out with. Oscar was a hanger-outer. Oscar was beautiful. He'd hang out and Woody would have to pay his cab fare.

SHELLY MANNE   It always comes to mind with Woody's band that it was a "bad" band. I'd come to work at night, really feel like playin', get on the stand and look down the line and there'd be five guys asleep. But it was a good band. That was an exciting band. I remember when I joined, the first time I played with that band, Woody called me from Washington, and Al Porcino and myself drove down. That's when I first played with the band. I joined the band right after that. We played at some theater in Washington, D.C. But that was a fun band. I mean fun musically because we played good charts. There were many good performances in Woody's band, with all those great players. I know every time Jug [Gene Ammons] played, he was exciting for everybody. The whole band would stop and listen. And Bill Harris. When Bill Harris played, he just would light a fire under you.

LOU LEVY   Guys left. Al left, Zoot left. Then Gene Ammons came into that band and Billy Mitchell. The band was different, but it was good. We made some good records. Capitol records, "More Moon" and some of those things. "Not Really the Blues," Johnny Mandel's great arrangement, which unfortunately we had to shorten because they didn't have LPs. I remember we had to cut out Earl Swope's trombone solo and a lot of the arrangement.

❖❖

Tenor saxophonist Billy Mitchell was working in New York with Milt Buckner's group in early 1949.

❖❖

BILLY MITCHELL   About February of '49, I went back to Detroit, and then Woody Herman called me. I went on the stage with Woody Herman from about February until November. Bags [Milt Jackson] was with the band, and Gene Ammons was leaving, so they wanted somebody to take Gene Ammons's chair, and Bags recommended me. Now what happened was I went from Detroit to Chicago where they had sent for about three or four people, and he auditioned them all, and I was the last one. I'll never forget it, I remember it so well—Pearl Bailey was in there following us that night, and I didn't meet her then, and I've never met her since, but I do remember her yelling out that night when I made the last set. She said, "Ah, you finally got one." So I stayed there till November.

It was a very bad experience for me; I didn't like it at all. At that time there was still quite a bit of Jim Crow out there, and I found that, where other people dealt with it, Woody didn't deal with it at all. He just ignored it. So at a lot of places it was very uncomfortable for Bags and I. He could have taken a lot of weight off of us. But the crowning thing was—I never will forget it—was one night in Kentucky they closed the restaurant to feed the band before we played for their affair. They sent seventeen dinners into the dining room and two into the kitchen for me and Bags. Woody didn't say nothing; he sat down and ate. So I left that night—I said I've had it. I got so mad, that night I threatened to kill Abe Turchen. He told me what I should accept.

But I remember in '67, I went out with Basie for a little while. Basie finally got Sal Nistico to take the chair, and he hired him away from Woody Herman for fifty dollars more than Woody was paying. And who should Abe Turchen call up, trying to find a replacement for Sal—but me! I said, "You don't remember me, do you, man?" He says, "No, no, have we met before?" I said, "Don't you remember in 1949 when you said because of guys like me and Oscar Pettiford and Ernie Royal you were never gonna have colored guys anymore in your band?" I said, "I'm the one who threatened to kill you." He says, "Oh, yes, oh, yes. You know what, you must come over some time, and have lunch." Life is funny, man.

TERRY GIBBS   I'll tell you, I love Woody Herman now more than I ever did. When I first started my big band, then I started to love Woody 'cause we gave him so much trouble. That band. Especially that band. And Woody was great. Woody would never book as many one-nighters as other bands because the band was such a great jazz band that we played a lot of clubs, and he'd lose money. You know, those days, the one-nighters paid you money. And the bus was always a scene. But I appreciate Woody more after I started my own band. A guy like Conte [Candoli] would show up ten minutes late in my band. He was my closest friend. I would say, "Conte, what are you doing? To me of all people, I'm your friend." He'd say, "I'm sorry." So I realized what Woody had to go through 'cause Woody had a bunch of guys; out of the eighteen guys about eleven really were strung out. Woody put up with a lot of shit that I wouldn't at all. We started a show with six guys; we had six guys there. He had every right to fire them. But Woody knew the band was good. To him it was like—we had Mary Ann McCall singing with the band. How much better can you do? There was not a guy . . . no dead wood in the band. Everybody was a good player— in the band, not just individually. It was the best white band around those days. I don't think there were any bands that were around— even Count Basie didn't have a band as strong till later on when he got Joe Williams.

Dizzy's band was raw. Well, I don't think Dizzy had the experience that Woody had with a band. 'Cause Diz didn't care if the ensembles were sloppy. In fact, at the end of the tune on the old records, you had Diz holding a high note, he'd fall off before the band—it was never a clean cut-off. But Diz wasn't looking for that because he was looking for the excitement and the soloists also. Woody had a band for years, and Woody learned from those bands. We all did. I learned a lot from Woody.

LOU LEVY   Woody was great. Woody had the patience to put up with all those crazy—the crazies. It was a wild band. You would think they didn't respect Woody, but I think—when he played his clarinet, I'm sure he didn't play as good as Al Cohn, but what's the difference, it fit.

❖❖

The clarinet did not really come out in the bebop period.

❖❖

WOODY HERMAN   Very few people have the facility to play, the kind of technique. Probably the one guy who survived it and could do it bet- ter and still does it better than anyone else is Buddy [DeFranco].

LOU LEVY   To this day he is a great bandleader, one of the best. How many are there? Woody Herman, Count Basie, the late Duke. I'm not so sure he had that band under control either. I like Woody a lot. I really think he's super. Love him. I'm crazy enough to even get along with Benny Goodman. Then when the band broke up, Woody took a small band to the Nacional Hotel in Havana, Cuba. That was Milt Jackson . . .

Bill Harris, Conte Candoli. I couldn't go on that Because Ralph Burns took the job—he was the arranger—so unfortunately I missed a good thing.

ZOOT SIMS   When I got fired from Woody's band, Giuffre was with Buddy [Rich], so we changed places. I left Chicago, and I joined Buddy in some town in Pennsylvania. It was a very long, lonely ride, I remember, 'cause I hated to leave the band after all that time, but I wouldn't beg for my job, and I had the feeling that the band was—just some kind of feeling that I had that, that was about it anyway. I don't know why. A lot of people left quite soon after that, but that always happens with bands. Sticking together means a lot for any band. All the great bands were together for a long time like Duke and Basie and Lunceford; and Goodman for quite a while, in the early days. I think it means a lot if you've got the right guys to begin with.

This was '49. When we finished that gig with Buddy at a theater in Pennsylvania, and we came to the Paramount. Then I think we broke up, and that's when I started to stay in New York. Put my card in and all that. 'Cause I worked with Buddy a lot since then . . . small bands. But this was the big band, I was a little let down, I mean it wasn't as good as the Herman band was, especially the arrangements weren't as good as Woody's.

AL COHN   Buddy's band? Yes, I went out to California with that band and back. He's not the easiest guy to work for. Every night for seven months, he'd take his long drum solo, no matter what else happened during the night. At that point he was marvelous, every night for seven months. You know he hated most other drummers. I mean he had contempt for most drummers. He just felt they were all "fumferers." Or bebop. He hated real bebop drummers. This is interesting. Of course I think part of it was he'd hear guys talking about this guy or that guy, yeah, yeah, and he would say, "That darn bebopper." The guy he liked that everybody else like was Tiny Kahn. Tiny wasn't a typical bebop drummer and he wasn't a technical drummer either. So there was no rivalry there. Tiny was the least competitive with any drummer, anyway.

❖❖

Kahn came from Jo Jones. And Buddy certainly loved Jo Jones.

❖❖

AL COHN   But Tiny was younger than Buddy and that was sometimes enough to incur his wrath. He said something about he thought Tiny was a bebop drummer, "but he isn't, he's just a swingin' drummer." Buddy certainly knows about drums.

AL COHN   I joined the band at the Arcadia Ballroom in New York. Took Allen Eager's place. It was during the spring of 1947. I had just come off three—January, February, and March—a grueling three months with Alvino Rey. We had some pretty good soloists in the band. Earl Swope and later Rob Swope and Tommy Allison and Charlie Walp, trumpeters. Good players. Jerry Thirlkild on alto.

❖❖

Jerry Thirlkild was crazy. Around Mt. Vernon they called him "The White Bird."

❖❖

AL COHN Jerry Thirlkild started a fire on the plane. We went to California on a plane. He was complaining he was cold and everybody was complaining that it was cold. It took us about twenty-four hours to make this trip. It stopped every half hour to refuel. And he tried to start a fire in the middle of the plane. In the aisle.

❖❖

Terry Gibbs went from Rich to Herman.

❖❖

TERRY GIBBS I quit Buddy's band, and we made a trip. We had to drive back from San Francisco to New York. I got back about two in the afternoon. I said I'll never ever go on the road again. I got a call from Woody at five. I took a plane to Chicago, joined the band the same night that I got back. That was great.

But Buddy Rich, I'll never forget one time with Buddy. Buddy was nasty in those days. Boy, was he nasty. He'd pick on the band. Whatever it was, it was bad. He was just picking on everybody. And he was gonna make a star of me. "You're gonna be a star. You're driving in my Cadillac with me." And the rest of the guys would travel on the bus, and it used to go about fifteen miles an hour and break down every eight miles; you know one of those. We made fifteen dollars a night when we worked. Now I'm driving in Buddy's Cadillac, and we get a little mellow. We get mellow, and every time we get mellow, I say to him, "You know, Buddy, the guys in the band—we got Johnny Mandel, we got Al Cohn, we got so many good players, the guys wanta play. Why don't you come on tonight and say, 'Hey, guys, let's play.' 'Cause the guys wanta play. You're not doing it." He said, "Really!" That night he came on stage, "Yeah, guys, let's play." The guys didn't believe it. Boy, the band would roar because Buddy's band—everybody who went to Woody's band came from Buddy's band. That was like a school for us. Al Cohn, Earl Swope. And so the next night, I'd be back in Buddy's Cadillac. He drives like a hundred miles an hour to the next job, and we were there, and we get a little mellow again. I say, "Hey, Buddy, tonight when you come on, let Johnny Mandel play. 'Really?' " Bang. " 'Hey, Johnny, you got the next chorus.' " Bang.

Now about for about five nights in a row, I was telling Buddy Rich what to do, and the sixth night, I start to tell him, and we're going through a desert, and I'm afraid of a snake or a cockroach. So finally, we're going through the desert, and at the darkest point I say, "Hey,

Buddy." He says, "Hey, wait a minute." He stops the car. "I've heard enough of this shit for a week. Get out of my car." I say, "Get out of your car on a desert?" He said, "You'll get the bus. It's coming." I say, "Hey, wait." The car sped away, and I'm standing in a desert all alone. I waited four hours. Panic. In my life—four hours. Nothing at all. Every time I heard a noise, I kept jumping 'cause I couldn't see anything. And I'm so afraid. There were snakes in the desert. Finally, the bus showed up. I got in the bus. And we laugh about that. Buddy and I laugh about it. He left me there. For four hours. Like I tell you, he drove a hundred miles an hour, and the bus went fifteen miles an hour. So I had to wait. They were like two hundred miles behind us. Oh, I'll never forget that in my life. I was panicked.

❖❖

Although it was far removed in intent and content from the Herman and Rich bands, even the monolithic mid-'40s Stan Kenton orchestra reflected the influence of bebop through its sidemen.

❖❖

SHELLY MANNE   Right after the war, when I got out, I joined Stan's band from a quartet we had on 52nd Street. In fact, the day before I joined Stan is when we made the 52nd Street album for RCA.*

We had a quartet with Ed Finckel, Bob Carter, Allen Eager, and myself at the Deuces. And I joined Stan from that group. You could tell all the guys, I remember, really distinctly, when I joined the band on the bus, all the guys wanted to absorb everything that was happening on "the Street," and they knew that's where I had been playing for years. They'd come to me and question me and ask me about Diz and Bird and that kind of music and everything. 'Cause they had been on the road. They hear about it, but they're not where it's happening. It was a great curiosity and great desire for knowledge about the music. Everybody went on the road with a little case of the 78s and a phonograph. The minute you get in, you plug in, that's it. It starts to play in the hotel. But I think all this, from that era, all the guys playin' that kind of music in the little bands going into big bands strongly influenced the big bands. Even in a strange way, I don't call Stan Kenton's band a bebop band by any means, but when Kai joined the band—Kai Winding—he established that whole trombone sound. The whole way of phrasing. And me joining the band, it established a whole new rhythmical thing in the band. Different players. Of course Art Pepper later.

The strange thing about the big bands, a lot of them that were established, well-known big bands like Benny Goodman's band for instance, I don't think Benny would hear of that kind of playing at that period. In that period he was more involved in straight-ahead swing, even with strong Dixie roots in the band actually. Duke's band like-

*with Coleman Hawkins.

wise. They were in another world. Duke's band was a thing of its own almost.

Anyway it was an exciting time. It was a scuffle a lot of times. It was a scuffle tryin' to save any money or existing. I remember we played Balboa, we had to search around for apartments that were reasonable enough. We were gonna be there for a month or so. I think after all my years on the road with big bands, when I finally left Stan for the last time and stayed out here, I think I had fifteen hundred dollars in the bank or two thousand dollars. I thought I was swingin'. But I mean, that's for a lot of years on the bus. For seven, eight years sittin' in the back of a bus.

GERRY MULLIGAN   By the end of the '40s the thing that was the most disturbing to me was that I could see that the bands, the dance bands, the name bands, were not going to survive. That's what was really upsetting to me. That had more to do with my anxiety about life than anything else. Except that without ever thinking about—I want to do this or what I want to be in life, man, I never thought about another thing—seriously, other than being a bandleader and writing music for bands. Dance music. So the big band got cut off from its own source, which is dance music. But it's funny because the band kept evolving and getting bigger. Starting in the '20s they would have like four or five horns, and then the stock band got to be two trumpets and a trombone and three saxes. Three or four really. Then in the '30s it got to be four brass and four saxes, three or four rhythm. And then five brass. Then they got smart, and it got to be four trumpets, three bones, and five saxophones. It just kept going. And do you know, part of the thing that really depressed me and I always hated being called West Coast Jazz because to me the influences out of the West Coast in jazz were personified by Stan Kenton's band. And Stan's band to me was some kind of way symbolic of the end of the bands as I loved them. It had gotten too big and too pompous. You know, it took itself so seriously. Like just something terribly Wagnerian about it all. Well, I once said, thinking I was being humorous, that Stan is the "Wagner of Jazz" and then realized afterwards—because he had done a thing with the transcriptions of the Wagner pieces, and tried to conduct them—that he really saw himself that way and didn't see any humor in it at all. But I hated what that band stood for because it was like the final evolution of wrongly taken points. The way the band kept growing. And the absolute maximum for any kind of use was the five saxes and the three or four bones and the four trumpets. The main reason . . . there's *one* you can do with four trumpets you can't do any other way, and that's four-part harmony, which only four trumpets together sound . . . OK. The only function for the fifth trumpet is an alternate player. But Stan's band kept getting bigger and bigger—to five trombones. Now five trombones is the most asinine.

That's why I didn't like Johnny [Richards'] band [either]. For just that reason. The only one of those bands that I liked at all was Boyd Raeburn's, and that's because Handy and Mandel wrote some interesting things for it. But the rest of the bands were just too preposterous. But Stan's band was just so unmusical to me.

❖❖

The first time Kenton really began to swing was when his band got some other arrangements like Shorty Rogers's and Mulligan's, and then it sounded like Woody's band rather than Stan's band.

❖❖

GERRY MULLIGAN   I wish that band had recorded those things I wrote at that rehearsal—those rehearsal periods. Shelly was playing drums. And Shelly was one of the only two drummers, I think, that Stan never did mess with. But by that time Shelly had left the band long since, and was just helping him out. So he played the way he wanted to. 'Cause Stan *always* messes around with drummers. Oh yeah. He made them play very loud and told them *exactly* what he wanted. He even carried his own cymbals, 26-inch or more and thick as a bicycle wheel. Ecch. And Shelly is just such a beautiful player; Mel [Lewis] was the other one. But anyway, it was symbolic to me of the end of the dance band. It was so pretentious. It was the last straw. It was suddenly we're looking down our nose at dance bands. One dance I ever went to with a girl in my life. The rest, I always went by myself. And was standing around. And the bands I heard, like Teddy Powell—Ventura and Irving Fazola and Ray Wetzel were with the band.

They had a terrific band. But the bands that came through, even as I was in high school in Reading, Pennsylvania. There was still one ballroom there that periodically would bring bands in. And there were *endless* number of interesting things going on, in the bands. Good players around. The thing now is not so good, but Vaughn Monroe would come through. Terrific band. Some bands would be more interesting in a musical way, but some bands would be musical and do primarily a show or be a dance band or whatever. Each band was different. There was another one I was just thinking of. Oh, Tony Pastor had a good band. Bobby Sherwood's band I loved. They were so innovative. Specially in his ballad arrangements. But to see all of that going, and all of the real inventiveness, and also taking away from its function. The first records that Stan's band made that I heard were "Her Tears Flowed Like Wine" and "Tampico"—stuff like that. It was still more related to their Lunceford influence. But to see the bands petering out. There were a couple of attempts to—during the late '40s. Artie Shaw put a band together for a while. And he was trying but finally when he took the band out people were not interested in anything except to hear the old things.

AL COHN   That was a good band. Gene Roland arrangements. Johnny Mandel arrangements. Artie's band was always structured. He never let it breathe. He didn't think along those lines. He used to put the vocalist down if sometimes she sang a note that wasn't in the chord. I don't know if that was to show that he really knew his chords.

❖❖

Lee Konitz was in the band of another clarinetist-leader, Jerry Wald, in the early 1940s. He hung out with tenor player Stan Kosow, a Lester Young disciple who carried records with him on the road, and lead alto saxophonist Les Clarke.

❖❖

LEE KONITZ   Jerry wouldn't let me play. He didn't dig the way I played. I said, "How come you don't give me any solos?" So he'd throw me a bone. He sure could hit those high notes though. He had a plastic reed on, I believe, and he could sock those high notes every time.

I started with Teddy Powell. I took Charlie Ventura's chair. Milt Bernhart was on the band, and I was fifteen or so, and everybody was either in the service, or at that time half of the band at least had split en masse, and I had very little experience—but I could read and get some semblance of a blend—and then I was confronted with concert changes, and it was really beyond my experience, and I was told—Boots Mussulli was on that band—and I was told the first night I got up to play "Body and Soul," Teddy Powell went off into the wings and banged his head against the wall. There was a nail in the wall. It was very difficult for me, being so young. I was the butt of a lot of distorted humor, I realized later. But overall it was okay. I enjoyed that experience very much. That was a short-lived band. Teddy Powell got busted by the IRS, and so I was only on the band for a month. But I was a good poker player—so I got those bearings quick, and I was able to do the job. I think Teddy Powell was '43 and Jerry Wald, '44. Jerry's was a good band and I played some nice music, and I really didn't need to play solos. Every once in a while I thought it would be nice if I had a crack. I just enjoyed being part of the band and traveling around. For the most part it was just exciting to me to travel around and stay in flunky little hotels and to sometimes "ghost," as they said— trying to save some money by doubling up with someone—and going and playing in Florida, and deep-sea fishing as a kid. None of the music was really offensive to me. It was all nice dance music.

❖❖

Then in 1947 Konitz went with Claude Thornhill, a band that was actually playing modern jazz arrangements.

❖❖

LEE KONITZ   The thing about that band that is most important, I suppose, in this whole transitional period, is that Gil [Evans] was, in fact, teaching the men how to play bebop. That was the music—the bands before that I had played in certainly weren't playing anything resembling that kind of music. This was a totally new experience. Although I thought of Claude's band as basically a ballad band. That was its forte. It was a school situation to see that all happening.

❖❖

So many musicians were into the new music and interested in playing it. Even the sidemen in some of the most commercial bands were, on their own, trying to play it and listening to it in total absorption.

❖❖

LEE KONITZ   I don't know that there was that much going on in Claude's band. I had a distinct impression of dance-band musicians doing whatever was asked of them. I don't think they went out of their way to learn this music. Louis Mucci has been a student of the trumpet more than the music itself. Gerry Mulligan was in the band only briefly. So there was no real inspiration that way. It was just Gil was a mover . . . And Claude—I don't think I said a half a dozen words to Claude the ten months I was on the band. I think he was either juiced—I never drank with him, so I didn't get too much more than to twinkle at each other on the bandstand in a friendly exchange. It's weird.

He was a shy guy. His wife traveled with him quite a bit of the time. So they were off by themselves. Gil conducted the rehearsals. On the job Claude would kick off the tempo, and then sometimes just sit there, thinking about something else. I only saw him get angry once—at Joe Shulman in Atlantic City.

❖❖

Claude Thornhill was many things; pianist, arranger, leader, and unique personality. He extracted a marvelous tone from a piano.

❖❖

GIL EVANS   He could play the piano with no vibrato, and that's what the band did. He could make the piano tone fit into the arrangement.

BREW MOORE   He was some kind of freak genius. He could take the worst, out-of-tune piano and make it sound in tune.

GIL EVANS   His time was sensational on slow numbers. He had a certain way of slowing down fast jazz figures. But no matter what the tempo was he always set the right one.

❖❖

Thornhill favored varied tonal colors, and this led him to employ one of the larger ensembles among the standard dance bands of the day. In the pre-war period he once had seven clarinets in the reed section. Another combination consisted of five clarinets, three flutes, and a tuba. It seems that the great New Orleans clarinetist, Irving Fazola, became phobic whenever Glenn Miller walked into the Glen Island Casino, and would immediately leave for the downstairs area, remaining there until Miller left. Thornhill hired Jimmy Abato to make certain he would have at least six clarinets on those occasions.

Fazola also figured in the introduction of the French horns, but this was a more pleasant experience for him. Thornhill had instructed the two horn players to sneak out and play an obbligato he had written to back Fazola's solo on "Summertime." Reportedly, Fazola was so taken with the new sound that he bought a bassoon. The French horns, one of Claude's surprises, became, of course, a Thornhill trademark.

❖ ❖

CLAUDE THORNHILL   Perfect intonation in the sections and balance of the overall sound of the orchestra were emphasized. With the exception of certain pieces in our arrangements, the orchestra played without vibrato. Vibrato was used to heighten expressiveness. Even before we added French horns to the band, the feeling and sound were there; the trumpets and trombones, often in hats, imitated the sound, and did it quite well.

GIL EVANS   Thornhill was the first among the pop or jazz bands to evolve that sound. Claude was the first leader to use French horns as a functioning part of a dance band. That distant, haunting, no-vibrato sound came to be blended with the reed and brass sections in various combinations.

When I first heard the Thornhill band, it sounded, with regard to the registers in which the sections played, a little like Glenn Miller, but it soon became evident that Claude's use of no-vibrato demanded that the registers be lowered. Actually, the natural range of the French horn helped cause the lowering of the registers. A characteristic voicing for the Thornhill band was what often happened on ballads. There was a French horn lead, one and sometimes two French horns playing in unison or a duet depending on the character of the melody. The clarinet doubled the melody, also playing lead. Below were two altos, a tenor, and a baritone, or two altos and two tenors. The bottom was normally a double on the melody by the baritone or tenor. The reed section sometimes went very low with the saxes being forced to play in a subtone and very soft.

❖ ❖

The unique Thornhill sound and style indeed succeeded in creating something different. Certainly no other organization in the wide area referred to as "Popular Dance Orchestras" ever used instruments such as French horn, flute, and tuba in quite the same way.

Tubaist Bill Barber had joined Thornhill in mid-1947, adding yet another dimension to the rich ensemble. Evans gives credit to Claude for the idea, although the leader liked the tuba to sustain chords while the arranger wanted to use it to play moving, jazz parts. Mulligan was an Evans suggestion, both as saxophonist and arranger. He contributed several fine jazz charts to the book, but they were not recorded until 1953.

In 1948 large orchestras, hampered by the record ban in communicating new material to a large listening audience, were losing out to singers, who were able to beat the ban by recording supported by a cappella choirs. Big bands were folding, and Thornhill was one of the casualties. Claude went to Honolulu, where he had been stationed during the last part of the way. Evans has spoken of a nervous breakdown and "Claude letting some doctor talk him into shock treatments." Evans remembers writing to him in Hawaii and sending him solos by Parker, Davis, Gillespie, and Bud Powell, transcribed from records, for him to work on at the keyboard.

❖❖

GIL EVANS   Then came the story, that Claude had sent word back by hummingbird that the band was going to reorganize.

❖❖

Essentially the scope of the Thornhill orchestra in the years of 1946–1948 encompassed the older interpretations of classical themes; the mellifluous ballads, instrumental or vocal; an occasional novelty; and the new jazz of the period as introduced into the band by Evans. To help play his arrangements of Charlie Parker's "Anthropology" and "Yardbird Suite," Miles Davis's "Donna Lee," and Sir Charles Thompson's "Robbins' Nest" came young modernists Konitz and Red Rodney. The up-tempo charts, for all their harmonic richness, were swung with a singular lightness.

❖❖

GIL EVANS   Claude was a complex arranger. After the war he never really got writing again. He leaned on me, and he didn't want to. I let him because I wanted the experience. He liked the modern jazz, but it wasn't what he wanted to play. He wanted the old "Where or When", "Snowfall" style. He liked things to float and hang—clarinets moving very quickly over a sustained background.

❖❖

It was out of the Thornhill orchestra that the famed Miles Davis Nonet emerged in 1948. The focal point was Evans's apartment on West 55th Street—one that Thornhill had rented just prior to his 1940 band—and the first Davis recording session for Capitol contained Gil's arrangements and was peopled by Konitz, Mulligan, tubaist Barber, and French hornist Junior Collins, all Thornhill alumni.

Johnny Carisi was one who frequented the West 55th Street cellar apartment and contributed to the Davis band's book.

❖❖

JOHNNY CARISI   We used to fall by. And between Gil and Mulligan, I think they conceived that instrumentation, which is kind of logical from a very practical instrumental viewpoint. It's six horns which are more or less octave arrangements of each other. Certainly the trumpet and trombone, it's the same pitch an octave apart. The alto and baritone, the same thing. The French horn and tuba, because the tuba is, in a sense, although not exactly, if you want to really go deep into it, a big French horn. Gil had already been dabbling with the French horn in Claude's band. Well, the tuba is in that same family. The problem was to get a tuba player that could play delicately enough, that wasn't a German-band-sounding tuba. But which is hard to do. The tuba is a conical-bore instrument, and it has different properties from straight-bore instruments. There are certain low-pedal notes that you could play on that you can't play on straight horns for instance. I think that between Gerry [Mulligan] and Gil they figured it out. It probably started with Gil, and Gerry was very quick on [snaps fingers]: "Wow, of course, why not, the trumpet and trombone; alto and baritone; and the French horn and the tuba."

They got a few rehearsals together and everybody—well, they wanted two or three things. Gerry wrote more than anybody. Gil wrote a couple of tunes, either his own or he mostly did arrangements of other people's things. John Lewis did a couple. Gerry did some of his own and did some George Wallington [hums]*—that's George Wallington's tune. And I wrote them, altogether, about three things, two of which never got on because they never got them, they never had enough rehearsal time to ever actually work them out, but "Israel" was the one that really got a good shot at it. By the time they made enough noise to get a recording thing at Capitol, it was ready to be played. Originally I wrote "Israel" for Woody Herman's band, which I never got to him at all, but in other words, it was a big-band thing that I was writing.

❖ ❖

The closest Benny Goodman had gotten to bebop was a 1947 recording by his big band of Mary Lou Williams's "Lonely Moments," but he didn't make a real move until he hired Wardell Gray to join his sextet during 1948. The other member of the front line was, of all things, another clarinetist, Stan Hasselgard, who had come from Sweden the year before to take an art history course at Columbia University.

Goodman had heard both Gray and Hasselgard in California in 1947: Gray at a Gene Norman jazz concert, and Hasselgard at a jam session. In the summer of 1948, both came east and took part in a V-Disc, with Mary Lou Williams on piano, called "Benny's Bop."

Hasselgard left college when his funds ran out in New York. In Hollywood he became associated with Barney Kessel who, more than anyone in New York, brought him around to thinking in new directions. With Red Norvo, Hasselgard and Kessel recorded four sides for Capitol under Stan's leadership in December 1947.

*"Godchild."

❖❖

BARNEY KESSEL   Stan came to L.A. and was very enthused about playing. I've always loved to play and have never lost my enthusiasm for playing music, but there have been barren periods in L.A. when there wasn't really too much going on, and this was during one of those periods that he came there, and I was working and doing studio work, but was not playing around very much, and he was so enthused about playing that it got me enthused, and we simply created places to play, and we would play different places. He got a chance to make a record for Capitol, and he asked me to write an original for it, and he wanted to play with me—he had heard some of my records.

I noticed that he did not read music, he was completely self-taught, and I've been told—because I don't know the clarinet that well—by clarinetists that he played many incorrect fingerings, in which he just lipped the clarinet, and just found a way to get these notes out. It was not really the right way at all, but he made it come out right.

❖❖

Hasselgard was killed in an automobile accident about two months after his 26th birthday. On November 23, 1948 the car in which he was riding with June Eckstine, en route to California, crashed near Decatur, Illinois. From his Capitol records and in-person work with Goodman, it looked like he was going to be *the* modern clarinetist. He was the only clarinet player Goodman ever featured alongside himself. Before he ventured into the modern idiom, Hasselgard had been a Benny Goodman-style player.

❖❖

BARNEY KESSEL   Sure, and he had a very lovely sound, too. I don't think keys really mattered too much. He didn't even know that this was a different key. I was always very interested in—never knew of it, never knew exactly what it was—just as a layman off on the side, I've always been interested in his role and his association with Benny Goodman. I don't know if Benny Goodman considered him a protégé or whether he was actually helping him.

I don't know what the attraction was there. Whether he wanted to help him in his career, or whether Benny himself was learning something from this, in a different way entirely, or what, I don't know.

CHICO O'FARRILL   After the war it was easier to get records. I came to the U.S. in 1948, but by 1947 I was so deeply steeped into the idiom that in 1948 it was no trouble for me to join Benny Goodman three or four months after I came here. When he had that bebop band. In fact I was working at the time with Gil Fuller in writing some things for Dizzy. Gil was writing at the time for Dizzy, and he introduced me. How did it happen—I was working with Benny Goodman and—how did I get together with Dizzy—I really don't remember. It was one of those things. I didn't know anybody. I met Fats Navarro. Fats was very much a mentor to me, you understand. People were just hanging around at the Lasalle Cafeteria, Charlie's Tavern, those places. For some reason or other Fats took very much a liking to me. He started telling me about the music business and do this and that. In other words he taught me some of the ropes. He was a very sweet person.

I don't remember him being especially shy, but I think he was a wonderful person, very warm, and of course I have wonderful memories of him. I'll never forget that when Benny Goodman organized that '48 band, Fats was supposed to be in that band—you've heard the story—he was late for one rehearsal, and Benny was like—then the second rehearsal he was late again, and the third rehearsal Fats was late again. So he's walking up on the bandstand, and Benny said, "Fats, get up. You're fired." I was very happy that Fats was going to be in that band. Then he wasn't, and I was very sad about it. Another person that was very influential in my career was Stan Hasselgard. He was with Benny, and he took a liking to my writing. He saw some of the things that I was doing with Gil Fuller, which, incidentally, some of it was "ghost" writing. Gil would say, "Look, score these five pages or these forty bars for Count Basie" or for whatever it is—he had a stable of writers—and Stan found out about it and heard some things that I did and liked it very much, and he introduced me to Benny Goodman.

❖❖

O'Farrill wrote "Carambola" for Gillespie and "Undercurrent Blues" and "Shishkabop" for Goodman.

❖❖

CHICO O'FARRILL   "Undercurrent Blues" was really the most important thing that he ever did of mine. The medium of records is very important because you become familiar, and you are really eager to find out and learn—records can be a great help. So by the time I got here all I had to do was—just like polish a little bit here and there, get some things out of my concept, but I was ready for it. In fact I remember actually the one thing that really blew my mind was, being a big-band writer, you know, Dizzy's recording of "Things to Come." I think nowadays if you played that record, like, very few bands would be able to play it correct. It was that particular feel that they had for it. Events happen at a certain time with certain people that will never be duplicated again, the set of circumstances. It might have to do with the social climate of the times and so forth. Like, for example, the Jimmie Lunceford orchestra. It sounded like that because it was at that particular time in the development of jazz that it was supposed to sound like that. You can take all those arrangements and get the best musicians, musicians that are even familiar with that style, and it would never sound like that. Recreate some of it but never exactly.

From a professional point of view, career-wise I'm talking about, the Goodman band was a thrill to me because it was a big step. I expected to come to New York and struggle for about five or six years before I got to write my first jazz arrangement for an important band. So I had been here about five or six months and here I am, I joined the "King of Swing," quote, unquote. So in that sense I was very proud of my achievements, and I was very green at the time with certain things, for example, writing commercial arrangements, vocals, and the hits of the day, but I did learn a lot, and they were a wonderful bunch of guys, and especially I remember—how could you forget?—Wardell Gray. I mean this guy was so fantastic. So my feeling was that I was learning so much and that my career was being advanced in a very important way for me. As it happened—it's funny you know—when Benny broke up that band I didn't latch on to another job right away. I thought once you worked with Benny Goodman all doors open, and to some extent this is true, but to a certain extent it's not true, either. So it was a lot of fun for me traveling with a name band, going to Hollywood, to the Palladium, sometimes you would get to sign some autographs for some fans. At that time the big bands were starting to go through big crises, and I remember also that, that band was—I think in terms of Benny's usual bands—it was a unique band because he never again repeated the experiment. He went back to his old ways, and I think he felt very alien in that band. I used to bring in arrangements, and guys like Doug Mettome, Wardell Gray, Eddie Bert, Buddy Greco— they would cut the chords with me, and they would know what was happening, and Benny would get to the solo, and he would be completely detached from what was happening within the rest of the band. I think he actually felt embarrassed, if there's such a thing as embarrassment in Benny. When Benny's solo turn came about, I tried to simplify the harmonies a little bit without making it too incongruous all of a sudden.

It was a normal band. There was the usual number of misconduct or whatever it is. Benny would give "The Ray"* to some of the guys. There was nothing new—it was the usual Benny Goodman band. I remember that, to a certain extent, there were some rebellious characters in there, to some extent they were right. Like Wardell Gray sometimes felt the brunt of racial discrimination in a very strong way. He was the only black in the band. Actually, even though Benny has been famous for being the first one to break the racial barrier, but still Wardell did feel the brunt of it sometimes, so he tended to be, at times, very—how do you say—ill-humored, or he sometimes drank too much and so forth, but I remember that Wardell was a wonderful guy, and, in fact, I can remember one time we were traveling from Las Vegas to Los Angeles to do our first recording for Capitol, and being young and ambitious, I wanted to write for Stan Kenton, and I told Wardell, "I can't stand this band anymore and I want to write some more ad-

*The stare that Goodman used on someone he felt had made a mistake.

vanced things and Benny doesn't let me write." He'd say, "Look Chico, be smart. This is making a name for you. Build your career, build your name, take the money and run and then do what you want. Don't quit all of a sudden just like that." Which was something I will always be grateful to Wardell for.

I remember also one time I wrote an arrangement for the band on "Goodnight, Sweetheart," and I really went pretty far out. So one day, we ran it through once, and Benny said, "What is this, Chico, you trying to give us harmony lessons?" I think, actually, the whole idea, frankly, is that Benny believed that the direction, in terms of commercial success, at that particular time, was going into that particular bop-oriented thing. And the band did well because, naturally, in those days, any Benny Goodman-fronted band would have done well. But I don't think Benny did it really for purely artistic reasons. There was also commercial reasons behind it. When we saw that it didn't make any difference whether he played "Flying Home" or whatever—he went back to his old ways.

❖❖

The 1945–1946 Count Basie band included tenor saxophonist Illinois Jacquet, trombonist J. J. Johnson, drummer Shadow Wilson, and trumpeter Joe Newman. It was not, by any stretch of the imagination, a bop-oriented band, but these four were reflecting the new music in various ways. Johnson's solos on his own "Rambo" and also "The King" demonstrated his translation of the Parker-Gillespie method to the trombone. "The King," a feature for Jacquet, found Illinois incorporating bop figurations in his playing to get along with the Herschel Evans and Lester Young influences in his background.

❖❖

JOE NEWMAN   I worked with Jacquet first with Hamp's band. Then we went with Basie's band. Before that he had made these records with Norman Granz for Jazz at the Philharmonic, and his "Blues(Part 2)" became the hit of that whole series. And he was wise to this, so he decided he was going to leave the band. We were playing the Aquarium. So he talked to me: "Why don't you come go with me? I'm going to form this band." So I left to go with Jacquet. It started off at first it was just Jacquet and myself, and we picked the rhythm section in each town we went. Norman [Granz] was booking him. Leo Parker came in the band. In Washington, D.C., we played there, and Norman didn't get there in time. People were storming the door to get in. So I went in the ticket box, and I was selling tickets for it. I was standing in money this deep, I'm telling you, like fifty dollar bills. If I had been a crooked guy, I could've took anything, there was no way they could tell. But Norman came, and he didn't even say thank you to me. It didn't matter. I didn't really care. I'm just saying he didn't, and I could have really ruined him. Leo Parker came that night, and he sat in with us, and Jacquet asked him to join the band. Then it was the three of us. Jacquet had always liked J.J., and he was amazed at the way J.J. could get over his trombone, and he became a member of the band, and John Malachi was the piano player at that time. And Shadow Wilson before that. Shadow had come in before this, so this was really the band. Then Russell Jacquet wasn't doing anything, and Jacquet brought him in the band, and then later on John Lewis came into the band. We traveled all over the country.

"Black Velvet," "Robbins' Nest," "Bottoms Up"*they were hits. The thing about that, we didn't have any written arrangements. Most of those arrangements, I mostly made up. Like I'd set the riffs, and I'd make the out choruses. Actually the idea for the bridge to "Robbins' Nest" was mine. We were recording, and Jacquet had run out of tunes to record. He didn't have anything. It was Sir Charles's (Thompson) birthday, and he was sitting down at the piano, fooling around with this melody. He says, "Let's play this, man." So we say, "Okay." We got to the bridge, he says, "Whatcha gonna do with the bridge?" So I started off [hums tune], and then Sir Charles answered me. So we made it up that I would start it off, and Leo Parker would answer me. It was just some regular formations, the way the chords ran. But it was simple, and it fit the first part of the melody, and that was it. I never got any credit for it. You don't really care during those days; you're more into being a part of it. So that's really how that happened.

"Black Velvet" was an arrangement because Jimmy Mundy wrote the arrangements. This was when Jacquet finally started to pay for some arrangements. But he had made his money. After that it wasn't too much, but all the time this guy used to make so much money. We'd play one-nighters, and he'd come back to New York, and he was staying at this room up on St. Nicholas Avenue, and he had this big bureau drawer—wide as this, man, and about as deep—and it would be full of money. At night he'd get on the bed, like King Midas, sitting in all of this money: "Look at that *money!* Rich. King, king" [imitates Jacquet]." I don't know, it really never bothered me, the money aspect of it. I guess I was too dumb, but I was more interested in the music end of it. I made more money than most everybody else was paying at that time, but it still was nothing. We rode in cars, a DeSoto Suburban.

❖❖

It was really a small big band.

❖❖

JOE NEWMAN   It was, it really was that. With J.J. and Leo Parker and Russell Jacquet there, we had three brass and two reeds, and one time

*"Bottoms Up" and "Robbins' Nest" were recorded for the Apollo label before Jacquet signed with RCA Victor.

Ray Perry was with the band. He played alto when he wasn't playing his violin. He mostly played the violin for solos.

❖❖

The mode of that band, though, was kind of boppish.

❖❖

JOE NEWMAN   Russell wanted to be Miles Davis. Whenever he played a solo, it was patterned after the style of Miles. Then I was so boppish, too, but I was still kinda leaning more to, I guess, more to swing.

You know the company was fast too. Leo Parker was undoubtedly the best baritone player I'd ever heard, too, at that time. He could get over that baritone. He didn't sound like a baritone. He played it like a tenor more or less, and he had such fire in him, whatever he played. Plus he played good ballads. J. J. was another big influence during that time because he really had all the bop things. He did write some bop tunes. I remember we did a record in Detroit early one morning with Sonny Stitt and Russell Jacquet. It was his record. Russell stayed up with Sonny Stitt all night to make sure he made the record date 'cause Stitt was strung out. We used to go to Detroit all the time with that band. They really loved us there.

The Jacquet brothers would get in a fight. That's something. You couldn't believe it. We'd finish a dance down South in a tobacco warehouse, and the people were rough down there in a lot of these towns. They'd drink, and they'd break the bottle and throw it on the floor, and Jacquet and Russell would get into an argument. The next thing you know, fists would be flying, and they would be wrestling. They'd be rolling all over the floor, in the glass and never get cut. That's like a guy fights and gets up with his cowboy hat on. They never got cut.

❖❖

The Russell Jacquet date with Stitt, Johnson, Leo Parker, and Sir Charles Thompson was done in 1948 for a local Detroit label by the name of Sensation, but it reached the general public on King Records, a Cincinnati outfit destined to become one of the most important rhythm and blues companies in the record business.

Most jazz records were made in New York and Los Angeles in those days, but Charlie Parker's quintet recorded "Bird Gets the Worm," "Klaunstance," "Another Hair-Do," and "Bluebird" for Savoy in Detroit on December 21, 1947. Detroit was a city that really took bebop to its bosom, at least in the black community. In the 1950s a steady flow of superior young musicians came out of Detroit. They had grown up in their home city during the previous decade in a musical climate powerfully colored by the Parker-Gillespie influence. The first wave, however, was already visible and influential in the persons of Hank Jones, Milt Jackson, and Billy Mitchell. It was a city with high schools whose music programs fostered much talent, and enough nightclub venues to allow fledgling jazzmen to learn on the job.

Billy Mitchell was born in Kansas City but he grew up in Detroit.

❖❖

BILLY MITCHELL   I came to Detroit when I was two years old, in 1928. I was around ten or eleven around 1937, 1938, about the time that *Camel Caravan* was just starting to popularize swing music around the country with that Benny Goodman program. Radio was very important. But I was involved with music all my life in one way or another. When I was young, in the church—everybody comes up singing in the church. Then there was always fooling with it one way or another, playing the player piano, trying to follow the keys. I knew exactly what I wanted to do and never wavered from it really.

I began studying music in the public schools. Actually I started in Michael Intermediate School. I was lucky. That has so much to do with it—how you get started. They had a very good music program there. At the time I went in, there were a lot of people on the Detroit scene still, in my classes, people like Tate Houston, who's deceased now; Julius Watkins was sort of one of our teachers. He came out a little later—Major Holley. Quite a few came out of that school and then went on to the high school, Northwestern, or if they wanted to take music, specifically, they went down to Cass Tech, which was a pretty good school at that time. I went to Cass.

It had what for that time was a very advanced music program. I would say it would compare with some of the college programs of today, really, most definitely, and would compare favorably.

I started out playing clarinet. I switched to saxophone early on. Before I got out of intermediate school I started out playing the tenor, and it's been my favorite ever since. I'd get an alto every once in a while, and I might play a job on it or make one record on it or something like that. I always keep up. But tenor was always my instrument. But they're all saxophones; you get a kick out of playing all of them sometimes. I had a cousin who was into music. His name is George Favors, and he played in a band in one of the finest clubs in the city. At that time it was known as Club Zombie. They had a fine, ninepiece band—a fellow named Harold Wallace . . . I'd go with him to rehearsals. Nobody became known from that band. We were playing for acts, people like Billy Eckstine, Lena Horne, Foxx and White. I went on the road with my first gig at fifteen. Then when I went into this band, which is where I really get a good training . . . You know Otis Finch,* tenor player? When he left in '43 or early '44, he went with Fletcher Henderson, and I got Bill Evans in the band, that was before he was Yusef [Lateef].

The area [Detroit] was wide open. In those days the war was going on, people were working, they were employed. All the nightclubs were

*Drummer Candy Finch's father.

going, and every little tavern had a trio or a five piece band and a singer. A nightclub had those shows and things in the back. They had a master of ceremonies and a comic and a shake dancer. There was a lot of activity. That was everywhere in the Middle West, not only Detroit. You could find the same thing in Chicago, Pittsburgh, St. Louis. It seemed there was more happening then. I imagine there's just as much going on today, or more.

You got to remember this was all-black activity, too. This was before black musicians and black entertainers hit the white jackpot. Many of the same things are going on now but we lost those things; they're definitely not going on in the black community now as they used to.

But at this time, this was the changing of an era. That was the Swing Era, the big-band era. At that time the people who were idolized were the big bandleaders and the few soloists who were able to emerge. There was Hawkins, Prez, Ben [Webster], Don [Byas]. But then, there were quite a few others that people don't mention anymore. They forgot about Joe Thomas, who's still alive and kicking. Arnett Cobb was out there, and Illinois Jacquet was a strong influence at that time. People like Ike Quebec; anybody that's New York and was being recorded at that time was heard to some extent in the other places. Another thing, at that time the records we were hearing were the ones that were made before that time because at that time the recording ban was on. So there weren't any records being made anywhere but here [New York], and most of them if they were being made here were bootleg or black market.

I don't think I ever modelled myself after somebody. All that I ever consciously attempted at imitation was Coleman Hawkins's "Body and Soul" and Illinois Jacquet's "Flyin' Home," because you had to know them to get jobs. You had to know those two to get a gig anywhere. But I had never consciously imitated anyone. I've admired lots of people. I have my favorites.

After I left Nat Towles's band I went back to Detroit in '46. It was at that time I met people like Kenny Burrell and then a lot of the people I had known out of Detroit all of my life. I knew Bags [Milt Jackson] long before that, although not well. Till '46 and '47 I worked around Detroit in a lot of little spots around there: Club Bizerte, Old Time Inn, Civic Center. So that's '46, '47 . . .

I was working with bandleaders at that time who were prominent in the Detroit area. For about two years I spent mostly with King Porter, a trumpet player, one of the top little groups in the city, just five pieces. We worked all the clubs, even the big ones that were downtown. I also spent a little time during that period with, you remember the old society orchestra leader Leroy Smith? He's deceased now, but he was at that time on a level like Meyer Davis. I worked with him for a short while. Then I came to New York in '48 with Lucky Millinder's band. I left that city a couple of months with that, and I left that and went

with Jimmie Lunceford's band to make the first memorial tour. I left
that and went with Milton Buckner—we had a small group at that time;
myself and Julius Watkins were the front line.

❖❖

After returning to Detroit and then joining Woody Herman for
about ten months, he once again came back to Detroit.

❖❖

BILLY MITCHELL   Before I left the first time the scene was—I was working
with groups that were playing in clubs that were more show-oriented
than actually jazz-oriented. Not all of them. In a lot of them, we were
the show. The band was the show in that case. As far as show, man,
we played music and the trumpet player sang, but that was it, that was
the show. It was geared to the tunes that were the popular things of
the day. There was some jamming going on, but the time of the extended solo—Bird and them brought in different things, they brought
in the time of the extended soloists and so forth. For example, in those
days it was almost unwritten law that you played two choruses and then
sat down. Whereas today, two choruses, ain't nobody took a deep breath
yet. So that era hadn't come in—that era came in for us in Detroit.
Like I say, in a sense, we ushered it in. That was late '49 when the
Bluebird era started. There was a fellow named Phil Hill. Now the
Bluebird, by the way, happens to be in the neighborhood I grew up
in. It was a neighborhood tavern; it was sixty years ago and still is now.
It's been there at least sixty years now. There was a fellow named Philip
Hill, Art Mardigan. Philip was a piano player.

❖❖

That was the rhythm section on one of Wardell Gray's Prestige
records when Bob Weinstock went to Detroit to produce it in 1950.

❖❖

BILLY MITCHELL   Phil had the band, and it was a neighborhood place. That
was the time all of us were going through some kind of problem or
another; mine came a few years later. Anyway, something happened,
and we stopped working there, and the lady asked me to form another band. That was when I formed the band at the Bluebird. In the
original band was—it could have been anybody working with me at
various times: the Jackson brothers, Oliver and Ali; and then Alvin
Jackson* came much later. But when the band finally did get settled
down, I had a quartet. It settled down to where I had Terry Pollard
and Beans—and I'm trying to remember who came first, Elvin or Thad
[Jones]. I think Elvin came first maybe because I needed a drummer.
So I had a quartet with Elvin, Terry Pollard, Jerry Richardson, Rodney Richardson's brother. They called him Beans.

It might have been that Oliver was working for me first, but he was
underage. I know Elvin came in. I don't know who was first but I know

*Milt's brother.

the way that Thad got hired. I told the lady that owned the place that I wanted to stretch out and put another piece in. She said, no, she couldn't afford it. So I told her, "Listen, I think it would be a good move and increase business. I'll have him come in and work this weekend and if you don't think we should keep him, you'll pay nothing and I'll just pay him and we'll say no more to it." So Thad came in and worked the first weekend, and at the end of the weekend the lady walked up and said, "Yeah, definitely." She paid me to pay him that weekend, and from then on that was it. That was the group. We had a five-piece group. Naturally, genius is a rare thing, and, brothers, we had a tremendous musical direction as well as everybody there being hard players. Then we had the advantage of having Thad Jones's imagination. So for five years we had the ultimate group. We had such a variety of musical things going, and we had so much talent and so much original music. As a matter of fact, we were nationally known and had never been out of Detroit. It was the place for jazz. It was the place for creative jazz music, and it was also the training ground, or one of the main training grounds, for a lot of the people who came up during that era and are the mainstays, or should be the mainstays of the music today. I'm talking about Tommy [Flanagan], Terry and Kenny [Burrell], and Barry [Harris], Kiane [Zawadi], Paul Chambers . . . . . . Doug Watkins . . . . . . all those people, Curtis Fuller, they all came right through there. A saxophone player I like so well, Joe Henderson. Fats [Navarro] came through there. It was a training ground for everyone, and Detroit was a hip musical town with hip music people. It believed in music at that time, Detroit did.

❖❖

There was a white counterpart to the Detroit black music scene in the '40s, and these musicians were thinking along the same lines, listening to Dizzy and Bird. Leo Osebald was a tenor man often mentioned in the pages of *Metronome* when someone would write a specific article about jazz in Detroit.

In 1960 when musicians and critics from New York, on their way to a Detroit jazz festival, were greeted at the airport by a group featuring Osebald, they were impressed with his fluency, natural swing and unpretentious mixture of Prez and Bird. He sounded somewhat like Al Cohn.

❖❖

AL COHN   I didn't know him but I knew Art Mardigan and Doug Mettome—a lot of the guys in the '40s. I thought they were all crazy. They all wanted to be pimps and the drugs . . . there were a whole bunch of midwestern guys that were into—oh everybody's idea, their ambition was to get a hustler to work for them. Then they could just play their horns. Only it didn't work out that way. Chicago was like that. But it was really one small group.

❖❖

In the '40s Chicago was a city with a great amount of jazz activity. The North Side was white and the South Side black, but the black travling groups played up north at the Argyle and the Crown Propellor Lounge as well as the South Side clubs, and Chicago's white musicians went out south to jam and sit in. They also mixed in the local big bands. Between his stints in the Eckstine and Herman bands, Chicago's own Gene Ammons worked all over the city with his combos.

❖❖

LOU LEVY I had a sister four years older than me that studied the piano, and I got jealous that she had something to do, and somehow I got into piano lessons—I was about ten or eleven years old—got into high school and somehow got into the jazz band in high school. I didn't really know how to read music very well, but they needed a piano player. My father was a ear piano player—G-flat, all the black keys. He played a lot of wrong changes, but he was a lot of fun. I think the first thing that affected me was when I went to my sister's confirmation party at the Sherman Hotel, the Panther Room, the College Inn, and I was eleven years old and heard Glenn Miller's band, and that was the greatest thing that ever happened to me in my whole life— "In the Mood" and "Pennsylvania 6-5000." There was an instrumental choreography worked out where the trombones would go up like this and the saxophones—and the music would go this way . . . I heard this smooth, beautiful band, and thought, God, what a great way to spend your life. So that's how I got started. Before I heard Count Basie, Benny Goodman, I heard Glenn Miller and whatever other band you want to name.

And in Chicago they had the *Chesterfield Show* or the *Camel Caravan* at the Civic Opera House. They used to have Harry James's band, and Glenn Miller would play the shows at the Opera House, which held 6500 people, and I used to get tickets and go to see the shows. Used to go for free. Totally fell in love with big bands. Big bands before small bands.

I played in the high-school band, and then I started to listen to— the guys in the band would say, did you hear this, did you hear that, and that also included some classical music. Then I was exposed to Stravinsky, Ravel, and Debussy—so that's impressionistic and far out for me—at the time it was far out and that really impressed me. The harmonic concept part of that turned my ear on, not that I was ready to handle it all, but it knocked me out. *The Firebird Suite* . . . *The Rite of Spring*, I think that influenced my jazz playing. I think it was a real important part—not to jump the gun and go on to six years later, but when I heard Paul Hindemith that really affected my playing, and then I heard Bartok.

❖❖

Guitarist Jimmy Gourley (born in 1926) is about two years older than Levy. He came up in the same musical milieu as the pianist.

❖❖

JIMMY GOURLEY   I quit high school about six months before I was to graduate, and I was to go right in the service. I quit school, and I was really starting to get into playing. I was playing more and more, and that was interesting me more and more. I got a chance to go on a band. I had something like six or eight months to go. Some of the cats in the school band were already out playing. We went to Oklahoma City. It's where I first went, and it was fantastic. It's a strange town with the Indians and all that. It was wide open because of the war, and they had players down there. Of course everybody knew Charlie Christian. All the black cats. Beautiful, they saw I played guitar, they said, "come on," you know. There was a club right across the street from the hotel, and we'd go jam. They would say, "There's a guitar player from Chicago in town," and I couldn't play, man. I was just reading, taking my first solos really, just leaping out there. There was another club, a roadside joint outside of town where we had a good band, with a little skinny chick singer who sang, "Dream about a reefer five feet tall." Cats took me outside. Man, I'd never even seen anything like that. I just froze up. They were real nice—"Come on, man." I don't know what I expected to happen out there, and I didn't make it. I sure wish I had because I can imagine what it must have been at that time out in Oklahoma. They must have had some ripsnorting grass. I'll never forget this when the cat said, "What's *your* kick, man?" when I turned it down. After that, the Navy and then, two years later, out. There all the cats were on the scene playing—Lou Levy in Chicago.

LOU LEVY   When I was working with Harold Fox. We had Count Basie's arrangement of "Basie Boogie" and I used to play it. So Harold Fox, being such a character, named me Count Levy—isn't that great?

JIMMY GOURLEY   Yeah, "Count" Levy. That's what we called him for a long time. I fit right in because they were all the cats I had played with in high school because I had lived up north. I kept all those contacts, so I knew a lot of people. A lot of them had to go in the service. Of course there was Junior Mance, a whole lot of good players, Jug, Johnny Griffin. That scene was goin' on too, a good scene. You wouldn't believe it, man; it was crazy.

There was this Jay Burkhart band at that time, which was a pretty good band. It got much better and on that band was Lou; Eddie Badgeley, a very good trumpet player; Gail Brockman was on the band who was beautiful, man; a good trombone player whose name I can't remember and occasionally Jug would play with the band. Cy Touff, Sandy Mosse, later on Joe Daley. [Bass trumpet, tenor sax, and tenor sax, respectively.] Joe was always like, "Get ahead, man." At that time he was very much into Charlie Parker. As was everybody else. That's how I came back into it. That Burkhart band was crazy. Everybody came through that band. I remember a couple of nights we had Sonny Stitt playing first a lot; Gene Ammons in the tenor chair; Gail Brockman, who was always there, and the band was just kicking. Naturally in that big band all kinds of cats came through it because we only worked two nights a week. There were some cats who couldn't make it or something so you got all different kind of guys. The first time I heard Doug Mettome was when he came in on the band one night. Nobody knew him—he was there before anybody else.

There's the Jimmy Dale* band, too—Harold Fox, "the band that rocks." That was a funny band, a mixed band which the Burkhart band was, too. Harold had all the gigs in "Brownsville," and Burkhart had the light part of town, but they'd all kick in. Jimmy Dale's band was a funny band. One night there'd be nine tenor players—Harold would just hire everybody. God, the solos were just like unending. It was a good band, a lot of good players, Wesley Landers on drums. That night, nine tenor players, boy, every tenor player in Chicago. Johnny Griffin. That's what was going on. When Illinois Jacquet came in town and we'd all go to see and hear him because J. J. was on the band.

LOU LEVY   Through high school I started working with local bands and playing big-band arrangements—Count Basie arrangements, Lionel Hampton arrangements. I worked with a guy—his real name is Harold Fox. The band consisted of a lot of local guys, a lot of good local guys. We had Gene Ammons, who is now dead, a beautiful player. Through that band came a lot of real good players. I somehow got into that band, and we were playing all these big-band arrangements. Now Harold Fox, to make a long story short, he had this tailor shop on Roosevelt Road in Chicago, and he made all the band clothes for people like Lionel Hampton, Stan Kenton, maybe Count Basie, Billy Eckstine; and through working with him in the local Chicago band we'd get all these arrangements. He'd make uniforms for them and get arrangements. So we got to play all these arrangements. Sort of learned a lot about music just playing those arrangements, different styles, listening to the records, playing with these guys. Then, in high school, I was working with a band in Evanston, Illinois, and one night a guy took me over to his house and played me a record of Dizzy Gillespie. I think I was fifteen or sixteen. I didn't know what it was, but loved it. I thought, "I got to find out about that." Then Lee Konitz lived in Chicago, and Lee took me to the record store owned by a guy named Phil Featheringill, and played a record for me of Charlie Parker, "Groovin' High," the first Charlie Parker record I ever heard, and that

*Fox's band was known as the Jimmy Dale band.

changed my whole life, and I knew what kind of music I wanted to play. Throw in all the little decorations in later life like Hindemith and Bartok, but it's still Charlie Parker and Dizzy Gillespie. The first record I heard of Dizzy—before I heard Bird I heard Dizzy—"Disorder at the Border," with Coleman Hawkins and Clyde Hart. I could whistle that solo to you right now.

❖❖

In those days Chicago was a jamming town. Loosely-knit cadres of musicians would travel around like roving bands, looking for places to blow. They'd always have their horns with them. In New York musicians would more likely rent a studio, with everybody chipping in some money. In some other places it may have been another scene, but in Chicago there seemed to be this and sitting in on someone's gig—which is universal when you can do it—but so many bars in Chicago had entertainment then, and the piano and sound system were there. Sometimes even drums. If the bartender, or manager, was agreeable—after all, they were getting free entertainment for the club—you'd have an instant session. It was mostly a bunch of guys who never attained any kind of recognition beyond Chicago. A lot of them were strung out—that was one reason.

❖❖

LOU LEVY   I remember guys walking around with their horns. It was a blowing town. I think Chicago then sort of reminds me of the Village now, there's something going on everywhere—all kinds of piano bars, but even more then because they had quartets and quintets. This is mostly duos and trios.

I remember going on and sitting in at the Yes Yes Club on South State, which was then the striptease row, that was worse than *Deep Throat*, by comparison. Forget it. If my mother ever heard I was there . . . I remember going there and sitting in with Sonny Stitt and Ike Day—super drummer. Wilbur Campbell.

JIMMY GOURLEY   I used to go way out south, within 7600 South, I used to walk to the IC [Illinois Central], which is another train we had to take to get into the El, with my guitar and amplifier I walked three blocks with. Take that train, get off of that train and get on another train. If you're way up north and playing you did it so you could play. So that's what I had to do, and that's what we did for a long period, a couple of years from '46 to '48, '49. But then we talked about how it got all broken up because of the law. Everything became something else. We had to be a little independent to keep playing. You had to really go into that because you couldn't do anything else once you start traveling. I wasn't always working so I ended up working in the daytime and, God, naturally that didn't last, man. Jesus, I couldn't make it. I'd try. I said I gotta straighten up. I needed money. "I gotta do something," but I couldn't make it because I was still playing. There was a period when we were working and always together—Lou Levy, Jimmy Raney, Gary Miller, Red Lionberg, Gene Friedman. I had a car. Anything you'd do your mother would say, "Where were you?"—coming in at eight in the morning. "Listening to records." How could you say you were listening to records all night till eight in the morning? That's all we were doing, and playing and talking about playing. It just seemed for me, anyway, that was the only thing to do, and it seemed like for everybody else, because that was what was happening. The Bird records were coming out one by one and, man, you'd lay on them. I remember one 78 record could last you a couple of months.

Jimmy Raney, he was like unbelievable at that time, man. He was ready, man. He was already saying . . . damn, there he was and I was moving right up. That's who I hung out with and who I played with— Lou and those people. I got the great, right sounds. Everybody was listening to Prez. It was a great scene and it was a very fertile scene.

❖❖

Raney was on Jerry Wald's band with Al Haig in 1944. The pianist took him to hear and see Lester Young in the film short, "Jammin' the Blues," and to 52nd Street. Later, they formed a strong playing association, recording together and as part of Stan Getz's group.

❖❖

AL HAIG   He stayed at my house. What was happening to Jimmy was that he was just floundering around with some strange Southern, I don't know, hokey-pokey style of playing that he'd brought up from Kentucky. At that time I was listening to Dizzy and going to 52nd Street, and because I'd befriended him in the band he was interested in where I was going to every night.

So I said, "Well, I'm interested in that new trumpet player, Dizzy Gillespie." So he knew about as much as I did then because it was kind of long before Dizzy appeared again on the Street since that broadcast. He was sitting in. So it was just a question of going to 52nd Street and catching him when he was there. That was the problem. Anyway, Jimmy and I became very good friends and still are. He just reworked his whole style. He went back to Chicago and just did the whole thing right from scratch, and as a result he's become actually one of the most—the peer of bebop guitar players I would say. I don't think anybody else is.

LOU LEVY   Anyhow, Jimmy Raney and Al Haig were around Chicago a lot then. Ronnie Singer—unfortunately that was one of the great losses. Fantastic. Great talent. He would have been one of the all-time greats.

JIMMY GOURLEY   I didn't know him very well, a great player. He was saying as much as Jimmy was at that time. We used to go out and play. He'd take his guitar, and we had the amplifier when we finally got organized and got out to the jamming scene. He was so hung up that he'd come out to where I was playing to play because everybody got a little afraid of him because he was going through such a drug scene.

It had to do with family pressure. He was young. He was younger than we were. He was going through that terrible scene. What a player.

LEE KONITZ   There was Jimmy Raney and Lou Levy, and situations that included them a lot of the time. Of course, they were well into the music. I don't know why this is exactly, but shortly after I heard this music, I came to New York, in '47, and heard it there, and it became very familiar to me in some way, very quickly, so that by the time it came to New York, every time I heard Bird I had the impression that I'd heard that before. It was never the kind of adventure that I'd gotten from some other people. Warne [Marsh] for one, for example. I can listen to him endlessly and never really have the impression that he's stringing the licks together, etc. But, at that time, Jimmy and Lou Levy sounded very clichéd and hackneyed to me with using that material. I was involved with Lennie [Tristano] at that time, and I had an overall outlook on the players that were in the bebop as being in the past, some way. It's weird. The main players were Lester Young derivative and, as you know, there was quite a lot of activity in Chicago, and my association with Lennie had me playing in some of these situations pretty young.

❖❖

Ronnie Singer and his wife committed suicide in New York. I believe they had a suicide pact. I met him briefly in Chicago, and then I met him briefly again in New York and heard him play a couple of times; once with Red Rodney at the Open Door, in the early '50s. In a lot of ways I think he was closer to Charlie Christian than some of the other modern players who took off from Charlie Christian, and yet he was still more himself, too. He had a spirit, a sound that reminded me of Christian, that kind of raw sound and power.

❖❖

LEE KONITZ   I just played a few times with him, didn't know him well, but he had something special. I was never able to get with that group of people because I wasn't getting stoned and they were always scary to me. Something that they were into that I had not the slightest concept about for quite a long time. I never found out what that was about. Fortunately, I wasn't that curious. I really felt on the outskirts of those people, and their interests. That's why I was reluctant to talk about this because I've had, in many respects, a very insular kind of life. Even though I was involved with the bands, the people, I was generally running off and taking an hour of practice or do something by myself, instead of really hanging out and choochin'.*

*talking.

JIMMY GOURLEY   Of course the New York bands came to town too. Bird finally came to town. Sonny Stitt had been there for a while but was living there more or less underground. It was a frantic scene. The first time Bird came to town was a two-week engagement at the Argyle Show Lounge—Max, Miles, Tommy Potter, and Duke Jordan—and that was the first time he really hit town after Camarillo.

Boy, the band was just dynamite. There was a trumpet player named "Hotsy" Katz, Howard Katz. He had an apartment right around the corner from the Argyle, and his folks had a fruit stand outside of town, and they were gone, so we'd just stay there, go to his place between sets and come back. Bird just tore it up, it was so good. Sonny Stitt had been there before, and I remember we were saying, "How can Sonny be saying so much?" and Bird came to town and just wiped him out, fantastic.

The very first night was the first night when I tried snorting—Bird's opening night. Out in the car a cat had one thing, and we were passing it around to everybody. By the time we drove back to the Argyle Show Lounge, I was out of it. I had had one moment of complete high and then [makes sounds of being sick]. And I missed out on opening night. I was right outside the joint, but I just couldn't think of going in, and I had my uncle's car. Who comes out at the end of the night but Don Lundahl or somebody like that who lived out south who I was gonna drive back, or who was gonna drive me back because I was sick as a dog for hours. He's got Bird with him. He said, "Bird wants to go south, man. Can you take him?" "I can't drive." Bird says, "I'll drive," and he drove like a fucking maniac in my uncle's car. My heart was in my mouth. I came back every night to hear him after that. All the musicians were there every night.

LOU LEVY   We weren't allowed to go in there, but we made arrangements to get in. My friend [Katz] lived a block away from the club, so we could go over there and do whatever we had to do and go over there and listen to Bird. I walked in there one night—I played pretty good by Chicago standards because bebop was new and Chicago wasn't into bebop that much. From listening to all this I had a little bit of a jump on the younger guys anyway. Somebody told Charlie Parker that here's a kid that plays pretty good, and they let me sit in. Now here I am, sitting in with Charlie Parker and Miles Davis. I think I almost froze. That's the only time I've ever been almost scared in my life. I lived through it, but at the end of the set Charlie Parker said, "Hey, kid, can I buy you a drink?" I said, "I don't think I'm old enough to drink." So I had a Coke, and he talked to me, and he was really great—that big strong voice of his, that's almost overpowering in his personality. He said, "Have you ever heard of Bud Powell?" I said, "I've listened to Al Haig a lot and Nat Cole and I've heard about him but I haven't really heard him yet." I remember he put his hand to his mouth and blew a kiss to heaven. He said, "Go out and get yourself a Bud Powell record." He wasn't putting me down but just steering me on the right path. And I did that. And that's why Bud Powell's my favorite piano player.

I used to work in the Silhouette Club in Evanston—well, it's the border line, Chicago and Howard Street. I worked there in 1948 with Georgie Auld, Tiny Kahn, Frank Rosolino, and Max Bennett—a fantastic group. Bird would finish earlier than we did, and he would come all the way from the Beehive on the South Side, and come up and play the last set with us. Charlie Parker standing next to me. I didn't know what to think, except I loved it. And he was such a great guy because he—great and crazy at the same time—he used to stand next to me and look down at me and say, "Yeah." This is a few years after he told me to get the Bud Powell records. I think he appreciated the fact that everybody sort of dug his message. They were trying to play like him. At least people showed that they appreciated him. He appreciated that. I'm not trying to build up my own ego—when I was with Woody Herman and he came into the club—the Royal Roost—with Miles Davis, Bud Powell, and Dizzy Gillespie, and he called me over after the set and he said, "We liked you best," only because I was more into them than anyone else, and they appreciated that.

❖❖

There were a couple of records Levy made with Chubby Jackson—the band that went to Sweden—and his solos on "Boomsie" and "Dee Dee's Dance,* in particular, have that crazy intensity of the bebop period. He captured an essence in those solos.

❖❖

LOU LEVY   I guess it was that thing that Charlie Parker told me, "Go out and get a Bud Powell record." The intensity was there. It really was—not only the harmonics and the ideas, but it was the way you played them.

❖❖

There was a famous wire recording of Bird with Dizzy's band at the Pershing Hotel's ballroom. Chicago hipsters would take people to trumpeter Miff Cunliffe's pad, as on a pilgrimage, to hear it.

Miff also had recorded Dizzy's band with Miles, and Miles was way up in the stratosphere, playing like Gillespie.

❖❖

JIMMY GOURLEY   I was there both nights. With Bird it was unbelievable. James Moody was falling off his chair, just flipping, and Bird was just playing all the time. He only stopped when Dizzy played. They played through all the arrangements. Fantastic, just one night.

❖❖

*included in *Bebop Revisited,* Volume 1 (Xanadu 120).

These nights became legends. Another legend around Chicago was Ira Sullivan, who is just beginning to receive international recognition in the '80s.

❖❖

LOU LEVY   Ira Sullivan. Right, today could blow most people off the stand. Plays alto, tenor, trumpet, drums, vibraphone—it's ridiculous. He's really something else. A real natural. I don't think he can read a note. Maybe he's learned how to read a little, but anyhow he's a demon, fantastic.

❖❖

Like Detroit's Cass Tech, Chicago's Du Sable High and its famed Captain Walter Dyett, turned out many musicians who went on to international recognition: Benny Green, Gene Ammons, Johnny Griffin, and Clifford Jordan, among others.
   Junior Mance didn't go to Du Sable, but he did go on to make a name for himself, first in Chicago with Ammons, and then with Lester Young, Dinah Washington, Cannonball Adderley, Dizzy Gillespie, and on his own.

❖❖

JUNIOR MANCE   I was born in Chicago but lived and grew up in Evanston. My first influences were Albert Ammons, Pete Johnson, and Meade Lux Lewis. I worked underage all over Chicago. It was the summer before I graduated from high school. I was working in Waukegan with a traditional swing band. These young guys from Chicago were driving around looking for a place to sit in, and our leader let them. I heard this new music I'd never heard before that completely turned me around. There was this young saxophone player named Henry Pryor. He was around my age, sixteen or seventeen years old. That was my first introduction to Charlie Parker. This guy played so great. What I couldn't understand was that the other guys in the band —and they were in their '30s—put him down or looked sideways at him and said, "He's got no tone" and "He's just playing a lot of notes."
   With him was a young trumpet player, around the same age, named Robert Gaye, whom they called "Little Diz." It was so funny. After they left, the older guys said, "Don't listen to that stuff. That's nothing but noise."
   We exchanged phone numbers and addresses, and I started hanging out on their gigs. Dance gigs. And there were just as many people listening as dancing.
   Then the first year out of high school, 1946, I joined Harold Fox's band. Lou Levy was there before me, but I don't know why he left. I was going to Roosevelt College. That's where I met Lou Levy, Hotsy Katz—he married Harold Fox's daughter—at Roosevelt everyone was into the bebop movement.
   At the time Billy Eckstine's band wasn't completely dissolved, but

gigs were getting fewer and fewer, and when Gene [Ammons] was in Chicago he'd play with Harold's band. And he was also working a job at the Congo Lounge on 48th and South Parkway next door to the Regal Theater. I think that's where I *really* got into it then because Gene hired me. Gene Wright was the bass player; a fantastic drummer named Ellis Bartee played Big Sid Catlett style. Gene, knowing all the heavyweights—Bird, Leo Parker—when these guys came through town they would come and sit in with us. For a teenager this was jazz heaven. It was like going to school. Also, during that time the jam session was a big, big thing in Chicago. Even before I joined Gene I could go out at night and go to a half a dozen places and play a set at each one.

❖❖

Mance did his first recordings with Ammons in October 1947 with "Harold the Fox" and "Shermanski" containing solos by him. Ammons had made his hit, "Red Top," in June 1947 before Mance was in the group. Gail Brockman, a veteran of the Hines and Eckstine bands, was the trumpeter; and the reeds, in addition to Ammons, were Ernie McDonald and/or Flaps Dungee. The latter, who had also been with Eckstine's band, solos on "Dues in Blues."

❖❖

JUNIOR MANCE   Flaps Dungee, he was something. An amazing musician. Very quiet and very laid back. Never was out there seeking a name, but he played better than most of the alto players around there. He had big ears, figuratively and literally. Looked almost like an elf. Little guy.

When Gail Brockman soloed in the Jimmy Dale band, it was almost like the E. F. Hutton commercial. The whole band would stop and turn around and listen. The *band* would applaud sometimes. He played such well-constructed solos. They say—and I find it hard to believe—that he didn't have a great knowledge of chord changes. Because he played a line that was so perfect on the chord structure of the tune.

❖❖

At this time Ammons was the most popular jazz musician in Chicago.

❖❖

JUNIOR MANCE   Jug was the King of Chicago. They had a disc jockey named Al Benson who had a program called "Battle of the Bands," a live show each Saturday, I think it was. Jug wound up being the "champ" week after week after week after week. Because of that we were working all the time. In fact, sometimes we would play—well, not actually play but make appearances—on three, maybe, four gigs in one night. I remember we were working steadily at the Congo, and Jug had *four* jobs booked that night. "Red Top" was still hot. I was wondering to myself, "How are we going to make these four jobs?"

The first three we made okay. We just went to each one, played about two tunes and closed it with "Red Top." Then we'd jump in the car and go to another one. They were all dances. The last one was in Gary, Indiana, which is about a half an hour drive from Chicago. We made it, but we couldn't get back to the Congo. Jug's car broke down. Oh, and he was also supposed to make another appearance at the end of one of the earlier dances. We didn't make that. That guy got uptight and took Jug to the union. In the meantime, the union had gotten word that we were working four jobs in one night, and in those days they were strict about that. You worked one job, and you didn't even work seven nights a week. They had a five-night week in Chicago. You didn't work the off nights. But we did 'cause Jug was so popular and *nobody* questioned it on the South Side. But he got caught, and Jug wound up getting fined five hundred dollars. But it didn't really change anything. We kept doing it, but being careful.

I was in the Army from 1951–1953. When I came back, Jug was "strung out."

❖❖

Ike Day was a phenomenal young drummer. I heard him at one of Joe Segal's Roosevelt College sessions with Ira Sullivan in 1949 and his drive was protean. When Sonny Rollins was in Chicago in 1950, he played with Day and described him with superlatives.

❖❖

JUNIOR MANCE   I saw Ike sit in with Woody Herman at the Savoy Ballroom in Chicago. He had never heard the book. He used to sit in with Basie all the time. He couldn't read music at all. And he would play the book like he'd been playing in the band all the time. Just amazing. And he was so young then. He was about twenty-two, twenty-three, twenty-four, something like that.

❖❖

St. Louis had a comparable young drummer in Oscar Oldham, who played with Jimmy Forrest. His only recording is *Jimmy Forrest/Miles Davis—Live at the Barrel* on Prestige. He died in his early twenties in an automobile crash. Day died as a result of drugs, as did Lank Keyes, a tenor player.

❖❖

JUNIOR MANCE   He was another of Dyett's students—on a par with Jug.

❖❖

Henry Pryor's death was drug related.

❖❖

JOE ALBANY   There was a little cat that was robbing a poorbox in Chicago. They used to call him "Hen Pie," Henry Pryor, played nice alto. Met him in California. But Chicago was his home, and a cop shot him six times.

❖❖

The late '40s, with the war ended, saw some American musicians settling in Europe, like Don Byas, who went over with Don Redman's band in 1946. A great wave of black musicians left the United States for Europe in the '60s. In 1951 Jimmy Gourley went the transatlantic route but for a different reason.

❖❖

JIMMY GOURLEY   In 1949 I did a lot of gigs around town, different clubs, Jackie and Roy, a couple of local bands. I remember at the Hi Note when I was there with Jackie and Roy and Carmen McRae, who called herself Carmen Kirby at that time.

Anyway, I left Jackie and Roy, went back with them and finally came over here [To Paris] in 1951. The scene had just disintegrated. It was great over here. The scene was so open like it had been in Chicago. There were talented players over here, too. They were trying to play, the same thing, except the whole Parisian scene and fantastic decor. I had the G.I. Bill, so I was a little independent. Eddie Petan* had been over here for one year. I was dying to get out, and the G.I. Bill was ending. Why not? I was free, and everything was disintegrating around Chicago with the drug scene. All my friends, all the players, people I wanted to play with, and who I'd spent all this time with, were wiped out most of the time. I was in that scene without doing it. Coppin' with them, them getting high while they were playing. Of course as that took over it prevented everything else. It got to be pretty much of a drag for somebody who wasn't doing it, so I split.

❖❖

Long before '51—by the mid-'40s—heroin was growing in usage by the young modernists.

❖❖

FRANKIE SOCOLOW   I was out on the Coast with Raeburn's band at the time and the band was laid off,—had no more work. We went to Hollywood for a while, kind of scuffled around, did a couple of odd jobs with the band and we just virtually had no bookings. The band was laid off. And I remember I got sick. I got the flu or something, and I was miserable and had no money, and we living hand to mouth, six guys in a room. It was like real panic style, as we used to call it in those days—the band was on a panic. I came home, and when I came home I was shocked by the whole thing, 'cause I had been gone for a year or two. When I came back—everybody, everybody was a junkie. And everybody thought I was a junkie. It was like guilt by association. It was pretty prevalent in L.A. but not like in New York. It happened in L.A., but here it was unbelievable. I didn't know what the hell hit me.

❖❖

The hard drug epidemic among the modern jazz musicians had its beginnings during World War II. They had no rights of exclusivity—doctors in Germany between World Wars had an un-

*pianist from Chicago.

usually high percentage of morphine addiction—but musicians were more in the public eye than people in most walks of life. Besides, jazz musicians had always had an image as wild livers—boozers and marijuana smokers (it was called "tea" and a gang of other things then).

It was the beginning of a drug culture that later was to spread more widely through another music—rock.

❖❖

HENRY JEROME   When Lenny Garment and I created this band all the guys had a great need to be "on" and outside of old square Henry, the bandleader, here. They were all "on." In Child's Restaurant—this was a very proper restaurant. Although it held a thousand people and was a mecca of dancing in Times Square, you just didn't do these things in Child's. It was under the Paramount Theater, and they used to line up all the way up Broadway—a thousand people. Everyone was very dance conscious. Now, we went in with this progressive band, and the guys used to go into this tunnel underneath the Paramount, and the end of the tunnel led into a Walgreen's drug store, which was on the corner of 43rd and Broadway.

The one thing that's never changed in the business, when a band is on the stand and they get off for their break, they never want to get back on, and the boss always wants them on in time, so you always have one person in the band go get the band and make sure that they come on on time. This band, being "on" and being very jazz oriented, and very against rules and regulations, they were never on time.

But this particular time I didn't know *where* they were, and the guy that I had to go collect them didn't know where they were. Finally we went down this tunnel, and we come out in Walgreen's drugstore, and there was a whole row of phone booths. And we had as uniforms chocolate brown pants and canary kind of yellow jackets with brown ties, and there's this row of telephone booths, all filled with the guys wearing the uniforms, all making phone calls. And, of course, what they were really doing was sitting in the telephone booths, getting "on" with the marijuana. The whole band was there—uniform phone calls. And people were lined up who really wanted to make a phone call.

I said, "C'mon, guys." But the bottom line of the story is—hey, I was used to all these things—lo and behold, I pick up the *Journal American* in those days with number-one Broadway column by Dorothy Kilgallen and there, in big, bold, black type it says, "What name bandleader at what well-known chain restaurant has everyone in the band smoking marijuana in phone booths in Walgreen's?"

I read the thing and I really was very, very nervous 'cause in those days it was quite a crime.

❖❖

Heroin or "horse," as it was soon to be known, had not become a big factor at the time of the Jerome band, but there was a trumpet player, Manny Fox, who has been often mentioned by musicians as being one of the first to become "hooked" and introduce others to horse.

❖❖

HENRY JEROME   We finished the set, and everyone got off the bandstand, and Manny was sitting there—he didn't get off the bandstand. So I don't know what's going on but, all of a sudden, two of the guys go up and they formed a chair with their arms for him to sit on, and they lift Manny off his chair, in the sitting position, and they carried him off the stand. He was frozen.

DAVID ALLYN   I remember Manny was fucking around with it long before I was. Before a lot of people.

AL COHN   I'll tell you a great story, an historic one about [drummer] Lou Fromm. Lou in those days was a—well, Lou was using drugs, heavy drugs, but Lou is a fantastic cat.

Lou was a Nietzsche reader and he really believed that Superman thing. And he did it pretty good 'cause he was a junkie and he always looked great. He was strong. He always looked healthy. He used to—in addition to everything else that he took—he took all kinds of vitamins, and he would go by the clock. His whole dresser was just filled with all kinds of pills. He didn't know what they were. So any excuse. You ask him, "What's this?" "Oh, this is a pill I take at 3:37 every day because it does that."

So, we were coming home on a train from St. Louis, coming to New York. It was Georgie Auld's band. And this is one of the times Georgie broke up. We just got out of town, had enough money to get us out of the hotel and get the tickets. So we're sitting in the club car, and Lou walks in. He orders a split of champagne with a tall glass, a high-ball glass, and he takes a paper sack out of his pocket and takes out this lid with green stuff, puts it in the glass, pours the champagne over it. Everybody says, "What's that?" He says, "Oh, that's just herbs, healthful herbs." So everybody accepted that, but they knew. He let it soak in the champagne for twenty minutes and then drinks it. So later that night, I was out, sitting in the club car, and he comes in, and he told me what it was. I was very innocent these days, I didn't know anything. He said that in the St. Louis Botanical Gardens, they have coca leaves. It's maybe one of the three or four places in the United States where they grow this stuff, and he went there and he cut them. He said he couldn't make the trip. He said, "I don't know how to make this trip without this." Which I remember struck me funny, 'cause I didn't have any trouble making the trip. I thought it was great. I was eighteen years old and away from home.

Later, he was busted in a very publicized case. He was with Harry James or Artie Shaw. He got busted for heroin and he made a statement that he can't play jazz without drugs. And then that got on the front pages.

The drug scene was very big and then there was a whole bunch of guys, the guys in Georgie's band. Joe Albany was on the band. A lot of notorious guys. Manny Fox was on Georgie's band. He and Lou Fromm were real tight. I remember the first time I ever saw Jerry Hurwitz. When I was in Georgie Auld's band in '44, we played the Commodore Hotel and Manny Fox and Lou Fromm, after work, we finished work and Jerry Hurwitz was sitting in the lobby with Fat Otto.

These guys—well Fat Otto was fat; Jerry was like so skinny and he looked so dissipated. His hair was kinda long for those days and he looked so weird, walked with that shuffle and really stood out in those days.

The big thing then was taking Benzedrine inhalers. Staying up for three, four days at a time and just playing. Not looking to mug anybody or rape anybody. Just playing for four days straight. The idea was to get as high as you can and play.

❖❖

The death of Sonny Berman, in January 1947, was particularly shocking because it was the first of many hard drug-related incidents that would follow in the ensuing years. Although junk was being used by a lot of musicians, most people didn't know about it. It was still a very underground thing, and I think that's why it was even more of a shock to everyone. But it certainly didn't deter people. More and more musicians got strung out after that.

❖❖

NEAL HEFTI   Oh, I feel that I'm very lucky that I didn't go that route, because he later on told me, before he died, that the very first night that he turned on was up in our apartment, and I didn't know it. You know I was asleep in bed, and he was in the other room. We always had a suite. Two bedrooms with sorta like a living room in between.

I'm sort of lucky in a way, if some guy's death can be good for anybody. It was good for me because, I don't know, I was willing to try anything in those days. I really was. And I did, and when that happened it sure sobered me up fast, very fast. And I think sometimes you do things because of aloneness. A guy might be lonely, and the gang is all lighting up, and you want to be part of the gang. And the gang is all drinking or whatever they're doing. There's a reason these things become epidemics because they probably fill a need at the time. Anyway, that stopped me cold. I had really never thought of it because I think I don't like the sight of blood anyway, and the thought of putting a needle in my arm is enough to really turn me off of—I don't even take pencillin when it's offered. I don't like any kind of shots. But in a weak moment, I could have gone for it 'cause I'm not all that strong.

❖❖

Although Charlie Parker did not advocate heroin use ("Any musician who says he is playing better on tea, the needle, or when he is juiced, is a plain, straight liar.") and, in fact, tried to discourage fellow musicians from using it, many were drawn to it simply because he was a user.

CHUBBY JACKSON   There were two cliques in a musical organization, the whiskey drinkers and the pot smokers, and ne'er the twain ever met. Then of course a lot of younger people were so amazed and fascinated by the likes of Charlie's playing that something told them inside that if they were to assume his personal habits that they could get close to him in an imitative manner. That destroyed so many younger musicians. Today's scene is more into the chemicals, LSD, quaaludes; the "chic" of cocaine.

❖❖

Leonard Feather wrote, "He [Bird] feels sorry for the kids who think: 'So-and-so plays great, and he does such-and-such; therefore I should do like he does and then I'll blow great too.' "

Despite this he was emulated. Introduced to horse during his early teens in Kansas City, Parker, before he was twenty, was a night-life veteran who got high on substances from nutmeg on out.

❖❖

AL COHN   I was working with Henry Jerome's band at Child's Paramount in 1945. One time one of the other fellows and I were standing in front of the place after work, and Charlie Parker was there. Charlie knew about the band; he came down a few times. And he said, "You got anything?" Well, it happened that I had two sleeping pills in my pocket. And I never take sleeping pills, but somebody had given me them. And this other fellow had two sleeping pills. So we each gave him our two sleeping pills. And he didn't—no questions asked, he just put them right in his mouth and swallowed them. Four sleeping pills. I think he knew what they were. I don't really know if he knew. But I figured he was probably hip about what any kind of pill looks like. He stood and talked for a while, then left.

MILT HINTON   I would usually meet Bird in Beefsteak's,* and he would begin to go off the deep end. And Beefsteak's, unfortunately, was a place, which most people don't know—the sellers of dope found out that the easiest, safest place to sell dope was in a bar where people drank—because the police weren't lookin' in a bar for junkies. So these guys would come into Beefsteak's to make their connections.

When they came in they would tell a guy, "Well, go back to the men's room, and meet me at the men's room," and the junkie would go the

---

*Beefsteak Charlie's—musicians' bar on West 50th Street.

bar, and he wouldn't buy a drink, he'd buy a Coke. And he would sit there waitin' for the pusher. And the pusher came in, and, of course, he would order a drink and go right straight back to the men's room. Well, the owners of Beefsteak's had no inkling of this at all, cause there was enough whiskey drinkers like me to keep the place flourishin'—Oscar Pettiford and Paul Webster and Hilton Jefferson—and even Joe Nanton—Tricky Sam—and we just all hung there, and the bar was flourishing with plenty of money on the bar for the bartender-owner to be quite satisfied, so anybody was walkin' back to the john. When the pusher would come in, he would walk right back—and I tell you, it was a long time before *I* was aware of this, sittin' there drinkin' beer. It was a cheap bar—two dollars would buy the whole bar a drink, and if we were short of change we just pooled our resources and just put about three dollars of change up there, and we just drank a beer and went on until the money ran out. So, consequently, not bein' involved in it we didn't even know what was happening with the junkies. That this was going on.

And so Bird would come in, and they would go back there. Even in later years, poor Billie [Holiday] would come through there, and see these guys comin' in there. By this time we were *really* aware of what was going down, and in the next hour or so, after Bird had been back in the back and made his strike, in the next hour or so, he was completely out of it, and he's sittin' at a table when a guy had a free lunch, he had sandwiches there. Now, he's occupying a table, and he's completely out of it, and he hasn't bought a drink, and of course, the bartender—you can imagine—"Well, this guy, he's sittin' here and he's out of it, and I never even saw him buy a drink." Of course, it was left to us to defend him and try to get him up and get him together and try to get him cool and get him out of there. But it was a long time before we really knew what was going on. This was in the early '40s.

GERRY MULLIGAN   At the time I went back to Philadelphia, after Krupa's band, I used to come to New York a lot and visit with Bird, and stay with him at a place up at 148th Street: a dreadful little room in the top floor of a place. It was just such a sad place for a man like Bird to stay. And you know for the longest time he kept the junk scene away from me. He didn't even want me to know that. And he'd excuse himself and go into the other room, turn on, and come back. But finally, and he did it as a warning to me, he said, "This is ugly. Keep away from it." One time he turned on in front of me. And he did it in the most horrendous way possible, with blood all over the place—it just was dreadful. So he made his point. I never even thought about turning on, at that period.

DEXTER GORDON   Bird and Lady [Billie Holiday]. Not that all this is their fault. I'm not saying that. But they were doing it, and Lady was an established idol, and Bird was the other coming idol at that time. And, of course, most of the cats then were pretty young, very young in fact, so they didn't have that experience.

JOE ALBANY   I had Bird refuse me stuff when I was sick, supposedly sick, which really makes you angry when you're all in the same scene. Because there's something new in music and because a lot of guys resent it and it made it unnatural to be different, it's hard to be different, so people tell you; so many were born and not many left now.

FRANKIE SOCOLOW   The new music became, I guess, the biggest single influence in our lives, and it's a way of thinking, it's a way of living. Just like when Diz first came on the scene he had this tiny little goatee. Every trumpet player in the world started to have one. Guys claimed, "Oh, yes, it's a very good thing to have one." Whether it was or . . . you know. But it's just bringing out a point—somebody who you admired to such a degree will influence your whole personal being. That's why a lot of guys became junkies. There was a tremendous reason why a lot of guys became junkies. There was a tremendous reason why a lot of guys who probably in their lives never ever would have dreamed of getting hung up with shit like that. Bird was a big junkie, and to be like Bird you had to be a junkie. I mean everybody smoked pot, but when it came to hard shit, it didn't really become popular, if that's the right word to use, until Bird and his emulators. He had such a tremendous influence on people because of his playing—naturally somebody that looked at him with the most adoring eyes, so to speak, would try to do anything to be like him. The only thing they couldn't do was play like him.

Everybody was friends. A lot of bad things happened. It broke up a lot of friendships; it broke up a lot of families; it had a very devastating effect, really, on an awful lot of people.

❖❖

Once someone gets strung out he has to have it in order to function. But there were times I figured Bird was so high, he was too high to play—even he couldn't play.

❖❖

FRANKIE SOCOLOW   The only time I saw Bird when he couldn't play was when he was really drunk. I saw him very stoned on shit, but needless to say he played his ass off. I'm not saying because of the shit . . .

CHARLIE ROUSE   I used to always think that you had to get high because that was the era that I came up in. You had to get high to play. But the older I get, man, I think if you're in your right mind and you've got your facility—because it's like, your instrument, your body's got to be in shape, too, to play. You're young at that time so you're strong so you can force that shit. When you got too high you couldn't play shit. You dig? So if you took a certain amount, and you wasn't too high and you were high. Then you had your imagination and your thoughts could . . . 'cause when you're improvising, when you're playing jazz, you play what you hear. So the rhythm or whatever is behind you, you hear something, and you go ahead and make it. And you may do it when you wouldn't do it sober. You wouldn't attempt it.

These were cats who didn't like the hard drugs—the heroin. They would leave. There were a group of cats that wouldn't even think about that. Diz wouldn't even think about the hard drugs but the "girl,"* because the "girl" put you in another frame of mind. Fats was the same way. It's the "C."

❖❖

Then there's pot. And we know that it does have mind-altering properties, but man has been altering his mind with drugs or alcohol ever since the beginning of time. If it isn't one thing it's another—the bark of a tree, whatever. He finds it. In *Jazz Masters of the 40s*, I wrote, "In spite (or because?) of [heroin] a great music was made." Maybe that's the only way to look at it. One critic reviewed the book and couldn't understand "because." Drugs do not necessarily help musicians play better, but the music could not have been the same without everything that went into it. Now I would take the question mark off "because."

❖❖

DEXTER GORDON   Yeah, there's no way. You have to accept that, that it definitely had an influence on the music, your life-style. That's what you're expressing. That's what you're playing—your life-style. So it definitely had an influence.

RED RODNEY   I think it was a good statement, "in spite of or because of." I think you should take it [the question mark] off because the leader of this music, Charlie Parker, was addicted. Heavily addicted. Badly addicted. It helped him get through some of the anguish and some of the feeling, I'm sure, did come out. But now we won't take Charlie Parker because he was a genius, so no matter how messed up he got, his genius would show. For example, "Lover Man," on that Ross Russell date, where he was completely out of it and still showed genius. All right, but I'm going to put all the rest of us who were foolish enough . . . It became the thing. That was our badge. It was the thing that made us different from the rest of the world. It was the thing that said, "We know, you don't know." It was the thing that gave us membership in a unique club, and for this membership, we gave up everything else in the world. Every ambition. Every desire. Everything. It ruined most of the people. It turned out that drugs had to be done

*Cocaine was known as "girl" or "C"; heroin was "boy" or "H."

away with and if it had to kill many of us, it was a lesson. Those that it killed served a good purpose because they played to the best of their ability. They did what they wanted to do, and their deaths weren't wasted, by no means. Many times of course, it was an untimely death, sure.

But then we had Clifford Brown who never used drugs and got killed at a young age. So any of this could have happened. I'll say, in my own case, and I know of a few others, I will never advocate the use of drugs. I think it is a horrible thing to do. A horrible situation to be in. I think it had a great deal to do with the music, and I think that a lot of the *good* things in the music were because of drug use. The tempos where guys really played on them, not the b.s. things. We had a lot of b.s. there, because people could sell bullshit at a high price. The truth is sometimes hard to give away. But the tempos for one thing. The tunes with the great changes in it. The intellectual part of it. Guys were always experimenting, and the drugs had something to do with that, too. When a guy is loaded and at peace, he shuts everything else out except what he's interested in. Being interested in music, he could turn out the honking of the world. And, "Hey, man, I just figured this out," and we'd try it that night, and it was great.

DAVID ALLYN Maybe they could listen a little more. I don't know. The power of concentration is higher, of course, or minute. And the blocking out of everything else, but you're also blocking a lot of other things out, too, like real feelings. You're numb. A goddamn wall.

RED RODNEY Unfortunately, it was a lot of sad things that happened from the drugs, and that showed in the music also. Hostility, pettiness, a lot of us became thieves, even though we didn't want to be. That showed. Our embarrassment showed. Our being ashamed of people that we liked knowing that we were hooked. Everything showed. Everything that happens to you through the course of the day or a week or a month or a year or your lifetime will show in your playing.

DEXTER GORDON Yeah, I mean it's not all bad. I think it can arouse you; it makes you concentrate very well. Because you heard those stories about Bird, like he's on the bandstand, and it's time for his solo, and Bird is nodding, sleeping, and the cats are tooting. There's a certain concentrative power with "smack" because just the existence of an addict is—you gotta use your mind so much. It really activates the mind to secure money and to find connections and sources of supply and so forth and play your games, do your little movements and all that shit. It was a very special way of living and also a special milieu.

❖❖

People always talk about why so many jazz musicians were strung out in the post-war period. Some believe it was because of the

frustration of trying to play a music that people weren't accept-
ing, or the pressure of being different. Others cite the influences
of the music environment—the people, the whole night-life underground, tracing it back to Storyville in New Orleans and working for the gangsters in Chicago.

❖❖

DAVID ALLYN   Well, it was definitely some sort of a withdrawal from the
people to be different. First it's a spike. Then what it does to you and
the concept of music goes into another bag. The minute junk comes
on the scene, that's another bag. The concept is different, but as you
look at it now, the junk that's used today in some of the kids that are
playing bad music, then it doesn't hold true does it? Well, it did something to the people that were learned and that came out of the school
that we knew, who went into the Charlie Parker school or Lennie
Tristano or whatever, but that's your jazz era. Coming in from out of
a world like I came off the Jack Teagarden band when I was a kid
like in my teens like Stan Getz did, like everybody. He was on the band
after me. But I mean that era. Then into Basie kind of a feeling. And
then like with Bird and Prez, that started to develop. Now you have
the learned music and the subtlety of jazz and then junk on top of
that. It started to produce something that was never reproduced. A
little later on they just forgot about that completely because they didn't
have that much talent. And when the junkies of today started to use,
well, what have we got to go back on—no fundamentals, not really.
Today, maybe, just recently, it's beginning to come into its own again,
so it started to evolve into something, but it's always from a learned
musician where you hear something creative. Because if you put junk
in a hillbilly, he's still gonna scream and call pigs, right? That's it. Ain't
gonna change him at all. But that whole era back there was like the
changing of the world. For me it was anyway. But all you do is stick a
joint in your arm, look out. Jesus Christ. Then, the respect goes, self-
respect. Rationality goes. You don't know what is right or wrong.

CHARLIE ROUSE   A lot of good musicians got messed up on that. All the
musicians that I know, basically, they were good people. It was just
that they were caught up—you get caught up into that shit and well,
Monk used to tell me, Monk always say, "Well, man, shit, if you don't
beat nobody, you can use drugs and stuff and you don't have to beat
nobody, it's just you." He thinks that way, you know? But basically, if
you're not a cat that will beat anybody, you just want to do it anyhow.
   There are some cats that are weak, man. Basically they wouldn't do
it if they wouldn't be on that. Well that's the way Thelonious thought,
man. He said, "You're jiving. You're not supposed to . . . Basically,
you're not supposed to beat nobody." But then, after they were off it,
or whatever, they'd give you their shirt or whatever, but it's just at the
time when they need it or something, everybody goes. Anybody goes.

❖❖

The Woody Herman band of 1947–1949, filled with more than a few "characters" and "bad actors," gave its leader his share of headaches.

❖❖

WOODY HERMAN   Well, there were a lot of problems because it was really the first real introduction in our band to people who were involved in the heavy drug scene. Up until then it was pretty mild. With the heavy thing it also builds a second society which is like every time we would make a replacement it got to a point where we would watch which group the new guy would go walking with. You knew right away after a while because you couldn't do bedchecks and check people's toilets. And then you either put up with it or you get rid of the person. But once it got into a heavy thing it almost becomes like a cancerous state of things. It was murder in some respects. At different points, with that band, my biggest gig was to keep everybody awake enough to blow. They'd be nodding halfway through anything. Very often I'd have to be like a den mother with them and try to plead with them because I didn't want them to wind up in jail, and I didn't want them to wind up in a hospital.

❖❖

Earl Swope was an athlete who used to work out in different towns. He used to find the gyms in the various cities. Then he got hooked. Red Rodney was one who *didn't* get hooked while on the Herman band.

❖❖

RED RODNEY   I was one of the few that didn't. I didn't get hooked until after that band. When I went with Bird. It took that. It took Bird. Standing next to that giant everyday, I probably said to myself, "I wonder if I jumped over . . ."*

DEXTER GORDON   Then there were a lot of cats that started later. That's another thing that surprised me. Cats that had seen us go through this shit. I'm talking about older guys like Ike Quebec and other guys, over thirty already. Even like Jug [Gene Ammons]. Jug wasn't using stuff at that time when we were. Then, in the band, he was the "Holy *One*," compared to us. I don't know if it was just a feeling of the times. I've thought about it often, 'cause it really caught on as an inside thing. Hey, but you're not getting high. Same thing with weed. Fats [Navarro] was a very nice cat. Very straight. Quiet, but active. He was pretty level minded. I was surprised when he started using stuff. He smoked all right but . . .

Also there's a much bigger social ramification to it. Because most all of the people that have been socially associated with drugs, have all

*To Parker's drug habits.

been minority groups—blacks, Jews, Italians, Mexicans. There were very few Anglo-Saxons. Until recently vintage. Which is why all of a sudden they started getting very humane about the problem. When kids from bourgeois neighborhoods, senators' daughters and sons—these type people, suburbia—start turning on, then it affects—"What, my son? How could this be? He's going to jail. What kind of . . . ?" That's when the shit starts happening. But all that, it was all right as long as it was minority groups that was using that. But I could see later on— the late '50s, '60s—it started spreading further.

❖❖

Gerry Mulligan, like Miles Davis, did not come to heroin in the first wave despite being around it. Eventually, he succumbed.

❖❖

GERRY MULLIGAN   Listen, there were some very corny guys around New York when I first came to town. And they had adopted Count's music and Prez and Bird. They had appropriated it all to themselves. It was like they had invented it all. Well [sighs]. I used to keep *far* away from those guys. Yeah, and there's really some—they were *bad* cats. And they weren't that good *musicians*. Not from anything I ever heard anyway. So there was a whole aura around the junk scene, and they apparently had a big effect, a big influence on a lot of the New York guys. Because I wasn't from New York in the first place, I was almost an outcast, you know, and was delighted to be so because these people really frightened me. They were too much for me. And I didn't like their attitude. Like that whole bullshit thing of like anything Count Basie's band did is all right. Duke Ellington is corny. What is that shit?

You know when the '47 Woody's band got started, that attitude prevailed in there, and they put Duke down. Anything that wasn't Count Basie was put down. They made Ralph Burns's life *miserable*. They finally got Woody so upset that I think Woody always had to get loaded before he would go on the stand. You know, Woody would be playing, and cornball Serge Chaloff would be making comments about his playing. Ridiculing on the stage. I finally told Serge one time, when I went out with the band to hear a one-nighter, and Serge started to say something ridiculing, of Woody. I said, "Listen, man, as far as *I'm* concerned, the record you're talking about, Woody's solo is *not* the worst solo on the record, so fuck you." You know, all that kind of opinionated bullshit, and ridiculing other players. What is that?

❖❖

I remember one night at Don José's* when some tenor player from Cornell came up. His name was McGee. I never saw him before or since. And a lot of the guys—I forget exactly who—held the attitude that on tenor you have to sound like Prez. McGee played

---

*studio on West 49th Street between Broadway and 8th Avenue that players would rent for sessions.

like Bird on tenor. They said, "On alto it's all right to sound like Bird but not on tenor." That's how rigid *they* were.

❖ ❖

GERRY MULLIGAN   Jerome* was into that kind of—he was one of the New York . . . bad influence—making a bad atmosphere at that Prestige date.† 'Cause he was so busy to jump on something for being corny. And on that thing, Gail Madden had gotten the rhythm section together. And she had the thing really together. She was using maracas as a sizzle cymbal. And she had those guys playing very well together. But Jerome's attitude in particular just destroyed the whole atmosphere. And it's one of the things that for a long time after that put me off of doing anything in New York. 'Cause the New York guys were so rigid. And the terrible thing, man, that their orientation, the idea that an all-star band in this town, if you didn't play Count Basie's stocks, you were dead. They couldn't play my charts worth a damn. None of them. One of the proofs of it is when Elliot [Lawrence] finally recorded some of the charts that I wrote, long after I wrote the things and long after the band was really terrific. But he got a bunch of the New York guys together and, of course, this is partially unfair, because they did not have adequate rehearsal time, and Elliot never invited me to come rehearse the band. Those guys could have played the things, but left to their own devices, it just didn't really come out well. Anyway, that kind of atmosphere prevailed in this town. The dopers were terribly hip, and anything that didn't fit their particular standards . . .

And their particular junk group was a very destructive one. And a lot of really weird things happened. A lot of guys died during that period. These people just didn't have any kind of sense of responsibility to each other or for what they were doing.

But I think that the reason a lot of us got involved with heroin later—you got to remember that some of us were *very*, very young. And it's one thing when you're functioning and looking at the world through 18-year-old eyes,—to suddenly find yourself twenty-one, twenty-two,—and you've cut out a life for yourself which is more than you can handle. There's nothing in my background that ever supposed that I would be able to cope with living by myself in New York, on the music scene, in the jazz scene. I just wasn't tough enough for it. That plus just general pressures—*internal* emotional pressures, if you will.

Take for instance . . . there was nothing that had anything to do with the normal scene that would have been, might have had a better effect on my head. I avoided getting with girls that wanted to get married because the idea of marriage was just—*really* impossible. And yes, that's the kind of a thing a man needs and a young man can use to

---

*trumpeter Jerry Hurwitz, later known as Jerry Lloyd.
†1951 Mulligan recording.

help with a kind of stability. Of course it doesn't work. But, that's like all part of the social forces at work. It's just a miserable, bloody life.

I think I managed to not be an adult in just about every imaginable area.

❖ ❖

During this time many of the New York musicians were living at home with their parents, and that took a lot of pressure off them. It allowed them to avoid certain responsibilities that were part of being on one's own.

❖ ❖

GERRY MULLIGAN   The only times that I ever got out from under the pressure of living here is when I spent time at one of the guy's houses. I used to enjoy hanging out with Tiny Kahn for that reason. 'Cause we'd spend time in his neighborhood over in Brooklyn. And it was like another world. Just to be able to get away from it, even for a couple of days. So I think that accounted for a lot of the appeal of junk. And for me, I got into it when I was really spending a lot of time writing, too. Because of the pressures and because of the noise and the chaos of the town, it was possible for me to turn on and sit and write for eighteen hours at a stretch. I would do that—I did that for years. Then it finally got to a point where junk just wouldn't work for that. You can't do that to your body or your brain.

A lot of the physical reactions—I used to kind of marvel at that, how different people would react to it. Because, specially in the early years of music, man, I didn't nod at all. But it was the first physical flash and then into quite wide awake, straight ahead, never once "heaved." I knew people that not only when they first started using junk, but all the years that they used it, every time they turned on, they'd heave. Then I finally kicked and used junk for the last time. And any time I have anything to do with narcotics* now, I heave [chuckles]. Because my reaction to drugs is so different now. And also it'll put me right to sleep. But it didn't work like that then.

To make any generalization about junkies, or musicians, for that matter, is bound to lead to all kinds of inaccuracies. But I don't know that there's a simple statement to be made about the use of junk at that point. You know it's hard to remember. And I realize now when I read things, how totally unaware and away from the world my thoughts were. The Second World War was just over, and there was absolutely no thought, or concern, or awareness on the music scene that this was the case. The musicians coming back from the Army— that's great—but the world was in a really incredible social disorder. And the kinds of political forces that were being unleashed on the world were coming to their own particular time—now. It's kind of incredible to be so totally unaware. It's hard for people now, after the political

*for medical reasons.

turmoil of the '60s, and the awareness that people have, because of the kinds of shenanigans that governments are capable of, to understand why people weren't aware in the '40s and the '50s, and they don't realize that it just was never presented to the people.

ART PEPPER   All the guys that played the jazz chair in the bands started using because they'd figured that it would make them play better. With me, I didn't start using heroin for that reason. My reason was because my first wife stopped going on the road with me, and I was lonesome, and I was an alcoholic then, and I drank every night. The only time I stopped drinking was when I just fell out someplace. That's what I was, an alcoholic. I smoked pot, took pills, I did everything but I didn't shoot stuff. The reason I started shooting stuff was that loneliness, being on the road alone and the sex drive that I had and not being able to satisfy it without feeling a terrible guilt feeling.

I guess when you're young and starting out, it's an adventure, seeing new places, and then it just becomes a series of stops along the way, and grind, and very difficult living. Of course, when your wife was with you it made it a little different. But most people don't have their wives with them. But a lot of them weren't married either, so they'd think, "What chick can I ball in this town?" If I would go ball a chick, I would have to leave her immediately, and then I would strip my body and just scrub it to kinda wash the guilt away. I knew that once I used heroin that I'd be lost. I knew there was no question, but I didn't do it because I knew I'd play better. I did it only because I was lonely and had to do something. I couldn't get into drinking at the time. I went up to the room, and they had some stuff, and my roommate at the time, Shorty Rogers did everything in his power to talk me out of it, and he finally just left the room—he wouldn't be a part of it.

He was already into it, but he didn't want me to get into it. Because I told him many times if I ever did it I would be gone. And he knew that I would. He knew my personality, that I was a very addictive person. I didn't do things just half. I went all out. And he didn't want to be there to see it. He did everything in his power to stop it, and this chick just wouldn't let it stop. There were other people there, too. They couldn't care less—they were all musicians: well known, big-name people—and this chick was the singer with the big band. She didn't care about nothing except that she wanted for me to feel good, and she was a sex maniac, a nymphomaniac. So she started playing with me, and took me into the bathroom so she could give me "head" and put out some stuff and chop it up so that I could sniff it. She was only wanting for me to feel good. She was a free spirit. That was her only thing was to feel good, and I knew that I was gone, and I was dead once I did it, but I just was so "drug." I couldn't get a drink. I was so unhappy. And that same night I had gotten the highest praise in my career as a musician, big praise at the job. I played extra well and played in a big place. Everybody was praising me. But then the praise ended, the people were gone, and I was left alone at the bar at the Croydon Hotel. I was all alone, drinking, drink after drink, and then I was . . . and there was no more praise—it was gone—and I couldn't stand it any more. I had to have another drink. I couldn't face it. I was all alone. The person I loved wasn't with me. I couldn't stand it. And so even though I knew my life was going to be ended, I didn't even care. Nothing could be as bad as the way I felt like then.

« 8 »

End of an Era

As the decade came to a close, changes were taking place in the music and the way in which it was being presented. The big bands were in decline, and the emphasis was on the small groups. Charlie Parker recorded with Machito's Afro-Cuban orchestra. The fusion of Afro-Cuban music and jazz was a continuation of something Jelly Roll Morton had begun in New Orleans during jazz's earliest days. He called it "the Spanish Tinge" at the time. From then on, there were many attempts to use Latin American rhythm and music in jazz. Duke Ellington presented some of the most successful mixtures during the '30s. In the late '40s Dizzy Gillespie was the catalyst, utilizing rhythms and melodic material in his big band.

❖❖

CHICO O'FARRILL   I think mainly a person like Dizzy will always be looking for something new, something that would take him away from that straight-four type of rhythm. In other words, I think that's the point you can trace the search for—how you say—to reach a rhythmic approach because, let's face it, up to about bop, those swing-band rhythm sections were the dullest rhythm sections you can think of. There was really nothing from the point of view of rhythm there, and I think Latin music, especially what you call Afro-Cuban type rhythms, have rhythmic counterpoint that is so rich and probably goes hand in hand with the search for also more intricate rhythms that the boppers were after.

❖❖

It has always been said that Dizzy was hipped to Latin music by Mario Bauza when they were in Cab Calloway's band.

❖❖

CHICO O'FARRILL   Mario has told me stories that he and Dizzy were roommates when they were with Cab Calloway, and Dizzy, to a certain extent, was very much intrigued already by this rhythm. I guess he would ask Mario, "Hey, what about the conga? How do you do this?" Conga rhythm sounds like a Cuban rhythm.

❖❖

Bauza, who in the '40s was music director for the Machito orchestra, figured in Gillespie's hiring of conga player Chano Pozo. Dizzy had realized after his second band—the 1946 edition—became established that he needed some additional percussion.

❖❖

DIZZY GILLESPIE   I decided I wanted one of those guys who played those tom-tom things. I didn't know what they were called then. So I contacted Mario Bauza because we were friends from way back. Mario took me down to 111th Street where Chano was staying. We talked about what he had heard about my music, and without any deal or anything, he came right on and started playing with us right then.

CECIL PAYNE   Chano Pozo came in and changed the feeling—not the feeling but the rhythm pattern of that band, playing "Cubana Be." Dizzy was concentrating on the Latin time, the different rhythm patterns that Chano showed. Chano would be singing all the time at the back of the bus.

The valet, Scratch, was always trying to learn him how to speak English. But he would speak it very good when he got mad. When he got mad, he spoke it all right.

❖❖

Gillespie has talked about how Chano would play in one rhythm, sing in another, and dance in a third.

❖❖

DIZZY GILLESPIE   I never knew how he could do that. He really was *the* man. This was a great creative period in our history, and "Cubana Be, Cubana Bop" was one of our most adventurous pieces. Three people wrote that, not only that but three people wrote it as one person. George Russell wrote the introduction; I wrote the middle part; and Chano and I did that *montuno* thing. It was just perfect, and it's still right now.

❖❖

"Manteca," if not as ambitious a work, was a hit for Gillespie in the Afro-Cuban jazz idiom, and his big-band version of "Woody'n You" was titled "Algo Bueno." Although Parker was not into Afro-Cuban music like Dizzy, he did use a rhumba beat when he played "How High the Moon" (as opposed to the 4/4 he used on its variation, "Ornithology") and "Barbados," an original blues which Marshall Stearns, in his *Story of Jazz*, credits to Johnny Mandel rather than Parker. (Mandel says this is incorrect. He may have written an arrangement of "Barbados" but, indeed, it is Parker's melody.)

On December 21, 1950, Bird was an unplanned part of Machito's recording of Chico O'Farrill's "Afro Cuban Jazz Suite." He had already recorded "No Noise," "Mango Mangue," and "Okiedoke"* with Machito in late 1948 and early 1949.

❖❖

CHICO O'FARRILL Machito was recording at the time with Norman [Granz], and for some reason or another, Norman asked me to write something for Machito then. It was something that was on the Mercury label called "Gone City"—it was actually in the spirit of "Things to Come" in the Afro-Cuban style for the Machito band. And Norman liked it so much that he commissioned me to write an extended piece of music featuring Machito's Orchestra. We had Buddy Rich, Bird, and Flip Phillips. It was a big thrill for me, naturally. I remember that the Machito band was a very rough band, but still the feeling was so good, and you didn't mind some of the wrong notes. Also, the original soloist was supposed to be Harry Edison, and "Sweets" walked into the studio, and we went through the first movement and he tried to play the solos, but it was a medium completely alien to his style, and he, himself, said, "Look, this is not for me." So that's when Norman said, "Call Bird." Somebody called Bird, and he came over to the studio an hour later, and he said, "Let me hear—where do I come in, here? Oh, I see." Bird, first take perfect. Just like that. You know he really was amazing.

❖❖

This wasn't the first time Bird had done something like that. In the summer of 1949 he recorded a Neal Hefti composition with an orchestra, including strings, under the direction of Hefti for Norman Granz's special album *The Jazz Scene*.

❖❖

NORMAN GRANZ "Repetition" was originally written with no thought of a soloist but, as so often happens on a jazz date, Hefti included Charlie Parker at the last minute. Parker actually plays on top of the original arrangement; that it jells as well as it does is a tribute both to the flexible arrangement of Hefti and the inventive genius of Parker to adapt himself to any musical surrounding.

❖❖

This session led Parker into the much debated *Bird with Strings*. Although some argued that Parker was pushed into playing with strings, it was something that he wanted and welcomed. Gillespie had recorded with strings in Hollywood in 1946, but the Jerome Kern estate blocked the issue of "Who," "The Way You Look Tonight," "Why Do I Love You," and "All the Things You Are." (They became available on *Dizzy's Delight*—Phoenix LP-4—in 1980.) However, Parker was aware of them and shared, with many jazz-

*should have read "Okiedokie," one of Bird's expressions.

men, the feeling that such a backdrop would give his work a certain cachet. Through Granz, oboeist Mitch Miller became involved.

❖❖

MITCH MILLER   I was then starting in the record business—it was either '48 or '49—and Norman Granz had his "Jazz at the Philharmonic" which was released by Mercury at the time. And Norman would tape his concerts, and he had the idea of doing Charlie Parker with strings. And never having recorded strings, he asked if I would produce it for him. He would be there, but I would produce it. I said, "Sure. I love Charlie Parker's playing."

We got the musicians in New York. And got Jimmy Carroll, who had done a lot of arranging for me, to do the arrangements. We were going to make the whole album in one day—ten to one, two to five, and seven to ten, with breaks. So we didn't go overtime, we had three sessions. In this era of a year to make an album—six months to a year—it just doesn't make sense to me. I don't know what these people are doing with all their time.

But we were rehearsing and balancing up at the Reeves Studio, and everything was going beautifully, and Charlie walked in, and he heard this music, and he said, "Man, that's too much."

And everyone was delighted, and he walked out of the room, and we thought maybe he's going to the bathroom, take his coat off, whatever. And he just walked out. And anyone who knows Norman, with the eyebrows and his pacing, he was going crazy, pacing up and down. Nobody could find Charlie Parker.

In the meantime we had the musicians hired for the three sessions. We continued to rehearse because all twelve pieces were arranged, and we finished the first session; we went into the second; still no Parker. Finally Norman thought let's salvage some of the money, try to get "Clair De Lune," something that would fit this combination we had 'cause we did have a harp. Well we finally gave up on that, and when we had the whole thing balanced we said we could do nothing but dismiss the musicians and hopefully find Charlie Parker sometime.

I don't know how many days afterwards—it wasn't more than a week I don't think—Norman caught up with Parker, and it turned out that he had been so overwhelmed by the sound that he felt he couldn't work with it. So Norman, out of a clear sky, says, "Why don't you play with him?"

So I said, "I can't improvise, but if they'll sketch out outlines for me, I'll be happy to do it."

They gave me some lead parts, and when Parker came back, since we had the balance, and we had a fabulous engineer—Bob Fine—and don't forget this was before tape so there's no editing, no nothing— the performance was it. And we came in and did all twelve sides— there were maybe eight on the album, but there were twelve sides then—in three or four hours. The whole album. There was nothing more than two takes. Most of it was one take. And, for me, that is the best Charlie Parker I ever heard.

❖❖

A highly subjective opinion, to be sure (and the reasons for Bird's defection could have easily been other than a flight from the "overwhelming sound") but, in the face of many who decried the "commercial" aspects of *Bird with Strings,* Parker played beautifully, despite the pedestrian arrangements—and, on "Just Friends," he produced a masterpiece.

In the late '40s, Parker also began to tour with Granz's "Jazz at the Philharmonic" troupe. He also maintained his quintet.

❖❖

AL LEVITT   Sometime around 1950 or 1951, Charlie Parker was hired to play with his quintet at Cafe Society Downtown. In his group were Kenny Dorham, trumpet; Al Haig, piano; Tommy Potter, bass; and Roy Haynes, drums. This club had a policy of having a quartet or quintet as the house band, whose function was to play for dancing, do a feature number as a show opener and to accompany the attractions when necessary.

I used to go there often as Cliff Jackson, the intermission pianist, would let me play with him on his sets. I was there on Bird's opening night, when the star attraction of the show was the Art Tatum trio, with Slam Stewart and Everett Barksdale.

It was obvious that Bird wasn't too happy about playing for the dancing. I overheard Roy Haynes and Kenny Dorham telling him to be cool, as they were only booked for two weeks, but if things went well they could be held over.

When the show started, Bird and Kenny Dorham came to the center of the floor, and Bird announced that they were going to play one of the tunes from his recently recorded album, *Bird With Strings,* which he hoped the audience would enjoy equally as well without strings. Then they would play "Just Friends" or "I Didn't Know What Time It Was," or one of the other standards from the record.

When Art Tatum came on, the trio opened with Tatum's famous version of "Tea For Two." Bird was standing off stage with a big smile on his face, obviously enjoying what he was hearing. Before you knew it, Bird picked up his horn, waited until the end of a chorus, then started playing and walking to the center of the stage at the same time. Art Tatum was shocked for a split second and then angrily said, "No, no, no, no." Bird looked a little disappointed, stopped playing, turned around and walked off stage. After the show, the quintet was supposed to play for dancing. Bird pulled up a chair and sat right in the middle of the dance floor and played all the bebop you wanted to hear. The audience loved it, especially all the musicians who had come to check out the scene. The quintet played a storm, it was great, but

needless to say, the management didn't feel the same way, and of course
the group only stayed for the original two-week contract.

❖❖

As the '50s continued, Parker played less with a regular group.
He did several tours, including one with Stan Kenton's orchestra
called "A Festival of Modern American Jazz," in which he replaced an ailing Stan Getz and was featured in front of Kenton's
behemoth.

Another all-star package toured on the West Coast.

❖❖

JIMMY ROWLES   I took this job because Charlie Parker was going to be there.
It only paid one-hundred dollars a week, and we had to ride in a bus,
and they had Dave Brubeck's quartet—and Shelly [Manne], Chet Baker,
and Carson Smith. Charlie Parker is supposed to show up in Olympia,
Washington. So we go all the way up the coast, riding in the bus. I
didn't know Dave Brubeck's outfit. I didn't even get acquainted with
Paul Desmond on that trip—now he's one of my best friends. We were
all saying, "He'll never make it." We were playing this job in Olympia,
and Bird showed up at about twelve o'clock at night. Now we go over
the border into Canada, and we played Vancouver or some place like
that. We're coming back from Canada, and we get to the border. We've
got to go through the mountains, and Bird is *completely* out of it. He's
laying in the back with his mouth wide open. We go through the whole
thing of getting through the border with this Mountie, and finally he
says, "That takes care of everybody but Parker. Where's Parker?" Well
this cat says, "He's not feeling well. I'll take care of that for him. He's
in the bus." The Mountie said, "Nope, gotta have Parker in here." He
said, "I can't move him." The Mountie said, "I'll get him." So he goes
out to the bus, and here he comes—Bird. Bird is, like, mad. He starts
asking Bird questions. He's got the pencil and paper. He says, "Your
age?" Bird is lying like hell, "25" or something like that. All of the
answers were wrong.

All of a sudden, right in the middle of the whole thing, Bird looks
behind him—cigarette papers and some tobacco. He says, "Give me
that." Bird takes one paper out, lays it down, takes the other side and
takes the sack and throws a bunch of it in there and closes up the bag
and goes like this—zip—one movement and he had a Camel. And then
he went like this—"Match." We fell out. It was beautiful.

❖❖

In the last years of his life Parker did not have a regular working
band. He would travel to cities as a single, picking up rhythm sections. Sometimes, as in Chicago, he would get a Junior Mance;
other times, as in Rochester, Walter Bishop had to come up from
New York to rescue him from a mediocrity.

It was during this time that Bird was living at 151 Avenue B
and becoming a presence on the scene in Greenwich Village. The

Sunday sessions at the Open Door, begun by Bob Reisner, became instantly legendary. Later, there was other, even more informal jamming, after Bird had split from home and was living at 4 Barrow Street with Ahmed Basheer and artist Harvey Cropper.

❖❖

AL LEVITT   Around that time there was a club in Greenwich Village called Arthur's Tavern on Grove Street. I think it still exists. Whenever I was free, I would go there and play. Bird was living with some friends in the neighborhood, and at the time he didn't even have a horn. He started hanging out there at night, as Jinx*, the pianist, was also a friend of his.

Pretty soon, different saxophone players would also come in to play, and when they finished their solos, Bird would borrow their horn and play too. This got to be a regular thing and lasted for nearly two months. I went there to play practically every night just to have the opportunity to play with Charlie Parker. During this whole time, the only words ever spoken between us was, one night during one of his solos, he turned around to me and in between phrases said, "I hear you, baby," and I answered, "Thanks."

He would play on whatever reed instrument anyone brought in. Jackie McLean sometimes came in, and they would both play Jackie's alto, or Brew Moore's tenor, or Larry Rivers' C melody or baritone sax, or Sol Yaged's clarinet. Bird just played on whatever reed instrument someone handed him.

Sometimes when there was no one there with a saxophone, Phil Woods, who was working across the street, playing for the strip show at the Nut Club with Jon Eardley [trumpet], George Syran [piano] and Nick Stabulas[drums], would come over with his alto during his intermission, and they would both play on Phil's alto.

A short time later, Bird was stuck for money to pay a taxi fare. He went into the Cafe Bohemia, which was just a neighborhood bar across the street from his small apartment, and told the proprieter that for a twenty-dollar loan to pay the taxi he would come in the next night with some musicians and play for free—which he did. The word spread around the streets that Bird was playing there, and soon the club was jammed. This gave the owner the idea to turn his bar into a jazz club, and for several years it was one of the most successful in New York.

❖❖

At the end of the summer of 1954 Parker was once again booked into Birdland with the strings but argued with his band, fired them and left the club. He attempted suicide, and on September 1 was admitted to Bellevue Hospital.

Discharged in his own custody on October 15, he went back to

---

*Jinx Jingles, a.k.a. Warwick Brown.

live with his wife, Chan, in New Hope, Pennsylvania, and showed up, looking fit, to play a concert for Reisner at Town Hall on the 30th of the month.

Bird played brilliantly that night. All in the audience were extremely regretful when the stagehands rang the curtain down as he was still blowing. The evening had started behind schedule, and union regulations do not sit still for spontaneous art.

Bird's last public appearance at Birdland on March 4, 1955, ended with an unstable Bud Powell causing Parker to leave the bandstand. When Powell himself walked off the stage, Parker took the microphone and called the pianist's name repeatedly. Then he left the club. Eight days later Bird was dead.

The decline of the big bands had started during the late '40s. By 1950 Dizzy Gillespie and Count Basie were heading small groups. Basie reorganized late in 1951, and Gillespie was able to lead a large orchestra in the 1956–1958 period which included two State Department-sponsored tours; but, basically, the big traveling bands which had produced so many talented players and new leaders, were finished as a major force. Some veterans of the big-band wars did try with fresh orchestras. For instance, Neal Hefti founded one in 1952.

How did Hefti feel about bebop and its whole influence on the music that followed? It was such a pervasive presence from the time that Parker and Gillespie burst upon the scene. All young musicians became involved in it, whether they were with a jazz band or a "Mickey Mouse" territory outfit.

❖ ❖

NEAL HEFTI   Well, it did become the influence. That was very true. That influence didn't last very long though. As a matter of fact, it was sort of a naughty word in the industry. You can do jazz sometimes if you don't call it that. If you want to call it rock 'n roll or country and western or whatever. Whatever is big today. If you want to call it that, you could do it. But bebop had a very, very bad—it shocked the music business. They didn't even want to see it go that way. They would put Dizzy and Charlie Parker down and anyone who sort of picked up on this kind of thing.

You see, bebop didn't last long enough for them to make any loot out of it, and this was a day when music publishers were owned by businessmen rather than musical people. I started my own music publishing company because the publisher that owned the music wouldn't print it. Thought it was valueless to print an instrumental. I remember the very first record I made was "Coral Reef" with my band. It was a very big seller. It didn't sell a million, although in my press releases I say it did. It sold about 400,000 singles.

You heard it all over. Disc jockeys used it for themes. Well, Billy May was starting a band, and he wanted a lead sheet of it, so I went up to the publisher, Jack Bregman, and I asked him if he was going to print anything with "Coral Reef" and he said, "Well, it's an instrumental. We generally don't print instrumentals." I said, "Well, would you go for an onion skin at least." Billy May was asking for it; Ralph Flanagan asked for it; Ralph Marterie: some of the bands that were sprouting up in those days, they wanted it. And we all thought, "If you play 'Coral Reef,' I'll play, whatever." And we could sort of, maybe, between the four of us, instigate some interest in bands. Well, he wasn't going for it. So I had to pay for my own onion skin to give these guys copies. So after that I started keeping my own copyrights.

There's a clause in the AGAC contract that says they either have to print, within a certain amount of time, or give you $200 and not print, or give you your copyright back. But you can cross that clause out, too, when you're signing these contracts. For instance, if you're gonna do a movie score, who's ever gonna print all of that stuff? They don't know whether they can or not. So they might cross that clause out. Well on my contract with those guys, it was crossed out. I didn't even understand contracts. So what I was trying to say, music publishers in those days, they would never think of taking stuff like Dizzy Gillespie music or Charlie Parker music and publishing it so that it looked like a piece of music. They might write it down in pencil and xerox it or put it out sort of like an underground publication, but they would really never print it as a piece of work, as a piece of music. So this was another reason that a lot of music in that era maybe really didn't get known the way that music later on became known. When writers started forming their own publishing companies, they wanted to see things printed, put out, look right, in this nature.

Of course the publishers associated it with everything that wasn't selling, too. So there was a financial downer to it. They associated that, and the people who were following that, as nonsaleable items. To them it looked like creeps with the glasses and the goatees and berets, standing like an "S," and it was too much for them to take all at once. They were still recovering from the war, and then there was a period of depression, too.

And that was another reason that people couldn't spend the money of those things. A lot of people were getting married now with money who weren't going to hear Dizzy Gillespie or Woody Herman or whoever, Neal Hefti, who were going to buy the refrigerator and the house. The Levittowns and these kind of things were selling, and hard goods were coming in and also, if you remember, there was a 20 percent tax if there was dancing or singing. That helped kill those kind of businesses, but it sort of helped little instrumental groups 'cause those are the only ones, if they were playing up there, fine, if they weren't singing or dancing. That was a big one. That was a biggie. Also the musicians' union really didn't like traveling bands all that much, 'cause they looked at that, the traveling band, as somebody who took jobs away from their local musicians. And so there was always that little feeling. Then, too, for instance, the New York Paramount, they made some kind of thing that only New York bands could play that place. All 802 [The New York musicians' labor local] played that place. Then they sort of modified it. Well, if we have all 802, we can't use Duke Ellington, we can't use—they say all right, traveling bands . . .

A lot of those guys never joined 802. You'd think they were, but to join the union, you had to be out of work for six months. That's not true anymore, at least it's not practiced. But in those days, I had to go to New York and stay six months without taking a steady job. I couldn't play in a band and get my card. And the same thing with Los Angeles. So they modified it. Well, all right, six months 802, six months traveling. But these were all little items.

I know that when I went out on the road with my band and we had records and DJs wanted to interview me, I had to be very careful, because I could end up with a $500 fine if I did an interview on a station that didn't have a staff orchestra or some sort. Maybe even a staff organist. And so the jockeys would get very salty and say, "Well, my God, Patti Page was here last week, and she couldn't have been nicer."

Patti Page doesn't belong to the A.F. of M., so there was a lot of this going on. So when I added all this up and I wasn't making any money, got two little kids, I decided to forget about it, very frankly.

❖❖

It seems as if the musicians' union is one of the unions that did more to hamper its members than help them.

❖❖

NEAL HEFTI   Well, it's a debatable subject. But you'll get some people who will agree with you. I'm inclined to agree. But I think I can't blame the musicians' union, I have to blame the musician, because the musician tells the musicians' union what to do, and the musician who may have spent five years on the road with a good band, if he's gonna settle down in Boston, doesn't want that same good band to play in Boston anymore. He becomes a different guy when he gets off the road. He says, "No, I don't want that band here. I don't want them to play the lush job. I don't care if they play one night for the public, but I don't want them to play the theater. I want to play the theater. I don't want them to play the country clubs. I'll play the country clubs. I don't want them to play the hotel. I'll play that. They can play one night of promotions only." And they will go to the musicians' union and say, "Do something. Do something or we won't vote for you." That's really what it comes to.

So all these things tended to happen all at once. And with the postwar depression and the 20 percent tax for singing and dancing, and the record companies didn't want to mess around with bands either very much. It was an oddity if you got yourself a record contract. I was an oddity, so was Billy May. As a matter of fact, it turned out that most of us who got record contracts were writers and they used us for other people, for other purposes on the label.

Practically every band that I ever worked with, at one time right after the war, tried to cut down to a small group. 'Cause I wrote for them, and I know. Basie did. Stan Kenton had a small group. At the Sherman Hotel in Chicago. I wrote my first arrangement for him for his nine-piece band on "How High the Moon" for June Christy, which I later expanded for his 18-piece band that he recorded for Capitol. That was the first one I wrote for him. About '46, '47, someplace like that.

Woody Herman had a six-piece band. I wrote for him when I went down to Cuba, and I tried to do it a little later. Tommy Dorsey took two bands and made one out of them. Jimmy Dorsey had to break up, and Tommy Dorsey had to make two bands into one. He had to form his own booking agency and buy his own bus to beat prices. I don't know if Harry James ever came down. He might have been one of the few who didn't.

Then you couldn't get the record companies—they weren't interested in recording bands because they knew that they couldn't go out and promote them. They knew that that band wasn't available, only a myth was available. So they went on to singers. And, also, there was another law passed, before I started my band, that a manager could only take 5 percent. So managers could only take 5 percent legally of a musician's income, so they were gonna go where they could get 20, 25 percent. The same managers that were gung-ho for bands, went right into singers. As a matter of fact, William Morris dropped their whole band department way before anybody else did. I think they saw the handwriting on the wall first, that financially the rug was taken out from underneath and only diehards would sustain.

❖❖

Then, of course, the singers became very popular in that period of the recording ban in 1943, when they would make records with a cappella choruses.

❖❖

NEAL HEFTI   A cappella or harmonicas, because some unions wouldn't take harmonica players. They were very quick to take them a little later, but they all had their problems. I know that if I were a big official at A.F. of M., I wouldn't know what to do because records were now replacing bands. A place that used to have a three or four-piece band now had a juke box. I learned how to play in clubs in Omaha. Go down and play in a place that had piano, drum and sax where you'd feed the kitty. I'd come and sit in and jam. Those places all turned to juke boxes later on, so it was a problem.

❖❖

Along with the decline of the bands there were new stylistic elements coming into the music in the late '40s and early '50s, pointing a new direction for the first half of the new decade. That was "cool jazz" fueled, nay Freoned, by the influence of Lester Young; the Miles Davis Nonet, and Lennie Tristano.

❖❖

GERRY MULLIGAN   As far as the "birth of the cool" is concerned, I think Lennie is much more responsible than the Miles dates. It's hard to say it's unemotional, because it's not exactly that, but there was a coolness about his whole approach in terms of the dynamic level.

LENNY POPKIN   For art to mean something it has to have spontaneity and feeling. I always had heard that, but I never learned that from any-body. Any book that I read about it always talked about it in terms of technique. Analyzed it in a very intellectual way. It didn't tell you any-thing about creating it. The teachers I dealt with were a very unhappy group of people. Lennie was the only teacher I have ever heard of—besides those who have become associated with him—that *started* with feeling.

❖❖

While Tristano's music could not be termed bebop as such, it cer-tainly was informed by it. He came from the same lineage and was shaped by several of bop's most important players.

❖❖

LENNIE TRISTANO   I'm not a historian. I'm not a sociologist. But I've been into jazz from 1929. The black people were doing their shit, whatever it was. The people who tried to analyze it, analyzed it wrong.

LENNY POPKIN   Lennie's method was to have his students sing the solos of Louis, Roy, Bird, Fats [Navarro], Bud, Prez, Billie, and Charlie Chris-tian. He based his approach on having you learn to improvise and how to express feeling spontaneously.

JIMMY ROWLES   I remember the first time I ever saw Tristano in Chicago, with Woody's band. He brought in an arrangement, and we ran this thing down. I can't remember the name of it. Woody never played it. He didn't like it. Lennie gave it to Woody, and I remember Sonny Berman sort of complained about something, the passage that he had to play that he thought was uncomfortable. And this guy, I had never heard of him before in my life. And we're playing this real weird piece of music he'd given us—a jump tune. Sonny said, "I can't make that thing. Anything I can do about it?"

"Well," Tristano said, "I wrote it down. I heard Sonny Berman play it on a solo on the radio one night." He was talking to Sonny Berman. He didn't know who he was talking to. Sonny just looked at him.

❖❖

Considering Tristano's knowledge and formidable ear it is possi-ble he was pulling a few legs. Before he left for New York in 1946, he stirred up a few brains. One of his star pupils was a young alto man.

❖❖

LEE KONITZ He didn't particularly care much for Dizzy, as I recall. He loved Bird. He never liked Monk. You know that. He was still talking about that in his 50s, talking about Monk being a lousy piano player.

At that time I remember Lennie saying that his ambition was to play tenor as good as Chu Berry. I heard him play tenor, incidentally, he was giving Emmett Carls a tenor lesson and playing Prez's chorus on "You Can Depend On Me" for him.

❖❖

Many of today's avant garde have a certain type of outlook. They say that bebop was the end of an era, while others looked at it as also a beginning—perhaps it was both—meaning the extension of a particular kind of harmonic music to its end point; then you got on to the modal, into the free form and "noise element" playing. Because, at that time, people saw it as the beginning of something else. They didn't see the evolution because they were too close to it, perhaps.

❖❖

LEE KONITZ I think that, in a way, Tristano might have been the end of that, but it was explored by more people than we know about, I think, but maybe in some—I mean there are reasons for that. In many respects that music wasn't as complete as the music that preceded it—in terms of being a definitive kind of expression, still transitory in some way. There was something about *all* of the music that preceded Tristano's music that was fixed, starting with Louis Armstrong, in some way. So that it had all of the powers that that kind of fix—if that's the word—and you could generally hear this same thing. Just play more confidently when you know what you're playing.

❖❖

Unlike rock, which although it drew its roots from black music [i.e. the British groups emulating the black bluesmen] ended up with a white audience, jazz has been an instrument of racial understanding.

❖❖

SONNY ROLLINS Jazz has always been a music of integration. In other words, there were definitely lines where blacks would be and where whites would begin to mix a little bit. I mean, jazz was not just a music; it was a social force in this country, and it was talking about freedom and people enjoying things for what they are and not having to worry about whether they were supposed to be white, black, and all this stuff. Jazz has always been the music that had this kind of spirit. Now I believe for that reason, the people that would push jazz have *not* pushed jazz because that's what jazz means. A lot of times, jazz means no barriers.

❖❖

Long before sports broke down its racial walls, jazz was bringing people together on both sides of the bandstand. 52nd Street, for all its shortcomings, was a place in which black and white musicians could interact in a way that led to natural bonds of friendship. The audience, or at least part of it, took a cue from this, leading to an unpretentious flow of social intercourse.

The new music definitely was indicative of a change in society as well as a change in the music. It was an expression of a new period, and a new era for black people in American society.

❖❖

BILLY TAYLOR   52nd Street definitely. It was a change because many black musicians, unless they were headliners, never worked 52nd Street, and when Dizzy and some of the other non-headliners for those days began—Ben Webster was not a headliner nor Sid Catlett or even Hawk, who was perhaps one of the best known. The Street really came alive if Billie Holiday or Art Tatum were there; on other occasions when they had the young Erroll Garner. The turnabout had been that 52nd Street had generally been a place where the guys who did studio, did other kinds of work, were pretty much the guys that played on the Street until things began to change during the war. Then during the war the black musicians began to play on 52nd Street, and by the time I got to New York the majority of people who supported the Street were blacks who were coming downtown in that regard to a midtown place because this was fun, and it was not the kinds of problems you had in some other places. If a black couple decided to go to the Blue Angel or one of the East Side clubs they may not feel as comfortable as in other places.

❖❖

And yet they did run into racial problems, especially with servicemen from the South. But it did open up more communication between blacks and whites.

❖❖

BILLY TAYLOR   On many levels. I've talked to a lot of people who came into jazz with the 52nd Street thing, and for them it has always been very democratic and the kind of music and social setting that really brought to the consciousness of a lot of people the contributions of the people who were from different backgrounds. Because it's kind of stupid to go to a club and see Zoot Sims playing with Sid Catlett and say that he plays okay for a white guy. That's ridiculous. It became apparent that there were guys who were just tremendous players on whatever instrument, and it wasn't just that the stamp of approval was put on them by Dizzy Gillespie or whoever. They were there because they could play. And they could do the job perhaps better than anybody else around for that particular occasion. I mean Al Haig and Zoot and Stan Getz and a whole bunch of other guys that were—Shelly

Manne was in the Coast Guard, and he would come in, and Sid [Catlett] would say, "Hey man, come on play." Well, they didn't invite a whole lot of servicemen up to play. You better believe that. And for this guy to come around and be asked to play was, you know, he could play. And there were many other guys like that.

SHELLY MANNE   Most of the incidents I remember involve Ben Webster. 'Cause when I was on 52nd Street I was twenty, twenty-one, and I looked like I was fifteen. The musicians had a strong camaraderie— black, white, it didn't matter—and Ben used to really take care of me. I mean he was almost like, when I was on the Street, a guardian. You know if somebody offered me a drink at the White Rose, he'd get mad. "He doesn't drink. Don't give him anything to drink. Or anything like that." But during that time, with a lot of servicemen in town and everything, there were some bad incidents. One night Ben walked right through the whole Onyx Club, directly to the back door, "do not pass GO." I mean knocking over tables to get at somebody who was bugging his piano player, Argonne Thornton. And Ben picked him up by the scruff of his neck and just held him off the ground while he talked to Argonne, and the guy started getting panicked because Ben was as strong as a bull in those days.

I just came back [from overseas in the Coast Guard] and the first place I headed was the Street to play. I was playing in my uniform when the Shore Patrol came in and it so happened that in the club that night was Big Sid, Al McKibbon, and Ben Webster, and I was sitting in with them. When the Shore Patrol took me off the stand, took me out, these three guys came and it must have looked like the "Fearsome Foursome" on the Rams. For those days—they make them bigger now—in those days they were big guys. And they were just making—they were protecting me. And when the Shore Patrol took me down to the guy I said, "Well, I just got back. I've been overseas for a year." And he bawled out the Shore Patrol and told them let me go back and play, but they wouldn't. It was a funny scene when those three guys came out to protect me.

It was after I moved out here to California that the strain started to happen. I think it was that blacks found new awareness of their freedom and their rights and everything, which created a very militant time. And, in fact, in some ways, it is still going on, which is rightfully so.

❖❖

It was understandable, but a lot of the white musicians didn't feel they were part of the white public that was harassing black people. And so they were hurt by this.

❖❖

SHELLY MANNE   When I started playing in New York, the first guy to ask me to sit in, or treat me good, was Leslie Millington, who used to be with Pete Brown's band. He later became a New York cop. And Arthur Herbert was a good friend of mine. He was really good to me. Arthur Herbert was the first guy in New York, when he was with Pete Brown's band, to say to me when I was sitting in the back of the old Kelly's Stable there every night. "Say, what do you do?" I said, "I'll probably be a drummer." He said, "C'mon, kid, play." There was nobody in the joint. And every night I'd go in, he'd ask me to play after that. And I'd play with Kenny Watts and his Kilowatts. That's where I got my first break. Ray McKinley heard me with that band and said, "Hey, kid, you wanta join a big band that's forming?" I said, "Yeah." And it was Bobby Byrne's band. But it was all through that association that those things happened.

And there was a one-arm trumpet player with Pete Brown. What the hell was his name? But these were the guys I hung out with all the time. In fact, we had a rhythm section in New York. We used to go around and play together all the time. It was with Eddie Heywood, John Simmons, and myself. Used to go to sessions and play. And it was never any thought about that kind of militant black/white scene. That was outside the music perimeter. I mean the music was here, that was something else. But then more and more guys became musicians. It was a lot of musicians that didn't know each other. It used to be all the musicians knew each other. At that time in New York anyway. And then more people got into jazz, and there was more a fight for jobs. It sets up almost a jealousy thing. Not just jealousy but a rightfully so, "Why isn't he hiring me? Or "Why is he hiring him?" And it started to become abrasive. There was a period—I guess it was the middle '50s—where Joe Gordon was on my band, and I remember going to some town and a bunch of very hip black cats came up and said to him, "What do you want to play with this band for?" And they gave him that kind of a time, and Joe was really upset about it. He came to me and told me. He was really upset.

❖❖

There are two sides of the coin. The same kind of people were saying, "Why is Sonny Rollins hiring Jim Hall?"

❖❖

SHELLY MANNE   Exactly. It was a very abrasive time, and I understood, and I'm sure most jazz musicians did understand. I remember it created a furor when Cannonball [Adderley] hired Victor Feldman.

❖❖

Frankie Socolow, like Manne, started out in jazz as a teenager who early on became involved in playing with older, established black musicians.

❖❖

FRANKIE SOCOLOW   I played a number of times with Monk up in Harlem. I was in high school at the time, and I used to go up there and come home about six in the morning and go to school. I used to walk around

Harlem at three or four in the morning with my horn. I used to get on the subway and go home. Because I wasn't even driving. And I was never frightened in any way. They saw you were a young musician coming up to play. Nobody would bother you. First of all, the feeling of hostility wasn't there. If it was there I certainly didn't feel it. It was a different time. After the war it started to change. Every war brings an end to an era. I'm not saying it ended that abruptly, but there were indications.

❖❖

52nd Street did bring everyone together, and when that ended it took away a certain focal point of the music. Then again, there have always been instances of black musicians creating a kind of music and white groups commercializing that music and making money off of it, and so there was hostility and bitterness.

❖❖

FRANKIE SOCOLOW   I'm sure there was. But then there were other guys that didn't feel that way. Guys like Diz and Bird. I remember when I was with Raeburn's band. We were at the Hotel New Yorker, and we used to have rehearsals every, let's say, Thursday night after the job. We'd start at about 2:30 in the morning and go to about six or so, five, whatever. Diz and Bird used to come down all the time and hear the band rehearse, and we got to be most friendly. And they used to openly compliment who they thought was good. Great people.

There's really no room for bullshit, When that music—I mean what did that music have to say? If a white guy played good jazz, actually it would be with a black feeling, 'cause the white guy that played with an authentic jazz feeling was playing black music.

ALLEN EAGER   I worked for over a year with Tadd Dameron at the Royal Roost. I was the only white guy in the band. Not because I was a token white, it was because they liked me, and I wasn't even up to them harmonically, but as far as the feeling and the swing goes . . .

RED RODNEY   The blacks have always been the forefront of jazz. They've always been the greatest on each respective instrument. But as far as the scene with the blacks and whites, when I first got in, there was hardly any ill will. I don't remember any. The attitude was just great. The camaraderie was wonderful. And as far as the white jazz musician, this was the one area in American life where there was honestly and sincerely no prejudice whatsoever. Nothing. We lived together. Ate together. Thought together. Felt together. And it was really the only area in American life where this happened. And then the black revolution came in, and with the black revolution the same black musicians understandably gave vent to their feelings and became very hostile, and they included the white jazz musicians with every other part of American life. This was unfair. The white jazz musician did not deserve this. And most of us understood it, but we were hurt by it.

With Miles Davis, I never knew how to take him. One day he'd be hugging and kissing me, and the next day I was whitey. But there are a lot of others I felt this with. It started in the middle '50s. And it really drove me away from jazz, because in that period, I went back to Philadelphia, and I had an office, society music, and made a lot of money with it. It was no jazz at all. It was bad music and good money, and every time I looked, I'd go down to see some old friends that would come to town in Philadelphia—Pep's and this and that—especially the black ones, I'd get a lot of static, ill will, and I just didn't feel there was the same feeling of camaraderie any longer. It's come back now though. The people I came up with, like those I felt hostility from and vibes from so to speak. Now I feel good vibes. So hopefully we're coming around.

❖❖

Los Angeles didn't present the same atmosphere for racial exchange as did New York, but the musicians who cared about the music found a way, and entrepreneurs such as Norman Granz helped in this direction.

❖❖

BARNEY KESSEL   I'd just gotten active playing in L.A. I just went to a lot of jam sessions. I would go because there were no guitar players that were making the jam sessions. Norman Granz really wanted Oscar Moore all the time, because Nat Cole used to work a lot of these jam sessions. He wanted Oscar because Oscar was already known and worked so well with Nat, but Oscar didn't want to go to these jam sessions. He did not attend them nor did he play them. He just wanted his free time. I was playing around town, and Norman asked me to play, so I began to play. Years ago I was playing in black clubs in L.A. with Nat Cole, J. C. Heard, Shad Collins, Al Killian, and then, later, many, many times played with people like Sonny Criss, Teddy Edwards, Wardell Gray. We'd be playing every night. Zoot Sims was there—Zoot and I, at one time, were on the scene playing all the time and most of the musicians were black. Jimmy Rowles was right there, too. There was a feeling of not only acceptance, but where you really felt they looked at you as an equal and that you had something to say.

❖❖

In *Jammin' the Blues*, issued in 1944, Kessel was the man in the background for racial reasons.

❖❖

BARNEY KESSEL   Norman asked me to be part of that and I was and we got into some problems because Warner Brothers, at that time, thought there would be a great problem in distributing that picture in the South, and not only would people boycott it but also the feature picture that would be shown with it—this picture was a short—they went into all sorts of things. They went into having me in the shadows. They did get to a point where we all—now it seems ridiculous—but we finally thought that the big, big compromise, which today would be out of the question, that they stain my hands with berry juice. I recall one time there is a picture of Lester Young and I sitting next to each other on the set, it's around somewhere—I think it appeared in a national magazine once—he was so white-skinned and he was sitting under a light, and I'm in the shadows, and he looked so much lighter than me. I said about Lester to all the other musicians, "I don't know if he should be here with us."

❖❖

Hollywood had other devices that it employed in order to avoid offending bigots. When the Count Basie small group of 1950 filmed one of those "band shorts" that were common fare in the movie theaters then, Buddy DeFranco was playing, but Marshal Royal was on screen—for Southern consumption.

This kind of thinking spilled over even into album-cover design.

❖❖

NEAL HEFTI   When *Basie Plays Hefti* came out, when he and I were in the baseball uniforms? We didn't think about it at the time but that was a no-no in certain sections.

❖❖

Even more controversial was the Pacific Jazz cover for *Countin' Five in Sweden* by Joe Newman. The trumpeter was pictured sitting with his wife-to-be, Rigmor, a Swedish woman. The second printing dropped this picture after a black record reviewer noted that the album wouldn't be sold in Mississippi.

When Howard McGhee was married to a white woman, he felt the results of these attitudes more directly from the Los Angeles Police Department, who knew he was a musician in the public eye.

❖❖

HOWARD MC GHEE   They beat the shit out of her—cop Grady, he tried to push her face into the ceiling, scar her up. They didn't like mixed colors.

Me an' my ol' lady, we went to a movie one night, and they came into the movie and took us down to the police station. They were picking up all the blondes. That's what they said. I said, "All blondes in Hollywood, you pickin' them up too?" They said, "Well, that don't have nothin' to do with it. We know what we doin'." They found out who we were, and they took us back to the theater. The next mornin', here they come to my house. I should have known it then, but what could I do. I had to let them in anyway. They could kick the door down and get in anyway. They arrested three of us for two joints. They said it was in the sofa, underneath the sofa. All the pot I ever did keep was over the toilet, in case anybody came in I could dump it in the toilet. In fact, we didn't have none.

I don't know what this cat told them or what. I went out and bought an ounce of pot. But I didn't like the count, so I took it back to the cat, got my money back. The next mornin', here come the police. They think I got pot. I figured the cat that sold it to me, told them he had sold some to me. They came to find it, but they didn't find it, so they planted some anyway. I think that's how it happened. I just told the judge when they took me in court—I knew what they were trying to do—I just went up and told him. Luckily he was a nice man. I said, "It's no use us goin' through this whole rigamarole. I'll tell you the whole situation if you really want to know what's goin' on, between these two officers. They didn't find nothin' on me. They didn't find nothin' in my clothes. All of a sudden they find something in underneath the sofa. If I was goin' to have some pot, I wouldn't have had it there. I know that they're tryin' to send me to San Quentin, and I know why. They done this because of my old lady. That's what this whole shit is about."

The judge actually went for me on my side. He was that kind. He says, "Well, it does seem kind of funny that they would take you out of the theater and then come to the house the next morning." So he cut me loose. I went home, and I waited 'til it got dark, and I packed everything I owned into my car, and me and my ol' lady, and the tenor player wanted to come to New York—I can't remember his name, so I told him, "O.K., I'll take you." I drove all the way on in to New York.

❖❖

In assessing the impact of bebop there are several aspects to be considered. One was "the war to make the world safe for democracy," as people were calling it. It was a fight against the Nazis and the forces of Fascism which represented bigotry and oppression. A black author, Roi Ottley, wrote a book called *New World 'A Comin'*, and many black people did feel that life would be better for them after the war.

There was a hopefulness reflected in the music, whether it was conscious or not. It was a very "up" expression. It had joy, beauty, and optimism.

❖❖

MAX ROACH   Black people aren't that optimistic, and they're not that pessimistic, either. You do the best with what goes on at the time. I don't think that the way the history of this country has gone sociologically— as a black person myself, I could never get overly optimistic, or by the same token, I'm not overly pessimistic, either. I make a living. The music is satisfying. You try to look at this goddamn society with as much as—being as pragmatic as possible. You have to be just, "Well, if I can eat today, good. If I don't get a job, I know I will get one. Shit, it's not gonna kill me," 'cause you don't want to commit suicide. I think everybody's like that. But the music itself has been a blessing. The music has always been kind of a saving grace, among other things, for people. Of course it was one area that you could participate in and you could make a living at.

❖❖

A lot has been made by certain writers trying to attribute specific political things to the music, but if it was not an altogether conscious social or political statement, the implications were there.

❖❖

DEXTER GORDON   I think all the cats were aware of the fact that what we were doing, what we were playing was new, was revolutionary. But of course I didn't know—and I'm not too sure how many of the rest of them realized—what a big impact this would make in the music world. We were all pretty young at that time. I mean we didn't really see in all that perspective, but we knew that we were in the midst of something new and something was being created and everybody had a kind of esprit de corps. Very proud, very excited about this. In a sense the cats were thinking this music was so great and so wonderful and putting all their hearts and souls into it, talking about a new and better world, and more colorful, more interesting, offering all this, and it was accepted to a degree and then again, there was always somebody putting it down, "All those funny notes," you'd hear that shit all the time, and there were a lot of people, older musicians who were putting it down. I really think it was the start of the revolution, the civil-rights movement, in that sense, because that's what the music is talking about. This is all the young generation, a new generation at that time. And they're not satisfied with the shit that's going down. Because they know there should be changes being made. And actually it was a time of change because it was wartime and people were moving back and forth all over the United States and constantly traveling—armies, war jobs, defense jobs. It was a time of great flux. And it was a time of change, and the music was reflecting this. And we were putting our voice into what we thought was about to be the thing.

❖❖

So much of jazz, throughout its history, has talked about change, travel, and related subjects. The '40s was a period where we had airplanes that could really move, and Charlie Parker had a tune called "Constellation." Whether or not that was on purpose, it typified the speed of that mode of transportation of the day.

Bebop, however, was not just an expression for the '40s. In various permutations it became and remained the main language or a major component of most contemporary styles short of the non-chordal and/or "freedom" players. The harmonic base of the musicians who embraced the modal may be different but even their

phrasing and vocabulary can be traced directly back to Parker and
Gillespie.

❖ ❖

BUDD JOHNSON   I still like bebop. It's harder to play than any of this other
kind of thing. When Parker and Gillespie got together they made a
wonderful team, an outstanding team, so naturally you have to like it.
I liked it—I like that style of music even today. It's more difficult to
play than this avant-garde because you have to run all the changes
correctly, and that's a bit difficult, because you must develop outstanding technique, and you must have this technique in order to play
what you feel inside and let whatever it is—come out.

Bebop is very demanding. Now you know, to play tunes like "Body
and Soul," to play tunes with all the changes and learn all those changes,
is very difficult. It's not just like you just picking up your horn and
going like [imitates horn]. So they create their own music to do that
with. And a lot of it is very, very good. But I would like to hear some
of those guys just take a tune with a whole lot of changes in it and run
it. Because now everybody figures everything is relevant. I can run this
against that. But you'll find a lot of the music out there, they get out
of the first chorus, bam, and they dwell on one chord and then they
play everything they know on that one chord, and they go to another
key and play everything they know on that one chord, and go crazy
on that one chord and back. Well, that's good, you know, but I still
think bop is more musical and more difficult to play than this music
because you had your melodies, you had form, something to build
upon. When you have a guy just makin' sounds on the horn like this.
I like to do a little bit of that, too. You know what I mean?

❖ ❖

There has been prejudice about bebop since it first happened, and
there continues to be, but it's one of the most beautiful musics
ever conceived.

❖ ❖

LOU LEVY   It's attractive to me because it's the final answer to good jazz.
If it's not attractive to other people, I just don't think they understand
good music. We could go into this forever, but I think bebop has got
all the answers. Bebop is the equivalent in jazz what Bach was in classical music. It's a total melodic line, done in the most logical way, and
very rhythmically and using all the time factors that you can—I don't
mean time signatures because that's just a fringe benefit—anybody can
work that out. But the thing is to—time over time crossing over bar
lines. Bach did that, the counterpoint thing, whatever it is. Bach was
sent to us, he was the first to me in jazz.

RED RODNEY   First of all, intellectually bebop is marvelous. The guys who
play it—almost every one of them are masters on their instruments.

Intellectually bebop was so fascinating and so tremendous, and Charlie Parker was the most intellectual of them all. The music had such high spirit. The intensity, the sensitivity of the music was just fabulous.

❖❖

Every period of jazz has had its center, although it has always been played in many parts of the country. New Orleans, Chicago, and Kansas City were centers. And although it came from different places, you have to say that bebop is New York.

❖❖

RED RODNEY   Bebop was a New York situation. Now you hear it all over and sometimes you go to Meridian, Mississippi, and go into a little club and, "Plow," you'll be knocked over on your fanny with three or four guys that are playing so great. But still, bebop is a New York . . .

And something happened, We—I think we turned the people off in some respect. The average person who didn't understand it. And I was guilty there as anyone else. We didn't entertain them. We came on like we're not show biz. "We're musicians. We're not entertainers." And in a way, that's true. But then, in another way, it's not. People that come into a club and want to hear jazz, they still want to be entertained by the person that's playing. And turning your back on them or not explaining what you're doing to someone who doesn't know is not a good way to keep them interested in coming back for more. And so I think we hurt ourselves there. And then, of course, we had the rock jockeys and the record promoters, and they just kept going and going, and help bury us all the way.

GERRY MULLIGAN   Part of the reason that the boppers got put down by the other musicians was because they scared the hell out of everybody. It was because they had a command of, a facility on their instruments, a technical facility, that the guys did not have. And when they heard Charlie Parker and Dizzy doing what they were doing, it just scared the hell out of most of the guys playing. Now even though there were guys around who could get around their horns, there was nobody that ever improvised with more drive, command, and fluid ability on his instrument—just sheer dexterity—than Bird. He was incredible. And I think when a man—the guys who were older when Bird was a young guy and came on the scene, heard him doing that and said, "Well, if he came along sounding like Johnny Hodges, terrific." But coming along doing what he was doing, I can hear the guys in their thirties and forties and playing all their lives, they know damn well they can practice eight hours a day for the rest of their lives, they would never have that kind of—and that's called fright. The jazz guys themselves were really very much frightened at the beginning. Then after they heard it for awhile they realized what was being played wasn't that difficult, it was just they'd never heard it before. It's like the first time you hear anything, especially something that's more complex than what you're used to, it takes a while to hear.

❖❖

It is interesting that the music begun in that period is thriving again today, and that people are playing it again, and that it's become more popular.

❖❖

ALLEN TINNEY   It's amazing. I really can't believe what I'm hearing, and what I'm doing—more so that I'm still playing because I was going to gently or gracefully move out of the business, like I saw the guys do when I was coming up. But it's really wonderful that this thing is being uncovered again. Of course, in a little different style, but still what we would call bebop or modern jazz. The reason why, I believe, that it maintained itself is because it was such a high level of musicianship. It wasn't just any yokie-dokie that could just get on a horn or piano and play it. They weren't considered jazz musicians, they were considered entertainers. If you honked your horn, you know, because there was a restriction on that. If you what they called "showboated," if you did any kind of fancy tricks or anything you were really sort of isolated, you were banned from the crowd. You just had to stand there and be real serious about it. It was taken right out of the entertainment role.

HOWARD MC GHEE   I think it [the message] was implied, and think socially it was done for a reason too, for social reasons, 'cause a lot of the guys had been, you know, they said takin' the whole picture of both races. Benny Goodman had been named the "King of Swing," so they had some cats that was playin' swing music. We figured, what the hell, we can't do no more than what's been done with it, we gotta do somethin' else. We gotta do some other kind of thing. Now if we could play "swing" and still execute and be right was the thing, that's what we all were thinking of collectively. So now, we play these things, we know that in order for a cat to play these tunes, he's got to be able to play these changes. He's gonna have to think in order to do this. So that's why we really latched on to it, because it made you use your mind more, because you had to learn the changes. That's why the cats out here play something like "Groovin' High," they don't know the changes, they just play the melody, they learn the melody and say, "Yeah, well I know the tune." But really, when it comes down to the solo they go avant-garde somewhere, they go off somewhere and forget about the chord. They think they're playing the tune. They're not, really. In those days, that's what we were thinking of. We'd go in and say, "Let's play "Confirmation," or something like that—clear out the young cats that didn't know what they was doin'. They never listened to what we were doin'.

The people, especially the G.I.'s who were coming back, had no idea that this was happening. They was over there fightin' for one thing, and we were over here tryin' to get our heads together as far as playing music was concerned. A lot of people couldn't fit into it. It was completely different for the average guy. A lot of musicians that were stationed in the Army, they came back and couldn't figure out what was happening. A guy would come and stand by the bandstand, his mouth wide open and looking at us, and I'd say, "This cat, he's looking at me. He really don't know. He should go look at Bird. That's where he should really be!" A lot of cats looked at Bird with their mouths wide open. "What's he doin'?"

Bird was an exception himself. He was like a messenger, in my eyesight. I don't know any, besides Louis, Prez, and Bird, maybe Hawk I ought to add in too—I don't know any messengers that's been out here any more influential than those writers.

BUDDY DE FRANCO   I think also the biggest problem is the more developed you get—the more harmonically developed you get—the further away from an audience you're going to get. And all of a sudden, you have just a select few. You have just a few people who have ears that are capable of hearing and following the thread. Most people just simply have to go by their gut feeling. Only. Now, Charlie Parker had, to me, the greatest swing feeling that there ever was, except he added to that the cerebral, the intellectual. And, to me, it was the greatest combination of real swing feeling and the intellectual approach to playing jazz. And that's what I always admired so much about him. If you wanted to isolate the physical from what he did mentally, it was just fantastic. And if you wanted to disregard what he did mentally and just feel what he did, you could do that also. And why in hell 90 percent of the population didn't pick up on that, I'll never know. That remains a mystery. I just think they were scared, maybe, be the cerebral part of it.

CHUBBY JACKSON   Music has always accompanied every era we've ever lived in. In the Herman band the Marines were coming; that's why there were Gozzo and Pete Candoli screaming. Then the *Stardust* era came back when guys were coming home and wanted to dance with their ladies. I don't have to tell you where society is and has been coming from because I don't think in our lives we've ever faced up to such chaos from the top on down. Now music gets on the bandstand and in this sheer defiance, things come out of a band that are almost ugly and have no feeling with anything at all.

I think we could use the word "academic" with bebop and get away with it because Dizzy was, and is, such a giant and, of course, Charlie Parker. Their melodic lines were furiously put together, and they were correct. Consequently, in the rhythm section the piano player started to arrive at some very, very wild harmonic concepts—altered changes, altered changes on altered changes. Then the piano player would generously whisper to the bass player, "Let's play an F-sharp to a B," and all of a sudden . . . See, from the simplicity let's say of the Basie band—because to me it's the simple, swinging band of all time—that band is based on dynamics and accents—nice little quarter-note patterns that can go from real soft to loud, and lovely solos—to when Dizzy brought his first bebop band in, with Ray Brown. I heard him on 52nd Street. By this time he's already putting in some very wild changes and playing wild melodic lines on top of those newer changes. At the moment it was a reach-out to get into some newer academic things as against some of the space-out things of today. I don't particularly believe in the term "free form." If I'm playing with you the first time it's completely free; we'll just eyeball it and if we get together, hot dog. Now, take it again, three to six weeks later. We're still playing with each other. All of a sudden, intuitively, you anticipate each other's moves because those things maybe worked a night before. And little by little the free form is just getting into a thing called form. I've noticed that with a lot of the guys that play free form, that they've been together a long time. You go hear them night after night, and you'll be amazed at the repetitions going on because they're almost intuitive. They feel good; they worked; they didn't get in your way. It's only when guys are sitting in and say, "Let's space out" and this one goes off in his direction, this one decides he's going to left field.

When on 52nd Street, from the era of Roy [Eldridge] and all those people, they were playing blues, and Dizzy came on in and wanted to play "All the Things You Are" and "I Concentrate on You." He was digging into some marvelous Broadway tunes, songs with some fabulous changes, and he was discovering his own approach because he's a marvelous arranger. He had it all down and was scaring everybody. They were afraid to get on the bandstand because they were afraid he was gonna call out one of those. But it was great for the younger players because it opened up—I keep using the word "academic"—I think bebop was one of the real steps of academic thinking. After that, music became more societal—the rift between colors, styles, ages. What hurt me most was when the human emotion of happiness and fun seemed to dwindle and disappear, because that's why I became a musician. I was having fun. I fell in love with Jimmy Blanton, and the Savoy Sultans. To get on the bandstand with a blank look is so distant to me, and it leaves me more than ice cold.

JIMMY ROWLES   I don't know what happened to me. I finally started to get into music in my own way and from the things that I've learned from everybody I've listened to. I started taking tunes apart, each tune. I'd practice all night when everybody was sleeping; practicing and saying there's got to be another change there. I'd finally change it and get this shit together. I know the older you get and the more you under-stand, you start to put the lyrics together and you start feeling with this shit, then you find the right changes and when you finally get to the right changes, then you say, "Now I'm going to start to play this m——f——in the right way." If you play "How Deep Is the Ocean?," you've got to play it with the right changes.

❖❖

In saying "the right changes" the bop player meant that you take the tune as written and then you use your knowledge as a player to augment it and get underneath it and inside it.

❖❖

JIMMY ROWLES   It had a whole lot to do with it. They helped me to learn how to put things together. The more you listen to it—listening to Bird and those guys. If it weren't for those guys there wouldn't be nothing. There wouldn't be nothing.

Epilogue

In 1951 Red Rodney had left Charlie Parker's quintet and formed his own group. His manager was a man named Ray Barron who, for a short time, had been *down beat*'s Boston stringer. Rodney's recording affiliation at the time was Prestige, and Barron was on the phone in President Bob Weinstock's inner office, talking to a club owner in some small town in the Boston area. "I got this terrific bebop band for you," he began. "Click," went the other end of the line.

Bebop, or bop, had never been that welcome a word, but now it was anathema, "business-wise," to a small-time club owner. He needn't have known that traditional cornetist Doc Evans had presided over a mock funeral for bebop in Minneapolis, or even have seen the picture of the event in *down beat*. The word scared him. And hadn't Dizzy Gillespie's big band broken up? And didn't Charlie Parker, when he had a job in Philadelphia at 8:30, leave New York from Charlie's Tavern at that time, or not show up at all?

Parker's involvement with drugs was widely-known, and within bop there were many of the bigger and lesser names who were "strung out" on heroin at one time or another during this period. Gillespie was not, but his zany behavior repelled some people as it simultaneously attracted others. In the minds of many, bop and drugs were inextricably linked, and this created another negative for the music.

Long before this association, bop had received bad publicity from uninformed quarters. *Life* magazine ridiculed Gillespie (never even mentioning Parker) in a 1947 article and, even earlier (March 1946), a Los Angeles disc "jerkey" named Ted Steele (New Yorkers were later subjected to his noxious personality and non-talent on television's WPIX in the early '50s), attacked bebop by banning it on radio station KMPC with the indictment that it "tends to make degenerates out of our young listeners."

His prime targets were pianist-vocalist Harry "The Hipster" Gibson and singer-guitarist Slim Gaillard. *Time* described bebop as "hot jazz overheated, with overdone lyrics, full of bawdiness, references to narcotics and double talk."

Of course Gibson and Gaillard were not beboppers. The longest bop lyric was "Salt Peanuts! Salt Peanuts!"; and they were undoubtedly unaware that Gaillard's "Yep Roc Heresay" was, in truth, his recitation of a menu from a Middle Eastern restaurant.

In the early '50s Gillespie, with a small group, was recording novelties such as "O Sho Be Do Be", and Parker was displaying erratic behavior, even when at the head of his "strings" group, but bop was far from dead. Parker and Gillespie were reunited three times in this period: once in the studio for Norman Granz in 1950, at Birdland in 1951, and at the famed Massey Hall concert in Toronto in 1953. The results, respectively, can be heard on Verve, Columbia, and Prestige.

If bop was not "dead" however, it was in a quiescent period with the advent of "cool" jazz, which, in reality, was "cool" bop, heralded by the "Birth of the Cool" recording sessions of the Miles Davis Nonet. Many former big band musicians from the Kenton and Herman orchestras settled in southern California in the early '50s and "West Coast" jazz, synonymous with "cool" jazz, was hatched. Much of the inspiration came from the Davis Nonet dates. In the forefront of the movement were trumpeter Shorty Rogers, alto saxophonist Art Pepper, and drummer Shelly Manne. When Gerry Mulligan, who had been involved directly with Davis's band, moved to Los Angeles from New York and formed his pianoless quartet with trumpeter Chet Baker, further impetus was added.

In general, musicians on the East Coast continued to swing with a more vigorous attack but while the Modern Jazz Quartet, spawned by the Dizzy Gillespie band, played such bop classics as "Woody'n You" and "A Night in Tunisia," it espoused a restrained, quasi-classical approach in quite a bit of its repertoire.

By the time Parker died in 1955, there had already been a reaction to "cool" by such groups as Art Blakey's Jazz Messengers and Miles Davis's quintet, followed by the Clifford Brown-Max Roach quintet. The term "hard bop" was coined to describe these groups. It was an inaccurate, and too-convenient labeling, but it was through these combos and Horace Silver's group, which had come out of the Blakey quintet, that bebop moved into its second important stage, one in which two giant figures, the tenor saxophonists Sonny Rollins and John Coltrane, would be fully revealed to the jazz public.

❖❖

Index

Interview material indicated by **boldface** headings